ExamInsight
For
Windows Server 2003 Certification Examination 70-290
Managing and Maintaining a Microsoft Windows Server 2003 Environment

Second Edition

CD-ROM practice exam provided by
BeachFront Quizzer, Inc.

Author:
Jada Brock-Soldavini, MCSE
with the
TRP Author Certification Success Team

Published by

TotalRecall Publications, Inc.
1103 Middlecreek
Friendswood, TX 77546
281-992-3131

NOTE: THIS BOOK IS GUARANTEED:
See details at www.TotalRecallPress.com

TotalRecall Publications, Inc.

This Book is Sponsored by Beachfront Quizzer, Inc.

Printed in United States of America
Printed and bound by Data Duplicators of Houston, Texas
Printed and bound by Lightning Source, Inc. in the USA and UK
Printed and bound by BookSurge, Inc in the USA and around the world

Paper Back
ISBN 1-59095-029-1
UPC 6-43977-02290-5

eBook
ISBN 1-59095-625-7
UPC 6-43977-61290-8

Worldwide eBook publication and distribution by:

The sponsoring editor is Bruce Moran and the production supervisor is Corby R. Tate.
Author: Jada Brock-Soldavini, MCSE

I would like to dedicate this book to my husband Michael and children Alyssa, Daniel and Christian. It is wonderful having you for a family. Thank you for your patience, love and support. I know it has been difficult at times. Also, I would like to extend my love, gratitude, and appreciation to my mother Betty Hite and Grandmother Ruth B. Smith for all of the hard work and sacrifices that were made for me growing up. I would also like to give thanks and appreciation to Alfred and Joan Soldavini who are always there to support me. I could not have done this project without your unwavering love and support. I love you all.

Jada Brock-Soldavini

ExamInsight™
For
Windows Server™ 2003 Certification
Examination 70-290

Managing and Maintaining a Microsoft Windows Server™ 2003 Environment

Second Edition

Jada Brock-Soldavini, MCSE
with the
TRP Author Certification Success Team

About the Author

Jada Brock-Soldavini lives in suburban Atlanta and works for the State of Georgia as a Network Services Administrator. She has co-authored or contributed to other numerous works pertaining to Microsoft Windows technologies. She has an A.S. degree in Computer Information Systems and has been in the Information Technology industry for seven years. She is also married to Michael and the mother of three children Alyssa, Daniel and Christian. In her spare time she enjoys cooking, writing and reading anything that pertains to Network and Security technology.

The TRP Author Certification Success Team

Deborah Timmons

Deborah Timmons is a Microsoft Certified Trainer and Microsoft Certified Systems Engineer. She came into the Microsoft technical field after six years in the adaptive technology field, providing technology and training for persons with disabilities. She is the President and co-owner of Integrator Systems Inc.

Alan Grayson

Alan Grayson has a Masters Degree in Systems Management, is a Microsoft Certified Trainer, a Microsoft Certified Systems Engineer and Microsoft Database Administrator and also holds a dozen other certifications.

Patrick Simpson

Patrick Simpson is a Microsoft MCSE, MCSE +I, MCT and a Novell Master CNE and Master CNI. He has been a Microsoft Certified Trainer for five years and working in the IT industry for approximately 9 years, specializing in network consulting and technical education. Patrick has written numerous certification study aids for both Microsoft Windows 2000 exams and for Novell certification exams.

Pat is married, has three children and is currently working for a technical consulting/education company in Green Bay, WI.

David Smith

David [Darkcat] Smith is Microsoft Certified Trainer (MCT) and Microsoft Certified Systems Engineer (MCSE). He has been working in the IT industry for approximately 15+ year, specializing in directory services design and administration. He also enjoys planning and implementing large scale rollouts.

Tom McCarty

Tom McCarty is currently an independent trainer, network engineer and consultant. He has worked in the computers and networking environment for 20 years as an administrator, end user support and instructor. Tom has the following certifications; MCSE on Windows NT 4.0, MCP+I, MCDBA, MCT on Windows 2000, and MCSA on Windows Server 2003. Along the way he has gained experience in Exchange 5.5 to 2000 upgrades, SMS 2.0 and NT to Active Directory migrations. In addition to Microsoft certification Ton holds CompTIA A+, Network+ and IT Project+ certifications. I always enjoy seeing the light come on in someone's face when they finally nail down something new.

About the Book

As an MCSE and practicing IT professional, I drew on my background to design this study guide specifically to help you *pass* the MCP/MCSE: Managing and Maintaining a Microsoft Windows Server 2003 Environment Exam 70-290.

Part of the TotalRecall IT ExamInsight Book Series, this manual functions as a "refresher course" that provides short summaries of core exam topics with a pre- and post-assessment quiz for each; is heavily illustrated with figures, diagrams, and photos; contains chapter summaries to reinforce key points; gives helpful tips for test taking; and lists a wealth of useful websites, articles and other learning aids found in no other book. Since it also includes lots of real-world material, you can continue to use it as a ready reference on the job.

So, if you are already networking with fellow professionals and just want a quick refresher course along with practice questions, this *ExamInsight* manual is the book for you. As a bonus for buying it, you get a 50% discount towards purchase of the popular BeachFront Quizzer test engine. This test engine includes practice exams drawn from a base of over 300 questions, along with explanations linked to relevant chapters in an eBook version of the manual. Many explanations also link to additional resources, such as web sites, articles, etc. The adaptive nature of the BeachFront Quizzer software is that it keeps generating types of questions that you find difficult to answer until they are no longer hard for you. By focusing on your rough spots, we will get you certified fast—or get money back! See the last page of this book for details.

For further exam practice, you can also pair this manual with TotalRecall's handy Q&A workbook *ExamWise for MCP/MCSE: Managing and Maintaining a Microsoft Windows Server 2003 Environment Exam 70-290.* It uses a unique format of two questions per page, with answers and explanations on the reverse page. It also includes 30-day free access to a BeachFront Quizzer online exam.

On the other hand, if you are just getting started and really need a thorough grounding in all of the exam topics, then try either edition of TotalRecall's complete "certification success system" that comes with the BeachFront Quizzer test engine—*InsidersChoice* to *MCP/MCSE: Managing and Maintaining a Microsoft Windows Server 2003 Environment Exam 70-290* with free download OR *InsideScoop* to *MCP/MCSE: Managing and Maintaining a Microsoft Windows Server 2003 Environment Exam 70-290* with a CD-ROM. Each edition includes a comprehensive manual and BeachFront Quizzer test engine with integrated eBook. You can choose whether you want the Quizzer as a free download or free CD.

All four books carry TotalRecall's proven guarantee—pass, or your money back!

Introduction

They have done it again, only this time it may be closer to being right. Microsoft's Windows Server 2003 in my opinion is hands down better than any of its predecessors (although not perfect, nothing ever is). They have really made this product function as it should in a networking environment. Most of the functions are easy to navigate and configure by using the Microsoft Management Console. I was around the industry when DOS was running desktop machines, Novell 3.xx was king of the hill and Windows 3.11 was around sometimes. Which, in all honesty was not that long ago. But considering what is available today with this release in comparison to 10 years ago, it is an incredible display of innovation and technology. I know that many technology professionals working in the field opted to wait out the Windows NT 4.0 migration to Windows 2000 Server and get their hands on the Windows Server 2003 software. If you are one of these people then I believe once you get into the book and also work this out in your test lab you will find that it was worth the wait. It is always helpful (though not necessary) to go through these study guides and try the settings in a test lab environment. Nothing is worse than applying group policy settings on a domain without first testing them out to see what will happen.

I hope that this book will assist you with the difficult job of taking the exam for 70-290. It is chocked full of information that will make you perform better and smarter in the Windows networking environment. Happy reading, and good luck with your technical endeavors. I hope this guide gives you valuable insight and helps you pass those tough exams.

Jada Brock-Soldavini

A Quick overview of the book chapters:

Table of Contents

Exam Information and Resources

Exam News

Exam 70-290 was made available August 14, 2003.

http://www.microsoft.com/traincert/exams/70-290.asp

The course provides a general introductory overview of this task.

You will need to supplement the course with additional lab work.

Audience Profile

The Microsoft Certified Systems Administrator (MCSA) on Windows Server 2003 credential is intended for IT professionals who work in the typically complex computing environment of medium to large companies. An MCSA candidate should have 6 to 12 months of experience administering client and network operating systems in environments that have the following characteristics:

- 250 to 5,000 or more users
- Three or more physical locations
- Three or more domain controllers
- Network services and resources such as messaging, database, file and print, proxy server, firewall, Internet, intranet, remote access and client computer management
- Connectivity requirements such as connecting branch offices and individual users in remote locations to the corporate network and connecting corporate networks to the Internet

Credit Toward Certification

When you pass the Implementing, Managing, and Maintaining a Microsoft® Windows® Server 2003 Environment exam, you achieve Microsoft Certified Professional (MCP) status. You also earn credit toward the following certifications:

- **Core** credit toward Microsoft Certified Systems Administrator (MCSA) on Microsoft Windows Server 2003 certification
- **Core** credit toward Microsoft Certified Systems Engineer (MCSE) on Microsoft Windows Server 2003 certification

Microsoft Online Resources

TechNet: Designed for IT professionals, this site includes How-tos, best practices, downloads, technical chats and much more.

MSDN: The Microsoft Developer Network (MSDN) is a reference for developers, featuring code samples, technical articles, newsgroups, chats and more.

Training & Certification Newsgroups: A newsgroup exists for every Microsoft certification. By participating in the ongoing dialogue, you take advantage of a unique opportunity to exchange ideas with and ask questions of others, including more than 750 Microsoft Most Valuable Professionals (MVPs) worldwide.

TotalRecall Publications

Recommended Preparation Tools and Resources

We make a wealth of preparation tools and resources are available to you, including courses, books, practice tests and Microsoft Web sites. When you are ready to prepare for this exam, here's where you could start.

Microsoft Classroom Instructor-led Course for 70-290

- Course 2274: Managing a Microsoft Windows Server 2003 Environment
- Course 2275: Maintaining a Microsoft Windows Server 2003 Environment

TotalRecall Online Instructor-led Course for 70-290

- Course TCFTC 70-290: Managing and Maintaining a Microsoft Windows Server 2003: MCP/MCSE Exam 70-290.

http://www.totalrecallpress.com/syllabis/70-290

WBTWise Self-Paced Training for This Exam

- Web Based Training: Managing and Maintaining a Microsoft Windows Server 2003: MCP/MCSE Exam 70-290

http://www.wbtwise.com/

BeachFront Quizzer Certified Practice Tests

- Visit www.bfqd.com Web site to download a practice test.
- Visit http://www.online-exams.com/ Software Web site to take a practice test.

www.totalrecallpress.com

The objective of this chapter is to provide the reader with an understanding of the following:

1.1 Manage basic disks and dynamic disks

1.2 Monitor server hardware

- 1.2.1 Tools used to manage hardware
- 1.2.2 Device Manager
- 1.2.3 The Hardware Troubleshooting Wizard
- 1.2.4 Appropriate Control Panel items

1.3 Optimize server disk performance

- 1.2.1 Implement a RAID solution
- 1.2.2 Defragment volumes and partitions

1.4 Troubleshoot server hardware devices

- 1.4 1 Diagnose and resolve issues related to hardware settings
- 1.4 2 Diagnose and resolve issues related to server hardware
- 1.4 3 Diagnose and resolve issues related to hardware driver upgrades

1.5 Install and configure server hardware devices

- 1.5.1 Configure driver signing options
- 1.5.2 Configure resource settings for a device
- 1.5.3 Configure device properties and settings

Chapter 1: Physical and Logical Devices

Introduction:

Windows Server 2003 gives Administrators various options to use when physical and logical disks need managing. You can perform tasks such as assigning drive letters, and creating partitions and volumes. Disks can be managed via the always present command prompt or the Microsoft management console. Before you begin to manage your disks you need to understand the different disk types, and how to Optimize and troubleshoot your disks. This chapter will also show you how you can:

- Manage basic and dynamic disks using the command prompt and the Computer Management console
- Configure shadow copies of volumes
- Configure and troubleshoot your Redundant Array of Inexpensive Disks RAID configuration
- Use the performance logs and alerts console in Windows Server 2003 to configure performance baselines and alerts for your hardware
- Troubleshoot hardware devices using the Control Panel and the Hardware Troubleshooting Wizard.

This chapter is full of information to assist you with the preparation for Microsoft 70-290 exam Managing and Maintaining a Microsoft Windows Server 2003 Environment as well as some real-world solutions for managing your Microsoft Windows Server 2003 disks and hardware devices.

Getting Ready Questions

1. On what operating systems can you have local dynamic disks?
2. How can you access Device Manager?
3. Under Server 2003, what type of fault tolerant volumes are available on basic disks?
4. For what do you use the FTOnline tool?
5. The Windows Server 2003 operating system uses which features to guarantee that the device driver has not been altered?

Getting Ready Answers

1. You can have local dynamic disks on Windows 2000 Server and Professional, Windows XP and Windows 2003. Operating systems prior to Windows 2000 (including MS-DOS, Windows 3.x, Windows 95/98/ME, Windows NT) as well as Windows 2000 Home Edition cannot support dynamic disks locally.
2. There are three ways to access Device Manager—through Administrative Tools | Computer Management; right-click My Computer | Hardware; and through the keyboard shortcut Windows Key | Pause.
3. None. Fault tolerant volumes on basic disks are no longer supported in Windows Server 2003.
4. The FTOnline command-line tool can be used on Fault Tolerant disks to mount and recover files on Windows Server 2003 systems that have been upgraded. Once the server has been rebooted the disks are not mounted by FTOnline.
5. The Windows Server 2003 operating system uses three features to guarantee that the device driver has not been altered and is in its original pristine state:
   - File Signature Verification
   - System File Checker
   - Windows File Protection

1.1 Manage basic disks and dynamic disks

Administrators have many options that can be used to manage basic and dynamic disks in Windows Server 2003. These options have not radically changed between versions of Windows 2000 Server and Windows Server 2003. Before you decide which type of disk to use, you need to understand the difference between basic and dynamic disks. Remember, once a basic disk has been converted to a dynamic disk it cannot be undone. Keep this in mind when you begin to convert your Basic disks to dynamic disks.

Table 1.1 below shows some differences between Dynamic and Basic disks.

Disk Type	Features
Basic	This type of disk is accessible by all Windows Operating versions as well as the command prompt. Up to three primary and one extended partition, or four primary partitions, can be created on a basic disk. Basic disk partitions cannot span multiple drives. It must be converted to a dynamic disk first.
Dynamic	Dynamic disks can also be configured to be fault tolerant by using RAID-5, mirrored or clustered volumes. Dynamic disk volumes are always referred to as dynamic volumes. Disks that use Universal Serial Bus (USB), Firewire, detachable or removable disks, or disks on portable computers cannot be converted into dynamic disks. It is not recommended that you convert a basic disk into a dynamic disk if there are more than one installation of Windows Server 2003, Windows 2000 or Windows XP.

Table 1-1: Differences between Basic and Dynamic Disks.

Before you begin to convert a basic disk to a dynamic disk, make sure that you first close any programs that are running on the disk. If you are converting a boot disk to a dynamic disk, remember that the computer will need to be rebooted for the changes to take effect. After the conversion process has taken place, the basic disk partitions will become dynamic simple volumes.

Note: Dynamic simple volumes cannot be converted back to basic disk partitions. Conversion is permanent.

It is always a good strategy to evaluate this in a test lab environment before you try to convert your disks. As noted, once they are converted from basic to primary, the conversion is permanent and the only way to undo this would be to remove the partition and rebuild it again. As well, ensure your backups are up to date before you attempt any changes on your Windows Server 2003.

Dynamic disks cannot be accessed directly by any of the following operating systems:

- MS-Dos
- Windows 95
- Windows 98
- Windows Millennium Edition
- Windows XP Home Edition
- Windows NT 4.0.

However, shared folders on a dynamic disk can be accessed via a network connection.

All versions of Windows XP Professional, Windows 2000 and Windows Server 2003 (including 64-bit versions) can access dynamic disks directly.

Before you convert a basic disk to a dynamic disk that contains shadow copies, use the following steps so that you do not experience data loss:

- Determine if the disk is a non-boot volume.
- Determine that the volume containing the shadow copies is not the same volume where the original files are stored.
- Dismount the volume that contains the original files and take it offline.
- If you do not bring the volume back online within 20 minutes then data will be lost on the disk that contains the shadow copies. This pertains only to on a non-boot volume. Boot volumes can be converted from basic to dynamic without losing shadow copies.

Figure 1.1 displays the Microsoft Management Console used to manage disks in Windows Server 2003. It can be accessed by clicking on **Start,** selecting **Administrative Tools** and choosing **Computer Management**.

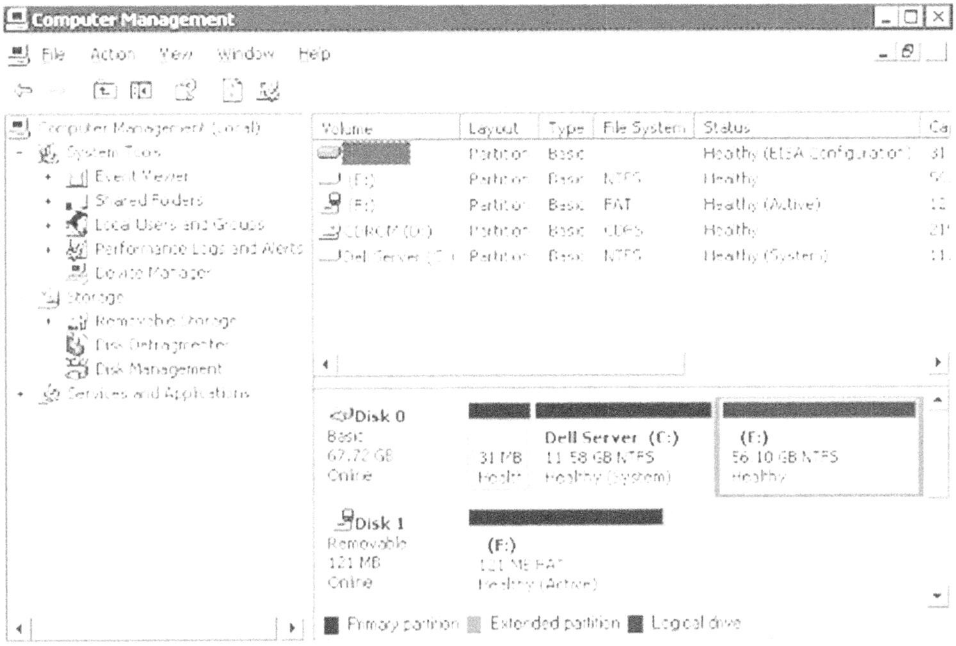

Figure 1-1: Computer Management—Microsoft Management Console (MMC).

The Disk Management Console shows all information pertaining to the disks installed on the server. By default, the screen shows the volume name, layout (partition) information, the type of disk either basic or dynamic, the file system type, the status of the drives, and the capacity of the drives. Depending on your console setup, if you scroll over to the right, you may also see the free space of the drives, percent free, fault tolerant information on the drives as well as overhead information on the disk drives. The console in Figure 1.1 is set to show you the information in the volume layout. You can change the view of a console by clicking on **View** in the top menu and selecting which area you wish to change (Figure 1.2). The Settings options are as follows:

- Top –
  - Disk List – Lists the Disks information
  - Volume List – Lists the disk information in a list by volume
  - Graphical View – Lists the disk views in a graphical format.

- Bottom –
    - o Disk List – Lists the Disks information
    - o Volume List – Lists the disk information in a list by volume
    - o Graphical View – Lists the disk views in a graphical format
    - o Hidden – Only available for the bottom pane. This option hides the bottom portion of the management screen.
- Settings –
    - o Appearance – This setting allows you to control how the console displays disk information. The option to color code disk region information such as RAID 5, Disk Spanning, and Free Space available and a myriad of additional information can be set using the Appearance option.
    - o Scaling – The scaling option can be used to show the display proportions in the details pane of the console for disks and areas located on the disk. The proportions can be set based on capacity using logarithmic scaling (which is the default), capacity using linear scaling and all the same size.
- Drive Paths – Drive Path settings for volumes
- Customize – Options that allow you to change or hide screen information.

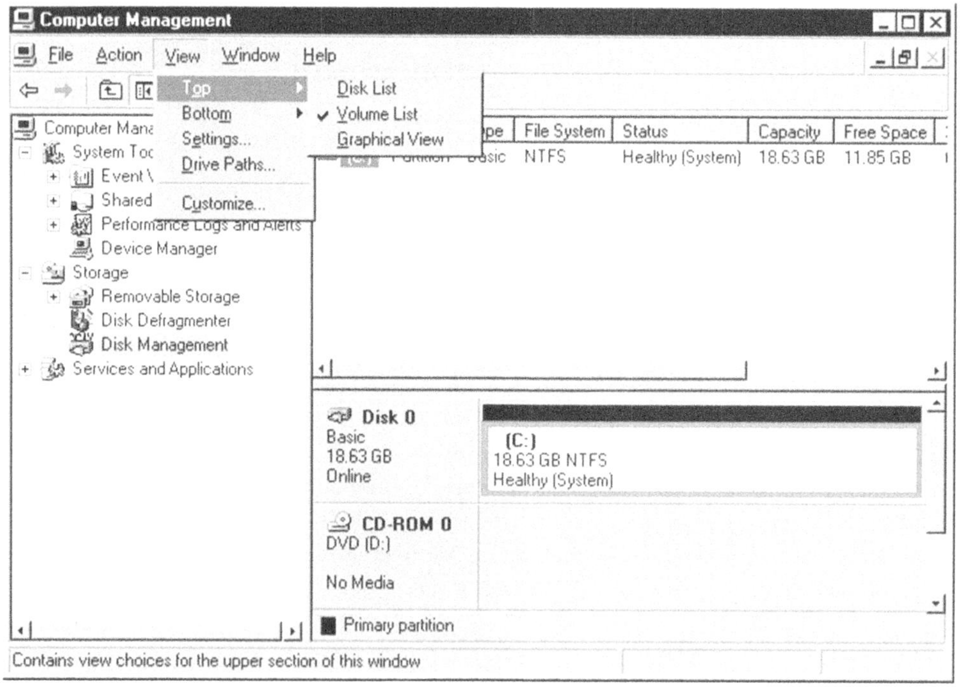

Figure 1-2: Changing the View of the Disk Management Console.

In Figure 1.3, the top view has been changed using the **View | Top | Graphical View** settings and the Bottom View has been changed to the Volume List view using the **View | Bottom | Volume List** option. You can also choose to hide the bottom of the screen by choosing the **Hide Option** from the list. This option is only available for the bottom half of the view. Other options include the **Graphical View** and **Volume List** view.

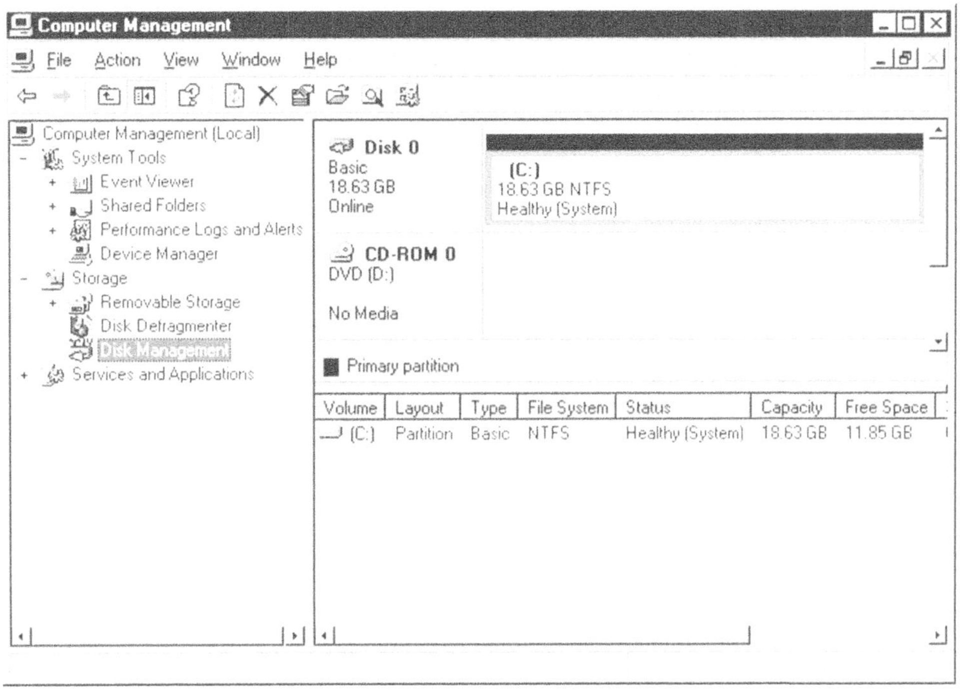

Figure 1-3: Changing the Views in the Computer Management Console.

Choosing **Action** from the top of the console will allow you to do the following tasks:

- **Refresh –** This option allows you to refresh the console screen.
- **Rescan Disks –** This will allow you to rescan your disks to refresh drive letters, file system information and volume information.
- **All Tasks –** This will allow you to **Configure Shadow Copies**.

Figure 1.4 shows the options that allow you to customize the view of the console screen. This allows you to add or remove the console tree, action and view menus, standard toolbar, status bar, description bar, task pad navigation bar, and add or remove the menus and toolbar snap-in menus.

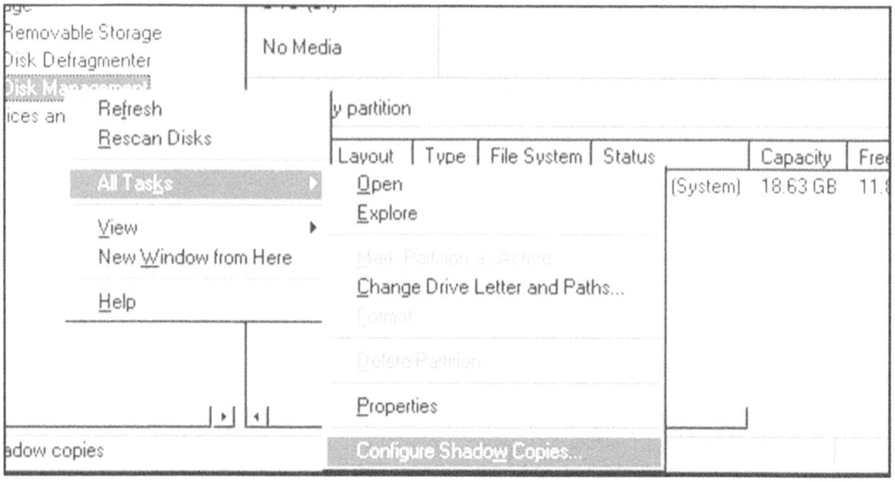

Figure 1-4: Creating Shadow Copies using the disk management console.

Figure 1.5 shows the options that allow you to customize the view of the console screen. This allows you to show or hid the console tree, action and view menus, standard toolbar, status bar, description bar, task pad navigation bar, as well as the menus and toolbar snap-ins.

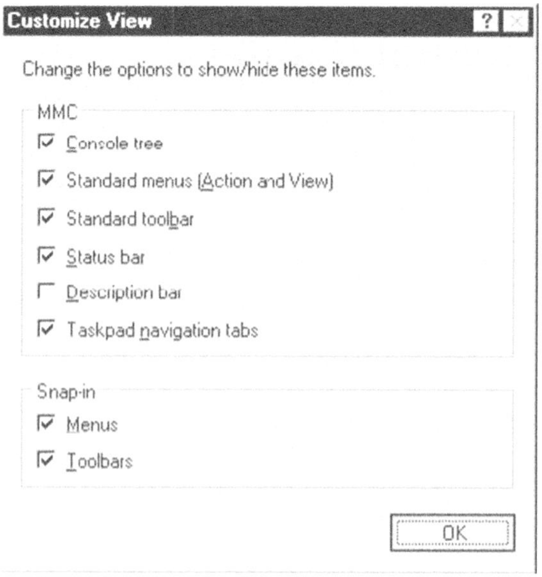

Figure 1-5: Customizing your View in the management console.

Once the view has been customized, click the **OK** button. You can also view the **Shadow Copy** settings if they have been enabled (Figure 1.6). Shadow copies, by default, create two copies of shared folders a day. This can be changed using this console.

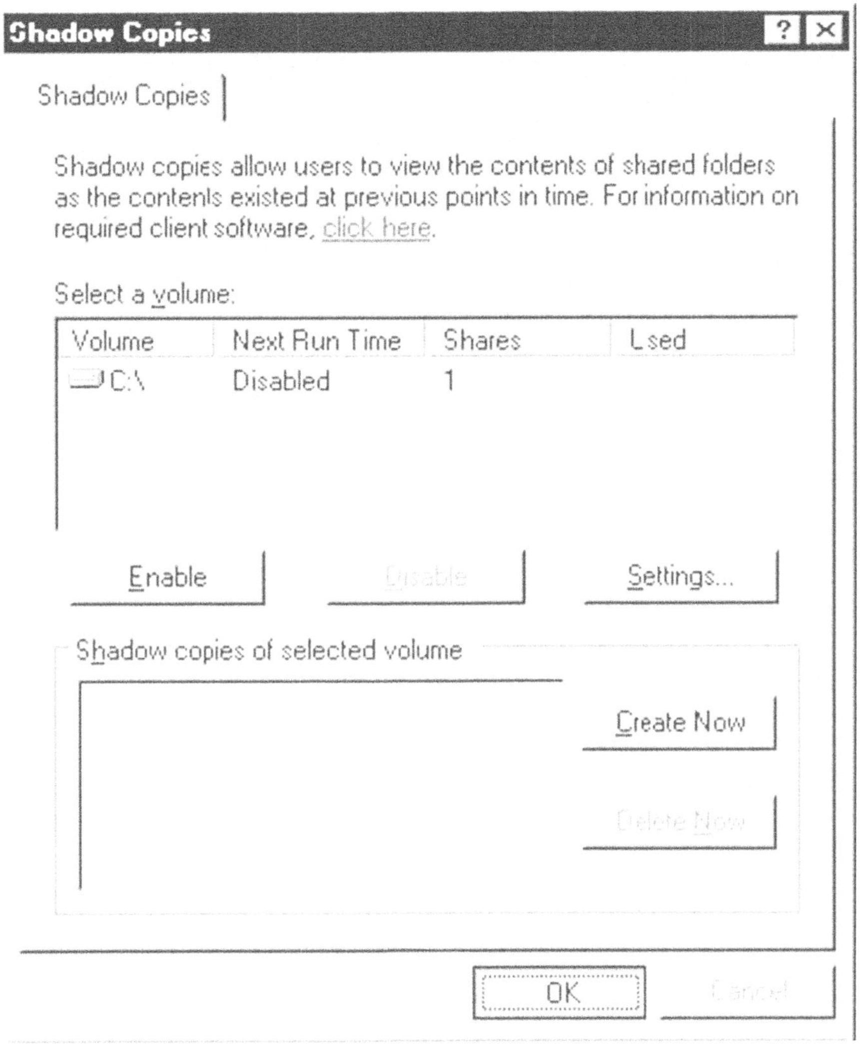

Figure 1-6: Enabling Shadow Copies using the Computer management console.

Note: To use Shadow Copies, Task Scheduler must be running.

Network Administrators can now take advantage of the Previous Versions software included in Windows Server 2003. The previous version software can be used to allow clients, who access shared folders on the network, the ability to recover files that have been deleted, in order to compare versions of a current and previous working file. To take advantage of this feature, software for accessing previous versions has to be installed on the client desktop. The software can be accessed via the following UNC on the Windows Server 2003: \\server\WINDOWS\system32\clients\twclient\. For x86 clients, choose x86 folder and double-click twclient.msi. The software will then install on the client machine. By default, copies are scheduled to be taken at 7:00 A.M. and 12:00 noon, Monday through Friday. If you retain the default schedule, save your work frequently. Why? Let's say that it is 4:00 p.m. and you need to revert. If you have not saved your work, you will revert back to the 12:00 noon file, and all subsequent work will be lost.

Table 1.2 below lists common RAID error messages, causes and possible solutions.

Error Message	Cause	Solution
Online/Errors	The dynamic disk has I/O errors on a region of the disk. A warning icon appears on the dynamic disk with errors.	If the I/O errors are temporary, reactivate the disk to return it to **Online** status.
Missing	If the disk status is **Offline** and the disk's name changes to **Missing**, the disk was recently available on the system but can no longer be located or identified. The missing disk may be corrupted, powered down, or disconnected.	Check to see if a hardware problem exists with the controller or a cable. Repair if necessary. Use the **Reactivate Disk** command to bring the disk back online. If this does not work then remove the disk from the system.
Offline	An **Offline** dynamic disk might be corrupted or intermittently unavailable. An error icon appears on the offline dynamic disk.	Make certain the dynamic disk is not corrupted. Also, check the Event Viewer for any warnings or error messages pertaining to the disk.

Error Message	Cause	Solution
Foreign	The disk has been moved from the local machine to another machine.	Add the disk to your computer's system configuration so that you can access data on the disk to the system by selecting the disk and then right-clicking on the Import Foreign Disk option. Volumes on the foreign disk will then be viewable and accessible.
Basic Volume with the Failed Status	The basic volume cannot be started automatically, the disk is damaged, or the file system is corrupt. Unless the disk or file system can be repaired, the **Failed** status indicates data loss.	Check the physical properties first then correct any problems if they exist such as controller card and cables. If the disks show they are Offline then try to return the disks to the **Online** status. The volume should automatically if this is successful and the status will return to healthy.
Dynamic Volume with the Failed Status	Dynamic Volume is showing offline.	Try to manually reactivate the volume.
Dynamic Disk is online but Dynamic Volume is in the Failed status	Check to see if underlying disks are online.	Reactivate the disk. But If the dynamic volume is RAID-5 or mirrored you will need to bring them online first or restart the mirrored or RAID-5 volume manually. After this has been done and then run Chkdsk.exe from the command prompt.

Table 1-2: RAID error messages and definitions.

You can now use these counters to monitor hardware on the server.

1.2 Monitor server hardware

Administrators have several options they can use to monitor server hardware in Windows Server 2003. Those options will be outlined in the following section. Some of those options include:

- Creating a baseline
- Hardware counters
- Performance Logs and Alerts.

An administrator can use counters to monitor server hardware after creating a baseline. A baseline is the level of performance for the server hardware under normal circumstances. Once the baseline has been established, you can use the counters to measure performance and give you an idea of how your server hardware is functioning. Counters can sometimes spike based on what is occurring on the system. Events such as services starting up or a system reboot could cause a spike or a temporary drop in performance. Do not get these spikes confused with an bottleneck. A bottleneck is a condition, often relating to a hardware resource, that causes the entire system to perform inadequately.

Microsoft suggests that you collect three types of data on the server to create a counter log. The counter log can be used to give you a total view of the server performance. The three types of data are:

- **Baseline Performance –** The baseline establishes what is typical counter values you expect to see when the system is behaving in a satisfactory manner. What needs to be established is a pattern of system behaviour when the system is idle as well as when common specific tasks are run.
- **General Performance –** This is used to identify short term developments such as memory leaks that occur after new software has been installed on a system . After a few months, you will be able to compute and average the server's performance and use that as a measuring tool for future capacity and growth.
- **Data for service level reports –** Depending on the type of company for which you work, this information can be used to make certain that systems in the organization meet specified performance and service levels.

Figure 1.7 shows some resource counters available that can be used to set up your system for monitoring using the **Performance** console. The Performance console consists of the System Monitor and the Performance Logs and Alerts console. System Monitor uses counters on different objects, such as the hard disk or processor, to gather system information. To access the System Monitor, click on **Start,** select **Administrative Tools** then choose **Performance.**

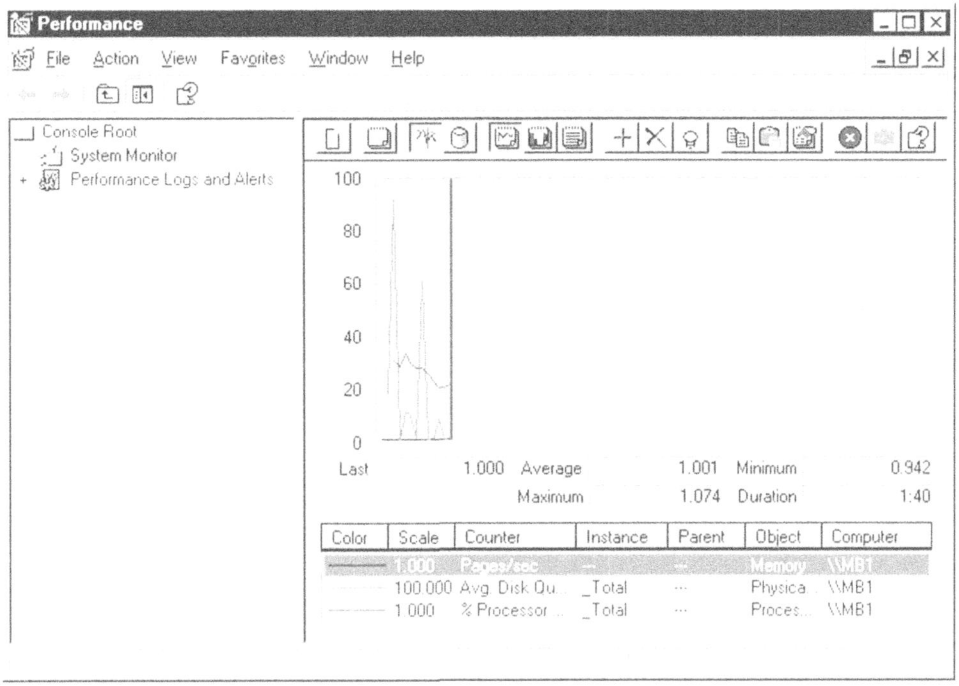

Figure 1-7: Opening the Performance Console to access the System Monitor.

When opened it will automatically begin to create a counter log by using the default counters displayed in the bottom right of the console. Additional counters are shown in the Table 1.3.

System Resource	Counter	Maximum peak
Disk	Physical Disk\% Free Space Logical Disk\% Free Space	15%
Disk	Physical Disk\% Disk Time Logical Disk\% Disk Time	90%
Disk	Physical Disk\Disk Reads/sec, Physical Disk\Disk Writes/sec	Check with Manufacturer for specifications
Disk	Physical Disk\Current Disk Queue Length	2 in addition to the number of spindles
Memory	Memory\Available Bytes	For larger memory computers, greater than 4 MB
Memory	Memory\Pages/sec	*n* pages/sec per pagefile
Paging file	Paging File\% Usage	Above 70%
Processor	Processor\% Processor Time	85%

Processor	Processor\Interrupts/sec	Depends on processor; 1,000 interrupts per second is a good starting point
Server	Server\Work Item Shortages	3
Server	Server \Pool Paged Peak	Amount of physical RAM
Server	Server WorkQueues\QueueLength	4
Multiple processors	System\Processor Queue Length	2

Table 1-3: System Resources, Counters and maximum peaks.

Microsoft has numerous counters available to create counter logs. Obtaining information on counters can be done when adding a counter. Selecting a counter will enable an "Explain" button. (You can see the button in Figure 1.8.) Clicking on that button will give you a detailed explanation of what each counter does. Let's take, for example, the "% Processor Time" counter from the Performance Object "Processor". Clicking the "Explain" button gives you the following details:

"% Processor Time is the percentage of elapsed time that the processor spends to execute a non-Idle thread. It is calculated by measuring the duration of the idle thread is active in the sample interval, and subtracting that time from interval duration. (Each processor has an idle thread that consumes cycles when no other threads are ready to run). This counter is the primary indicator of processor activity, and displays the average percentage of busy time observed during the sample interval. It is calculated by monitoring the time that the service is inactive, and subtracting that value from 100%."

System Monitor can now be configured to create a baseline. Just select the System Monitor, located in the left console pane under Console Root, in the Performance Console. The graph will appear to the right. The graph can be customized by using the toolbar above the graph. Right-click any blank area in the details pane and a shortcut menu appears that allows you to add counters, save, and view properties of the graph. The **Add Counters** option is shown in Figure 1.8.

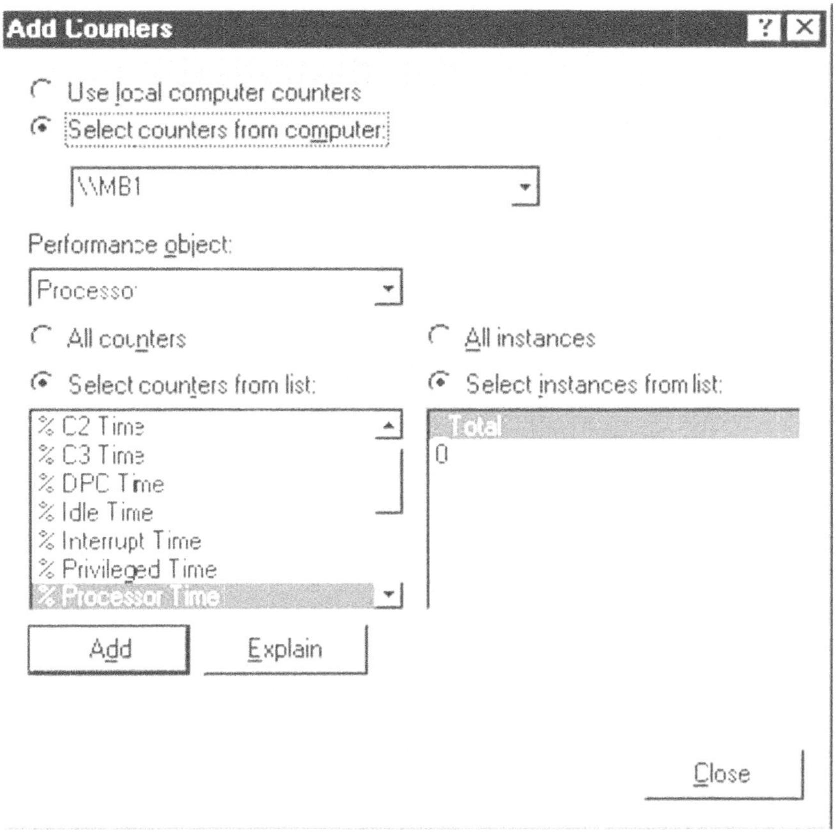

Figure 1-8: Adding Counters to System Monitor.

You will notice, under the Add Counters dialog box, you have the option of selecting counters from the local computer, or from remote computers (provided you have the administrative rights). For a remote computer, simply choose the **Select counters from** option and select the computer for which you wish to create counter logs. Choose the performance object you wish to measure performance on and the select the counters from the **Select counters from list** box at the bottom left of the screen. Selecting a large number of counters will impede performance for the simple reason that every single process and function that occurs on the computer is being measured. It is always a good idea, when possible, to test out potential counter groupings on a test lab machine before using on a production machine.

After the counter has been added click on the **Close** button. Figure 1.9 below shows the Toolbar from the Performance Counters and alerts console.

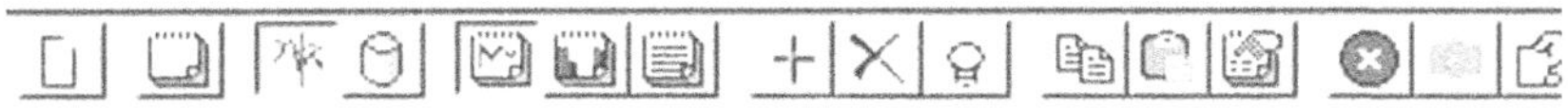

Figure 1-9: Scheduling shadow copies on volumes to run at various intervals.

The Performance Logs and Alerts option (Figure 1.10) can be used to monitor the usage of resources on the operating system.

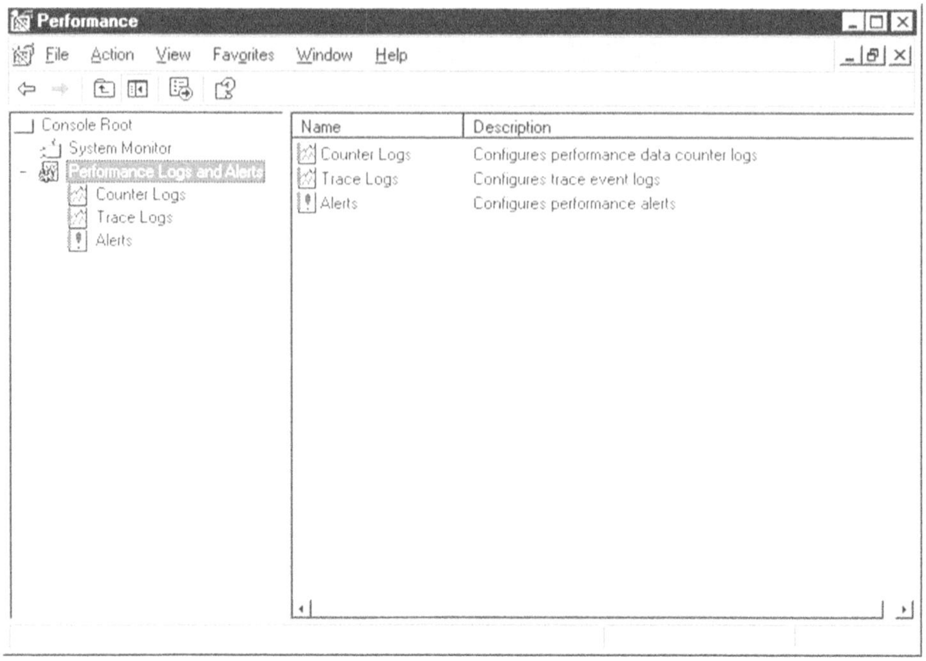

Figure 1-10: Performance Logs and Alerts option.

The Performance Logs and Alerts pane tool consists of three parts:

- Counter Logs- record data about hardware usage and activity on a system. New Counter logs can be created from the console by Double Clicking **Performance Logs and Alerts** in the pane and selecting **Counter Logs**.
- Trace Logs- measure data and record operating system events such as page faults and disk I/O activities on a continuous basis.
- Alerts- messages that are sent to the system administrator when a specific counter exceeds, or falls below, a predetermined setting.

All of the toolbar options have properties available that can be accessed by selecting the toolbar option and then clicking on **Properties** from the menu.

- The **General** tab allows views to be changed (Graph, Histogram or Report), modifying display elements (Legend, Value bar and Toolbar options). As well, the appearance can be made three-dimensional or flat, and borders can be added.
- The **Source** tab allows for data source information to be shown and database DSN information can be added. A Time Range option is also available if needed.
- The **Data** tab shows counter information and colors options, scale, width and styles can be modified.

- The **Graph** Tab will allow you to enter titles, vertical axis information, and display the vertical grid, horizontal grid and vertical scale numbers. The maximum and minimum vertical scale numbers can also be entered here.
- The **Appearance** Tab allows the color and font for the graph properties to be changed. Select a graph option in the **Color** drop-down menu and then choose the **Change** button. Tthe color wheel will appear, allowing you to modify these properties. Choose the **Change** option under the font text to change the font size and type.

Table 1.4 shows toolbar information pertaining to System Monitor in the Performance console.

Option	Explanation
	This is the new counter option and allows you to create a new counter log. This button can be pressed or you can hit the CTRL+E from your keyboard to open a new counter log.
	Selecting this allows you to add counters, save the counter log and view the properties of the log.
	This option allows you to view the current activity of the counters. This can also be accessed by selecting CTRL+T from the keyboard.
	This option allows you to view log data it can also be accessed via CTRL+L from the keyboard.
	Allows the view to be changed to a Graph View.
	Allows the View to be changed to a histogram.
	Displays a Report on the counters.
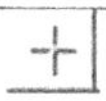	Opens the Add Counter option to allow you to select other computers and also add counters for various Performance objects.
	This is a delete option. When selected will remove counters from the graph.
	This is the highlight option and will highlight the graph when chosen.
	This option will copy to the clipboard the information that was highlighted.
	This option will paste the information that was copied in a statistical format. This is shown in Figure 1.11 after this table.
	This option shows the Properties menu tabs. It is the same as right-clicking the option from the toolbar.
	This freezes the display and also may be accessed by using CTRL+F.
	This option Updates data and is only available if the display has been frozen. If the display has not been frozen then this option is not accessible.
	This option displays the help files for the System Monitor.

Table 1-4: Performance Counters and Alerts toolbar information.

Figure 1.11 shows the output of the System Monitor graph from the Copy and Paste options on the toolbar. To Copy items into a file for viewing choose the Highlight option from the toolbar then select Copy command from the toolbar. Open a text editor (this example shows Wordpad) and **right-click** in the blank document. Select **Paste** (alternately you can use CTRL+V from your keyboard) to paste the information into the document.

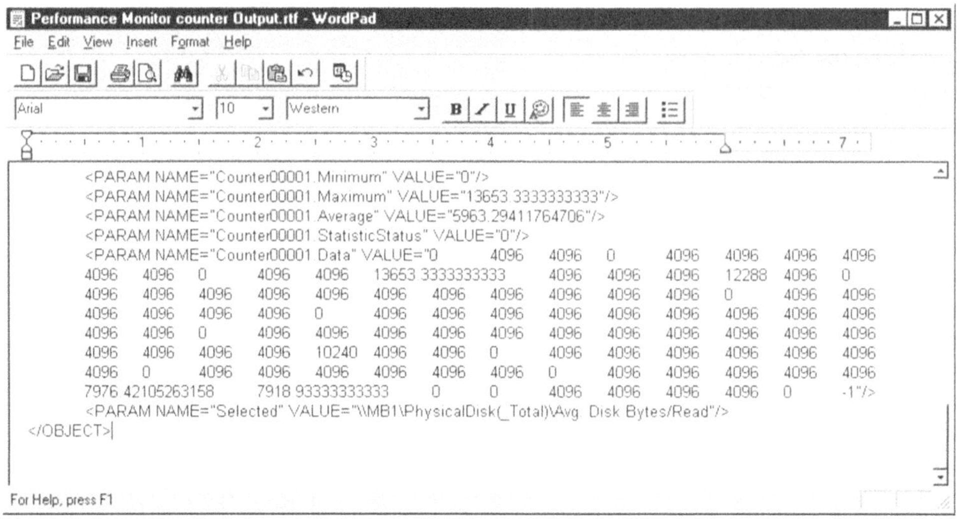

Figure 1-11: The Performance Monitor Output file pasted into Wordpad.

The Performance Logs and Alerts information can be exported into a Microsoft Excel file. Keep in mind that Excel needs total access to the information, so you will need to stop the Performance Logs and Alerts service.

Transactional-based events, such as Active Directory and kernel processes, can be produced into a report format using the Tracerpt tool. This downloadable tool will allow you to generate reports in the .csv format as well as in binary log format.

The following URL points to a very helpful resource on the Microsoft Web site—**Performance Counters Reference for Windows Server**:

`http://www.microsoft.com/technet/treeview/default.asp?url=/technet/prodtechnol/windowsse -- rver2003/proddocs/deployguide/counters_overview.asp`

This URL gives some new insight to the performance counters that can be used on a Windows Server 2003 system. The page is shown below in Figure 1.12.

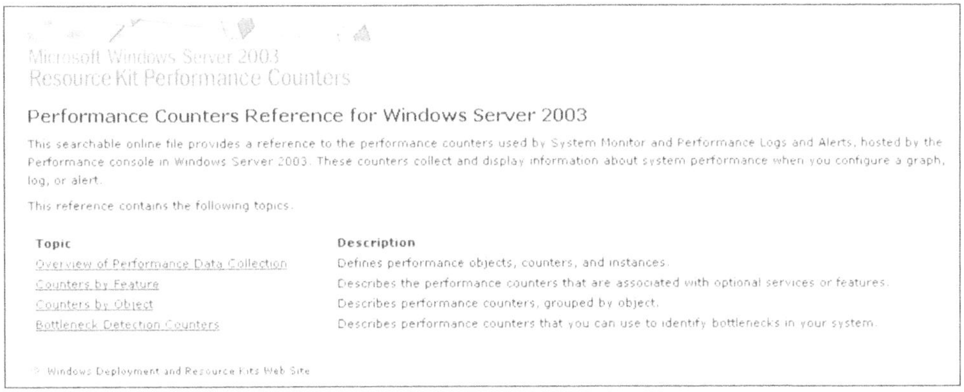

Figure 1-12: Windows Server 2003 Resource Kit Performance Counters.

It is also a wonderful reference for the many counters that are available for use on Windows Server 2003 systems.

Important to remember is the fact that two new security groups have been created in Windows Server 2003. These groups are meant to ensure that only trusted users have access to the performance data for viewing and manipulation. The two new security groups are:

- **Performance Log Users** have the ability to collect data from remote servers or computers using different accounts (such as the Administrator account).
- **Performance Monitor Users** have the ability to monitor performance counters locally from the server as well as from remote clients and do not need to have Administrative rights.

Log files can also now be appended to other log files and can be greater than 1 GB in size. To modify the log files, expand the **Performance Logs and Alerts** tool by double clicking. Three options will appear—the **Counter Log, Trace Log** and **Alerts**. Right-click on the **Counter Logs** to create a new counter log file and choose **New Log Settings** as shown in Figure 1.13.

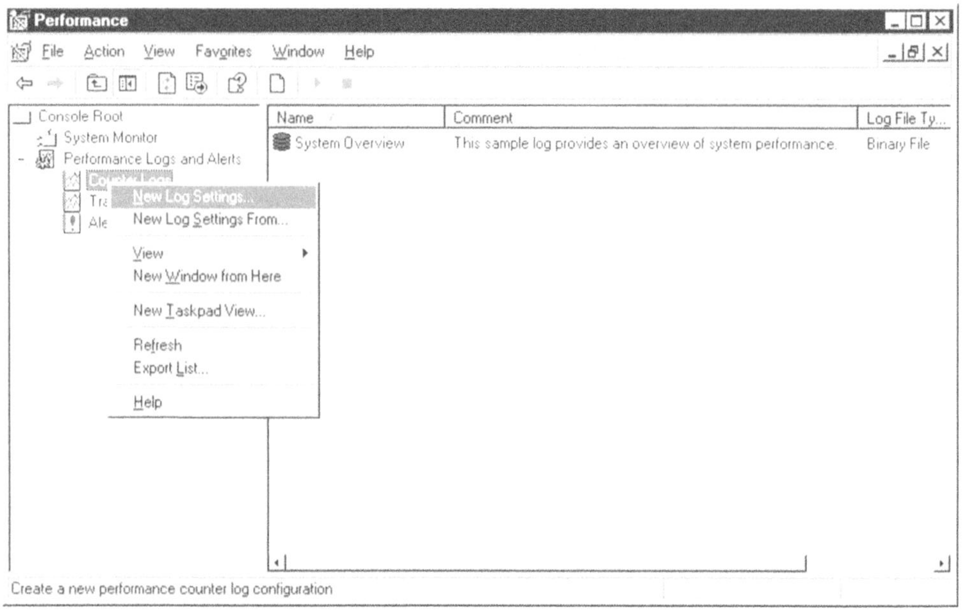

Figure 1-13: Creating a New Counter Log.

Enter a name for the Counter Log. In this example the name of the counter log is testlog.

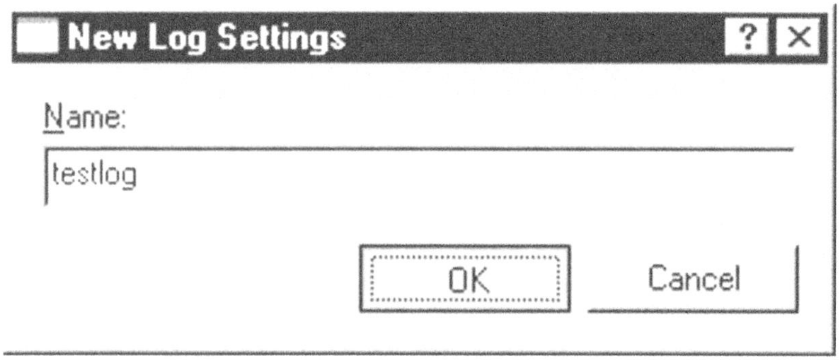

Figure 1-14: New Log Settings.

Click the **OK** button and the Screen shown in Figure 1.15 will appear. The **General** tab shows the current log file name, counter information and also shows gives clients the ability to run the counters on remote or the local machine under a different identity, such as Administrator, if needed, using the "Run As" command.

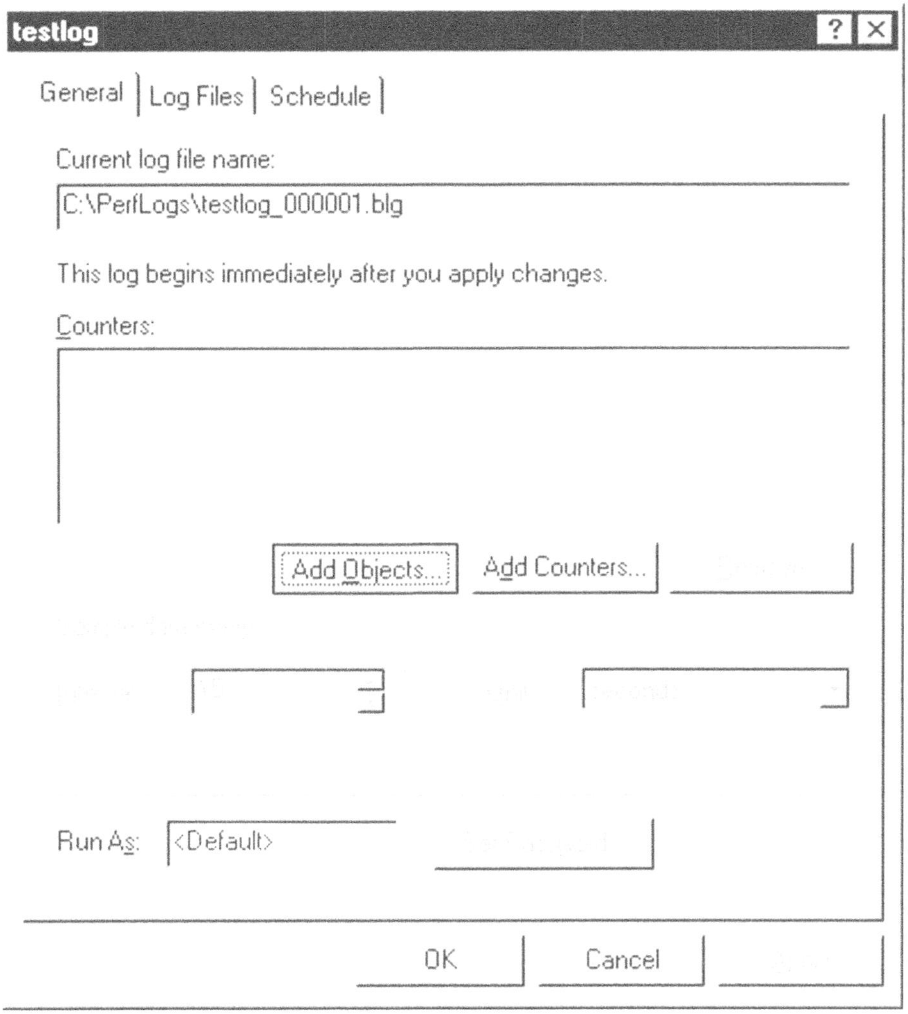

Figure 1-15: The General Tab for counter logs.

To add object and counters to the log file select, **Add Objects**. The **Add Objects** screen (Figure 1.16) will appear, which allows you to choose to add objects for the local computer counter. Alternately, you can select to add counter objects from other computers from the drop-down menu. In the example shown in Figure 1.16, I have selected the **Logical Disk** object from the list of available objects and then selected the **Add** button.

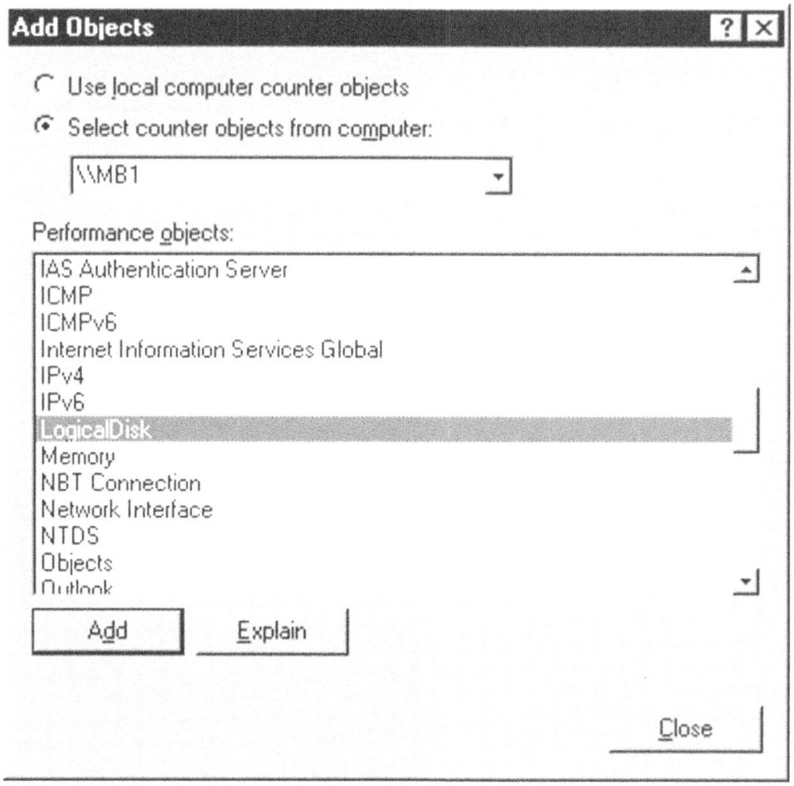

Figure 1-16: Adding Objects to the counter log.

As mentioned earlier, if you are not certain what the object counter's purpose is, you can select the Explain button to view the explanation of the object counter (Figure 1.17).

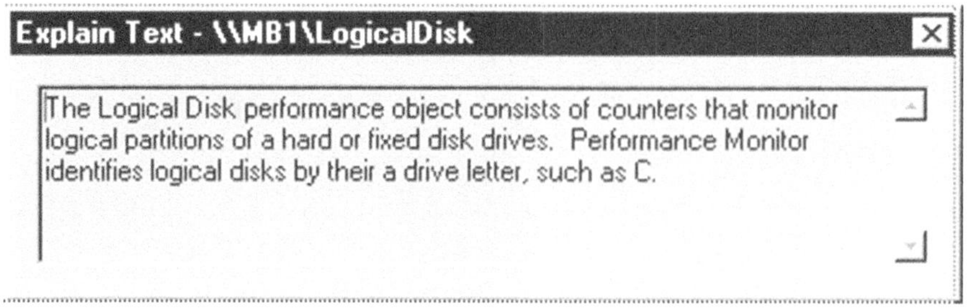

Figure 1-17: Viewing the explanation for the Logical Disk Performance Counter.

After you add the counter object, you will return to the **General** tab for the counter log. The newly added performance object will appear, as illustrated in Figure 1.18.

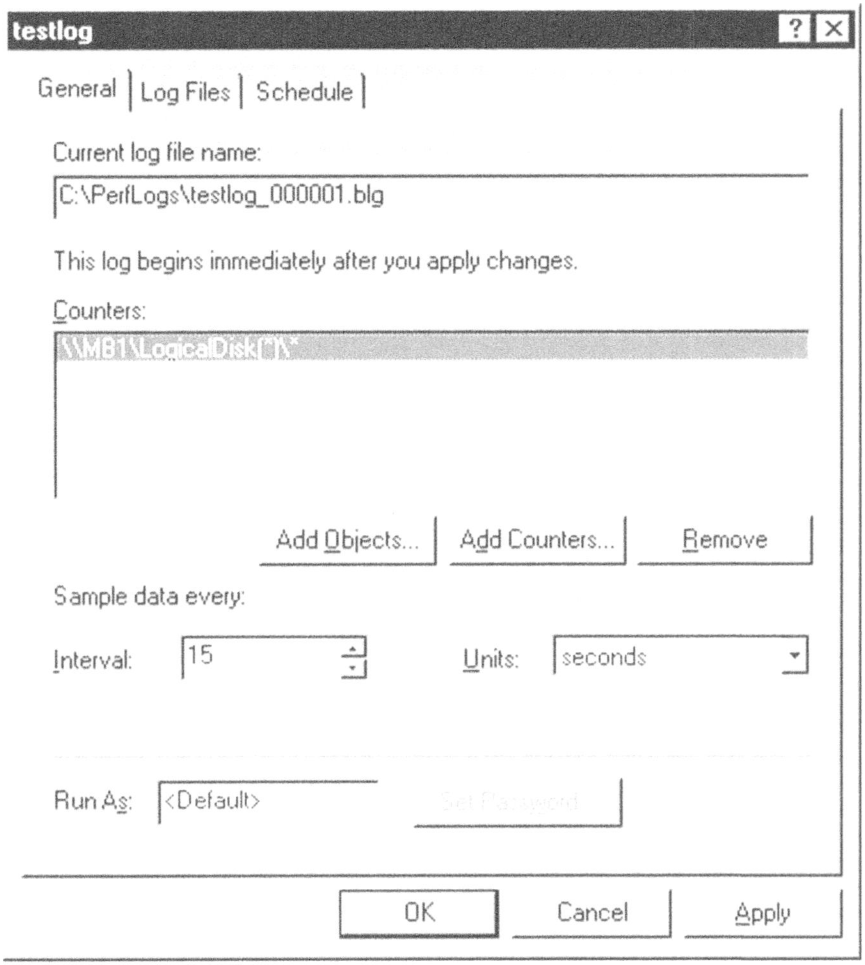

Figure 1-18: The newly added Logical Disk Performance object.

You can continue to add more objects by using the same method and you can remove objects by selecting the **Remove** button. After the Objects have been added to the counter log, you can add counters by selecting the **Add Counters** option. The process for adding counters is the same as adding performance objects.

Once the objects and counters have been added, you can change the rate that the data is sampled by increasing or decreasing the number in the **Interval** box, using the up and down arrows. You can also change the rate for the data sample by changing the **Units** measurement. The default measurement is by second; it can be altered to be by minute, hour or day. If you do not need to set an alternate identity, using "Run as", leave the box as **default** then click **Apply.** The next tab is the **Log Files** tab, illustrated in Figure 1.19.

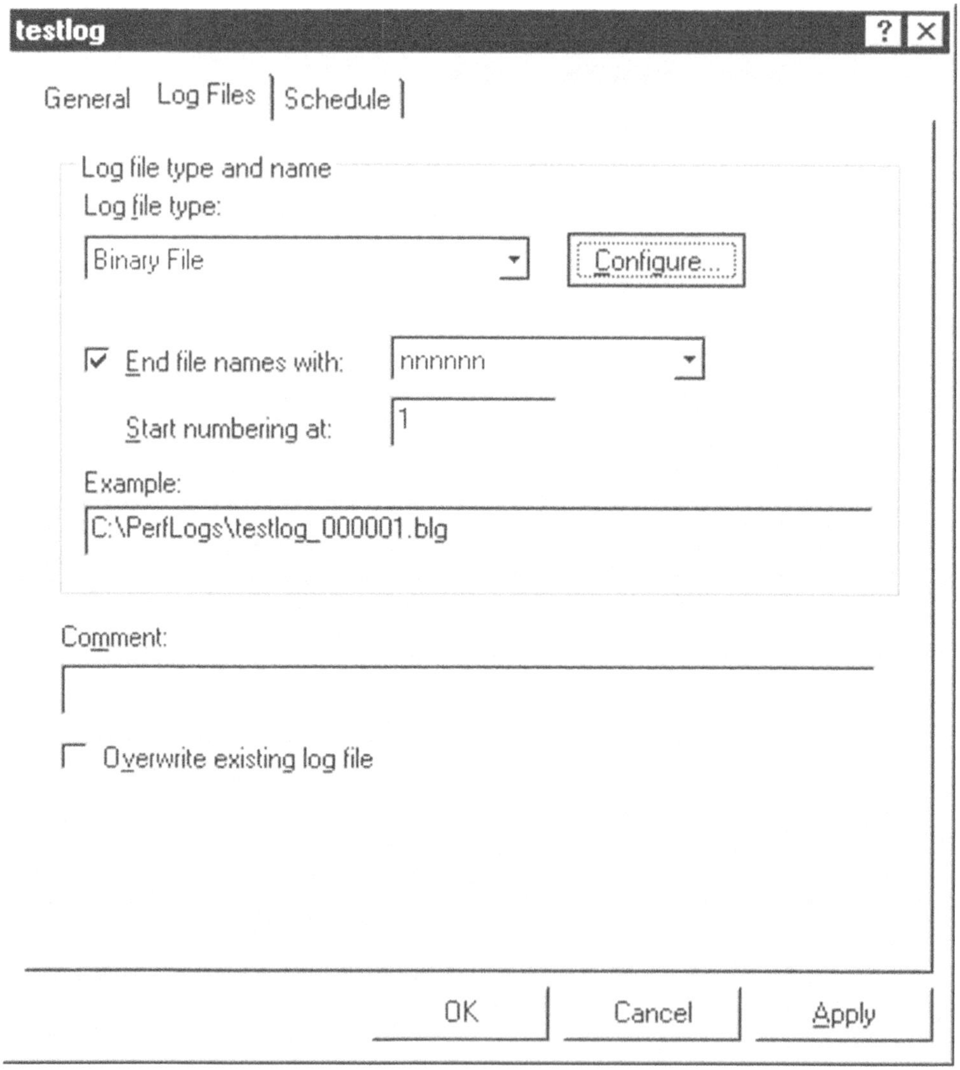

Figure 1-19: The Log Files settings for the Counter Log.

This dialog box gives you the option of changing the log file type from the default **Binary File** to either a comma delimited text file, tab delimited text file, binary circular file or SQL database (Figure 1.20). Select the option for the log file type that best suits your needs and select the **Configure** option.

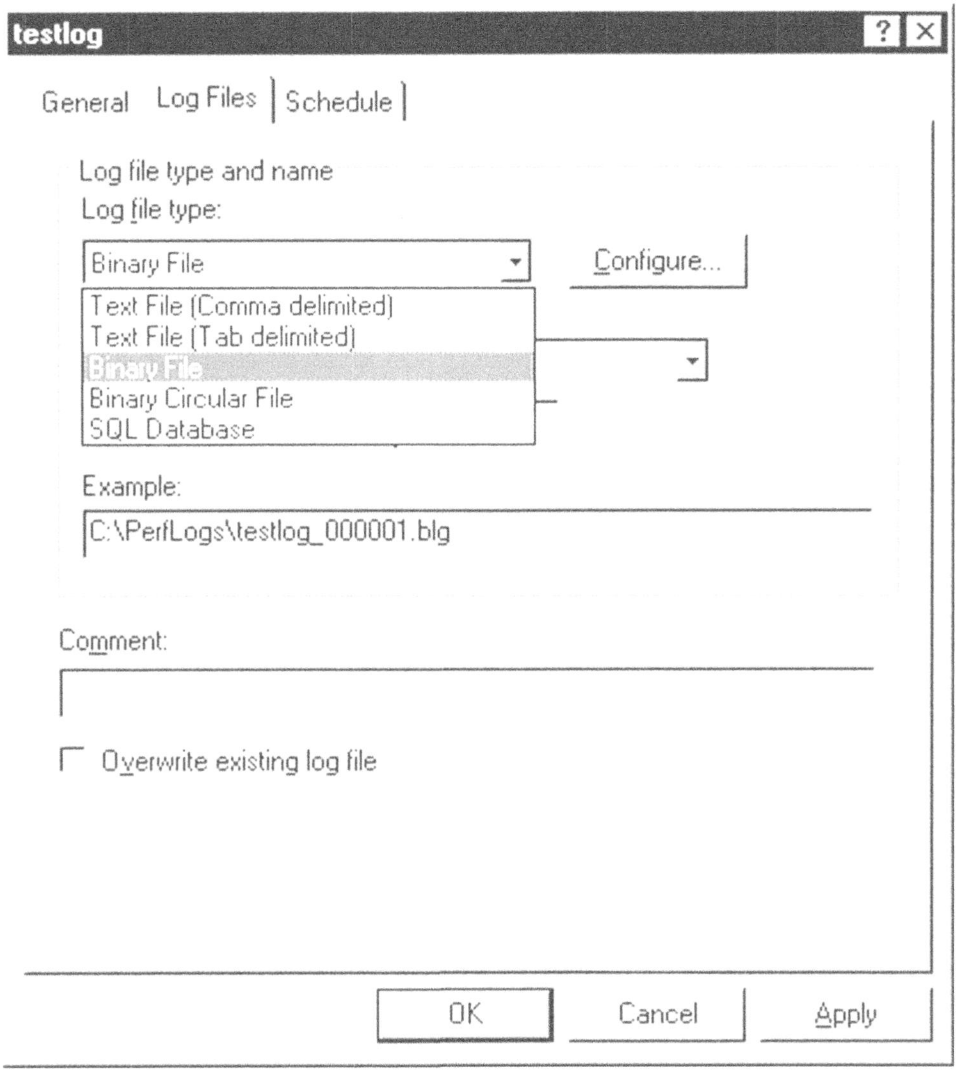

Figure 1-20: Selecting a log file type for the counter log.

The configure log file dialog box will appear (Figure 1.21). This box displays the default location for the log file, **C:\PerfLogs.** You can change this location, by clicking the **Browse** button and selecting a new location for the log file. The file name you assigned earlier is also displayed, and you are given the option to set a log file size limit (by default, it is set to "Maximum limit"). It is important to remember that log files can now grow to over 1 GB on Windows Server 2003, so make sure you set a limit if your available disk space will not allow for a log file of that size.

Once the information has been configured to your preferences, click **OK**.

Note: The **Configure Log Files** process is not mandatory; it can be left at default settings.

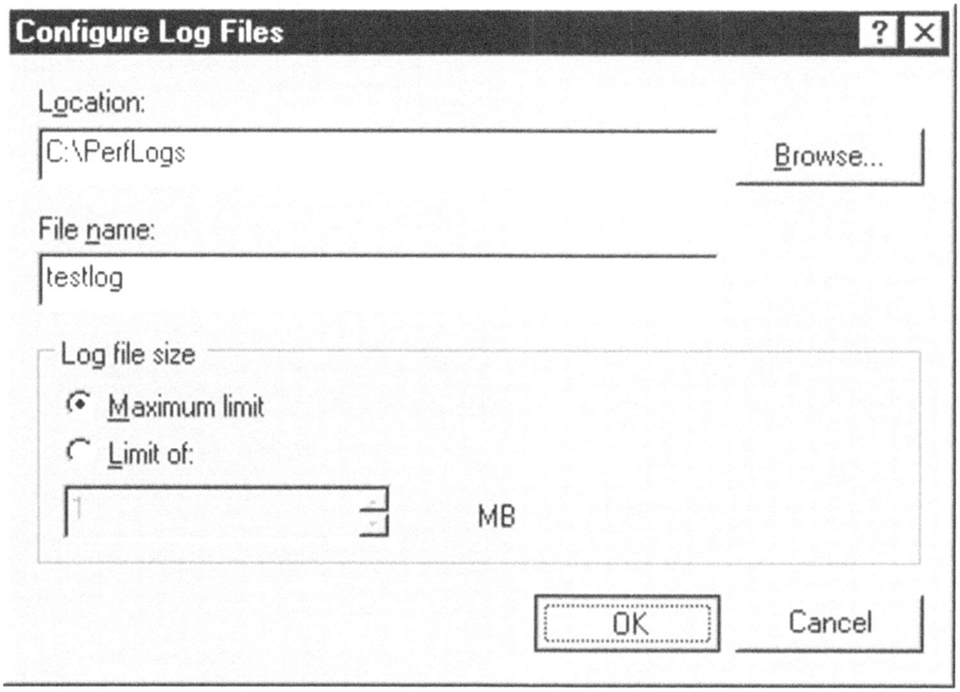

Figure 1-21: The Configure Log File screen.

The last option is the **Schedule** tab (Figure 1.22). This dialog tab allows you to preset a regular time for the counter log to start and stop logging. By default, the start time will be set to the time when you accessed the counter log settings. If you do not wish for the logs to begin and end at set intervals, you can choose the **Manually (using the shortcut menu)** option and start the logs yourself as needed. The **Stop** option is set to **Manually** by default.

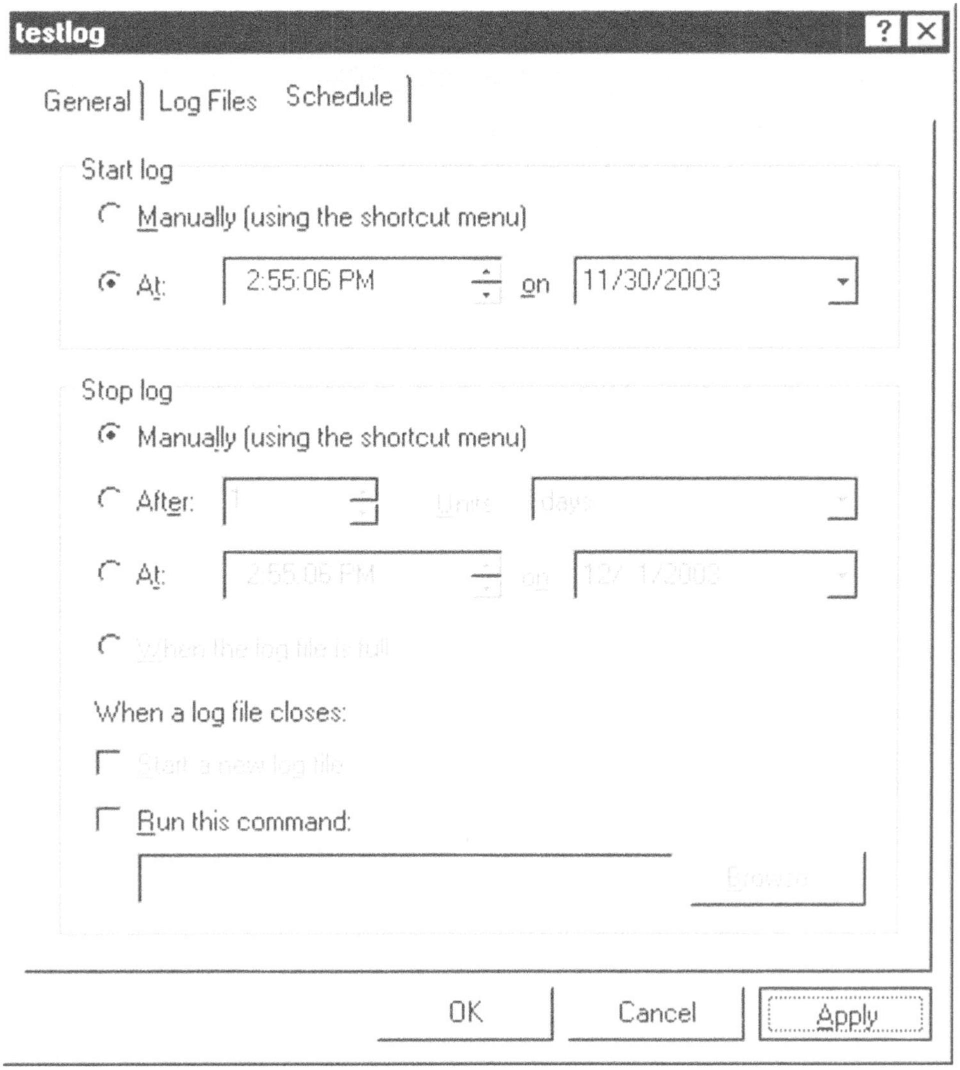

Figure 1-22: Scheduling a time for the logs to begin and end.

Another option available to you is the ability to start a new program or run a command when the log file closes. This can be configured by clicking the **Run this command** option. The **Browse** option will then allow you to browse to the application you wish to run once the log file has closed. Click the **Apply** button once to confirm the changes (if any) that have been made. You will return to the main Performance Logs and Alerts console (Figure 1.23).

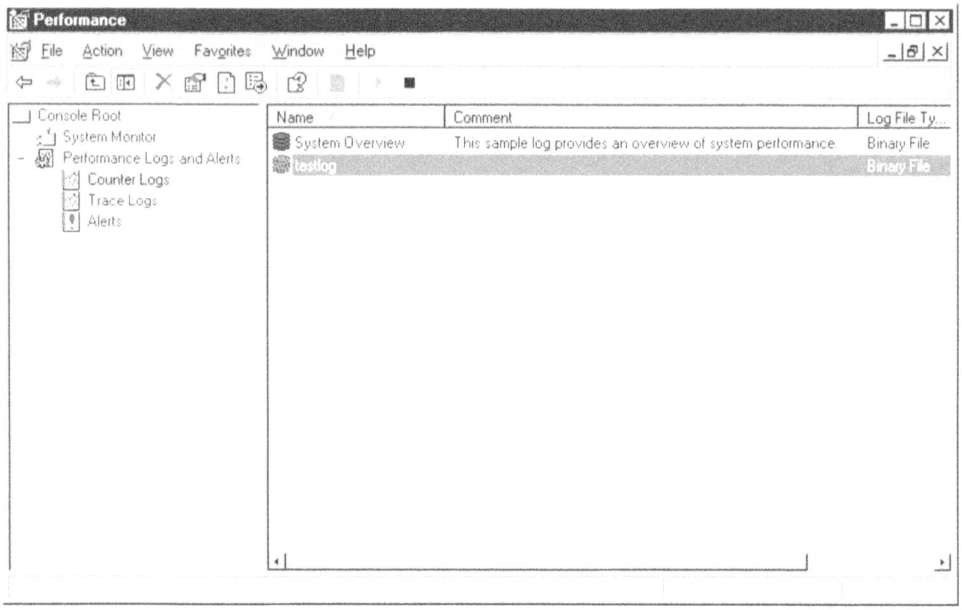

Figure 1-23:The newly created counter log in the Performance Logs and Alerts console.

As illustrated in Figure 1.23, the newly created counter log now appears in the console. If a log is running a Green icon will appear. If the log has been stopped then a Red icon will be showing.

Click the Start and Stop buttons to control the log file progress.

Our next task to walk through is the creation of Trace Logs. Right-click the **Trace Logs** from the left console pane. A shortcut menu will appear, as illustrated in Figure 1.24.

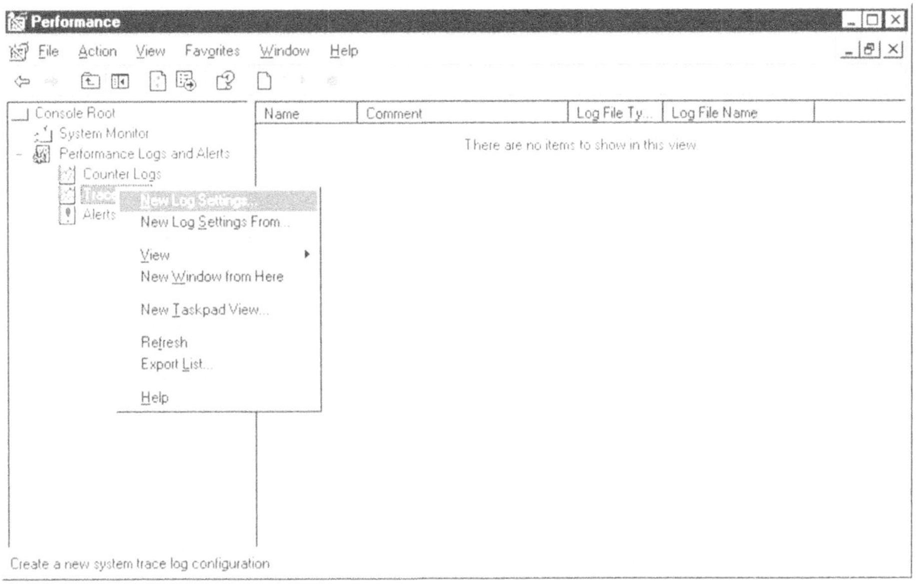

Figure 1-24: Creating a new trace log.

Choose the **New Log Settings** option (Figure 1.25) to create a new trace log. Adding traces is done in the same manner as we have just show in Counter Logs, so I will not go into extended detail again. Rather, let's look at some of the additional options shown on the shortcut menu.

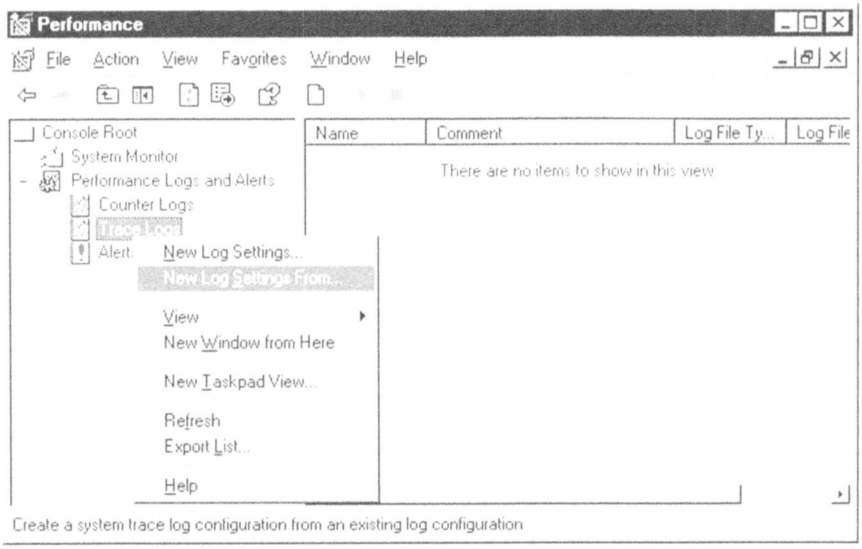

Figure 1-25: Creating a new trace log from prewritten options.

The first option we will examine is the "**New Log Settings From**" item, as illustrated in Figure 1.26.

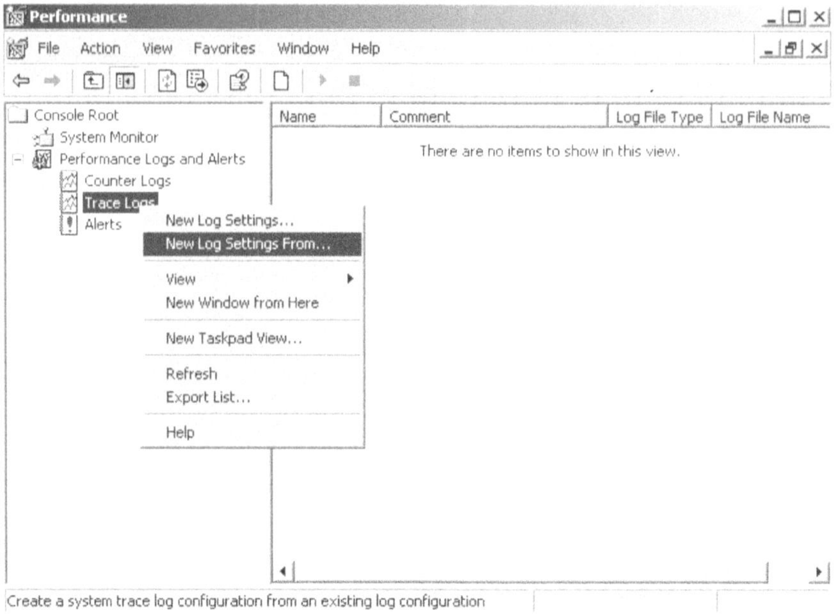

Figure 1-26: Shows the dialog View option.

Selecting this will allow you to open up to a location (for example, My Documents) where you can choose to select a file from which you retrieve log settings. If you select the **View** option (Figure 1.27), you will be allowed to change your pane view.

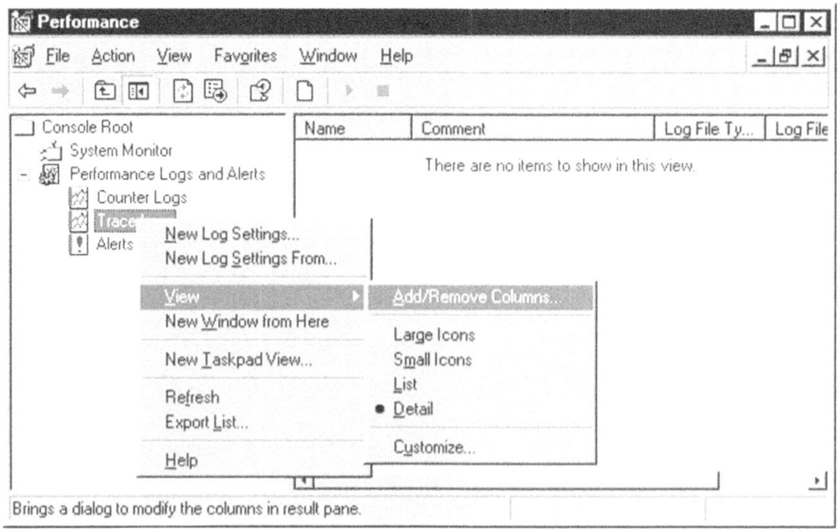

Figure 1-27: Shows the dialog View option.

For our "step through" example, we will select the "**New Taskpad View**" option, which is the fifth option on the shortcut menu. This is a clever tool and often underutilized. Selecting that option opens the **New Taskpad View Wizard.** When it opens, you will see the Introduction screen. Clicking **Next** will bring up a dialog box as shown in Figure 1.28. This dialog box gives you a number of choices, including whether you want to see a vertical list, a horizontal list or no list at all, whether you want to hide the "**Standard Tab**", as well as in what fashion you wish to see your task descriptions (either text or as an InfoTip). The choices for our sample are illustrated in Figure 1.28.

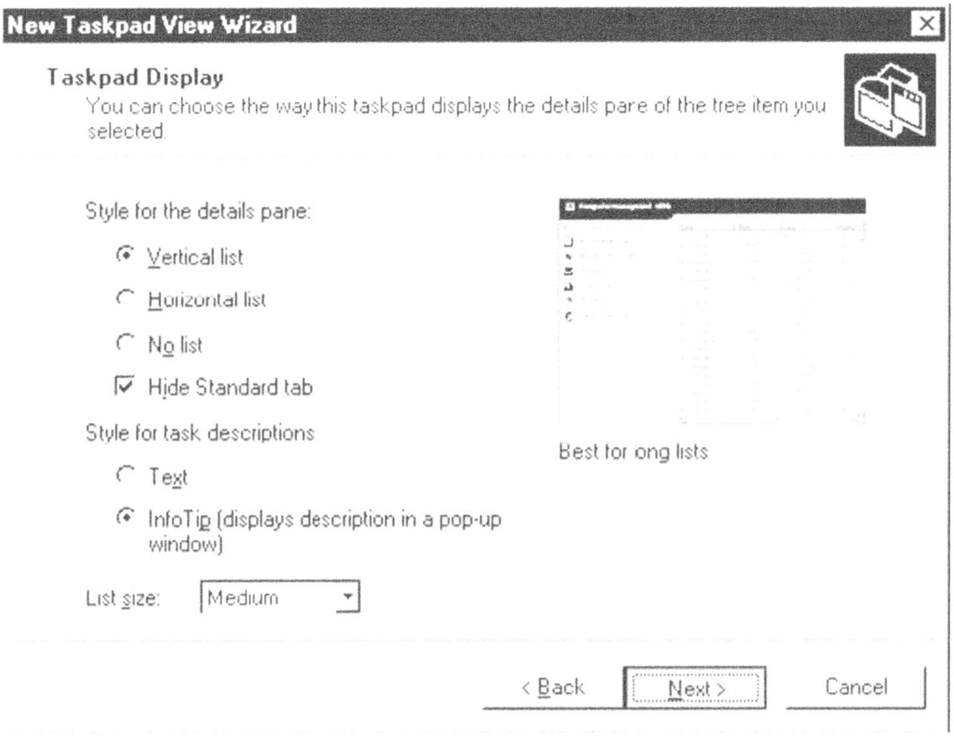

Figure 1-28: Shows the new Taskpad view option.

Clicking the "**Next**" button will bring up the dialog box shown in Figure 1.29. This box allows you to decide whether the new taskpad view will be applied to only the current tree item, or all tree items that are of the same type. Click "**Next**" and the final dialog box of the wizard appears, that allows you to give a name and description to the new taskpad view you have created.

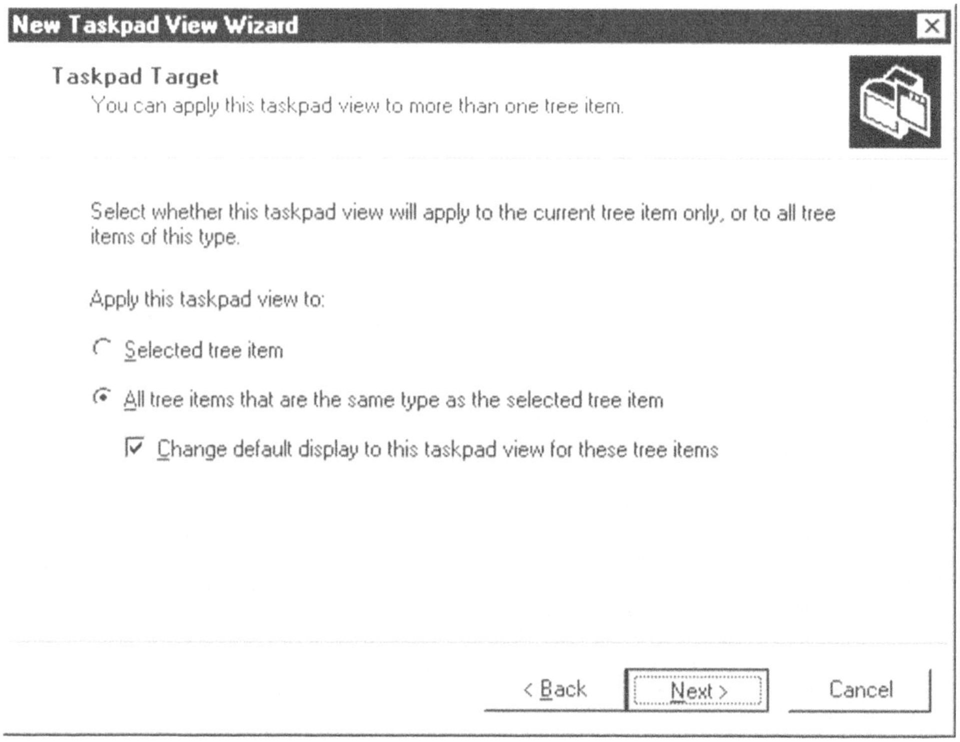

Figure 1-29: Configuring a new Taskpad view for the Performance Console.

Let's now take a look at creating a new Alert, which is somewhat different than what we have already done with Counter and Trace Logs.

Right-click the **Alerts** and choose **New Alert Settings** from the shortcut menu, shown in Figure 1.30.

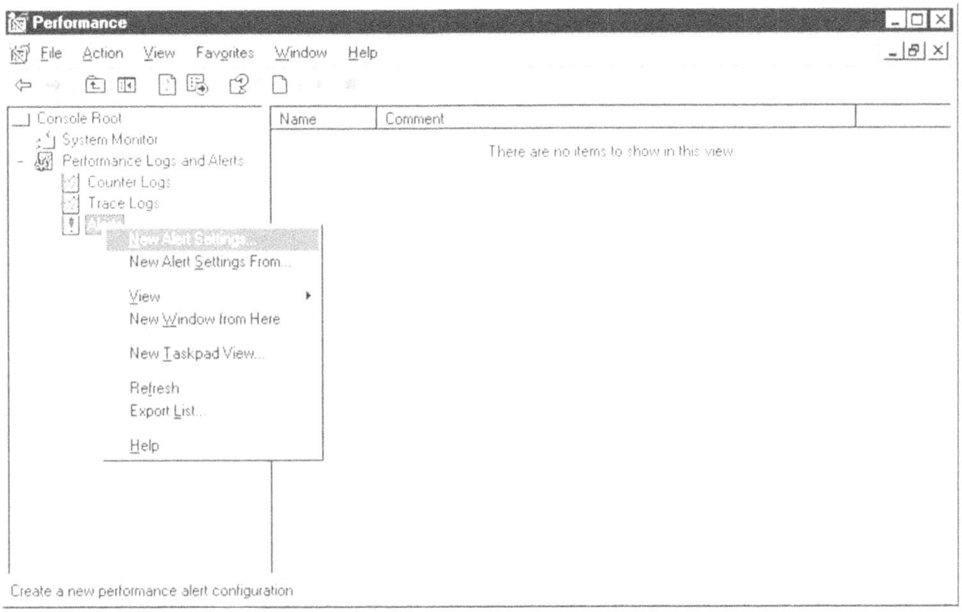

Figure 1-30: Creating new alerts using the Alerts tool in the Performance console.

The New Alert Settings console will appear, prompting for a name to be assigned to the new alert (Figure 1.31). In this example, we will use the name "alertest" for the name of the alert. It is important to remember that you cannot use the same name for different logs and alerts; for example, you cannot give a new alert the same name used for a counter log.

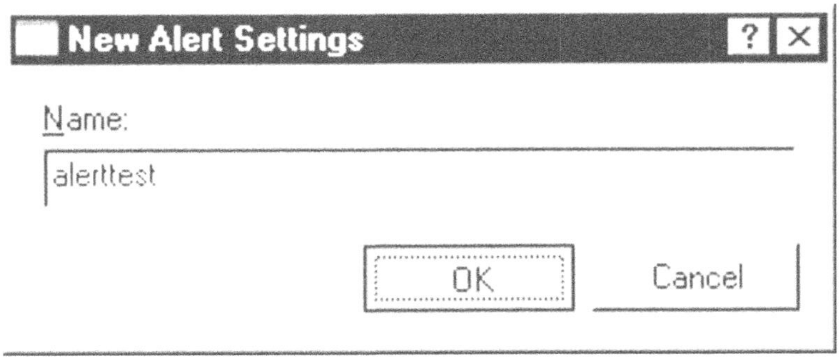

Figure 1-31: Entering a name for the Alert.

Once you have given your new alert a unique name, click **OK** and a properties dialog box will appear (Figure 1.32).

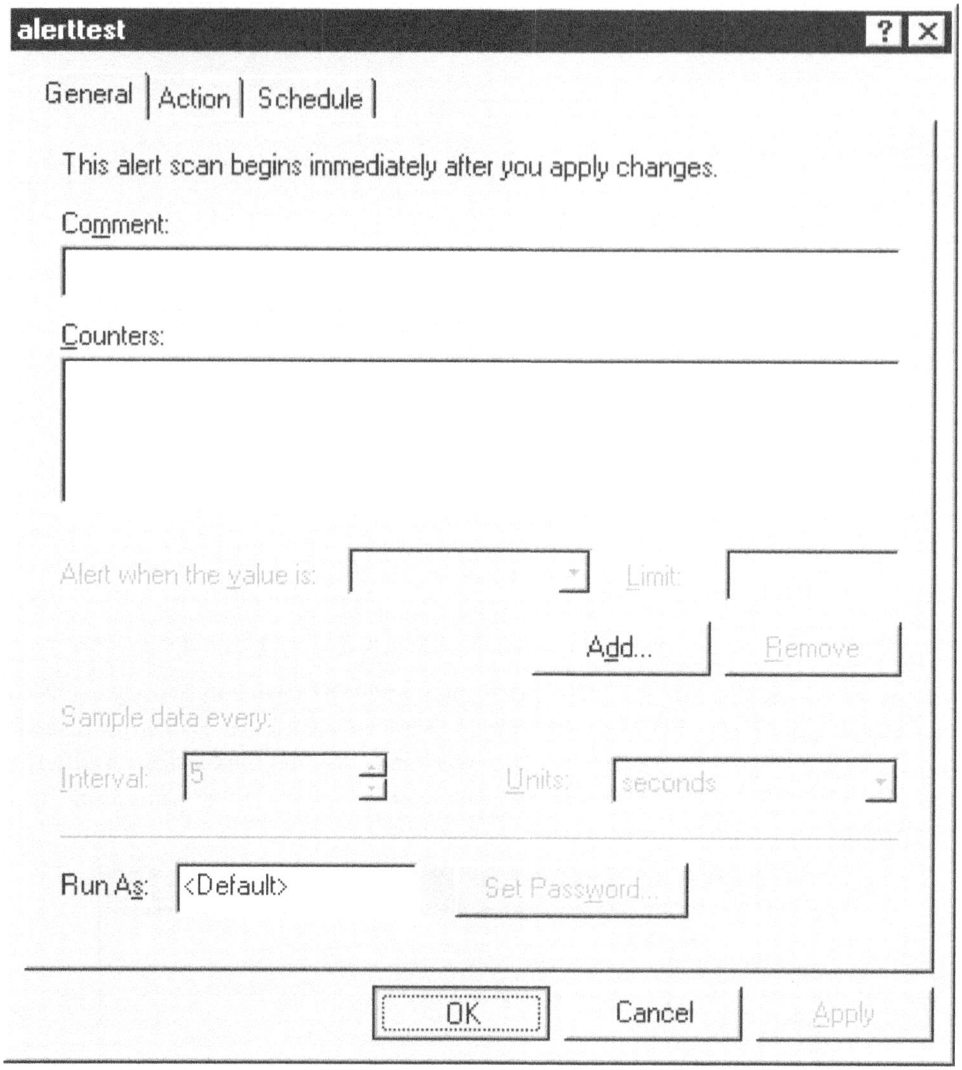

Figure 1-32: Entering Comments & Counters for Alerts using Alert properties menu.

Entering a comment is not mandatory, but it is a good idea. The comment should give a brief overview of what this alert is "all about." You will now add **Counters** to the Alert by clicking the **Add** button. An **Add Counter** dialog box appears (Figure 1.33).

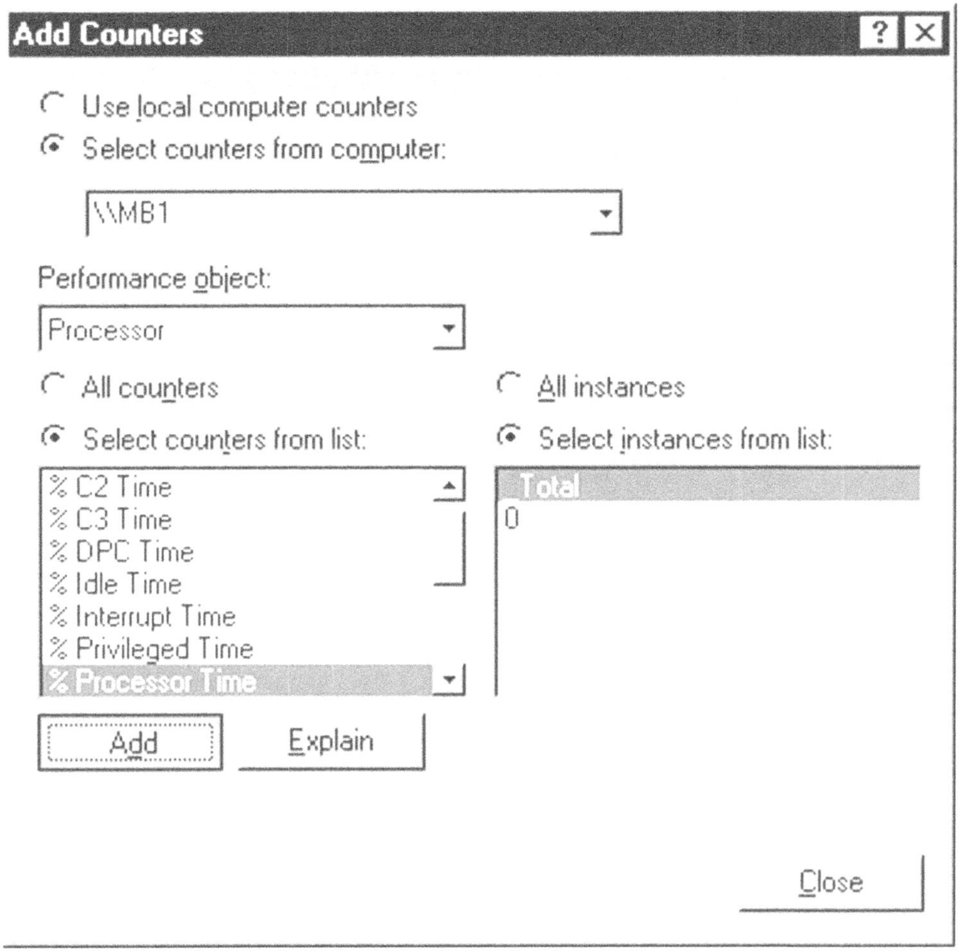

Figure 1-33: Adding Counters to Alerts.

This particular dialog box is identical to the one used for the counter logs, and the same procedures apply. To add a counter, locate the counter in the **Select counters from list** then click the **Add** button. As noted earlier, you can choose the **Explain** button to have a brief explanation appear about the selected counter, as illustrated in Figure 1.17. The counter can be applied to **All Instances** or a particular instance can chosen by clicking the **Selected from the list** option shown on the right side of the pane. Once the appropriate counter and instances information have been chosen, click the **Close** button.

You will return to the properties dialog box, General tab. For the example displayed in Figure 1.34, we chose the Logical Disk Free Space counter.

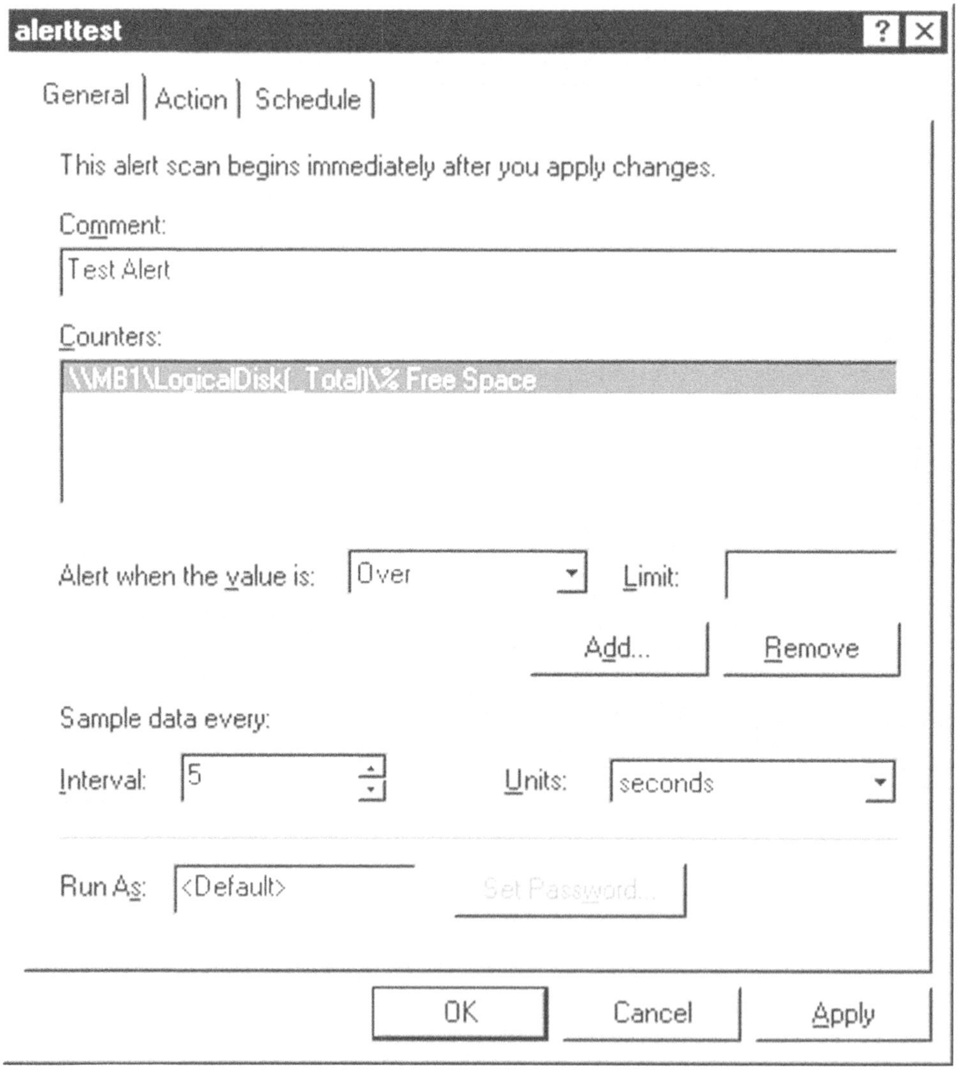

Figure 1-34: The Free Space Alert counter used to configure Alerts.

What you need to decide now is what factors will cause the Alert to be triggered. Is it when the counter goes OVER a predetermined amount, or when it is running UNDER a preset number. If, for example, you were monitoring free disk space, you may wish to receive an alert only when the amount of free disk space goes UNDER a certain figure. On the other hand, if you were watching the temperature of the CPU, you may wish to know when the temperature exceeds a certain level.

You choose either OVER or UNDER from a dropdown menu, and then enter a specific limit in the **Limit** box. The interval and Run As options are the same as for Counter and Trace Logs.

The next tab is the **Action** tab (Figure 1.35).

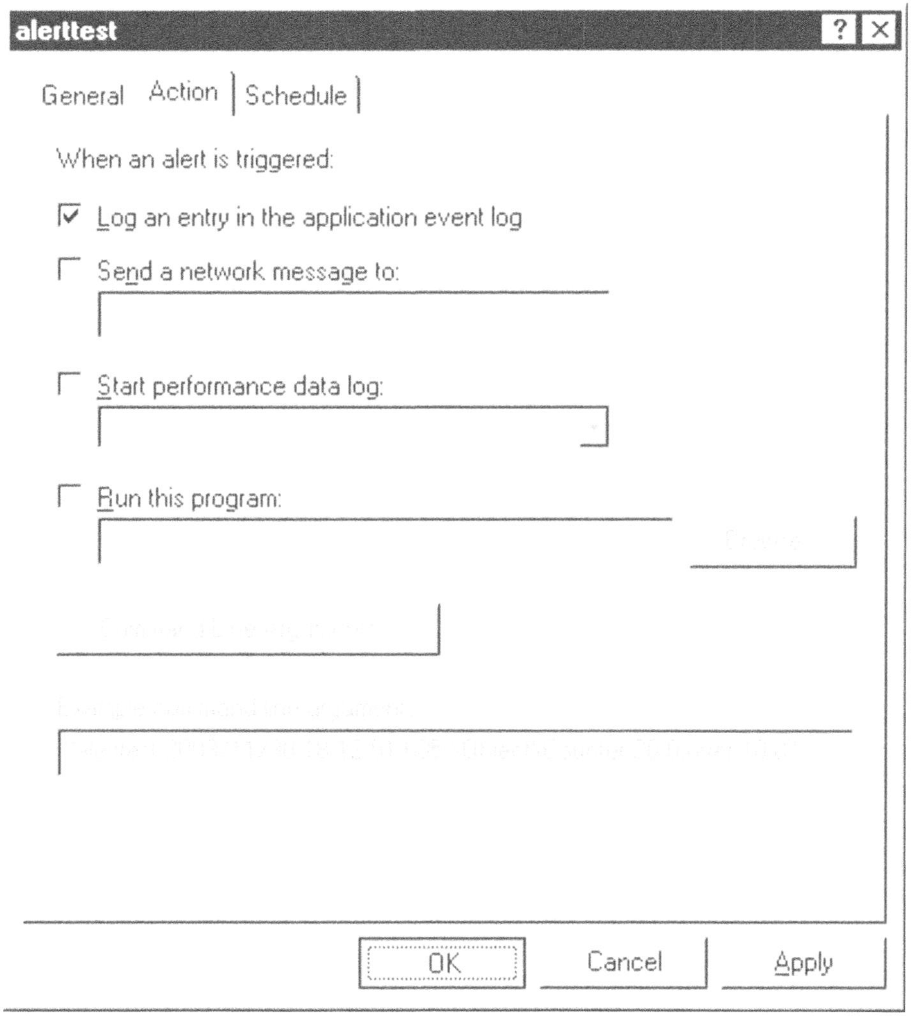

Figure 1-35: The Action Tab for Alert settings.

The Action tab specifies what action should be taken when an alert is triggered. To create an entry visible in Event Viewer (Application Log), **select Log an entry in the application event log**. This option is selected by default. As well, you can have the Messenger service triggered to send a message. To do this, select **Send a network message to** and type the IP address or name of the computer on which the alert message should be displayed. To run a counter log when an alert occurs, select **Start performance data log** and specify the name of the counter log you want to run. Your final choice may be to have a program run when an alert occurs. Choose **Run this program** and type the file path and name (alternately, click Browse to locate the file) The file can be a .bat, .exe other executable file type, for example, a program that will send a page to your pager notifying you of the alert.. Click **Command Line Arguments** and select the appropriate check boxes for arguments to include when the program you have specified is run. (This option is only available when you have selected **Run this program**.)

Figure 1.36 shows the options that are available when you click **"Command Line Arguments**.

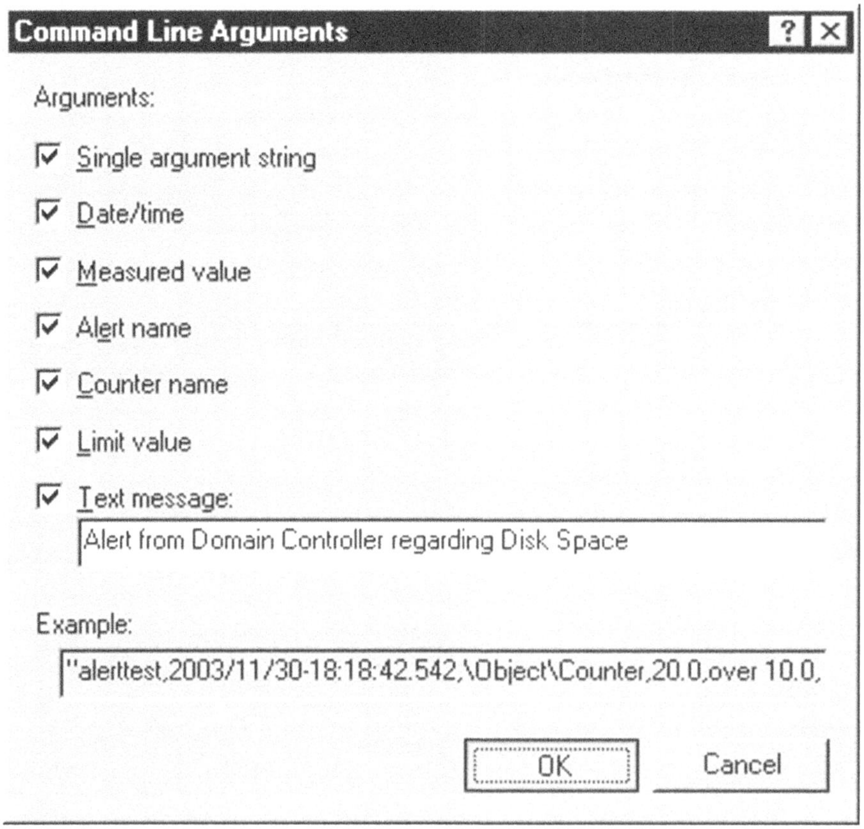

Figure 1-36: Command line arguments: Choose to Run this Program option.

By default, all boxes in the **Command Line Arguments** screen are checked except the Text Message Box. If, for example, you were activating a program to send you a page on alert trigger, you may wish to select this option and enter a text message in the dialog box. Click **OK** for the settings to take effect.

Figure 1.37 shows the newly created Alert in the console screen.

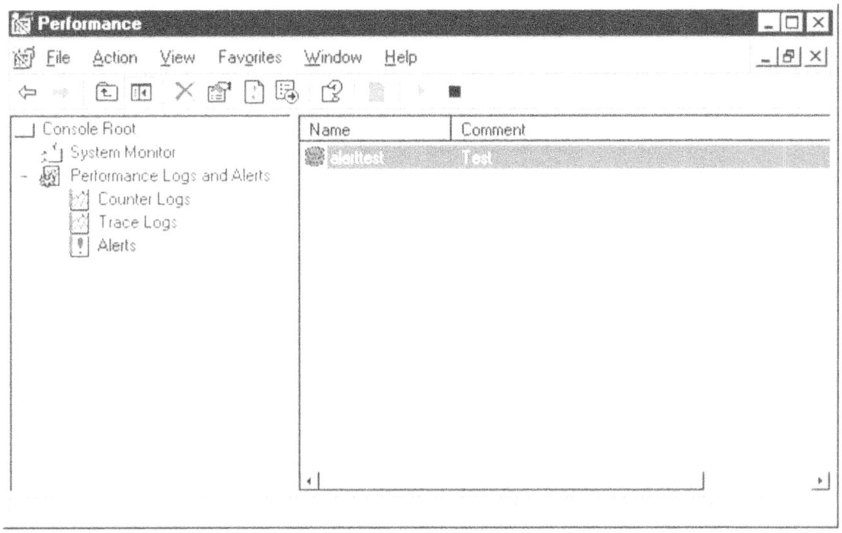

Figure 1-37: A new Alert created in the Performance Management Console.

This section has covered the basic information you can need to create baselines, monitors and alerts on your Windows Server 2003 systems.

You can save and close the Performance Management Console by clicking on **File** then **Save As** and enter a name for the Performance Console.

Pop Quiz 1.1

Pop Quiz 1.1 *Questions*

1. What versions of Windows can access dynamic disks directly?
2. Can a basic disk partition span multiple drives?
3. I have a dynamic simple volume that I wish to convert to a basic disk partition. How do I do this?
4. What three types of data should you collect on the server to create a counter log?
5. What is an alert?

Pop Quiz 1.1 *Answers*

1. All versions of Windows XP Professional, Windows 2000 and Windows Server 2003 (including 64-bit versions) can access dynamic disks directly.
2. Basic disk partitions cannot span multiple drives. The disk must be converted to dynamic first.
3. You can't. Dynamic simple volumes cannot be converted back to basic disk partitions. Conversion is permanent.
4. Microsoft suggests that you collect three types of data on the server to create a counter log—baseline performance, general performance and data for service level reports.
5. An alert is a message sent, usually to the system administrator, when a specific counter exceeds, or falls below, a predetermined setting.

1.2.1 Tools used to manage hardware

Hardware management can be performed through the MMC, Windows Device Manager and the command line. The following section covers the options available for managing hardware on Windows Server 2003 systems.

1.2.2 Device Manager

If you have worked in this field for over five or six years, you probably remember having to install and configure non-plug-and-play devices on your Windows NT or 95 systems. Remember the comment "plug-and-pray"? We spent a lot of time doing both when we hardware on a Microsoft operating system. More often than not, even if a device claimed to be "plug-and-play," you knew you would have to do some configuring on the system.

Well, times have definitely changed for the better! Installing hardware has gotten so much easier with each new release of a Microsoft O/S. Now, the term plug-and-play simply means that the Windows O/S will automatically configure the device to work with other devices on the computer in a manner that will not conflict with other hardware already installed.

Each device uses four resources, assigned by the Windows Operating System at the time of the installation of the device. The four resources are:

- IRQ (nterrupt request line numbers)
- DMA (Direct memory access channels)
- I/O (Input/output port addresses)
- Memory address ranges.

Once the hardware is installed on the Windows 2003, it is given a value. On rare occasion more than on device is assigned the same value (quite often the IRQ value), and the devices will conflict. Using the Device Manager you can manually change the settings for the device to correct the problem. It is not advised that you change plug-and-play device settings. Non-plug-and-play devices are not configured by Windows by default; they must be manually configured. There may be jumpers on a card, for example, which you can set manually, using the instructions supplied with the device. A particular jumper setting may set a device to a specific IRQ; changing the setting may change the IRQ setting. Non-plug-and-play hardware that has been manually installed cannot be changed automatically by the Windows O/S.

We are now going to take a look at the GUI tool, Device Manager. Device Manager first appeared with the Windows 95 operating system. It still has the familiar feel of that original Device Manager and it a great tool to use to configure and monitor hardware devices for errors.

You can open the Device Manager by any of the available methods:

- Click **Start,** select **Administrative Tools** and choose **Computer Management**. Select **Device Manager** from under System Tools in the left pane of the **Computer Management** Console.
- Right-click **My Computer,** and select **Properties** from the shortcut menu. The **System Properties** dialog box appears. Select the Hardware tab.
- Use the keyboard shortcut **WinKey+Pause**. (WinKey is the key with the Windows Logo). Again, the **System Properties** dialog box appears.

In the last two methods, once you are on the **Hardware** tab, select **Device Manager** button as shown in Figure 1.38.

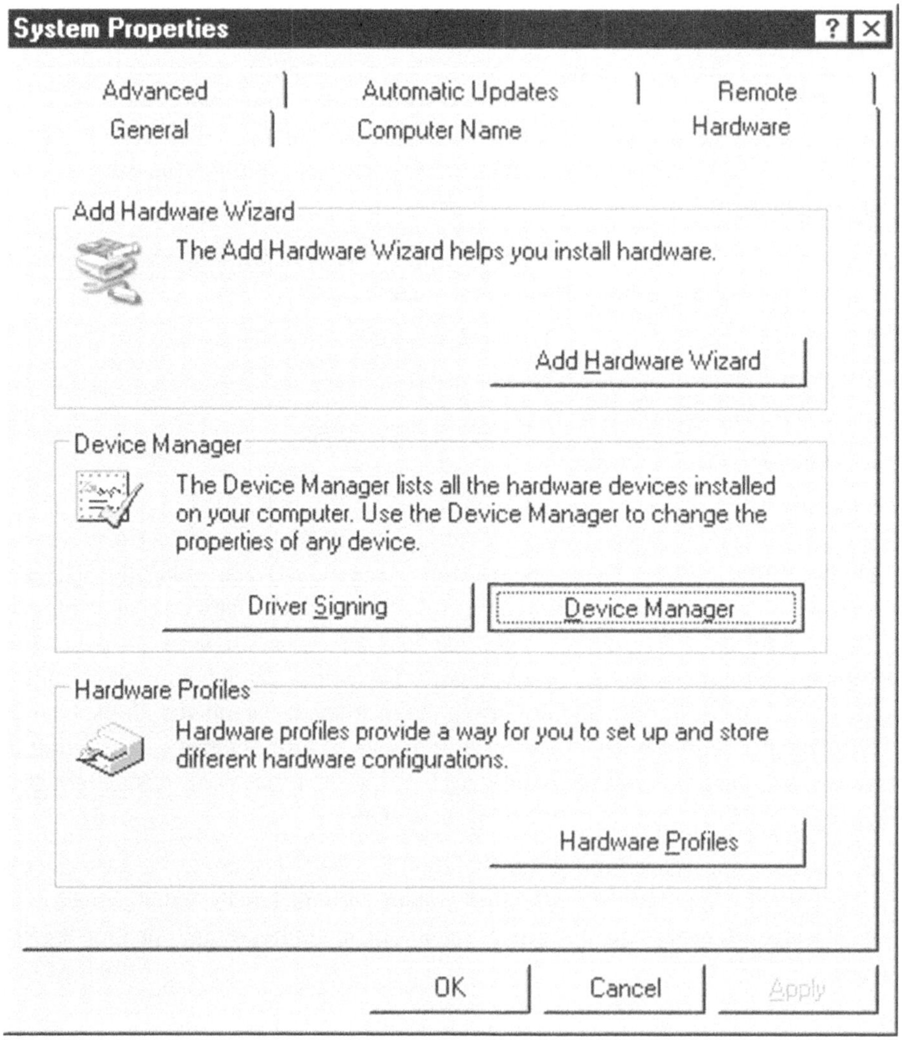

Figure 1-38: Selecting the Device Manager from the Systems Properties menu.

The device manager will open as shown in Figure 1.39.

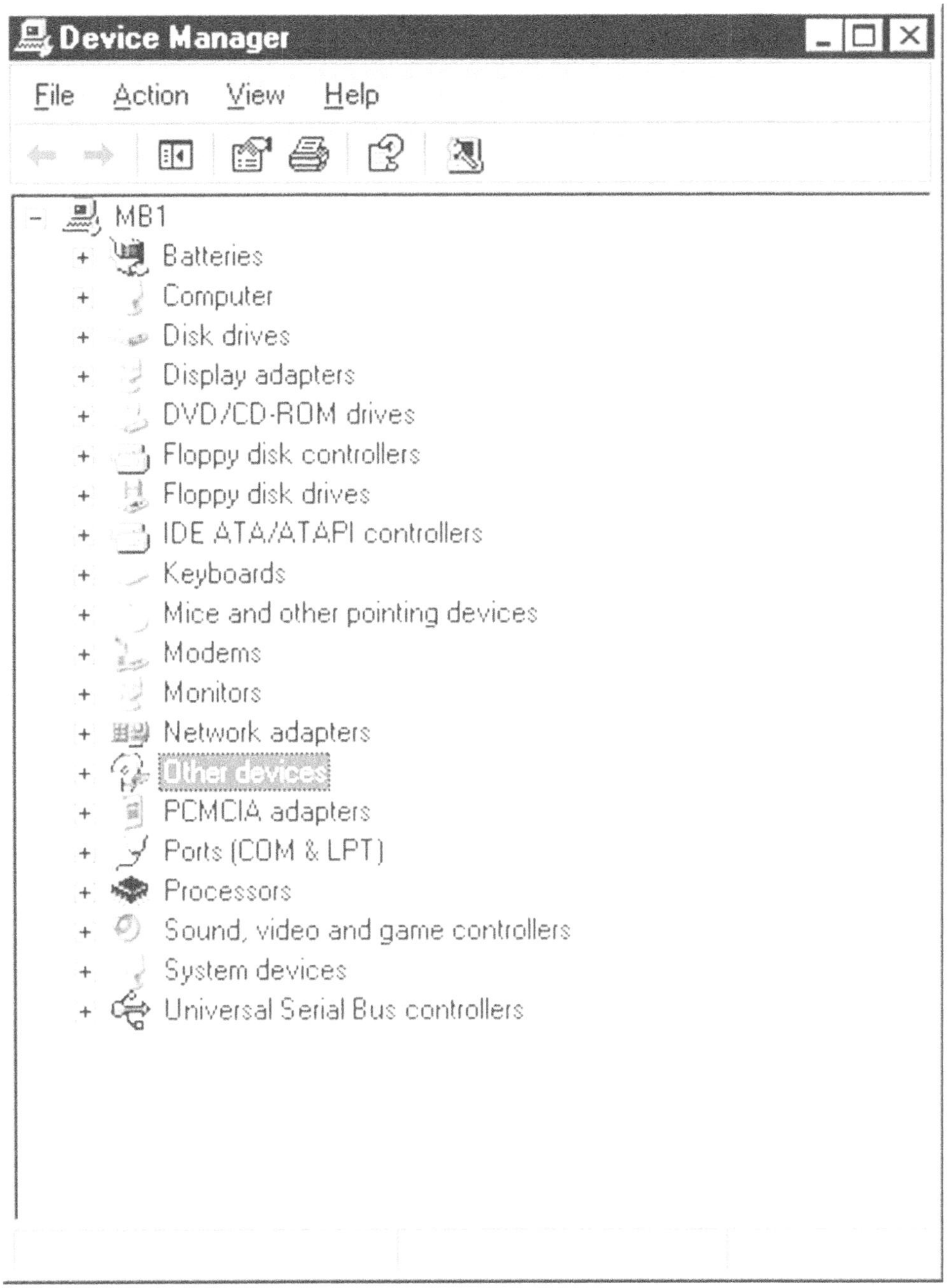

Figure 1-39: Windows Server 2003 Device Manager.

Before we begin, it is important to note that information pertaining to plug-and-play devices installed on the system are listed in alphabetical order. To view additional details, click on the plus sign to expand the devices. For the next example we will look at the Processor information in the Device Manager (Figure 1.40).

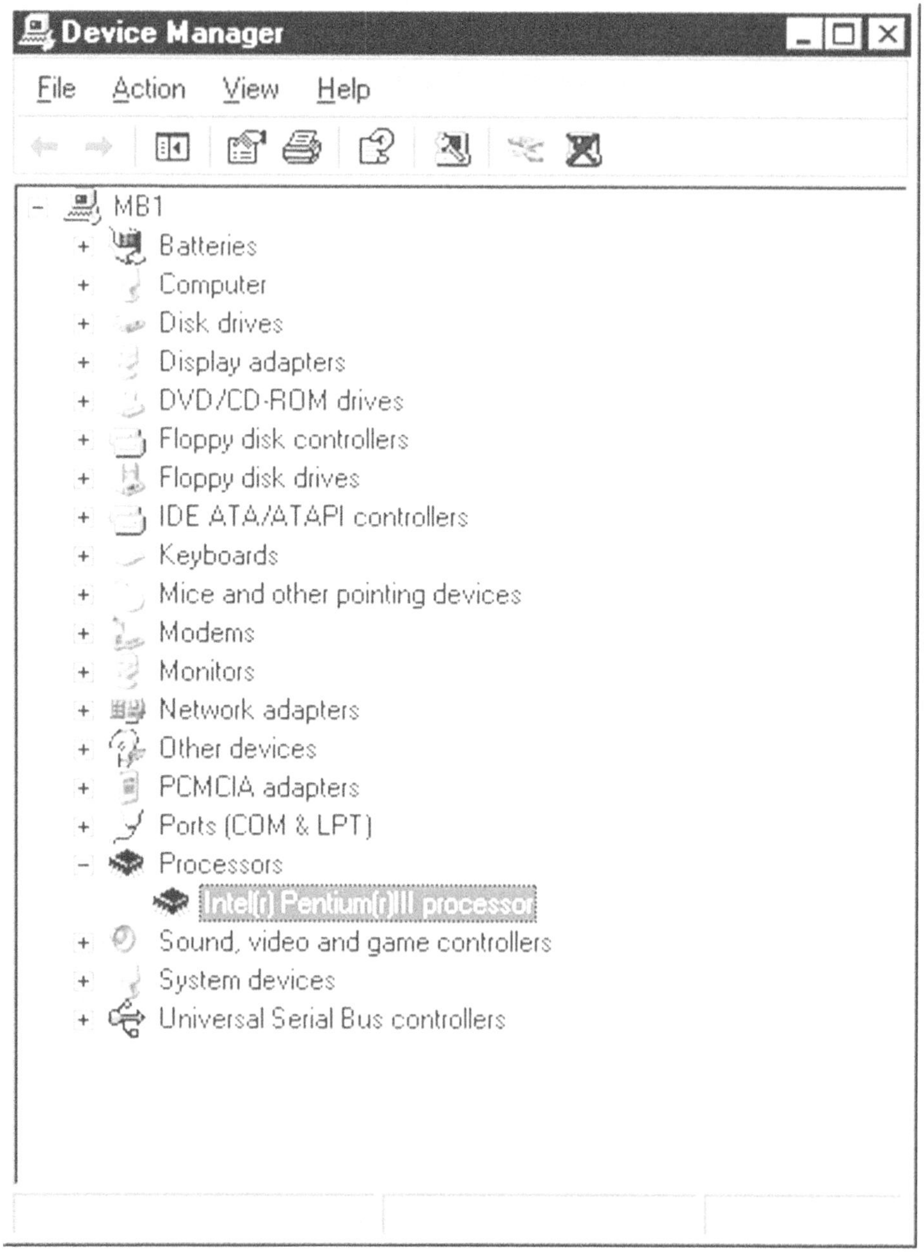

Figure 1-40: Viewing info on the System processor using the Device Manager.

The processor in this example is displayed as an Intel Pentium III Processor. On servers with more than one processor, all processors will be listed under the Processor option.

If you right-click **Processor,** the shortcut menu shown in Figure 1.41 will appear.

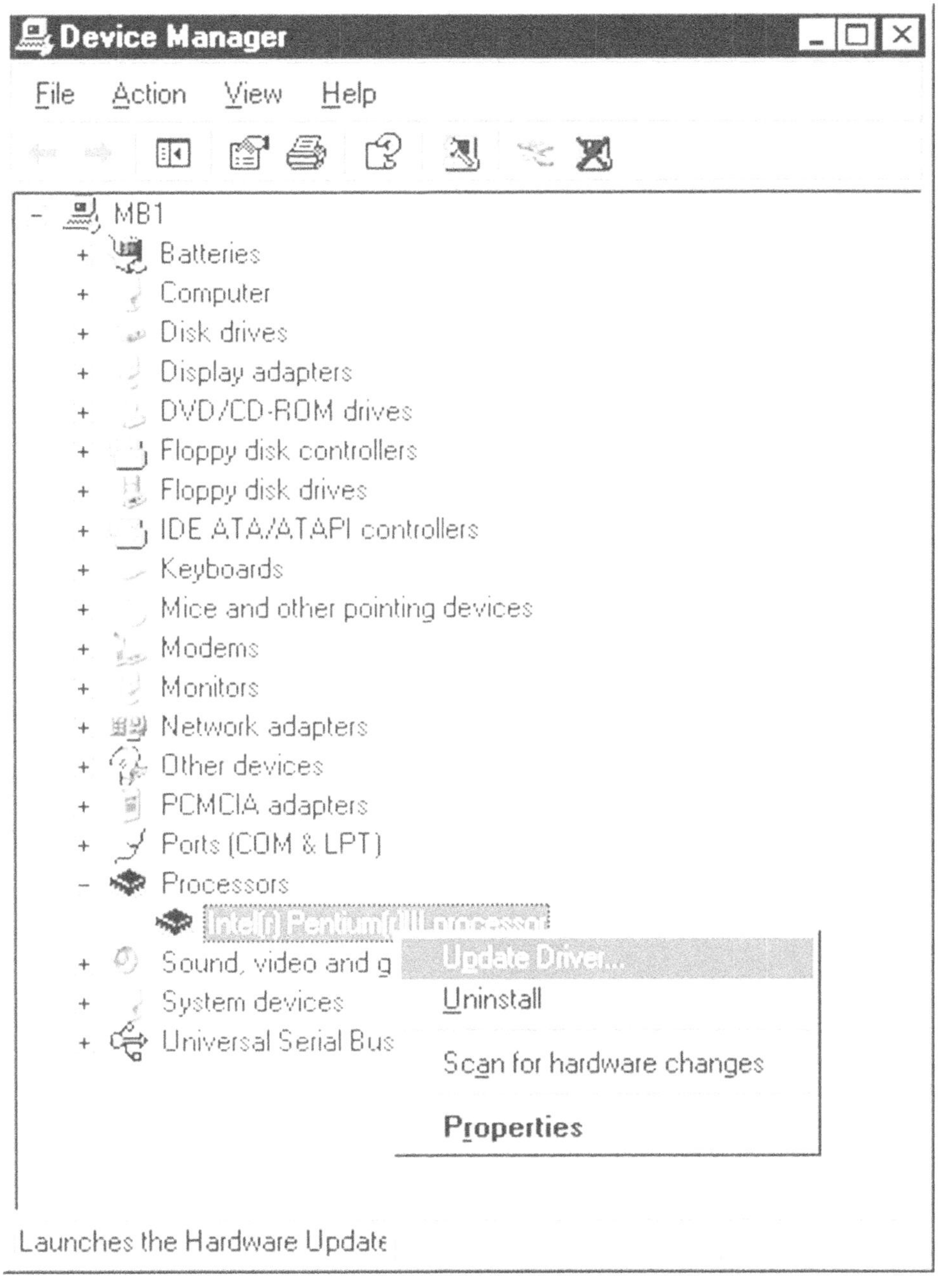

Figure 1-41: Options for the Processor in the Device Manager interface.

The options displayed in Figure 1.41 are the same options that will appear for all hardware—Update Driver, Uninstall, Scan for hardware changes and Properties. If you choose to update the driver, the Update Hardware Wizard will appear (Figure 1.42).

> **Note:** Caution must be exercised when updating certain hardware drivers as unexpected results may occur.

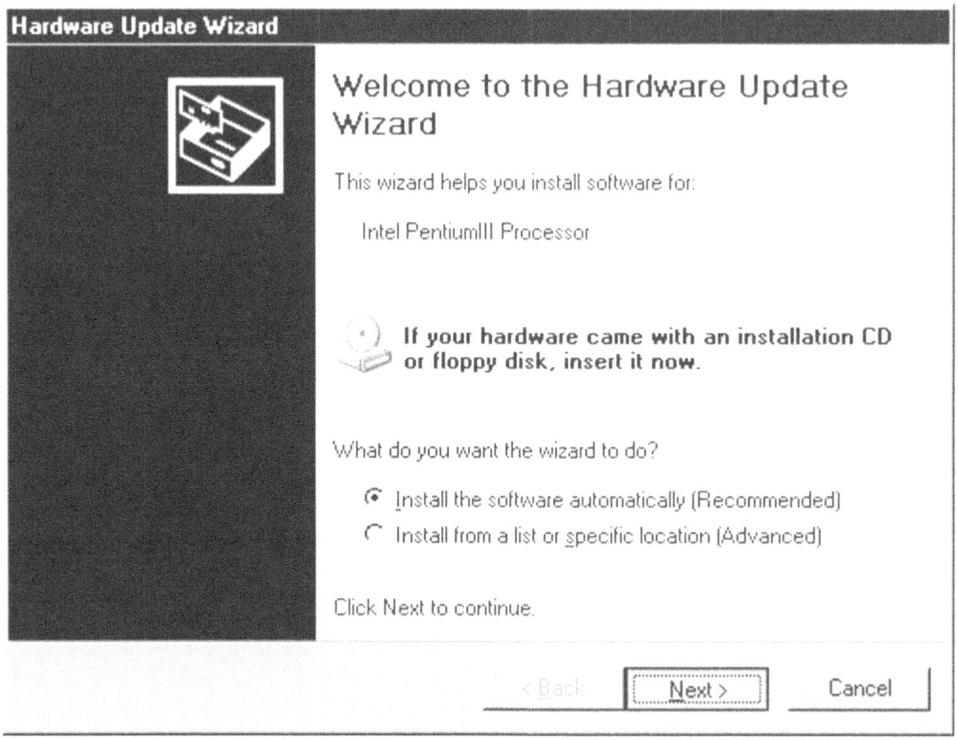

Figure 1-42: Hardware Update Wizard.

On the start page of the Hardware Update Wizard, you will be given two options for installation—the first is the automatically install the software (which is recommended) or the option to install from a specific list or specified location. After you have made your choice, select the **Next** option. For this example, we will install the software automatically. The wizard will then begin to for an updated driver (Figure 1.43).

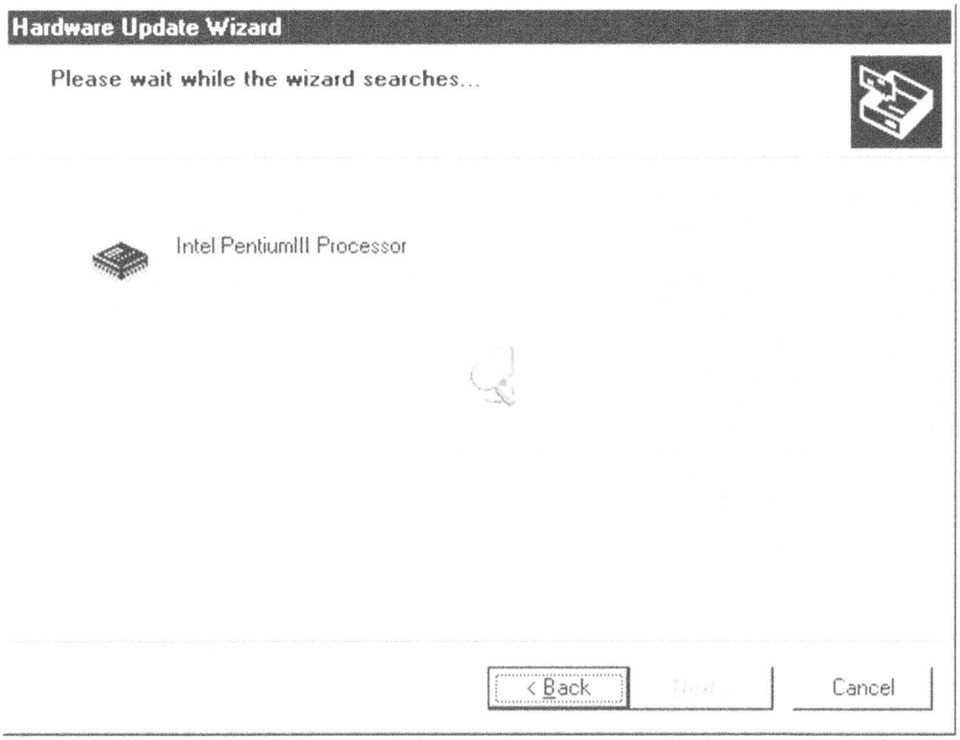

Figure 1-43: The hardware update wizard searching for new drivers.

Once the wizard finishes the search, it will either begin to install the new software or you will see a screen (shown in Figure 1.44) that states it cannot locate new software to install.

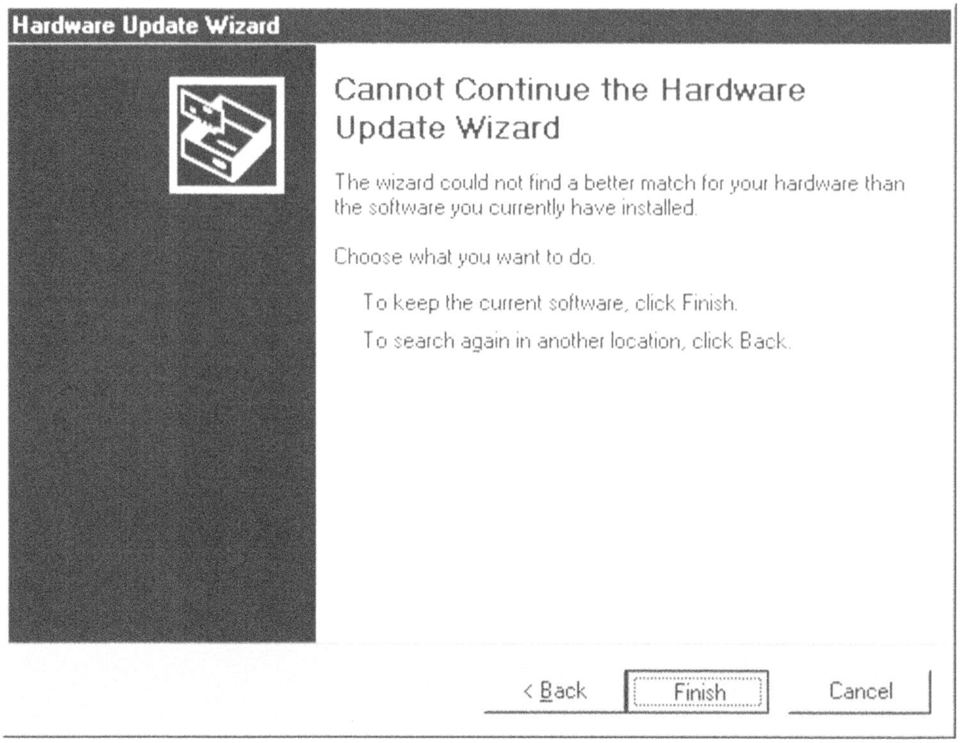

Figure 1-44: Hardware update wizard completed search.

You can now either select **Back** to have the wizard search in a new location or you can click the **Finish** button to keep the current software intact. For the purposes of this example, we will select the **Back** button and have the wizard search in a new location (Figure 1.45).

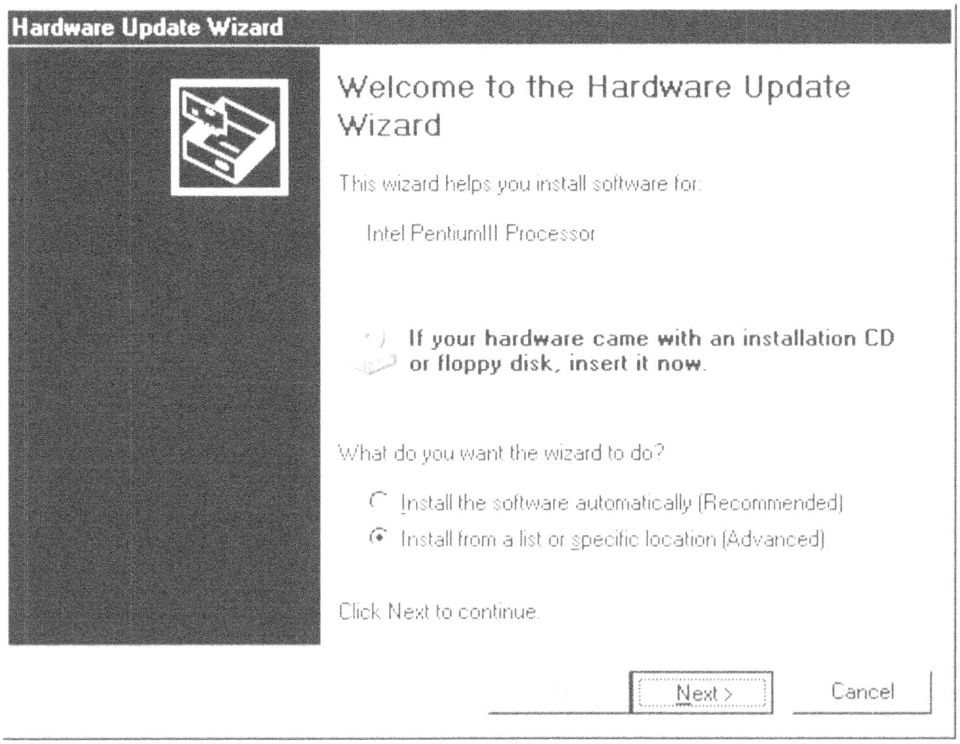

Figure 1-45: Hardware Update Wizard—specific location search.

Let's pretend that you have copied the new processor software to a shared directory on your server, C:\newsoftware. When you copied the software, you ensured that it was not in a compressed format and all files were located in the main folder. When you select the **Back** button, a screen similar to the one in Figure 1.46 will appear. You can now select the **Advanced** option to allow the wizard to search for the software in a different location. You can enter the specific search options for the driver you wish to install or you can choose to install the best driver from a list of drivers already on the system. In this example, we know that we have the software in the C:\newsoftware folder. We will therefore need to choose the **Include this location in the search:** option, and ensure that the C:\newsoftware folder is included in the search.

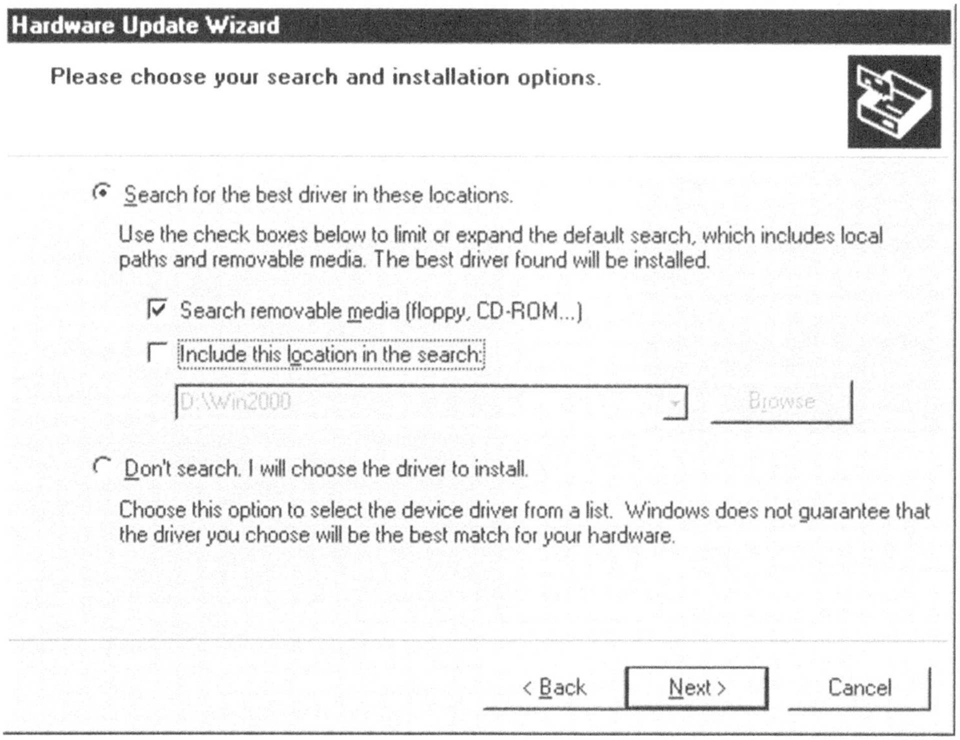

Figure 1-46: Choose the search & installation options.

You can either browse to the location of the driver, by using the Browse button, or manually type the location into the **Include this location in the search**. In our example, the **Search removable media (floppy, CD-ROM)** option needs to be unchecked, but if you do have the new software on a floppy diskette, CD-ROM or USB Disk on Key (which emulates an additional drive) you should insert the removable media into the appropriate hardware and leave the check mark intact.

Let's take a look at the option we did NOT use in this example—the **Don't search, I will choose the driver to install** option (Figure 1.47).

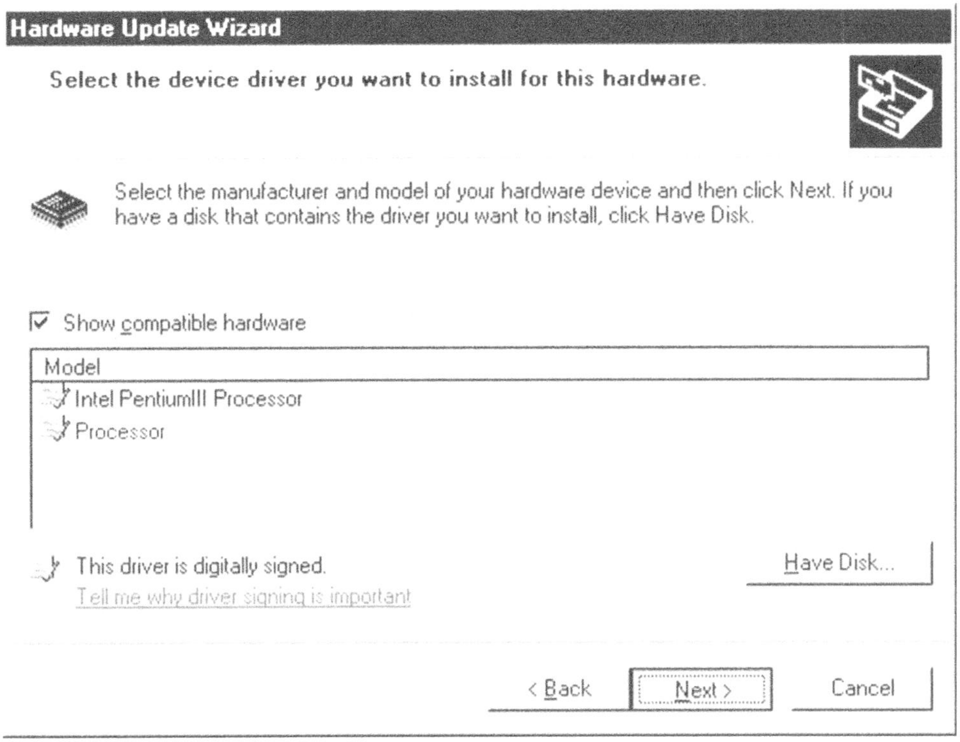

Figure 1-47: Selecting the Driver to be installed.

Selecting the Driver to be installed instead of searching media for driver information. Click on the **Don't Search, I will choose the driver to install option** and a screen like the one in Figure 1.48 will appear.

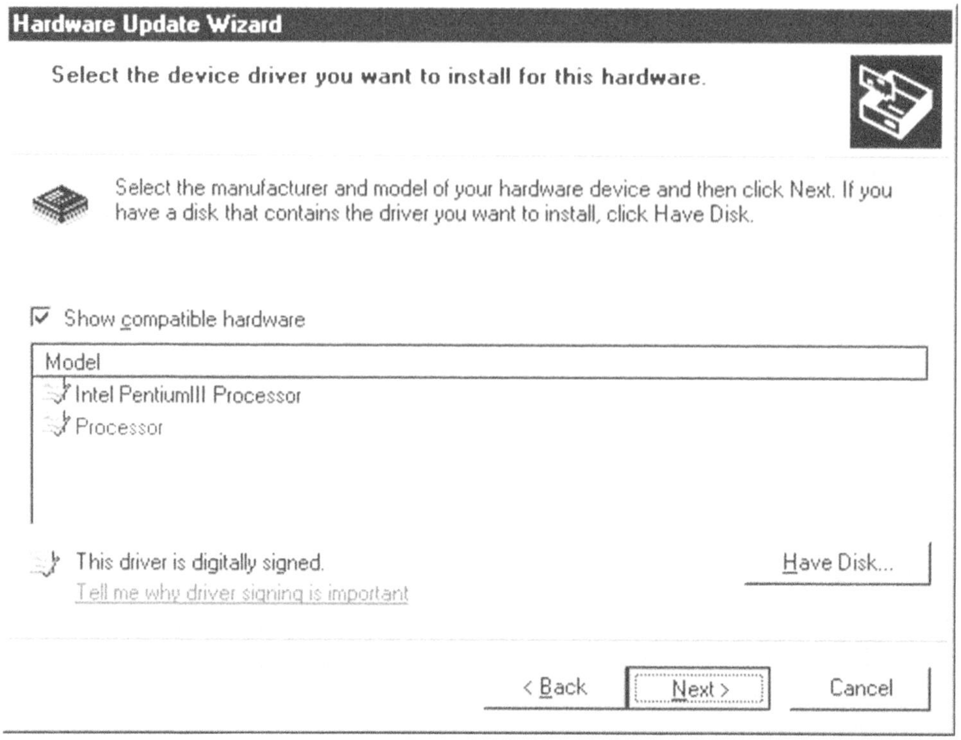

Figure 1-48: Selecting the driver to install from a pre-supplied list on the system.

As shown in the list displayed in Figure 1.48, in this instance you have the option to install the Intel Pentium III processor or the standard processor driver. Additionally, you would also choose to install the software from the **Have Disk** option.

Note the very important statement at the bottom "This driver is digitally signed." We will discuss information on digitally signing drivers later in this chapter (see section 1.5.1).

Typically, the browse location will appear at the top-level hierarchy of the system. We would browse to C:\newsoftware. (This is done only for the purpose of this example and you would need to browse to the specific location you wished to use on your machine.)

Once you have selected the appropriate folder that contains the software files, click on the OK button. The software wizard will begin to install the new software.

> **NOTE:** If the software files are not complete or in the proper format, for example specific .ini files are not in the location, then the OK button will appear as grayed out and you will not be able to use this option.

Once the wizard has finished, just click the **Finish** button. The process is now complete.

When you right-click Hardware in Device Manager, another option is available on the shortcut menu—the option to uninstall the object (Figure 1.49).

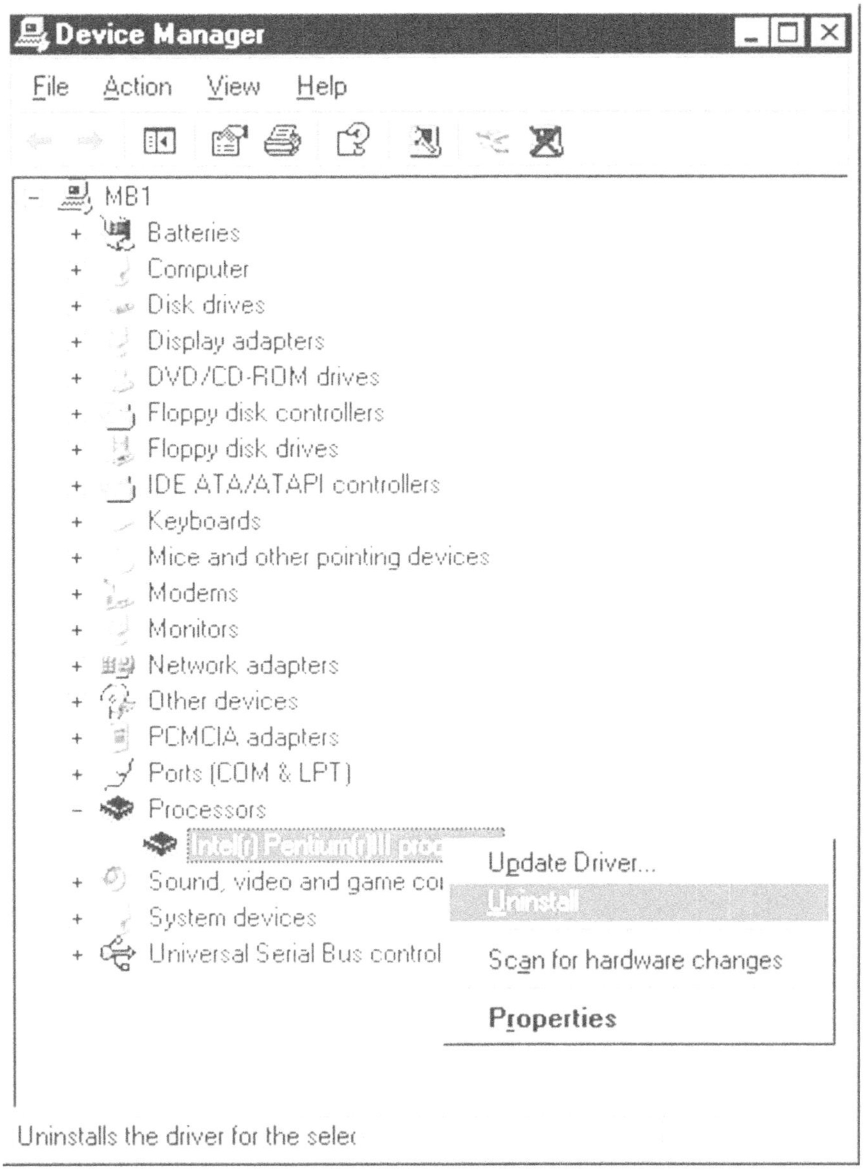

Figure 1-49: Choosing to Uninstall Hardware from the Device Manager.

If you choose to uninstall a device, do so with caution. Uninstalling a device can cause your machine to malfunction.

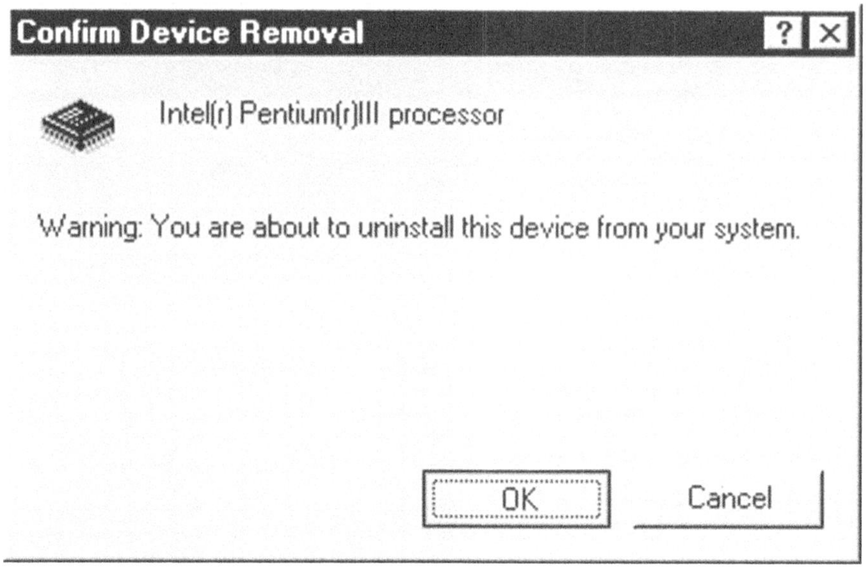

Figure 1-50: The Uninstall Warning Message.

Click the **OK** button if you are certain you wish to uninstall the hardware from the system. It is important to note that there is no "second warning." Once you have selected **OK** on the "**Confirm Device Removal**" dialog box, the object will be removed from the system and will be reinstalled only if you use the **Add New Hardware Wizard** option or reboot the Server for plug-and-play devices.

If you refer back to Figure 1.49, you will note that a modem is listed as part of the system. Figure 1.51 shows the device manager listing after the modem has been uninstalled. Note that there is no listing for Modem (between Mice and Monitors).

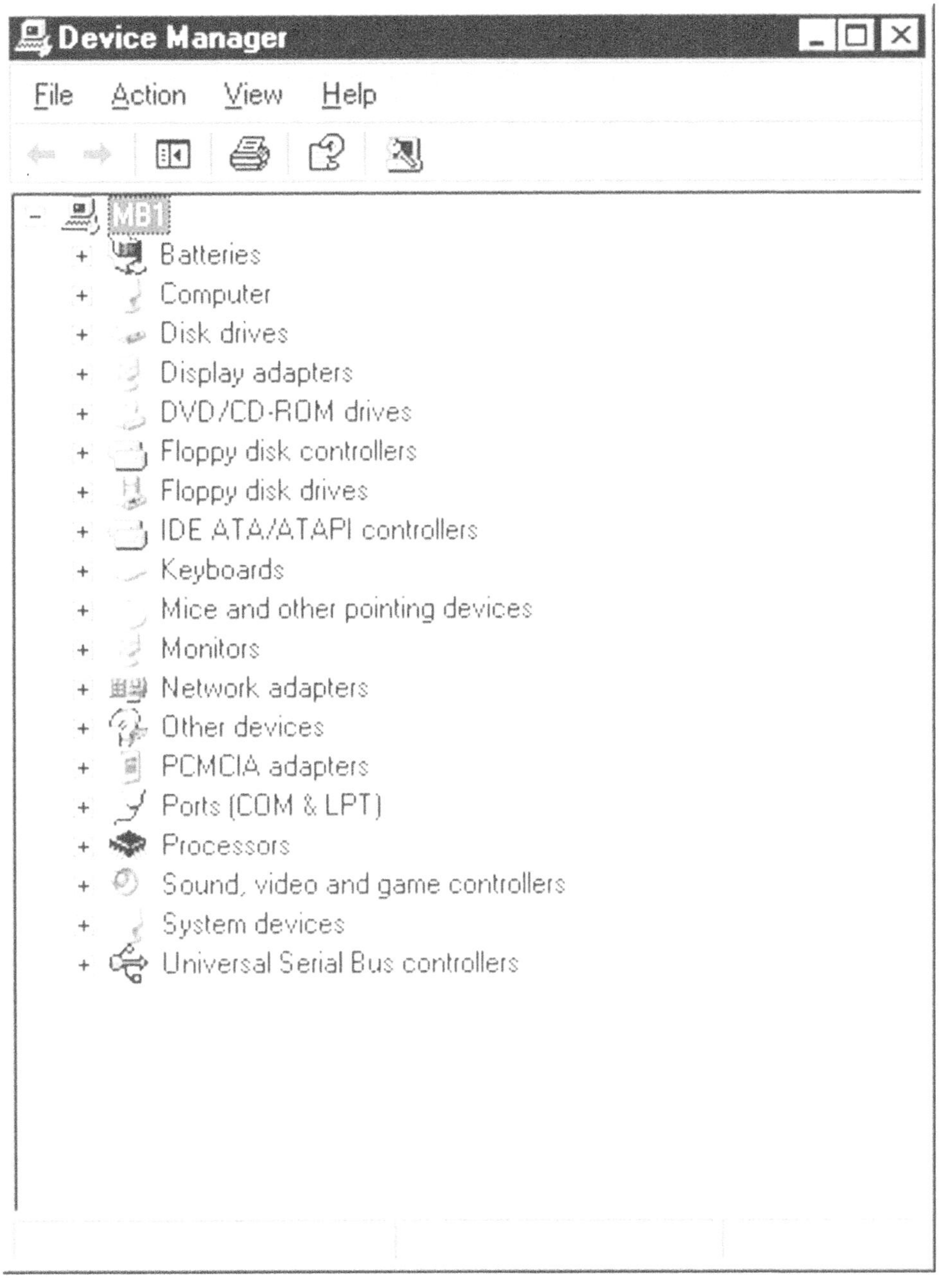

Figure 1-51: The Device Manager after a Modem Uninstall.

Once the hardware has been removed, you can scan the system for hardware changes. In this example, scanning for changes should reinstall the Lucent WinModem. Figure 1.52 shows the **Scan for Hardware Changes** option.

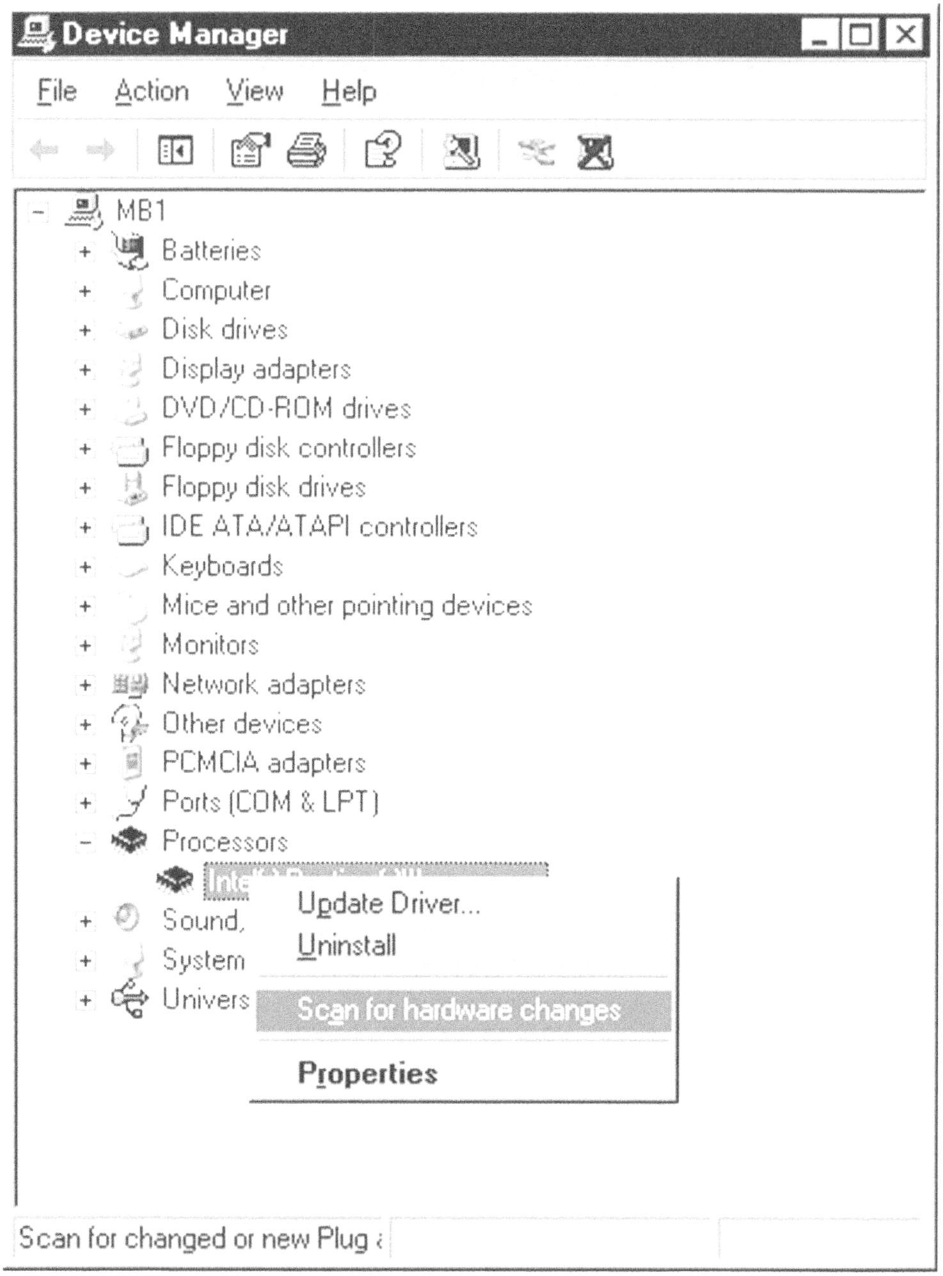

Figure 1-52: Using the Scan for Hardware Changes option from the Device Manager.

Selecting the option from the shortcut menu will cause the wizard to search for hardware changes. If new hardware is found, the Wizard will prompt you to install the software for the newly found device (Figure 1.53).

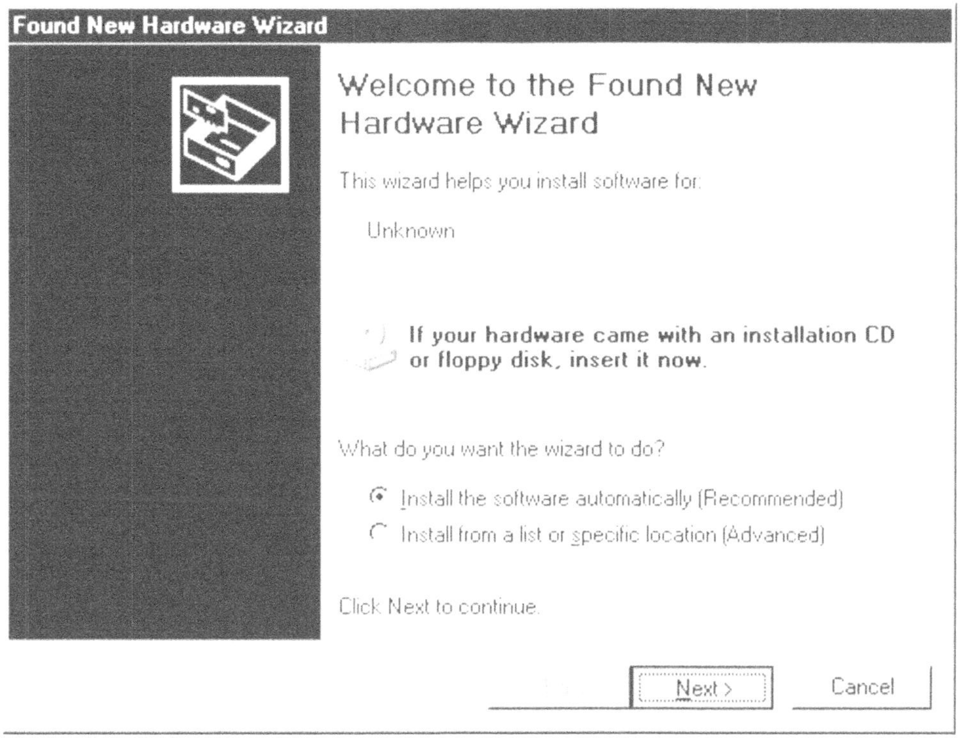

Figure 1-53: The Scan for Hardware Change Wizard.

We have already discussed how this Wizard works in detail (refer to Figures 1.42 through 1.47). The alternate location for **Scan for Hardware Change** is at the top of the Device Manager under the Action menu (Figure 1.54).

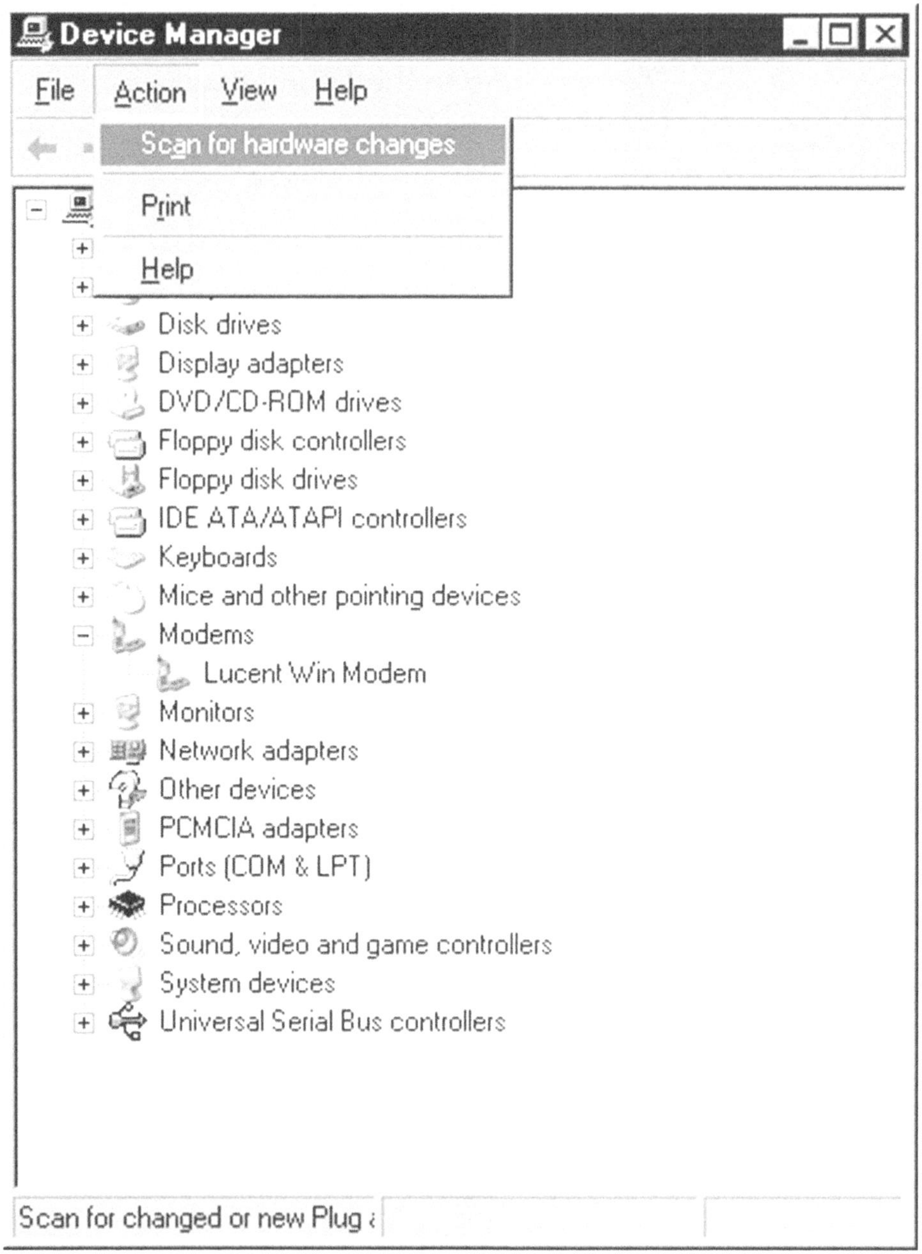

Figure 1-54: Accessing the Scan for Hardware Change Wizard from the Action menu.

In this example, when the **Scan for Hardware Changes** option was run, the Lucent WinModem was discovered and reinstalled. This is illustrated in Figure 1.55.

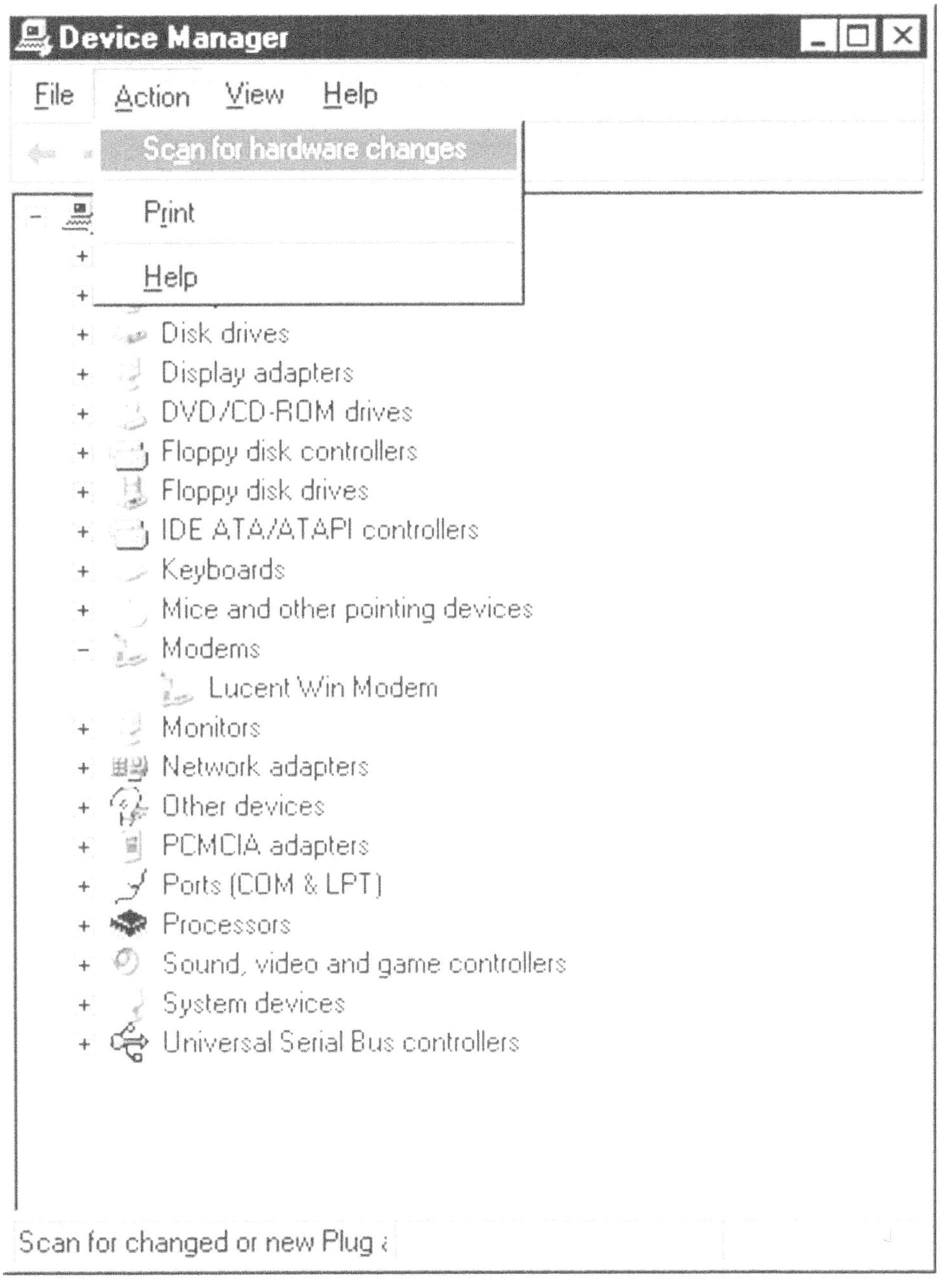

Figure 1-55: The reinstalled Lucent WinModem Hardware from the Device Manager.

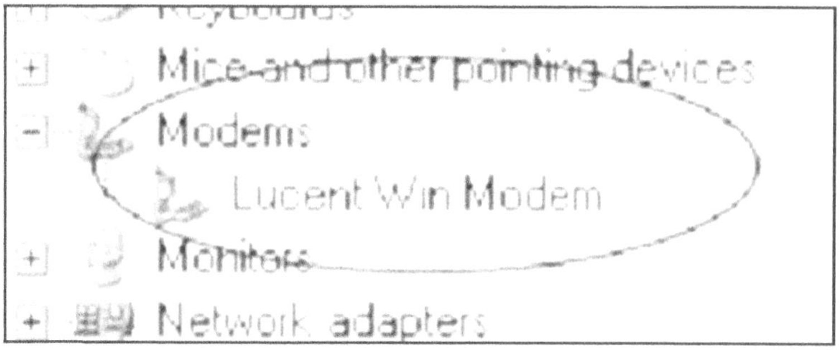

Figure 1-56: The device has no errors showing in the device manager.

A closer look (Figure 1-56) shows that the device is not indicating any hardware problems. We will discuss how Device Manager displays hardware problems a little later in this chapter.

The **Action** menu also will give you the opportunity to print information from the Device Manager by selecting the **Print** option. As well, there is a **Help** option. The menu items It also has the same menu items that can be accessed when you right-click hardware in Device Manager.

1.2.3 The Hardware Troubleshooting Wizard

The **Windows Hardware Troubleshooter** is a wonderful tool to help troubleshoot those hardware issues that you finding a challenge to correct. Open the **Device Manager** by any of the available methods:

- Click **Start,** select **Administrative Tools** and choose **Computer Management**.
- Right-click **My Computer,** click on **Hardware** then select **Device Manager**.
- Use the keyboard shortcut **WinKey+Pause**.

In this example, we will troubleshoot the COM Port hardware. Scroll down to the Ports (COM & LPT) and expand by double-clicking the **Ports (COM & LPT)** listing. Right-click the **COM1** port and select **Properties** (Figure 1.57).

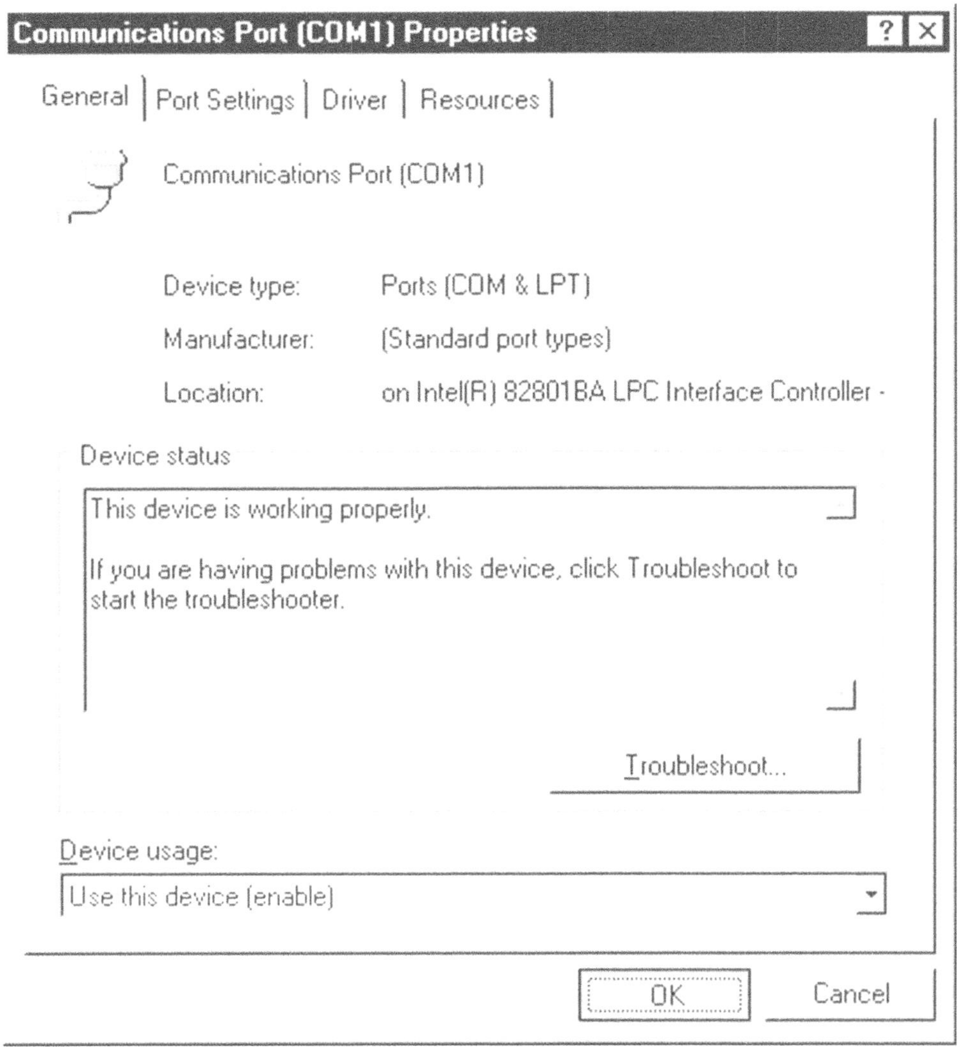

Figure 1-57: The Properties of the COM Port device.

If the device is not having a configuration problem, the **General** tab will show you that it is working properly, as is the case in our example. However, when the device is not functioning properly, Device Manager will display a warning icon (Figure 1.58).

Figure 1-58: Hardware device that has a warning, in Device Manager.

As well, if a hardware device has been disabled, Device Manager will display a red "X" over the icon. Figure 1.59 shows a IBM PC Camera that has been disabled.

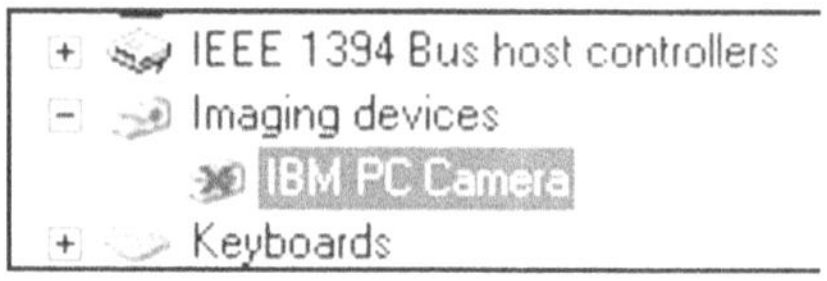

Figure 1-59: Hardware device that has been disabled in the Device Manager.

The hardware can easily be re-enabled by right-clicking the device and choosing the **Enable** option as shown in Figure 1.60.

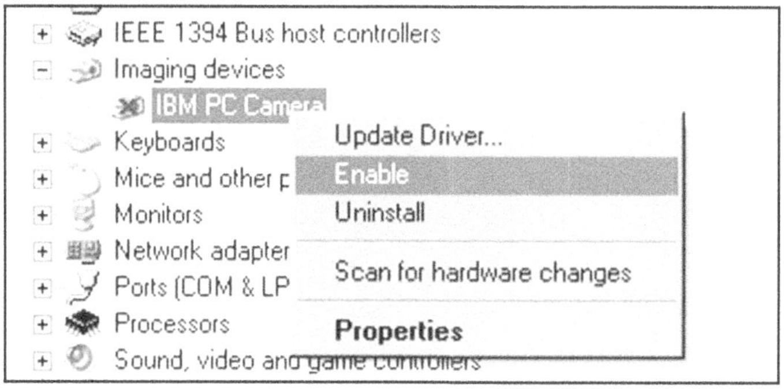

Figure 1-60: Re-enabling a device.

Once the device has been enabled, the red "X" will disappear and the device will be listed as normal (Figure 1.61).

Figure 1-61: The re-enabled device in the Device Manager.

If a yellow "exclamation mark" appears over the device, this indicates that the device needs some assistance. You can use the Hardware Troubleshooter help you resolve the issue.

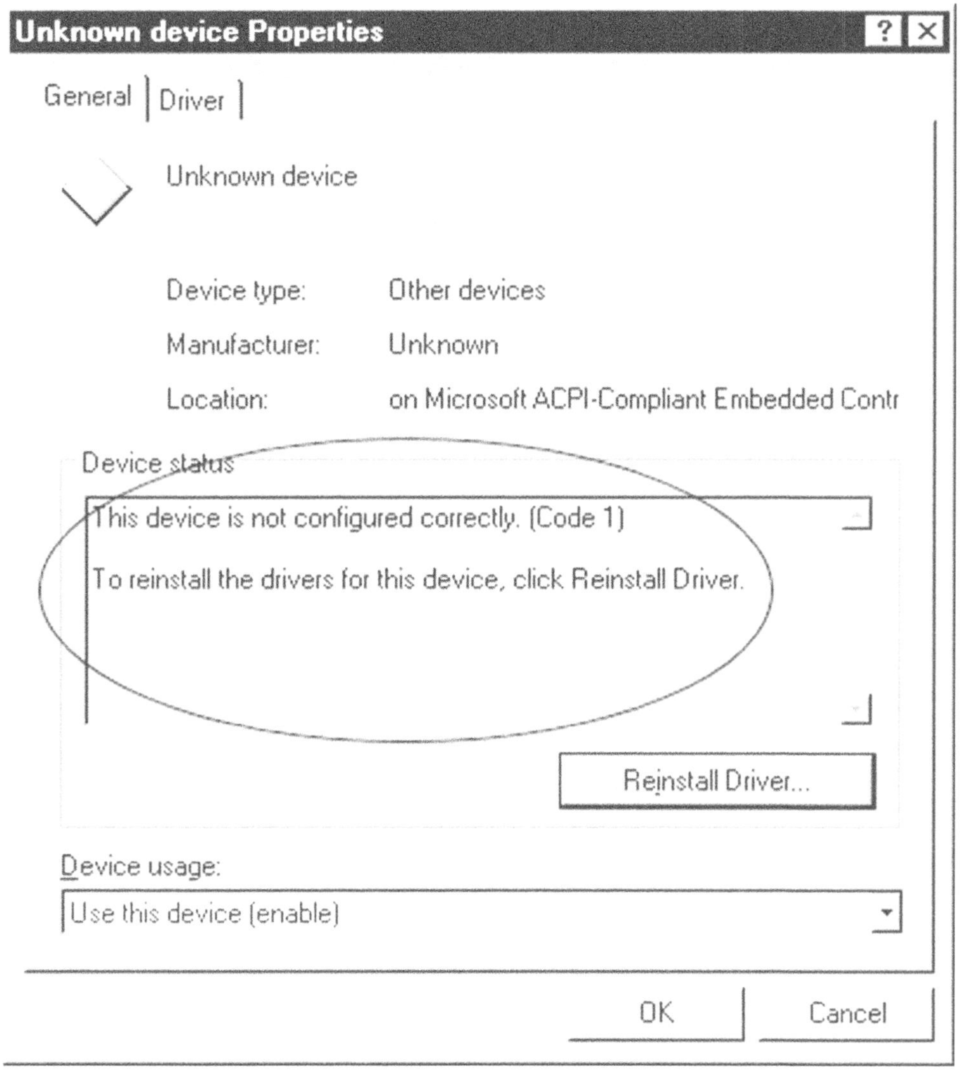

Figure 1-62: General Tab showing the device needs some technical assistance.

Click the **Troubleshoot** button and the Wizard will begin (Figure 1.63).

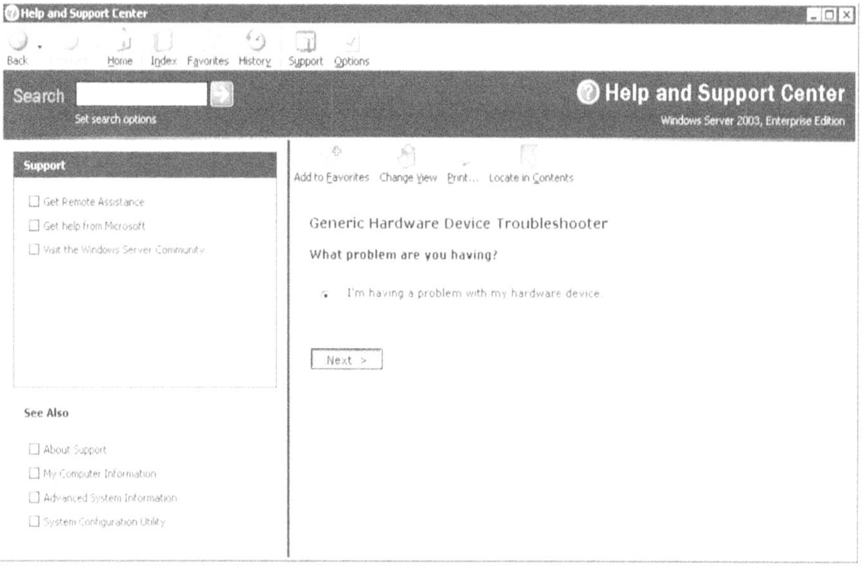

Figure 1-63: The Windows Server 2003 Hardware Troubleshooting guide.

Click the **Next** button and the Wizard will open the screen shown in Figure 1.64.

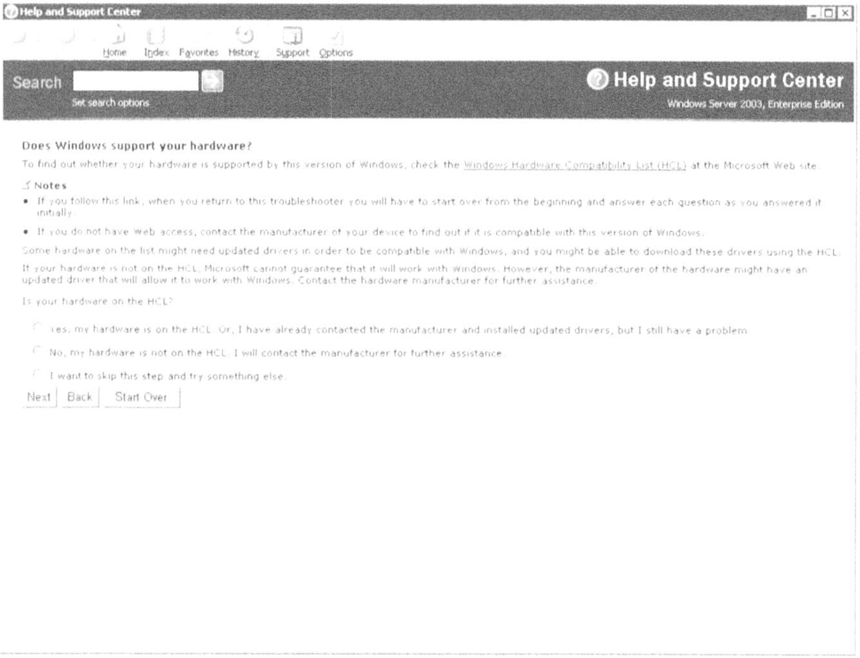

Figure 1-64: The Hardware Troubleshooter wizard.

You have the option of going to the Microsoft Web site to check the Hardware Compatibility List (HCL) at http://www.microsoft.com/windows/catalog/server/.

Three options are available to you on this screen:

- Yes, my hardware is on the HCL, or I have already contacted the manufacturer and installed updated drivers, but I still have a problem.
  (*This will take you to the screen displayed in Figure 1.65.*)
- No, my hardware is not on the HCL. I will contact the manufacturer for further assistance.
  (*Selecting this option will stop the Wizard.*)
- I want to skip this step and try something else.
  (*The wizard take you to the* screen *displayed in Figure 1.65*) For the purposes of this example, we will chose the **Yes** option (presuming that we have checked the HCL and the hardware is listed).

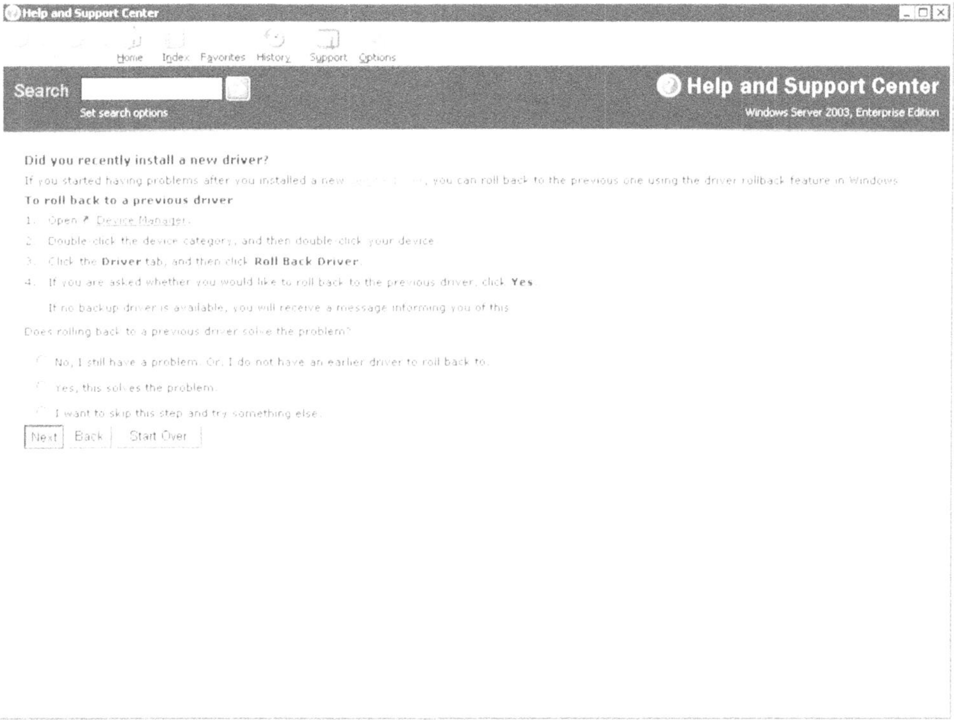

Figure 1-65: Hardware troubleshooting guide for devices.

This screen will prompt you for device driver information. You have three more options:

- **No, I still have a problem. Or, I do not have an earlier driver to roll back to.** If you have not installed the driver and are still having an issue. you can choose this option.
- **Yes, this solves the problem** option can be used when you need to rollback the driver to an earlier version. Use the instructions are listed on the screen.
- **I want to skip this step and try something else** will show the same screen as the one shown with the **No, I still have a problem. Or, I do not have an earlier driver to roll back to** option above. Figure 1.66 shows this screen.

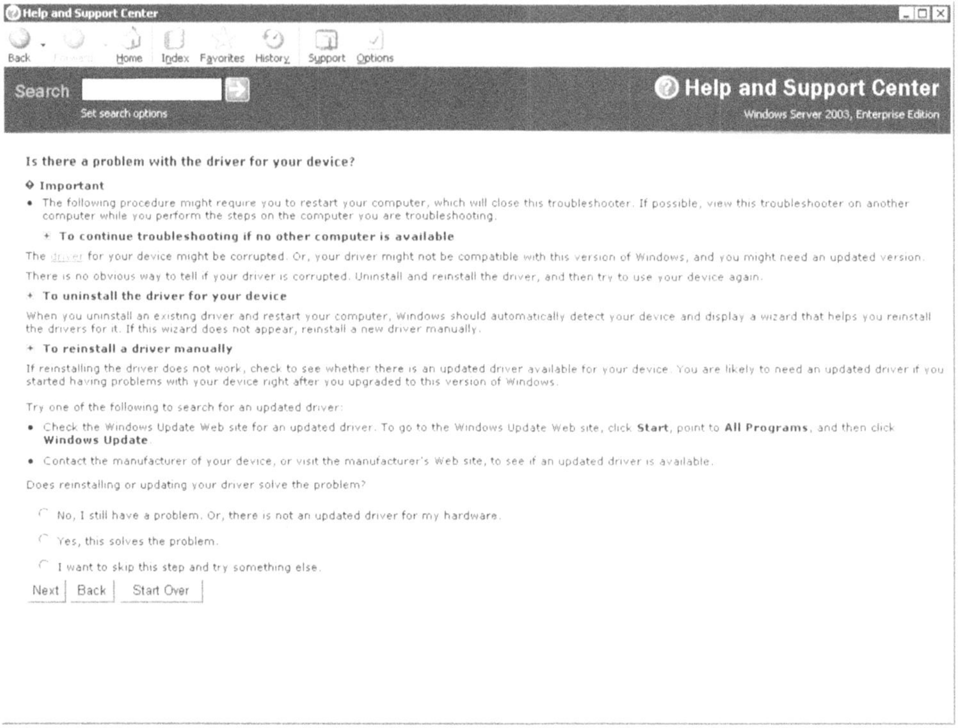

Figure 1-66: Choosing Device Driver troubleshooting options.

Choosing the **No** option will send you to the screen shown in Figure 1.67. It suggests that you contact the Hardware Manufacturer for assistance.

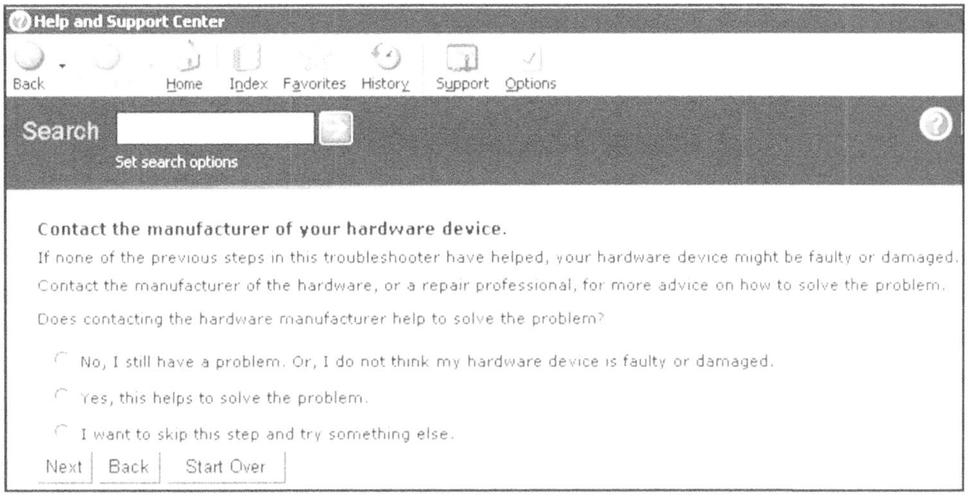

Figure 1-67: Troubleshooting the device with the Hardware Troubleshooting Wizard.

If you are still having a problem at this point, the device itself could be malfunctioning. Try putting in a new device to see if this resolves the issue.

Pop Quiz 1.2

Pop Quiz 1.2 *Questions*

1. Which four resources are assigned by the Windows Operating System at the time of the installation of a device?
2. What are the three methods available to open Device Manager?
3. In Device Manager, what does a yellow exclamation mark indicate?
4. What does a yellow question mark indicate in Device Manager?
5. In Device Manager, when a device is marked with a red "X", what does this indicate?

Pop Quiz 1.2 *Answers*

1. The four resources assigned by the Windows Operating System at the time of the installation of the device are:
   - IRQ (interrupt request line numbers)
   - DMA (Direct memory access channels)
   - I/O (Input/output port addresses)
   - Memory address ranges
2. You can open the Device Manager by any of the available methods:
   - Click Start, select Administrative Tools and choose Computer Management.
   - Right-click My Computer, and select Properties from the shortcut menu. Select the Hardware tab.
   - Use the keyboard shortcut WinKey+Pause.
3. A yellow exclamation mark indicates a device is having a problem and needs troubleshooting.
4. A yellow question mark indicates an unknown device.
5. A red "X" indicates that the device has been disabled.

1.3 Optimize server disk performance

Disk Performance plays a very important role in relation to performance on a Windows Server 2003. Implementing, maintaining and troubleshooting disk performance is a skill that will be used, time and time again, on servers within your organization. If you do not implement disk drive setup properly, your organization could experience data loss. The following sections explain how to use the software on a Windows Server 2003 to implement and manage disk drives on a Windows Server 2003.

1.3.1 Implement a RAID solution

Redundant Array of Inexpensive Disks (RAID) has been in use for years to allow network Administrators the ability to provide fault tolerance for data stored on hard drives. However, not all RAID configurations provide for redundancy of information. Some RAID configurations, such as striping, are used when performance means more to the network than fault tolerance.

Fault tolerant volumes are disks that use some form of RAID configuration to increase reliability.

Note: Fault tolerant volumes on basic disks are no longer supported in Windows Server 2003.

The following lists are split into most commonly used and less commonly used RAID types. If you are fortunate enough to have a server in your lab that has the hardware to support RAID, you can have the opportunity to experiment with the various RAID types in a controlled environment. This will help you in a real-world situation and find you have to rebuild a RAID setup.

- **RAID-0** – Known as disk striping, data is written across more than one disk but there is no redundancy of data (fault tolerance). It is most often used when the best performance is needed but no fault-tolerance is required.
- **RAID-1** – Known as disk mirroring, it consists of at least two drives that duplicate the storage of data. There is no striping—the data on the second disk is identical to the data on the first disk. Read performance is improved since both disks can be read at the same time. Write performance is the same to slightly slower as data is written to both disks.
- **RAID 5** – Known as disk striping with parity, it includes a rotating parity array; all read and write operations can be overlapped. RAID 5 stores parity information which can be used to reconstruct data and requires a minimum of three disks for the array. A low cost solution for data protection, it is best suited where fault tolerance is a necessity but performance is not critical. RAID 5 only works with Windows Server 2003 that have the dynamic disks enabled and it cannot be extended or mirrored.
- **RAID 10** – an array of stripes in which each stripe is a RAID 1 array of drives. RAID 10 gives even higher performance than RAID 1 but the cost is higher as well.

Less Commonly used RAID types.

- **RAID 2 and RAID 3** – These are similar RAID types. These use striping (no fault tolerance across disks). The main differences between RAID 2 and RAID 3 are that RAID 2 uses striping across disks with some disks storing error checking and correcting (ECC) information and RAID 3 uses striping and dedicates one drive to storing parity information.
- **RAID 4** – uses large stripes, which means you can read records from any single drive. It has no advantages over RAID 5 because it has write limitations.
- **RAID 6** – similar to RAID-5 but includes a second parity scheme that is distributed across different drives and therefore offers extremely high fault-tolerance. However it is not commonly used in networked environments.
- **RAID 7** – includes a real time embedded operating system as a controller, caching via a high-speed bus, making it similar to a stand-alone computer. However, only one vendor on the market offers this RAID type
- **RAID 53** – Similar to RAID 10, RAID 53 offers an array of stripes in which each stripe is a RAID-3 array of disks. This is a high cost solution.

It is important to remember that, if you are upgrading from Windows NT 4.0, Windows Server 2003 uses dynamic, as well as basic, disks and the terminology is different.

- The Windows NT 4.0 term, Volume Set, is the equivalent to a Spanned Volume on a dynamic disk in Windows Server 2003.
- The Windows NT 4.0 term, Mirrored Volume, is the equivalent to a Mirrored Volume on a dynamic disk in Windows Server 2003.
- The Windows NT 4.0 term, Stripe Set, is the equivalent to a Striped Volume on a dynamic disk in Windows Server 2003.
- The Windows NT 4.0 term, Stripe Set with Parity, is the equivalent to RAID 5 volumes on a dynamic disk in Windows Server 2003.

The Disk Management console is used by the Windows Server 2003 operating system to manage disks and can be accessed by clicking on **Start | All Programs | Computer Management.**

Locate the Disk Management console on the left preview pane and double-click to open (Figure 1.68).

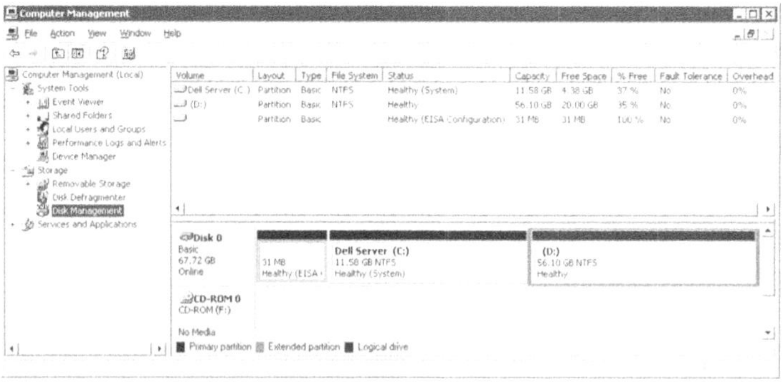

Figure 1-68: The Disk Management console.

The right side of the pane is used to show information pertaining to disk drives. The bottom of the right pane is used to show a graphical layout of the disks and can easily be modified by right-clicking on the drive (Figure 1.69).

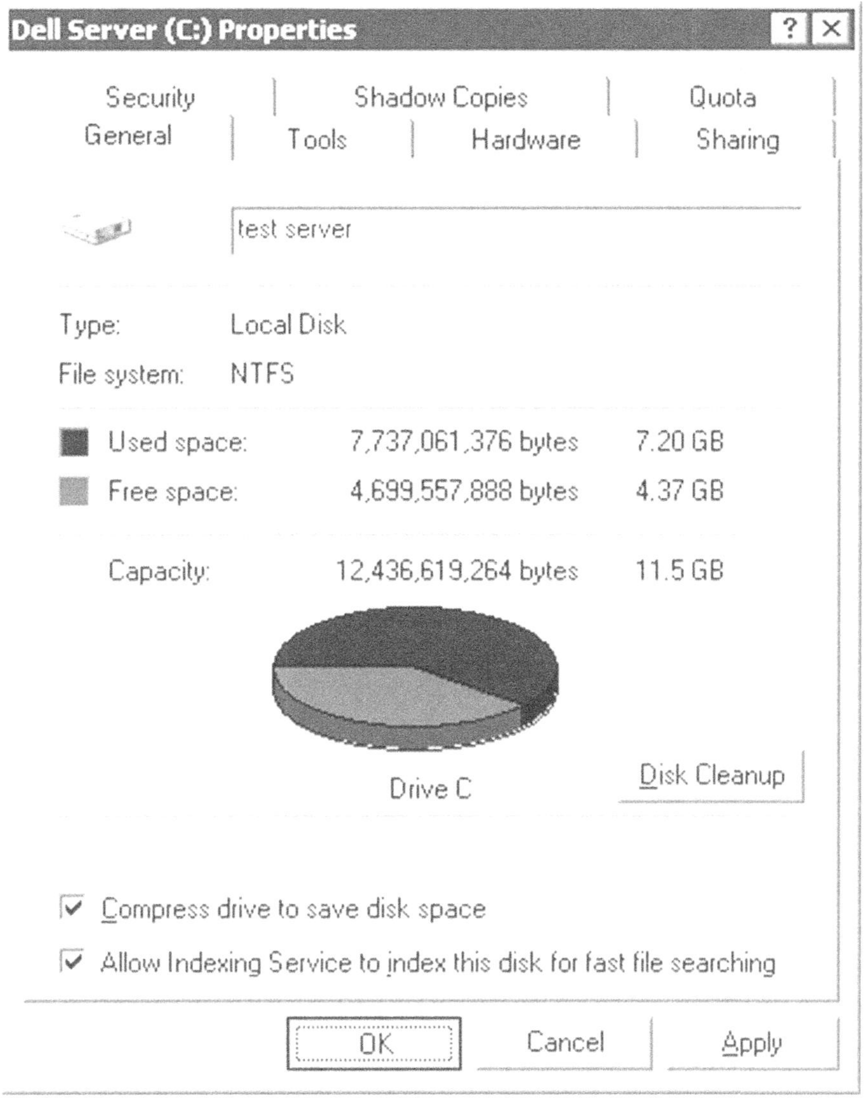

Figure 1-69: Modifying a hard drive using the Computer Management console.

The **General** tab allows you to:

- Name the volume
- View Used and Frees space in a graphical format
- Cleanup the Disk (remove temp files, empty recycle bin, etc.)
- Compress the drive contents which will save space
- Turn on Indexing to allow for faster searches on the drive.

The **Tools** tab allows for:

- Error checking on the drive
- Defragmenting the drive
- The option to backup the drive.

> **NOTE**: If you use Microsoft Exchange 2003 Server on the Windows Server 2003, you have the option to use the backup here to back up an online Exchange 2003 Information Store. This is a new feature included in Windows Server 2003.

The **Hardware** tab allows you to:

- View the hard drive hardware type
- Troubleshoot using the wizard hard disk drives. If you select the **Properties** option for the drive, you will have four tabs that show information for:
    - Device status
    - Policies
    - Volumes
    - Drivers installed.

  The policies tab should be of special interest, because it allows you to set optimization options for the disk. The options are to optimize for safe removal or to optimize for performance.

The **Sharing** tab allows you to set options such as:

- Sharing the drive for others to access
- Setting user limits on the drive
- Set **Access Permissions** (covered in depth later in Chapter Three)
- Set offline settings for access to information while offline.

The **Security** tab is used to:

- Add or Remove Users or Groups from the server
- It also has a setting in the lower pane for Administrative access permissions.

The **Shadows Copies** tab is new to the Windows Server 2003. It is used to create copies of shared folders from previous points in time. The **Shadow Copies** tab has the following properties:

- The ability to **Enable** or **Disable** shadow copies on Volumes. It also allows Administrators the ability to select a storage area and size limit (if needed) for the shadow copies. The copies may also be scheduled to run at specific times using the **Schedule** option after the **Setting** option has been chosen. Two copies are created per day by default.

The final tab is the **Quota** tab and it is used to set disk quotas of disk drives. Quota management is disabled by default and must be enabled for use. The **Quota Entries** option opens a new screen and allows you to set quota limits and warning levels. You can use this screen to add more quota limits and apply to specific users using the quota toolbar.

This console is also used to change drive letters. You can change drive letters by right-clicking the drive in the console and selecting the **Change Drive and Path** option.

FTOnline

The FTOnline command-line tool can be used on fault tolerant disks to mount and recover files on Windows Server 2003 systems that have been upgraded. Once the server has been rebooted the disks are not mounted by FTOnline.

1.3.2 Defragmentation of volumes and partitions

Defragmenting a hard disk drive can often improve performance and should be used often on the server. Right-click the drive you need to defragment and click the **Properties** button. Select the **Tools** tab, and choose the **Defragment Now** option. A new screen will appear (Figure 1.70) that allows you to choose the options for defragmenting the drive. You can choose to analyze the drive without performing defragmentation by selecting the **Analyze** option.

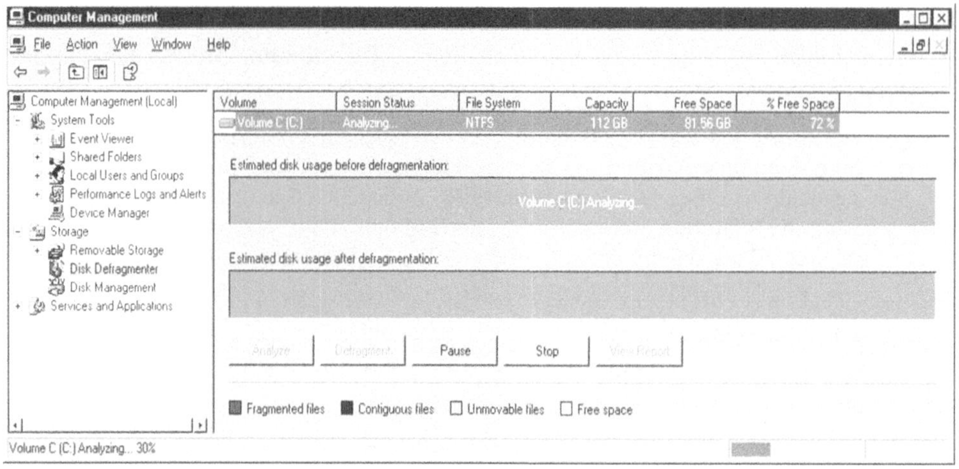

Figure 1-70: Analyzing a volume using the Disk Defragmenter tool.

The Analyzer can be stopped and restarted or paused using the options in the pane. If you wish to defragment the drive, you can use the Defragment option in the pane as shown in Figure 1.71.

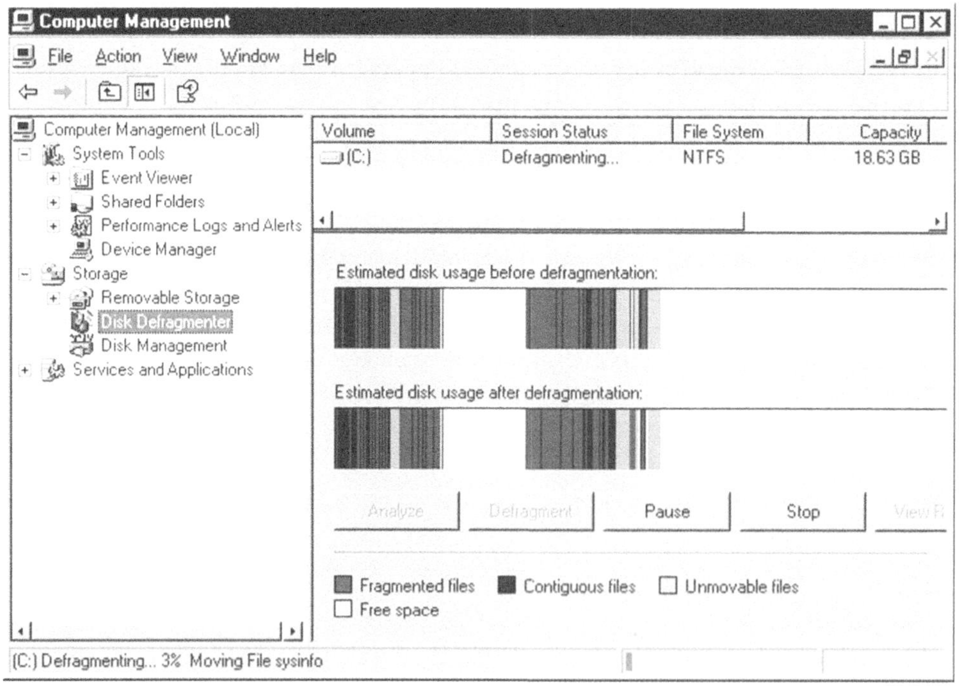

Figure 1-71: Defragmenting a volume using the Disk Defragmenter tool.

Note: You can use a scheduled task to keep the disk drive in a defragmented state, which will enhance the performance of the disk.

Pop Quiz 1.3

Pop Quiz 1.3 *Questions*

1. What are the four more commonly used types of RAID?
2. Of these four, which is NOT fault tolerant?
3. How do you access the Disk Management console?
4. What is FTOnline?
5. Why is disk defragmentation important?

Pop Quiz 1.3 *Answers*

1. The four more commonly used RAID types are RAID 0, RAID 1, RAID 5 and RAID 10.
2. Of these four, RAID 0 is not fault-tolerant, but provides performance enhancement.
3. You can access Disk Management by clicking on Start | All Programs | Computer Management.
4. FTOnline is a command-line tool that can be used on fault tolerant disks to mount and recover files on Windows Server 2003 systems that have been upgraded.
5. Defragmenting a disk will improve disk performance and should be done regularly.

1.4 Troubleshoot server hardware devices

Much of the troubleshooting of devices was discussed previously in the chapter. This section will cover some of the advanced troubleshooting skills needed in Windows Server 2003.

Using multiple monitors in Windows Server 2003

Windows Server 2003 supports the use of up to 10 monitors, particularly helpful if you need to view multiple programs on the same server. Let's walk through some of the steps you use when installing and troubleshooting multiple monitors:

- Open the **Control Panel.**
- Click **Display.**
- Make certain that the display type is not VGA by using the **Settings** option.
- If the monitor is VGA, check with the manufacturer of the card to see if drivers are available for Windows Server 2003.
- Make sure that the color depth is set to at least 256 colors (or at least 16 bits per pixel).
- Power off the computer.
- Check the additional VGA Card to make certain the VGA-disabled setting is selected. The instructions with the card should have how to make this change on the actual card. Install the secondary card into the server and connect the two monitors to the video cards.
- Make sure the monitors are powered up after they are connected to the server with the power off on the server.
- Power on the server.
- The primary card is controlling the first monitor (the one you are viewing) while the system is booting up into Windows Server 2003. The new video card should be detected and the drivers should be installed as long as the video card and monitor are both plug-and-play. Open the Display settings by right-clicking your desktop and selecting Properties, then Settings. Select the new monitor and choose the **Extend my Windows desktop onto this monitor**. This can be done for each monitor you wish to install. For further troubleshooting tips see the Microsoft Knowledge Base Article 328312.

1.4 1 Diagnose and resolve issues related to hardware settings

The Device Manager can be your best ally when you are trying to diagnose and resolve hardware issues on your server. The following sections pertain directly to solving hardware issues. If you are the type of technical person who enjoys building your own servers, make certain that you check the Microsoft Hardware Compatibility List (HCL) or make sure your parts have the Windows Logo, before you purchase them for the server. If you stick with the parts on the HCL, then you should not have many issues when installing Windows Server 2003 on your new machine.

1.4 2 Diagnose and resolve issues related to server hardware

In cases where an unknown driver is installed on your Windows Server 2003, you have a few methods available to troubleshoot them, such as:

- Booting the system in the **Safe Mode**—this should be one of the first things to try.
- System Information tool.
- Use the **Event log** to check for errors.

To boot the machine into Safe Mode while the server is booting up, just click the **F8** key on your keyboard. Choose the **Safe Mode** and press the **Enter** button. Check the Device Manager for the unknown device to see if it is still listed. If it is, try removing it from the list and rebooting, then reinstalling the driver software.

The System Information tool can also be used to troubleshoot driver upgrades and unknown devices on the server. To run the System Information Tool:

- Click **Start**, and then click **Run**.
- Type **Msinfo32.exe** and press the **Enter** key. The result is shown in Figure 1.72.

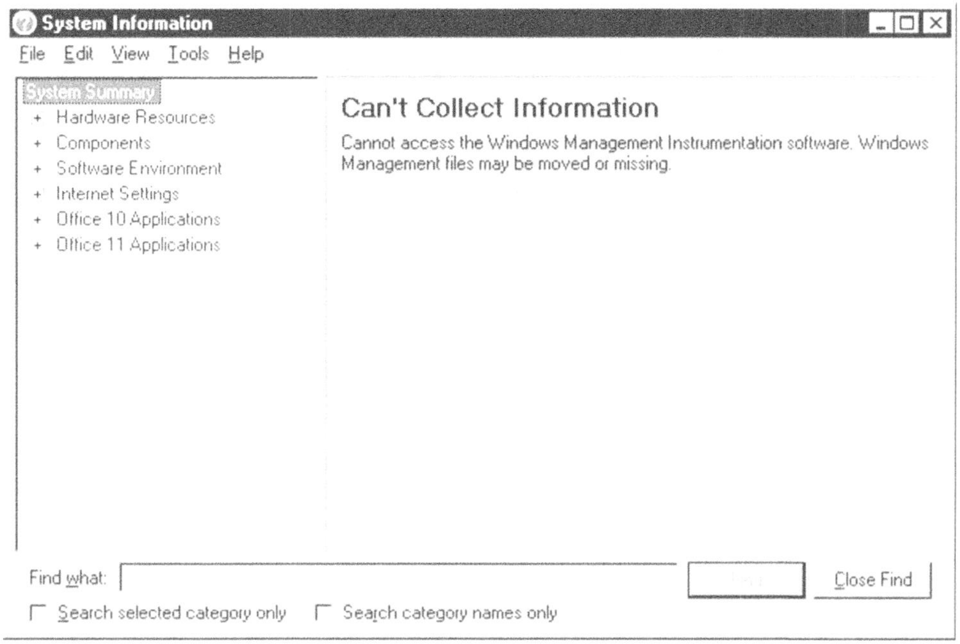

Figure 1-72: The System Information Tool.

As you can see from the right-pane, to access the Hardware Resources portion you must have the Windows Management Instrumentation (WMI) software installed on the server. The hardware portion of the tool will not work without the WMI software installed; however, the software function of the toll will work fine. WMI was formerly known as WBEM.

The WMI Software Development Kit can be downloaded at

http://www.microsoft.com/msdownload/platformsdk/sdkupdate/.

The Microsoft TechNet site also has a lot of information on WMI and how it can be used to run scripts. After you have WMI installed, click the **Components** folder. Devices that are installed on the server are displayed. Click the sub-component and the properties will be shown in the display pane. The columns listed below are shown:

- **Device** – This shows the name for the device and the driver associated to the device.
- **PnP Device ID** – Shows the device IDs such as PCI ID, ISA ID, and ID for unknown or other bus types.
- **Error Code** – Displays the error code associated with the problem. Using the Device Manager Error code you can determine what created the problem. Such as an unknown device error.
- **Problem Devices** – Will list three types of records can be shown depending on the device in question. The three types of disks are shown in the following boxes:

PCI PnP Device ID:

```
Device Name |
PCI\VEN_00000&DEV_0000&SUBSYS_00000000&REV_00\0&0000
| Error code
```

ISA PnP ID:

```
Device Name |?\PNP0000\0
```

Bad or Incompatible Device Driver:

Device Name | ROOT\UNKNOWN\0000

The **Setupapi.log** file can be used to assist you with identifying objects that could have created the **Unknown Device** in the Device Manager. Often devices may be listed as serial devices, but not be related to the serial port. This can happen if a partial plug-and-play ID is available and interpreted as a serial device. If software is the problem for the Unknown Device, use the device manager to remove the unknown device and reboot the server.

1.4 3 Diagnose and resolve issues related to hardware driver upgrades

For troubleshooting **Unknown Device** driver issues, you can use the Device Manager. Right-click on the device, open its properties, and you will see the **General** and **Driver** tab. The **General tab** will display the error message stating the device is not installed correctly and will give you the option to reinstall the driver (Figure 1.73).

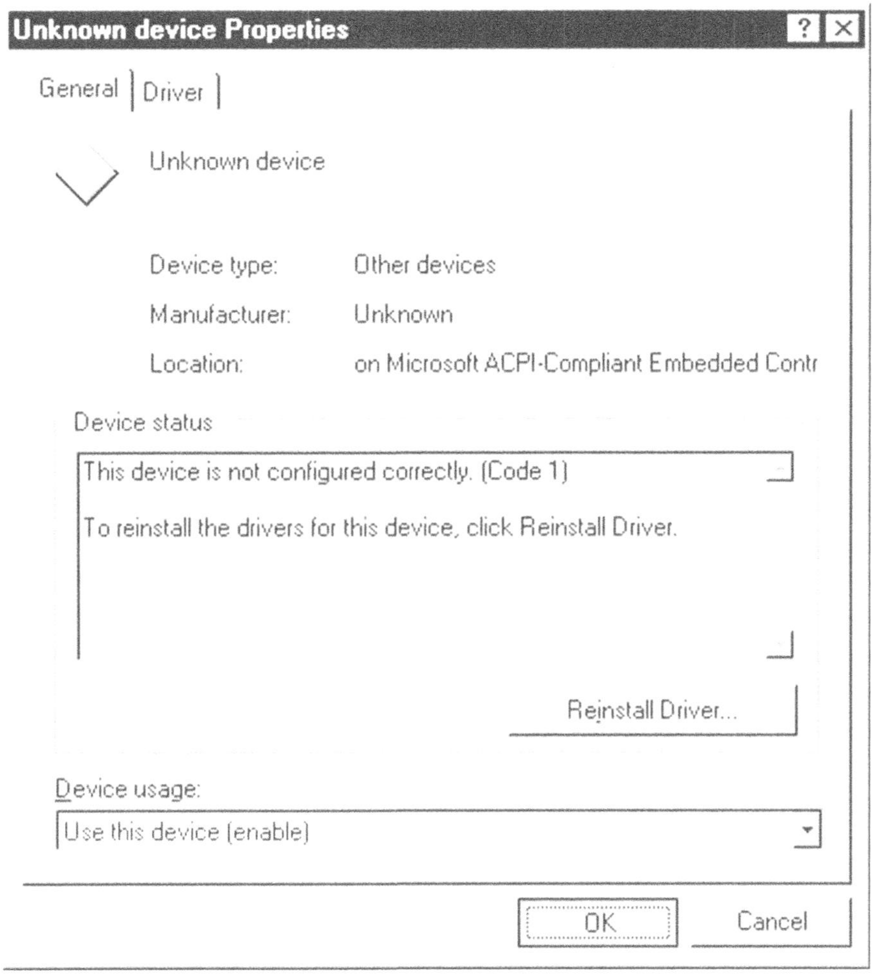

Figure 1-73: General Tab, Properties of the Unknown device.

The Driver tab of the Unknown Device gives you options to view driver details, update the driver, rollback the driver or uninstall the driver (Figure 1.74). At the top of the dialog box in our example displayed in Figure 1.74, you can see that the driver provider is unknown, driver date is not available, driver version is not available and the driver signer is not digitally signed.

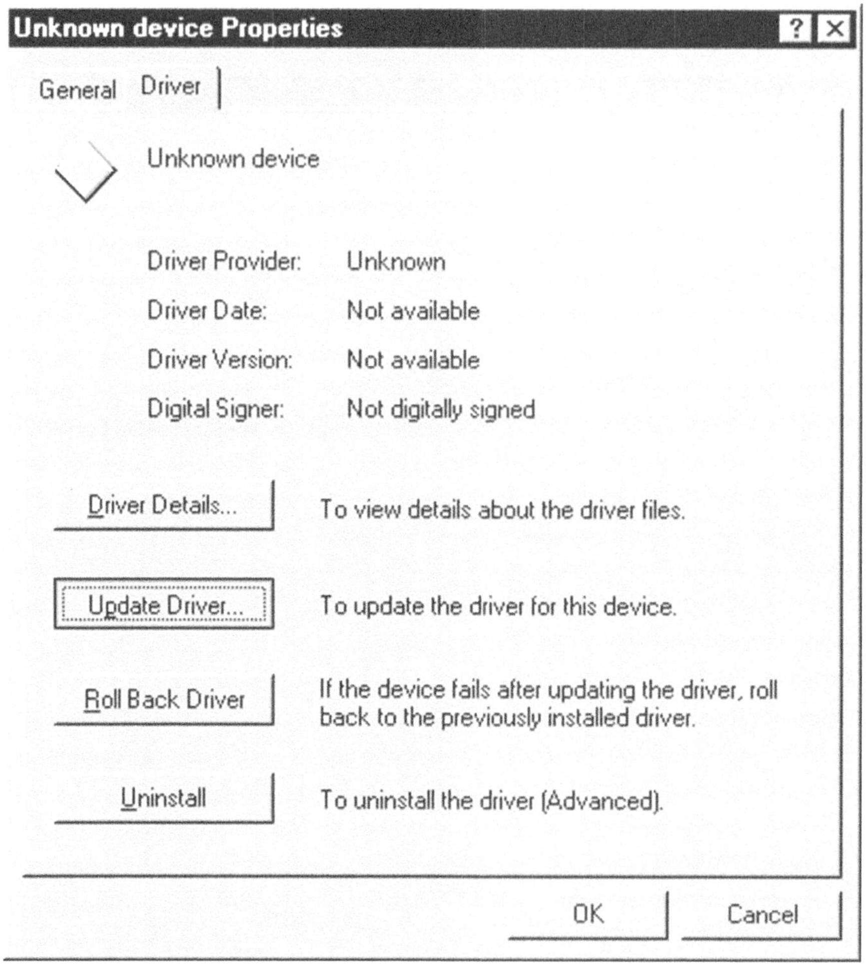

Figure 1-74: Unknown device Driver details.

Find an updated driver from the manufacturer (if available) and choose the **Update Driver** option to correct the problem. If , after you try this step, the device still is failing, use the **Roll Back Driver** option to roll back to the previously installed driver. The **Uninstall Driver** completely uninstalls the driver for the device.

Pop Quiz 1.4

Pop Quiz 1.4 *Questions*

1. How many monitors will Windows Server 2003 support?
2. What are three of the troubleshooting methods you can use when an unknown driver is installed on your Windows Server 2003?
3. How do you get to "Safe Mode"?
4. You have used Msinfo32.exe to access the System Information tool. However, you cannot access the Hardware Resources section. What must you do?
5. What is the difference between rolling back the driver and uninstalling the driver?

Pop Quiz 1.4 *Answers*

1. Windows Server 2003 supports the use of up to 10 monitors.
2. In cases where an unknown driver is installed on your Windows Server 2003, you can:
   - Boot the system in the Safe Mode.
   - Use the System Information tool.
   - Use the Event log to check for errors.
3. To access Safe Mode, just click the F8 key on your keyboard during the boot process and select "Safe Mode".
4. To access the Hardware Resources portion of the System Information Tool, you must have the Windows Management Instrumentation (WMI) software installed on the server.
5. The Roll Back Driver option will "roll back" to the driver previously installed driver, while the Uninstall Driver completely uninstalls the driver for the device.

1.5 Install & configure server hardware devices

Installing devices on Windows Server 2003 systems is much easier than it was in the years back before plug-and-play. If you check the Windows Hardware Compatibility List (HCL) before you purchase hardware, you can make certain that the hardware is on the recommended for Server 2003 and you should have no problems, unless the hardware itself is faulty. When installing hardware, always make certain that you use the proper safety precautions. If you need assistance with installing the hardware into the server, contact the hardware manufacturer. This section will show you how to configure and troubleshoot the device, after the hardware has been installed.

1.5.1 Configure driver signing options

To allow the Microsoft Operating System software to function properly with various manufacturers' hardware, the drivers for the hardware all include a digital signature. The digital signature can be described as a type of "approval" for the hardware. This means that the hardware has met specific testing level and that it has not been changed by another process on the machine. Some hardware manufacturers tout the **Designed for Microsoft Windows Server 2003** logo, which means that the product has been tested specifically for Windows Server 2003 environments. The Windows Server 2003 operating system uses three features to guarantee that the device driver has not been altered and is in its original pristine state:

- File Signature Verification
- System File Checker
- Windows File Protection.

Whether you are a newbie to the industry or you have worked in the industry for any amount of time, chances are you have most likely had to troubleshoot a system for driver problems. If the check points were not in place and you installed hardware that had not been tested with device drivers that have been digitally signed, you could end up with an extremely unstable server and frequent crashes.

This is not to say that all unsigned device drivers and hardware without the Microsoft Logo can cause a system to crash, but it is always wise to "err on the side of caution" and check the Microsoft site for a listing of compatible hardware to use on a server. Not all hardware is compatible with Windows Server 2003 systems.

To check for system compatibility, use the **msinfo32** tool. Click on **Start | Run** and type **msinfo32.exe**. The System Information tool will open. Select **Tools | File Signature Verification Utility** from the (Figure 1.75).

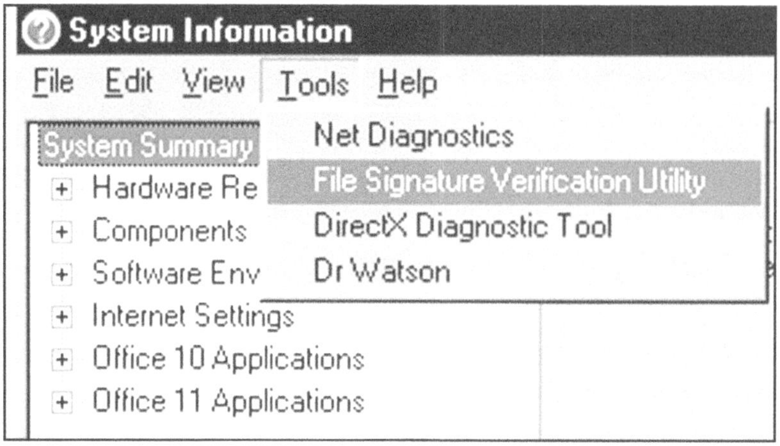

Figure 1-75: The first screen of the Wizard.

Once this has been selected, you can choose the **Advanced** option (Figure 1.76).

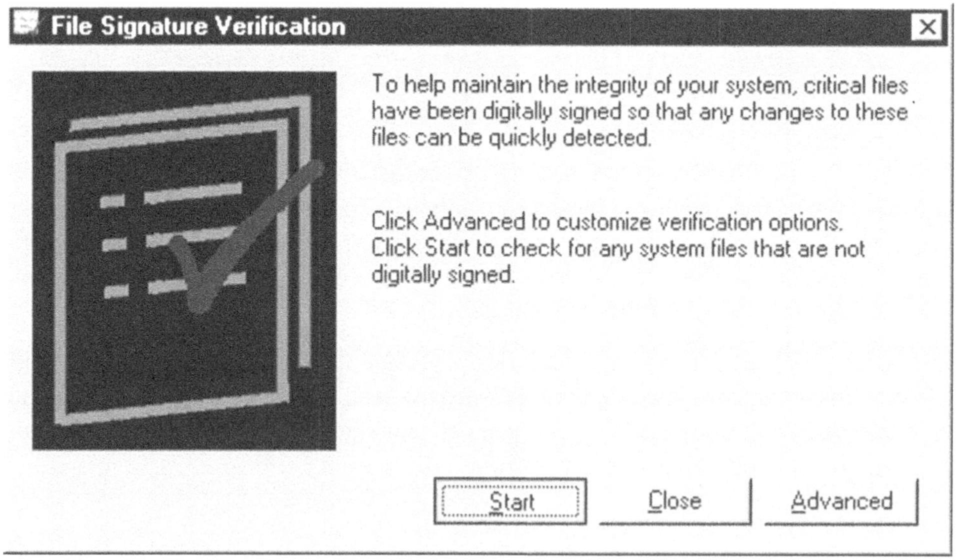

Figure 1-76: File Signature Verification wizard.

A new dialog box, with two additional tabs will appear (Figure 1.77).

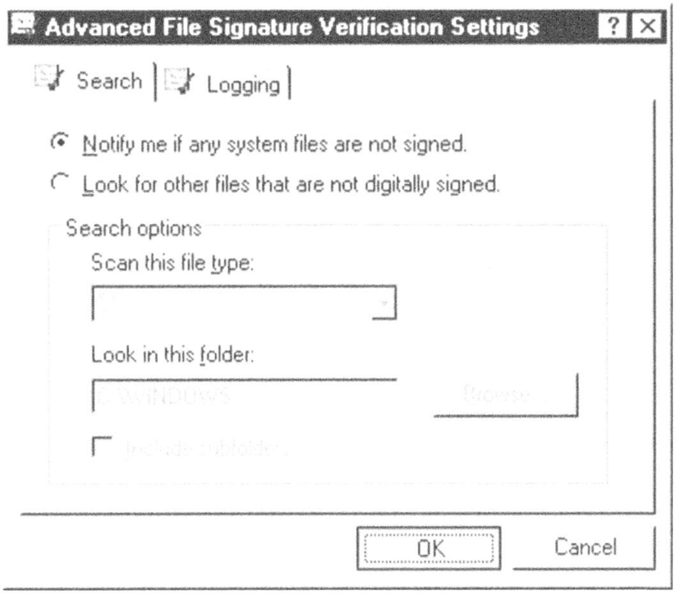

Figure 1-77: The Advanced properties of the Signature Verification Wizard.

On the **Search** tab, you have options to select for notification, search options and folders for the wizard to search. Now, let's look at the Logging tab (Figure 1.78).

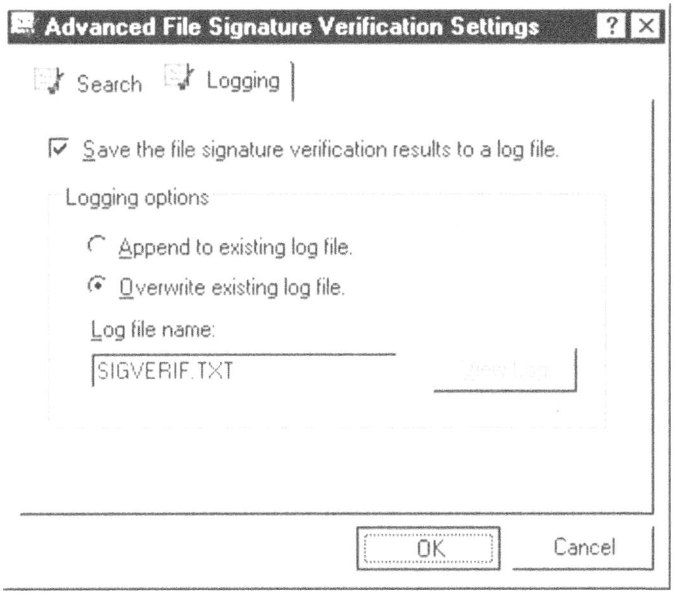

Figure 1-78: Logging option for the Advanced File Signature Verification wizard.

This tab is used to allow you to save the results of the file to a log file. The default log file name is **SIGVERIF.TXT.** After these settings have been selected, click the **OK** button to go back to the main screen of the wizard. Click the **Start** button and the scanning will begin (Figure 1.79).

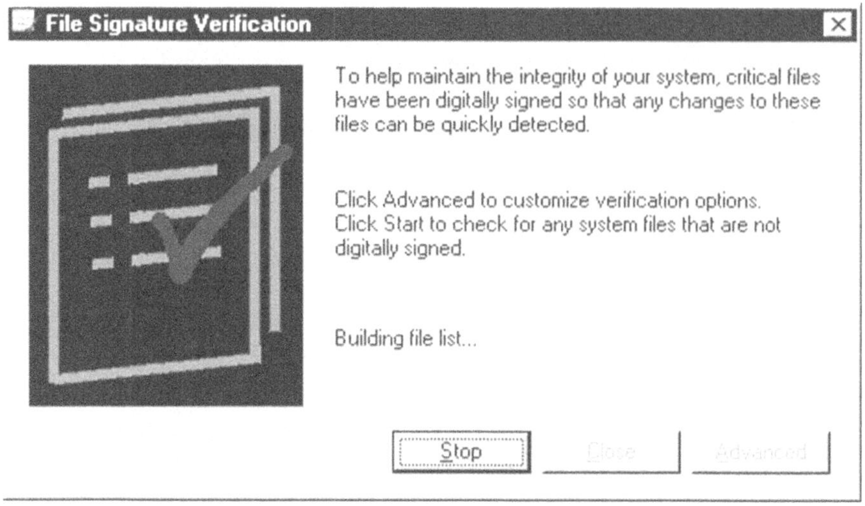

Figure 1-79: The File Signature Verification is beginning the file listing process.

After the file list has been built the scan will begin. Figure 1.80 shows the scan in progress.

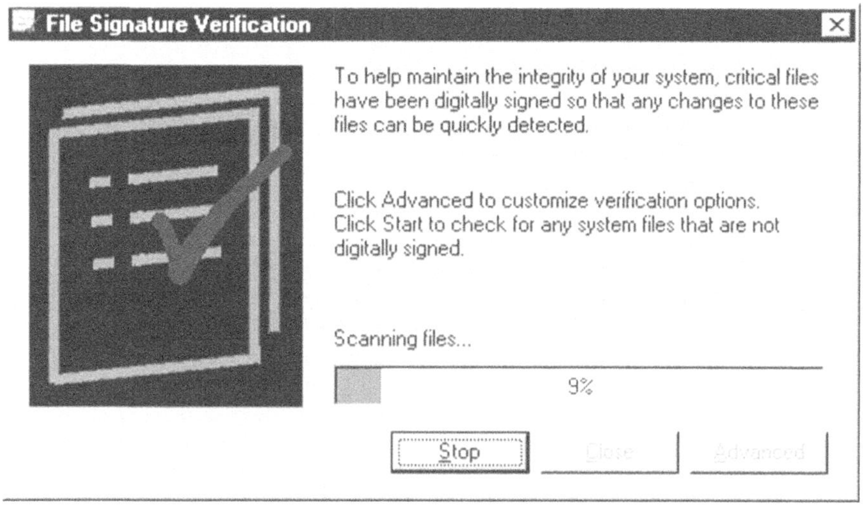

Figure 1-80: The File Signature Verification is beginning the scan process.

You can choose to stop the process at any time by clicking on the **Stop** button. After the scan has completed the results are displayed. An example is shown in Figure 1.81.

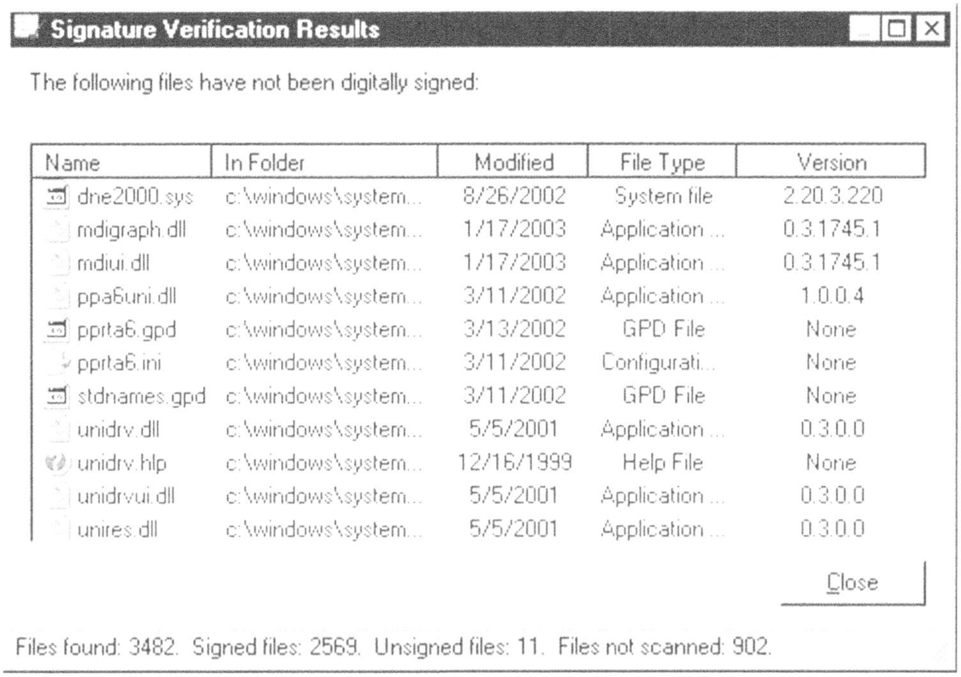

Name	In Folder	Modified	File Type	Version
dne2000.sys	c:\windows\system...	8/26/2002	System file	2.20.3.220
mdigraph.dll	c:\windows\system...	1/17/2003	Application ...	0.3.1745.1
mdiui.dll	c:\windows\system...	1/17/2003	Application ...	0.3.1745.1
ppa6uni.dll	c:\windows\system...	3/11/2002	Application ...	1.0.0.4
pprta6.gpd	c:\windows\system...	3/13/2002	GPD File	None
pprta6.ini	c:\windows\system...	3/11/2002	Configurati...	None
stdnames.gpd	c:\windows\system...	3/11/2002	GPD File	None
unidrv.dll	c:\windows\system...	5/5/2001	Application ...	0.3.0.0
unidrv.hlp	c:\windows\system...	12/16/1999	Help File	None
unidrvui.dll	c:\windows\system...	5/5/2001	Application ...	0.3.0.0
unires.dll	c:\windows\system...	5/5/2001	Application ...	0.3.0.0

Figure 1-81: The File Signature Verification results.

The displayed results show only the files that are on the system and are not digitally signed. The log file, as shown in Figure 1.82, is automatically created when you run the signature verification tool.

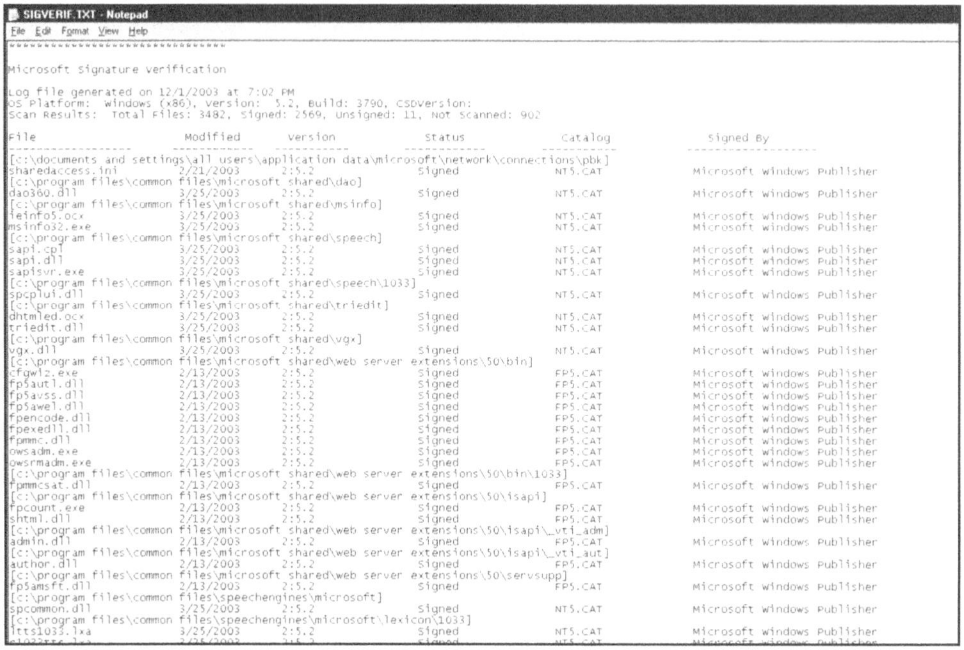

```
SIGVERIF.TXT - Notepad
File Edit Format View Help
********************************

Microsoft Signature Verification

Log file generated on 12/1/2003 at 7:02 PM
OS Platform:  Windows (x86), Version:  5.2, Build: 3790, CSDVersion:
Scan Results:  Total Files: 3482, Signed: 2569, Unsigned: 11, Not Scanned: 902

File                   Modified     Version      Status       Catalog      Signed By
------------------     ----------   ----------   ----------   ----------   ------------------
[c:\documents and settings\all users\application data\microsoft\network\connections\pbk]
sharedaccess.ini       2/21/2003    2:5.2        Signed       NT5.CAT      Microsoft Windows Publisher
[c:\program files\common files\microsoft shared\dao]
dao360.dll             3/25/2003    2:5.2        Signed       NT5.CAT      Microsoft Windows Publisher
[c:\program files\common files\microsoft shared\msinfo]
ieinfo5.ocx            3/25/2003    2:5.2        Signed       NT5.CAT      Microsoft Windows Publisher
msinfo32.exe           3/25/2003    2:5.2        Signed       NT5.CAT      Microsoft Windows Publisher
[c:\program files\common files\microsoft shared\speech]
sapi.cpl               3/25/2003    2:5.2        Signed       NT5.CAT      Microsoft Windows Publisher
sapi.dll               3/25/2003    2:5.2        Signed       NT5.CAT      Microsoft Windows Publisher
sapisvr.exe            3/25/2003    2:5.2        Signed       NT5.CAT      Microsoft Windows Publisher
[c:\program files\common files\microsoft shared\speech\1033]
spcplui.dll            3/25/2003    2:5.2        Signed       NT5.CAT      Microsoft Windows Publisher
[c:\program files\common files\microsoft shared\triedit]
dhtmled.ocx            3/25/2003    2:5.2        Signed       NT5.CAT      Microsoft Windows Publisher
triedit.dll            3/25/2003    2:5.2        Signed       NT5.CAT      Microsoft Windows Publisher
[c:\program files\common files\microsoft shared\vgx]
vgx.dll                3/25/2003    2:5.2        Signed       NT5.CAT      Microsoft Windows Publisher
[c:\program files\common files\microsoft shared\web server extensions\50\bin]
cfgwiz.exe             2/13/2003    2:5.2        Signed       FP5.CAT      Microsoft Windows Publisher
fp5autl.dll            2/13/2003    2:5.2        Signed       FP5.CAT      Microsoft Windows Publisher
fp5avss.dll            2/13/2003    2:5.2        Signed       FP5.CAT      Microsoft Windows Publisher
fp5awel.dll            2/13/2003    2:5.2        Signed       FP5.CAT      Microsoft Windows Publisher
fpencode.dll           2/13/2003    2:5.2        Signed       FP5.CAT      Microsoft Windows Publisher
fpexedll.dll           2/13/2003    2:5.2        Signed       FP5.CAT      Microsoft Windows Publisher
fpmmc.dll              2/13/2003    2:5.2        Signed       FP5.CAT      Microsoft Windows Publisher
owsadm.exe             2/13/2003    2:5.2        Signed       FP5.CAT      Microsoft Windows Publisher
owsrmadm.exe           2/13/2003    2:5.2        Signed       FP5.CAT      Microsoft Windows Publisher
[c:\program files\common files\microsoft shared\web server extensions\50\bin\1033]
fpmmcsat.dll           2/13/2003    2:5.2        Signed       FP5.CAT      Microsoft Windows Publisher
[c:\program files\common files\microsoft shared\web server extensions\50\isapi]
fpcount.exe            2/13/2003    2:5.2        Signed       FP5.CAT      Microsoft Windows Publisher
shtml.dll              2/13/2003    2:5.2        Signed       FP5.CAT      Microsoft Windows Publisher
[c:\program files\common files\microsoft shared\web server extensions\50\isapi\_vti_adm]
admin.dll              2/13/2003    2:5.2        Signed       FP5.CAT      Microsoft Windows Publisher
[c:\program files\common files\microsoft shared\web server extensions\50\isapi\_vti_aut]
author.dll             2/13/2003    2:5.2        Signed       FP5.CAT      Microsoft Windows Publisher
[c:\program files\common files\microsoft shared\web server extensions\50\servsupp]
fp5amsft.dll           2/13/2003    2:5.2        Signed       FP5.CAT      Microsoft Windows Publisher
[c:\program files\common files\speechengines\microsoft]
spcommon.dll           3/25/2003    2:5.2        Signed       NT5.CAT      Microsoft Windows Publisher
[c:\program files\common files\speechengines\microsoft\lexicon\1033]
ltts1033.lxa           3/25/2003    2:5.2        Signed       NT5.CAT      Microsoft Windows Publisher
```

Figure 1-82: The File Signature Verification sigverif.txt file.

This text file lists all files that were scanned and has multiple pages. It lists the file name, the date modified, version, status, catalog and program it was signed by. You can access the **Advanced** properties of the tool to change the name of the text file as well as the location of the file.

For the files not signed, the hardware manufacturer can be contacted. As well, a quick visit to the manufacturer's Web site might give you access to updated Windows driver files.

1.5.2 Configure resource settings for a device

Configuring resource settings for devices can be done by opening the **Device Manager** and selecting the device from the list. Figure 1.83 shows a hardware device that has a conflict.

Figure 1-83: Hardware device with a conflict in the Device Manager.

Figure 1.84 shows the Resources tab. This is accessed by right-clicking the device and choosing the **Set configuration manually** option .

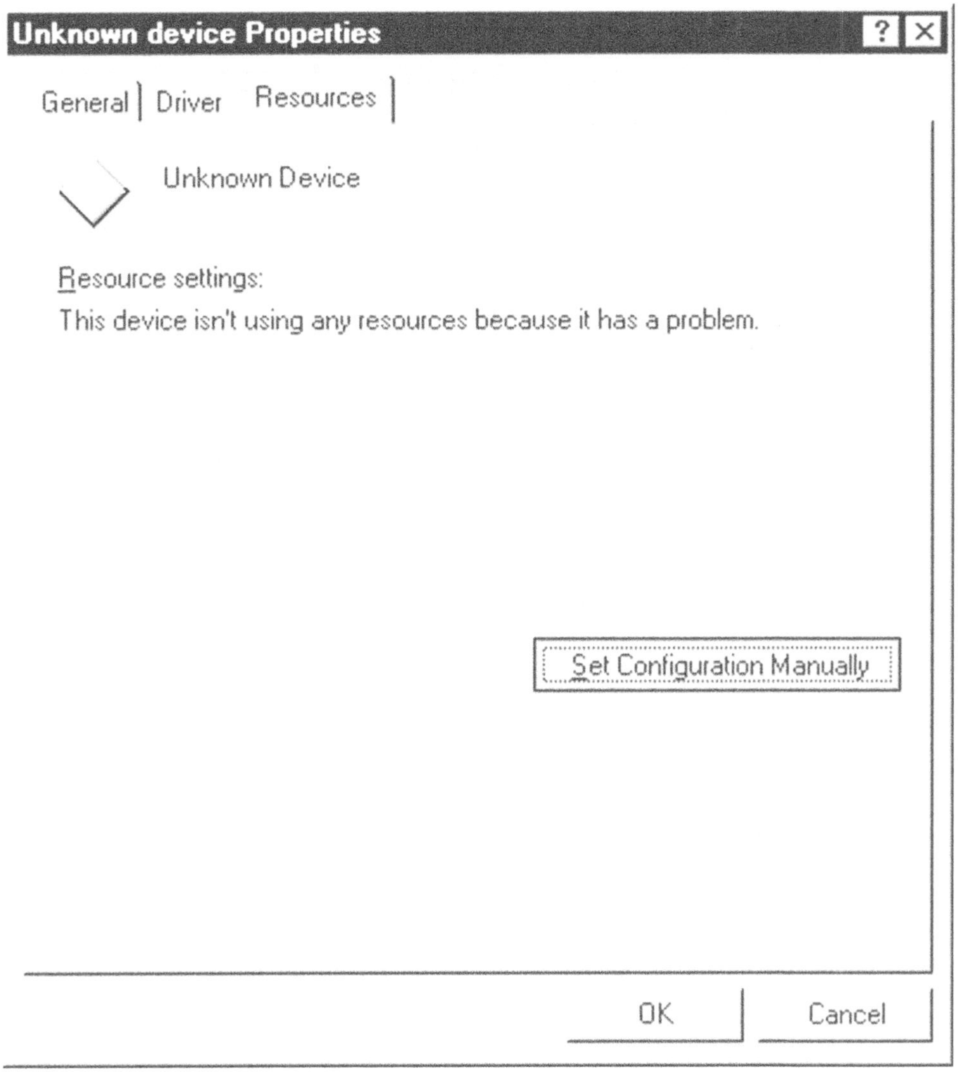

Figure 1-84: The resources tab of the Unknown Device.

After the **Set Configuration manually option** has been chosen, the screen shown in Figure 1.85 will appear, allowing you to select the options you wish to change.

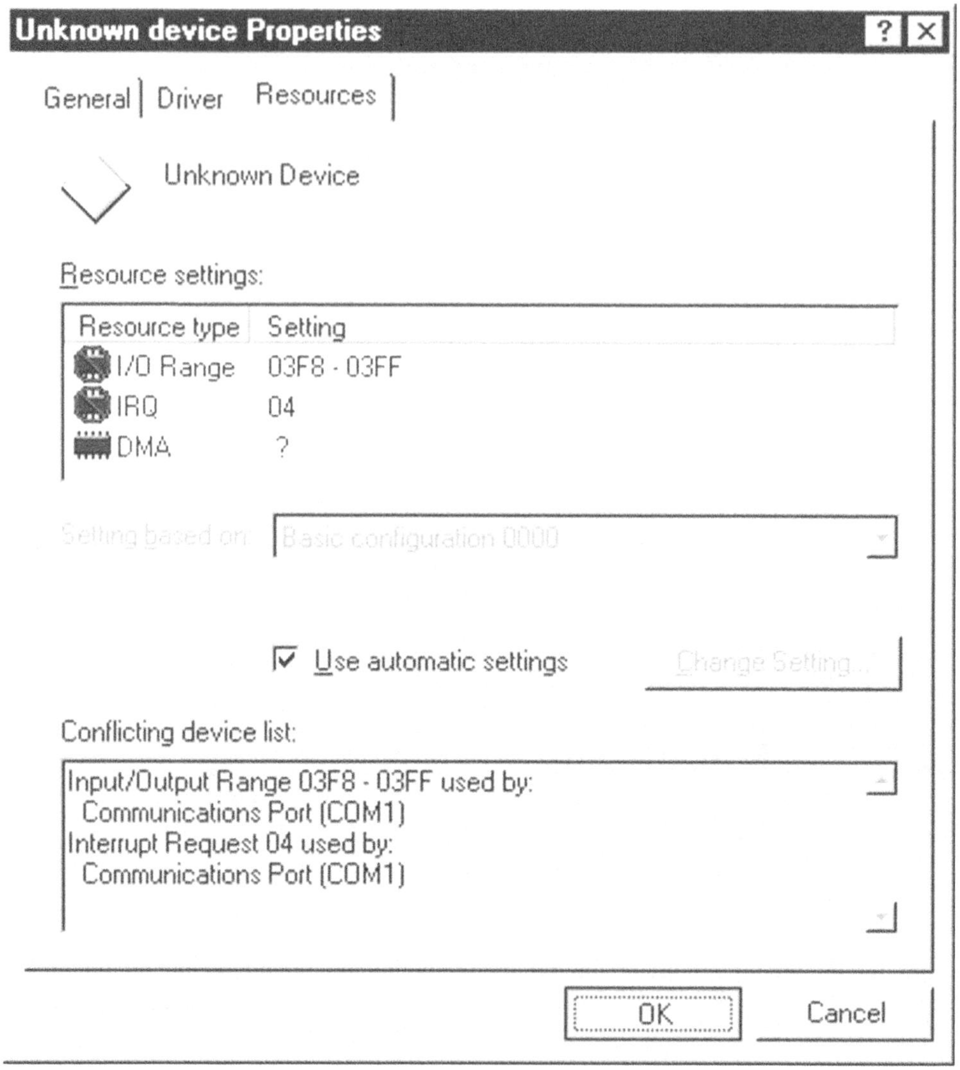

Figure 1-85: Changing resources manually on an unknown device.

Uncheck the **Use Automatic Settings** option and select the resource type that has the conflict. In our example, it is the **I/O Range** and the **IRQ** resource. Choose the I/O Range with your mouse (one click). Once it is highlighted, choose the **Change Setting** option and a drop-down menu will appear as shown in Figure 1.86.

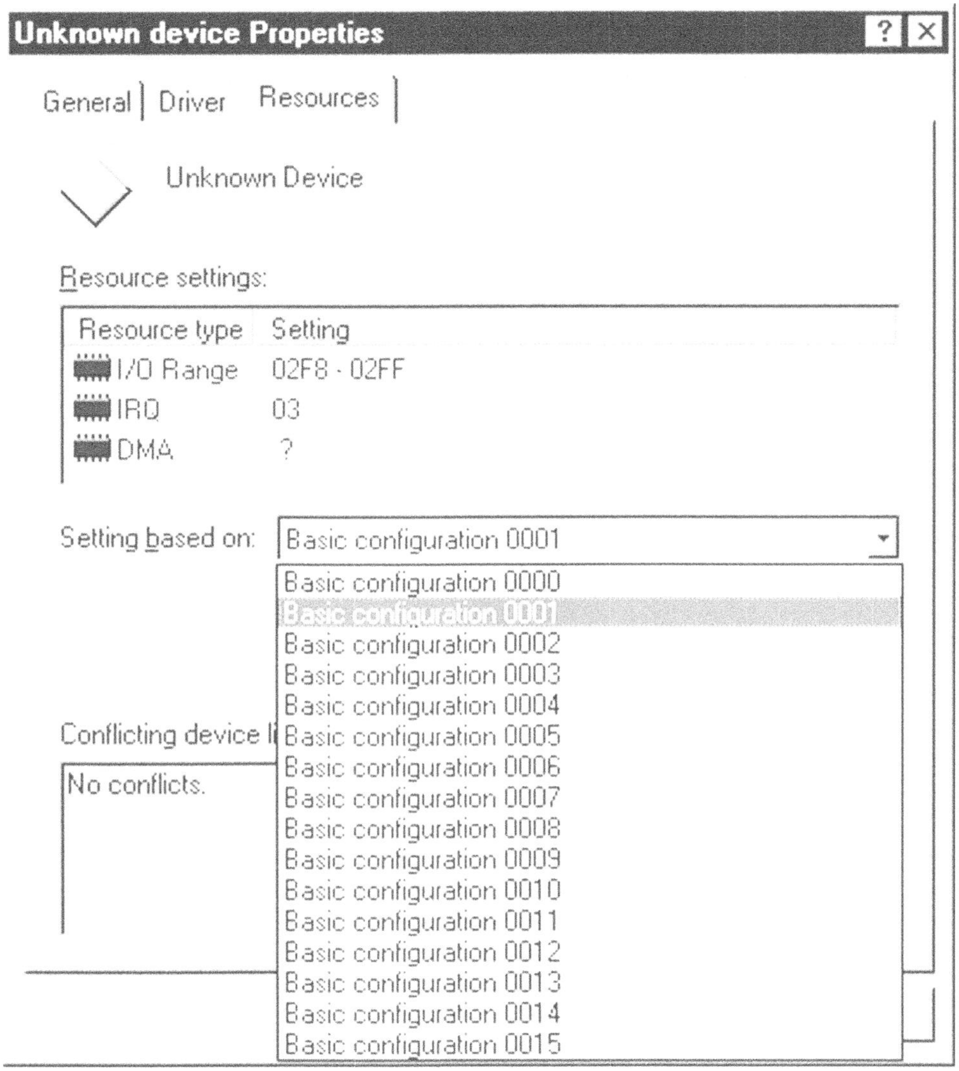

Figure 1-86: Forcing a change of settings on the Unknown Device.

In this example, the **Basic Configuration 0001** is chosen. Once it is selected the **I/O Range** and **IRQ** show no conflicts but the **DMA range** still shows a ?. This means additional modifications are needed (Figure 1.87).

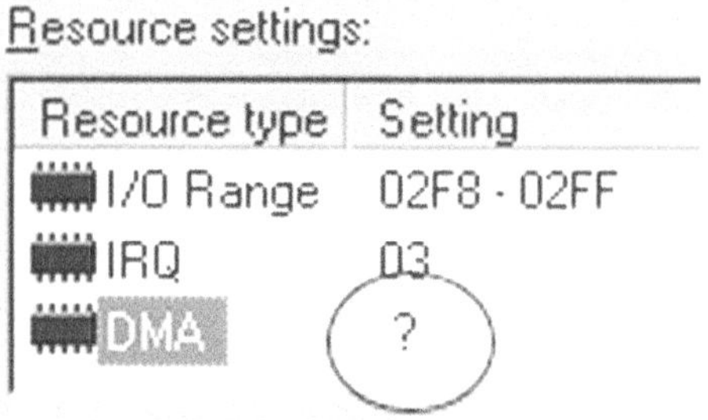

Figure 1-87: The DMA range with a conflict.

Click the **Change Setting** option again, this type selecting the **DMA** resource. A dialog box, similar to the one in Figure 1.88, will appear.

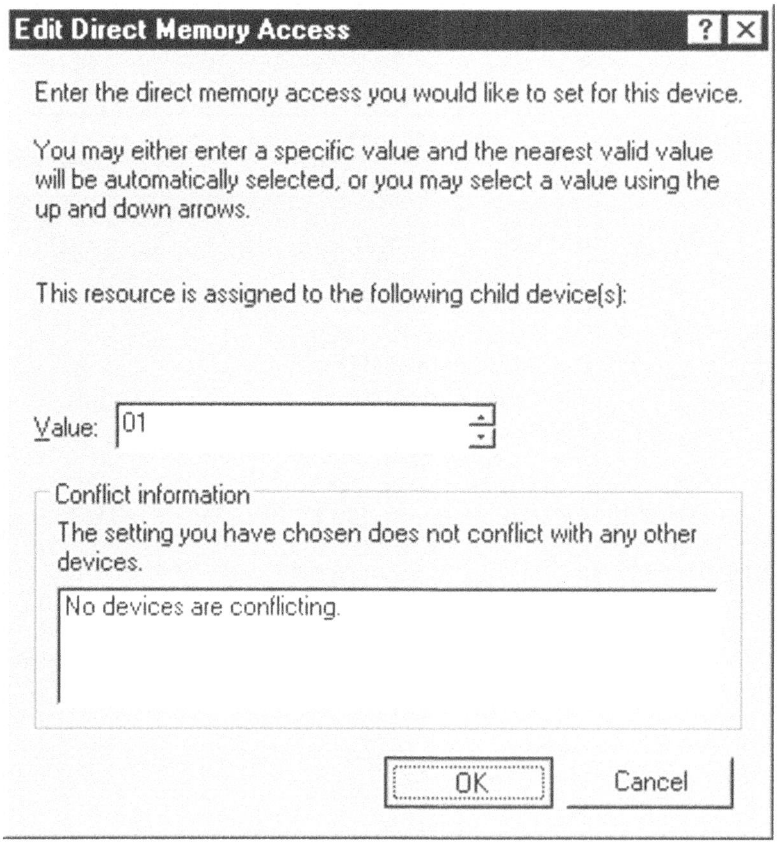

Figure 1-88: Entering a Value for the DMA range.

Use the up and down arrow keys to select a range for the DMA. While you do this, check the **Conflict Information** box to make certain it is now displaying the **No Devices are conflicting** notice. Click **OK** to make the changes. You will be to confirm the changes you have made (Figure 1.89).

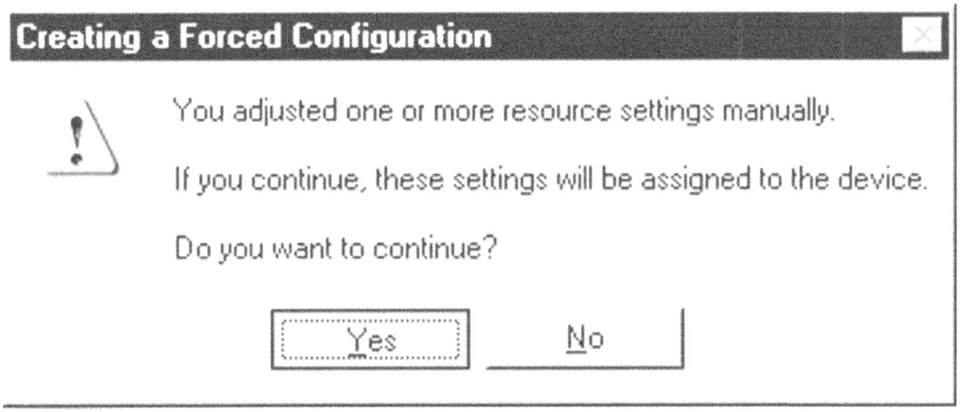

Figure 1-89: Creating a Forced Configuration on hardware.

Once you have chosen to apply the configuration changes, you will be prompted to restart the computer. Figure 1.90 shows this dialog box.

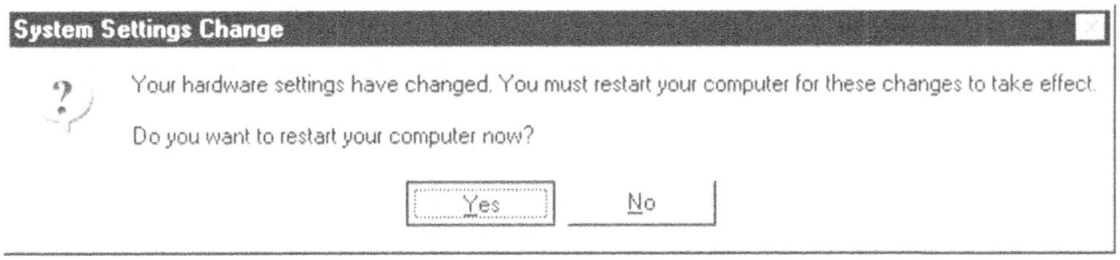

Figure 1-90: Restarting the Server after the Device resources has been modified.

Note that until the server is restarted, Device Manager will continue to show the Warning sign. Restart the server and check the Device Manager again for the hardware that was previously in conflict. It should now be displayed without any warning messages.

1.5.3 Configure device properties and settings

Configuring device property settings can be done by using the Device Manager on the Windows Server 2003. Open the **Device Manager** and select the hardware on which you wish to modify properties.

> **Remember** that most plug-and-play devices will not allow a change of settings.

The Automatic Setting option will be selected by default and will be grayed out, as shown above for the Network Adapter card installed on a server in Figure 1.91.

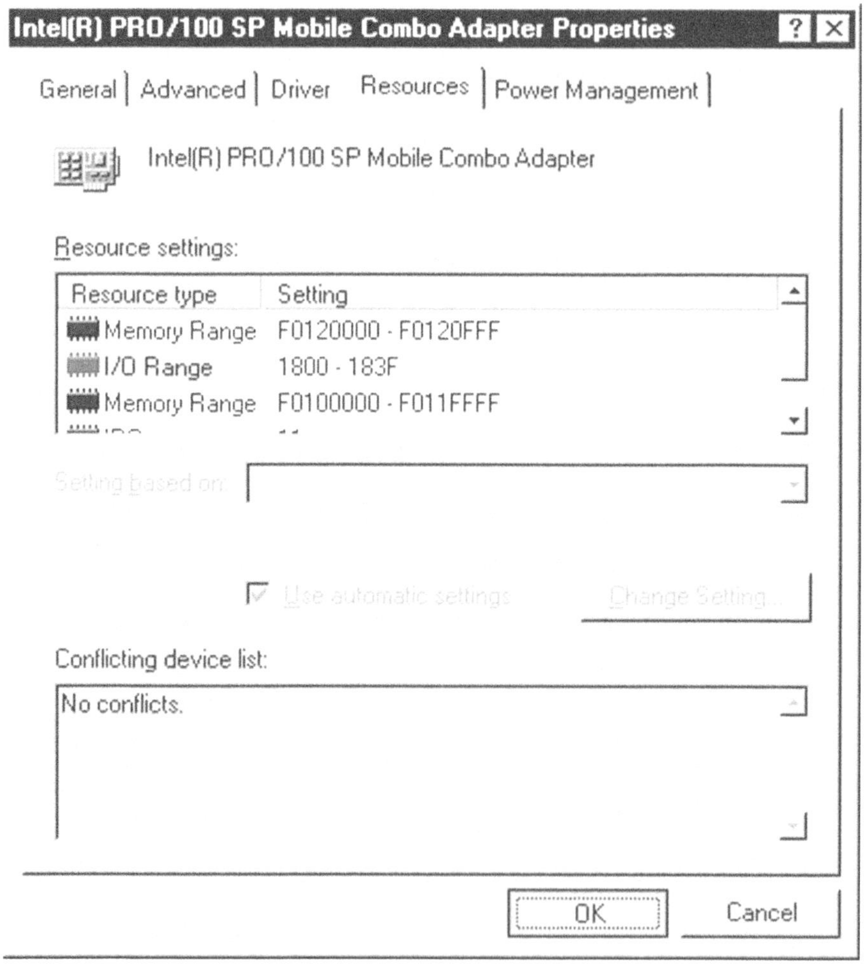

Figure 1-91: Automatic settings for a network adapter card that cannot be modified.

Figure 1.92 shows resources for a COM port installed on the system that can be modified.

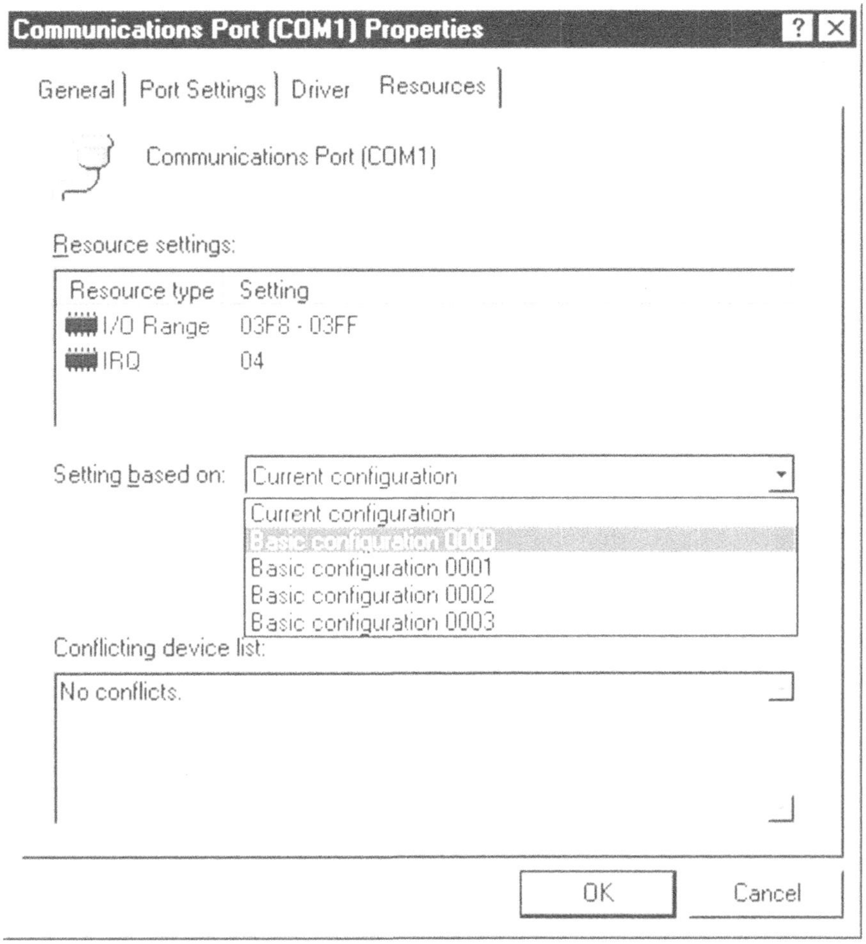

Figure 1-92: Modifying Resources for a COM port.

Using the **Settings based on** option, choose a **Basic Configuration** to use for the COM port. The IRQ was set to the default I/O Range of 03F8 and IRQ 4.

Note: Most times this is set by the motherboard BIOS. You will have to also go into the Setup properties of the BIOS when the server is restarting and change the Onboard Settings for the COM Port.

Figure 1.93 shows the I/O Range and IRQ changes.

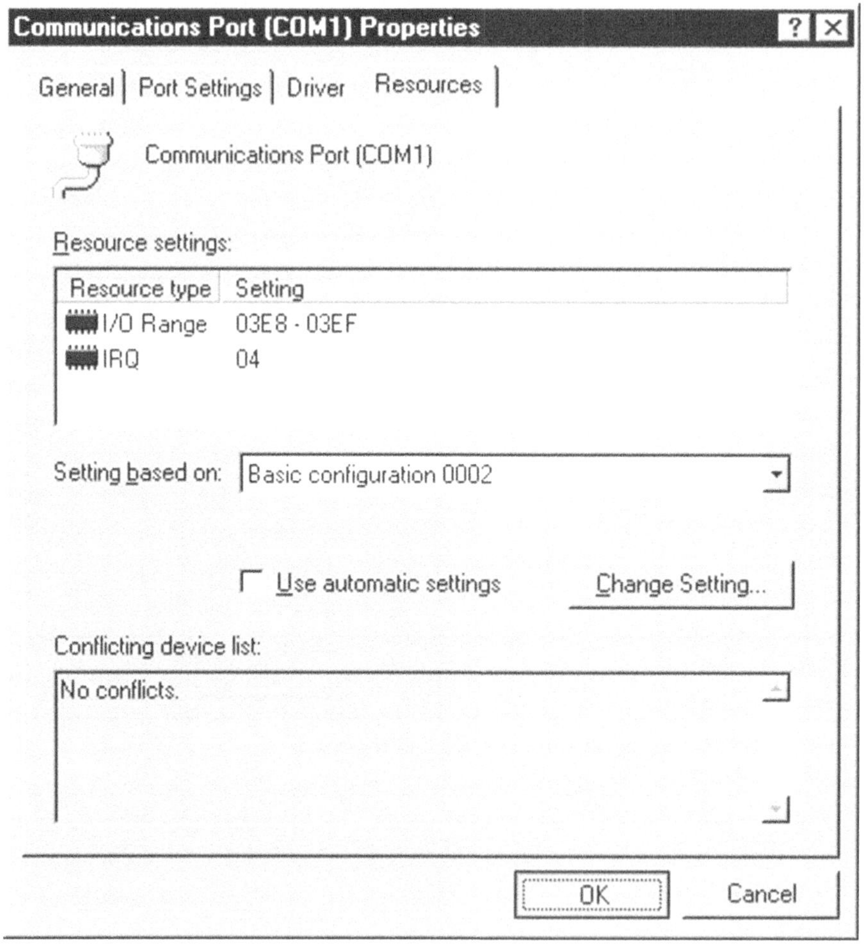

Figure 1-93: The new Resource settings for COM1.

Note that the I/O Range has been changed to 03E8 and the IRQ has been changed to IRQ COM4. These settings are the default settings for COM3 and would conflict if COM3 was installed on this server.

Chapter 1: Summary

Congratulations! You are ready to move onto the next chapter which will cover how to manage users, computers and groups. Check back to this chapter for a reference guide, especially when optimizing server performance and installing hardware on the server.

Chapter 1: Review Questions

1. You decide to create a logical volume on your Server 2003 machine using Disk Management. How can you accomplish this?

A. Go into Control Panel and select Computer Management. Right-click free space on an extended partition where you want to create the logical drive, and then click New Logical Drive. Use the New Partition wizard.

B. Go into Control Panel and select Disk Management. Right-click free space on an extended partition where you want to create the logical drive, and then click New Logical Drive. Use the New Partition wizard.

C. Go into Computer Management and select Disk Management. Right-click free space on an extended partition where you want to create the logical drive, and then click New Logical Drive. Use the New Partition wizard.

D. Go into Computer Management and select Disk Management. Right-click used space on an extended partition where you want to create the logical drive, and then click New Logical Drive. Use the New Partition wizard.

2. You attempt to access your G: drive, but you find that the status of the G: drive is offline with errors. What action should you take to change the status of the G: drive to online?

A. Double-click the disk, and then click Reactivate Disk to return the disk to regular Online status.

B. Right-click the disk, and then click Reactivate Disk to return the disk to regular Online status.

C. Right-click the disk, and then click Enable Disk to return the disk to regular Online status.

D. Double-click the disk, and then click Enable Disk to return the disk to regular Online status.

---

3. You attempt to access your H: drive, but you find that the status of the H: drive is missing. What action should you take to change the status of the H: drive to online?

A. Check for problems with the hard disk

B. Partition the disk

C. Reactivate the disk to Online status

D. Reformat the disk

E. Verify that the physical disk is correctly attached to the computer

4. You want to make sure that the junior network associates install only Microsoft signed drivers on the 2003 server that handles file and print services for the network. How can you do this?

A. In System properties, select the hardware tab. Click the driver signing button. Set the driver signing option to kill when you attempt to install.

B. In System properties, select the hardware tab. Click the driver signing button. Set the driver signing option to ignore when you attempt to install unsigned drivers.

C. In System properties, select the hardware tab. Click the driver signing button. Set the driver signing option to warn when you attempt to install unsigned drivers.

D. In System properties, select the hardware tab. Click the driver signing button. Set the driver signing option to block when you attempt to install unsigned drivers.

---

5. Which of the following situations with a NIC card could produce a bottleneck?

A. An unplugged NIC card

B. A NIC card that is set for 10 Mbps when it should be set to 100 Mbps

C. An older network card that is installed on a new server

D. A fiber channel NIC

6. How can you perform real time monitoring by using Task Manager?

A. Press CTRL+ALT+DEL, and then click Task Manager.

B. Press ALT+SHFT+ESC, and then click Task Manager.

C. Press CTRL+ALT+ESC, and then click Task Manager.

D. On the Processes tab, click a column name to sort by that column. Click the column name a second time to reverse sort by that column. On the View menu, click Select Columns to add counters to the Processes tab.

E. Click the Applications tab to monitor running applications. Click the Processes tab to monitor the running processes.

---

7. You need to install two expansion cards in your 2003 Server. One of the cards is a PCI plug-and-play compliant card and one is an ISA plug-and-play compliant card. What actions are necessary to configure these cards?

A. With the PCI card, simply plug in the device.

B. With the ISA card, simply plug in the device.

C. With the PCI card, you will have to manually configure the card.

D. With the ISA card, turn off the computer to install the device, and then restart the computer to initialize the device.

E. With the ISA card, you will have to manually configure the card.

8. You want to create a RAID 5 volume from free space from Disk O, Disk 1 and Disk 2. Disk 0 has 30 percent of its drive space free and Disks 1 and 2 have the entire disk free. Disk 0 is a basic disk and Disks 1 and 2 are dynamic disks and all are formatted with NTFS. What steps do you need to take to create the RAID 5 volume?

A. Convert Disk 0 to a dynamic disk.

B. Convert Disk 1 back to a basic disk.

C. Create the RAID 5 volume using all basic disks.

D. Create the RAID 5 volume using all dynamic disks.

---

9. Under what circumstances would you need to update a driver in Windows Server 2003?

A. If you need to convert to NTFS.

B. If you need to convert to native mode.

C. If a bad driver was installed.

D. If you have driver signing set to ignore driver updates.

10. Which of the following should you use to check device drivers, to see if they are installed correctly?

A. My Computer

B. Event Monitor

C. Task Manager

D. Device Manager

E. Internet Options

---

11. You have three SCSI drives. The first drive is a 80 GB drive with 10 GB free. The second drive is a 60 GB drive with 20 GB free. The third drive is a 50 GB drive with the entirety of the drive free. You want to build a RAID 5 array. How big will it be?

A. 10 GB

B. 40 GB

C. 20 GB

D. 80 GB

E. 60 GB

12. When implementing redundancy in a Windows Server 2003, which methods will work?

A. Implementing disk spanning

B. Implementing disk striping with parity (RAID 5)

C. Implementing disk mirroring (RAID 1)

D. Implementing disk striping (RAID 0)

---

13. You store backup tapes both off-site and on-site. You are presently performing a normal backup every Monday at 5 p.m. and incremental backups every work night of the week at 5 p.m. Three drives in your RAID 5 array fail Wednesday at noon. What should you do to restore the RAID 5 array?

A. Using the on-site tapes, restore the RAID 5 array with the normal backup from Monday.

B. Using the on-site tapes, restore the RAID 5 array with the normal backup from Monday and the incremental from Tuesday.

C. Using the off-site tapes, restore the RAID 5 array with the normal backup from Monday and the incremental from Tuesday.

D. Using the off-site tapes, restore the RAID 5 array with the normal backup from Monday.

14. Which of the following RAID configurations does not allow for a single disk to fail?

A. RAID 0 (Disk Striping)

B. RAID 1 (Disk Mirroring)

C. Disk Spanning

D. RAID 5 (Disk Striping with Parity)

---

15. Which of the following is a volume that Windows Server 2003 does not support?

A. Spanned

B. RAID 5

C. Half

D. Mirrored

E. RAID 0

Chapter 1: Review Answers

1. You decide to create a logical volume on your Server 2003 machine using Disk Management. How can you accomplish this?

   A. Go into Control Panel and select Computer Management. Right-click free space on an extended partition where you want to create the logical drive, and then click New Logical Drive. Use the New Partition wizard.

   B. Go into Control Panel and select Disk Management. Right-click free space on an extended partition where you want to create the logical drive, and then click New Logical Drive. Use the New Partition wizard.

***C. Go into Computer Management and select Disk Management. Right-click free space on an extended partition where you want to create the logical drive, and then click New Logical Drive. Use the New Partition wizard.**

   D. Go into Computer Management and select Disk Management. Right-click used space on an extended partition where you want to create the logical drive, and then click New Logical Drive. Use the New Partition wizard.

Explanation: To create a new partition or logical drive, select the Disk Management option in Computer Management. To create a new partition, right-click unallocated space on the basic disk where you want to create the partition, and then click New Partition. You can also right-click free space on an extended partition where you want to create the logical drive, and then click New Logical Drive. On the Welcome to the New Partition Wizard page, click Next. On the Select Partition Type page, click the type of partition that you want to create, and then click Next. On the Specify Partition Size page, specify the size in megabytes (MB) of the partition that you want to create, and then click Next. On the Assign Drive Letter or Path page, enter a drive letter or drive path, and then click Next. On the Format Partition page, specify the formatting options that you want, and then click Next. On the Completing the New Partition Wizard page, verify that the options that you selected are correct, and then click Finish.

2. You attempt to access your G: drive, but you find that the status of the G: drive is offline with errors. What action should you take to change the status of the G: drive to online?

A. Double-click the disk, and then click Reactivate Disk to return the disk to regular Online status.

***B. Right-click the disk, and then click Reactivate Disk to return the disk to regular Online status.**

C. Right-click the disk, and then click Enable Disk to return the disk to regular Online status.

D. Double-click the disk, and then click Enable Disk to return the disk to regular Online status.

Explanation: When a disk or volume fails, Disk Management displays status descriptions of disks and volumes in the Disk Management window. These descriptions, are as follows: Online, Healthy (either of these are normal), Online with errors (indicative of I/O errors on a dynamic disk—to resolve this issue, right-click the disk, and then click Reactivate Disk to return the disk to regular Online status), Offline or Missing (displayed when dynamic disks are corrupted, inaccessible, or temporarily unavailable—to resolve this issue, repair any disk, controller, or connection problems, verify that the physical disk is turned on and correctly attached to the computer, right-click the disk, and then click Reactivate Disk to return the disk to Online status).

---

3. You attempt to access your H: drive, but you find that the status of the H: drive is missing. What action should you take to change the status of the H: drive to online?

***A. Check for problems with the hard disk**

B. Partition the disk

***C. Reactivate the disk to Online status**

D. Reformat the disk

***E. Verify that the physical disk is correctly attached to the computer**

Explanation: When a disk or volume fails, Disk Management displays status descriptions of disks and volumes in the Disk Management window. These descriptions, are as follows: Online, Healthy (either of these is normal), Online with errors (indicative of I/O errors on a dynamic disk—to resolve this issue, right-click the disk, and then click Reactivate Disk to return the disk to regular Online status), Offline or Missing (displayed when dynamic disks are corrupted, inaccessible, or temporarily unavailable—to resolve this issue, repair any disk, controller, or connection problems, verify that the physical disk is turned on and correctly attached to the computer, right-click the disk, and then click Reactivate Disk to return the disk to Online status).

4. You want to make sure that the junior network associates install only Microsoft signed drivers on the 2003 server that handles file and print services for the network. How can you do this?

A. In System properties, select the hardware tab. Click the driver signing button. Set the driver signing option to kill when you attempt to install.

B. In System properties, select the hardware tab. Click the driver signing button. Set the driver signing option to ignore when you attempt to install unsigned drivers.

C. In System properties, select the hardware tab. Click the driver signing button. Set the driver signing option to warn when you attempt to install unsigned drivers.

***D. In System properties, select the hardware tab. Click the driver signing button. Set the driver signing option to block when you attempt to install unsigned drivers.**

Explanation: In System properties, select the hardware tab. Click the driver signing button. Set the driver signing option to ignore, warn or block when you attempt to install unsigned drivers.

---

5. Which of the following situations with a NIC card could produce a bottleneck?

A. An unplugged NIC card

***B. A NIC card that is set for 10 Mbps when it should be set to 100 Mbps**

***C. An older network card that is installed on a new server**

D. A fiber channel NIC

Explanation: Lack of memory is a major cause of bottlenecks. An older network card that is installed on a new server may cause a bottleneck. A failing hard drive may cause a bottleneck. A program that monopolizes a particular resource can be a bottleneck. An older multispeed network card may be configured for 10 megabits per second (Mbps) when it should be set to 100 Mbps and this would produce a bottleneck.

6. How can you perform real time monitoring by using Task Manager?

***A. Press CTRL+ALT+DEL, and then click Task Manager.**

B. Press ALT+SHFT+ESC, and then click Task Manager.

C. Press CTRL+ALT+ESC, and then click Task Manager.

***D. On the Processes tab, click a column name to sort by that column. Click the column name a second time to reverse sort by that column. On the View menu, click Select Columns to add counters to the Processes tab.**

***E. Click the Applications tab to monitor running applications. Click the Processes tab to monitor the running processes.**

Explanation: To perform real time monitoring by using Task Manager, press CTRL+ALT+DEL, and then click Task Manager. Click the Applications tab to monitor running applications. Click the Processes tab to monitor the running processes. On the Processes tab, click a column name to sort by that column. Click the column name a second time to reverse sort by that column. On the View menu, click Select Columns to add counters to the Processes tab. Click the Performance tab to monitor CPU and memory usage. Click the Networking tab to monitor network traffic to this computer. Click the Users tab to monitor the names of users who are connected to the computer.

---

7. You need to install two expansion cards in your 2003 Server. One of the cards is a PCI plug-and-play compliant card and one is an ISA plug-and-play compliant card. What actions are necessary to configure these cards?

***A. With the PCI card, simply plug in the device.**

B. With the ISA card, simply plug in the device.

C. With the PCI card, you will have to manually configure the card.

***D. With the ISA card, turn off the computer to install the device, and then restart the computer to initialize the device.**

E. With the ISA card, you will have to manually configure the card.

Explanation: You can install some plug-and-play devices by simply plugging in the device. For other devices, such as plug-and-play Industry Standard Architecture (ISA) cards, you must turn off the computer to install the device, and then restart the computer to initialize the device. Most devices manufactured since 1995 are plug-and-play. plug-and-play support depends on both the hardware device and the device driver. If the device driver does not support plug-and-play, its devices behave as non-plug-and-play devices, regardless of any hardware plug-and-play support. Non-plug-and-play devices are not supported by products in the Windows Server 2003 family.

8. You want to create a RAID 5 volume from free space from Disk O, Disk 1 and Disk 2. Disk 0 has 30 percent of its drive space free and Disks 1 and 2 have the entire disk free. Disk 0 is a basic disk and Disks 1 and 2 are dynamic disks and all are formatted with NTFS. What steps do you need to take to create the RAID 5 volume?

***A. Convert Disk 0 to a dynamic disk**

B. Convert Disk 1 back to a basic disk

C. Create the RAID 5 volume using all basic disks

***D. Create the RAID 5 volume using all dynamic disks**

Explanation: To create a RAID 5 volume, convert Disk 0 to a dynamic disk so that all disks are dynamic. Then simply right-click the unallocated space and select "New Volume."

---

9. Under what circumstances would you need to update a driver in Windows Server 2003?

A. If you need to convert to NTFS.

B. If you need to convert to native mode.

***C. If a bad driver was installed.**

***D. If you have driver signing set to ignore driver updates.**

Explanation: You need to update a driver in Windows Server 2003 if you have driver signing set to ignore driver updates or if a bad driver was installed.

10. Which of the following should you use to check device drivers, to see if they are installed correctly?

***A. My Computer**

B. Event Monitor

C. Task Manager

D. Device Manager

E. Internet Options

Explanation: Use Device Manager to check device drivers, to see if they are installed correctly.

---

11. You have three SCSI drives. The first drive is a 80 GB drive with 10 GB free. The second drive is a 60 GB drive with 20 GB free. The third drive is a 50 GB drive with the entirety of the drive free. You want to build a RAID 5 array. How big will it be?

A. 10 GB

B. 40 GB

***C. 20 GB**

D. 80 GB

E. 60 GB

Explanation: With RAID 5, smallest free portion available determines the parity portion of the array (which in this case is 10 GB on the first disk). Since 10 GB is the biggest parity segment we can have, the other portions must be the same size. So, the RAID 5 array will use 30 GB (10 GB + 10 GB + 10 GB), but, you will only be able to use 20 GB of that.

12. When implementing redundancy in a Windows Server 2003, which methods will work?
A. Implementing disk spanning
***B. Implementing disk striping with parity (RAID 5)**
***C. Implementing disk mirroring (RAID 1)**
D. Implementing disk striping (RAID 0)

Explanation: Implementing disk mirroring (RAID 1) and disk striping with parity (RAID 5) addresses the need for redundancy and fault tolerance in a Windows Server 2003.

---

13. You store backup tapes both off-site and on-site. You are presently performing a normal backup every Monday at 5 p.m. and incremental backups every work night of the week at 5 p.m. Three drives in your RAID 5 array fail Wednesday at noon. What should you do to restore the RAID 5 array?
A. Using the on-site tapes, restore the RAID 5 array with the normal backup from Monday.
***B. Using the on-site tapes, restore the RAID 5 array with the normal backup from Monday and the incremental from Tuesday.**
C. Using the off-site tapes, restore the RAID 5 array with the normal backup from Monday and the incremental from Tuesday.
D. Using the off-site tapes, restore the RAID 5 array with the normal backup from Monday.

Explanation: You store backup tapes both off-site and on-site. You are presently performing a normal backup every Monday at 5 p.m. and incremental backups every work night of the week at 5 p.m. Three drives in your RAID 5 array fails Wednesday at noon. Using the on-site tapes, restore the RAID 5 array with the normal backup from Monday and the incremental from Tuesday.

14. Which of the following RAID configurations does not allow for a single disk to fail?

***A. RAID 0 (Disk Striping)**

B. RAID 1 (Disk Mirroring)

***C. Disk Spanning**

D. RAID 5 (Disk Striping with Parity)

Explanation: RAID 1 (Disk Mirroring) and RAID 5 (Disk Striping with Parity) allow for a single disk to fail. RAID 0 (Disk Striping) and Disk Spanning do not.

---

15. Which of the following is a volume that Windows Server 2003 does not support?

A. Spanned

B. RAID 5

***C. Half**

D. Mirrored

E. RAID 0

Explanation: Windows Server 2003 supports RAID 5, spanned, and mirrored volumes.

Managing Users, Computers, and Groups

The objective of this chapter is to provide the reader with an understanding of the following:

2.1 Manage user profiles

2.1.1 Local user profiles

2.1.2 Roaming user profiles

2.1.3 Mandatory user profiles

2.2 Create and manage computer accounts in an Active Directory environment

2.3 Create and manage groups

2.3.1 Identify and modify the scope of a group

2.3.2 Find domain groups in which a user is a member

2.3.3 Manage group membership

2.3.4 Create and modify groups by using the Active Directory Users and Computers Microsoft Management Console (MMC) snap-in

2.3.5 Create and modify groups by using automation

2.4 Create and manage user accounts

2.4.1 Create and modify user accounts by using the Active Directory Users and Computers MMC snap-in

2.4.2 Create and modify user accounts by using automation

2.4.3 Import user accounts

2.5 Troubleshoot computer accounts

2.5.1 Diagnose and resolve issues related to computer accounts by using the Active Directory Users and Computers MMC snap-in

2.5.2 Reset computer accounts

2.6 Troubleshoot user accounts

2.6.1 Diagnose and resolve account lockouts

2.6.2 Diagnose and resolve issues related to user account properties

2.7 Troubleshoot user authentication issues

Chapter 2: Users, Computers, and Groups

Introduction:

Managing Users, Computers and Groups in Windows Server 2003 can be performed by using built-in consoles and command line utilities. The following chapter will give you insight on how to manage these administrative tasks within your organization.

Getting Ready Questions

1. In Windows Server 2003, how can the location for user profile storage be accessed?
2. In a Server 2003 Active Directory environment, do legacy operating systems (such as Windows 95 or Windows 98) now have computer accounts?
3. What does the acronym AGGUDLP stand for?
4. What is the difference between disabling and resetting an account?
5. What is considered a minimum password length for a strong password implementation?

Getting Ready Answers

1. In Server 2003, the location for user profiles storage can now be accessed by right-clicking on My Computer and choosing the Advanced option then User Profiles from the System Properties box.
2. Computer accounts are still not assigned to older legacy operating systems such as Windows 95 or Windows 98 machines in a Server 2003 domain. These operating systems still operate as participants in, rather than members of, the domain.
3. The acronym AGGUDLP stands for:
    - ***A***ccounts are members of
    - ***G***lobal groups, which in native mode can be members of other
    - ***G***lobal groups, which in native mode can be members of
    - ***U***niversal groups, which are in turn members of
    - ***D***omain ***L***ocal groups, which are the group scope that is granted resource access
    - ***P***ermissions.
4. Disabling an account renders it unusable. Resetting the account causes it to synchronize to bring it up-to-date.
5. A minimum length of seven characters is considered for password strength. It is also a good idea to have the passwords meet strong password requirements.

2.1 Manage user profiles

Microsoft Windows Server 2003 uses user profiles to allow Network Administrators the ability to create and maintain user desktop settings. User profiles are used to automatically desktop settings for a user logging into a client machine. A good example of this feature's use would be if more than one user uses the same computer at various times of the day, such as morning and afternoon shifts. This will allow the two users to have their own customized desktop settings, such as shortcuts, mail settings, video resolution etc. This feature can also be used to create mandatory user profiles. Mandatory user profiles are used to allow clients the ability to change desktop settings while they are using the computer but once the user has logged off of the system the changes which were made to the desktop are lost. Microsoft Windows Server 2003 has added additional functionality for improved use of user profiles. Some of these improved features are:

- The location for user profiles storage can now be accessed by right-clicking on My Computer and choosing the **Advanced** option then **User Profiles** from the **System Properties** box.
- Additional Group Policy functionality.
- From the Group Policy Microsoft Management Console MMC you can now access User Profile policies.
- Prevent users who have roaming profiles configured from obtaining their roaming profile on a specific computer. This means that the profile loaded on that specific computer would be local only.
- Allow the Domain Administrators to obtain full control over the profile directory that belongs to a user. In Windows 2000 the Administrator had no file access right as a default.

The section below covers the differences between the Local User, Roaming User, Mandatory User and Temporary user profiles used in Windows Server 2003.

2.1.1 Local user profiles

Local user profiles are profiles that are created the first time a user logs onto a computer. These profiles are not roaming profiles, which are stored on a server and are accessed by a user, no matter what machine is logged onto; rather they are stored locally on the computer hard drive. Changes made to this profile while a user is logged onto a machine are specific to that computer and will not "roam" with the client.

2.1.2 Roaming user profiles

Roaming user profiles are created by a domain administrator and stored server-side. Any changes in shortcuts, mail settings, display settings, etc. would be updated to the profile located on the server. From any machine on the domain that a client logs onto, this profile will be available for their use. Roaming Profiles cannot support encrypted files.

Creating a Roaming user profile

Creating a roaming user profile is accomplished by following two steps—create a test profile and then copy the test profile to the network server. Use the steps below to create a test profile.

1. Before you begin, make certain you are logged onto the machine as an Administrator.
2. Click on **Start,** choose **Administrative Tools** and select **Computer Management**.
3. Click on **Local Users and Groups,** then select **Users**.
4. Right-click on **Users,** then choose **New User**. Enter a name and password for the user.
5. Use the mouse to clear the **User must change password at next logon** box.
6. Select the **Create** option and then choose **close**.
7. **Log off** of the computer and then log back on as the user name that was previously created in this step. A local user profile has now been created and the next steps are to configure the environment (desktop settings, shortcuts, appearance) and then copy to the network server.
8. From the server that will store the network profiles, create a folder such as the following: \\network_server\profiles\username.
9. Click on **Start** choose **Control Panel** and select **System**.
10. Choose the **Advanced** tab and select **Settings** (located in **System Properties** under **User Profiles**).
11. Choose the **Profile** under the **Profiles Stored on this computer** option and select the **Copy To** option.
12. Enter the **Path** to the profile, which was created in Step 8.
13. Select the **Change** under the **Permitted to Use** option.
14. Enter the **Name** of the user account created in step 4, then select **OK**.
15. Click **OK**, then **OK**, then **OK** again.
16. Open the **Computer Management** console by clicking on **Start** then choosing **Administrative Tools**.
17. Open the **Local Users and Groups** console and double-click on the **Users** button.
18. Find the **user account** that was created in Step 4 and select the **Profile** option.
19. Enter the **Network Profile Path** in the profile path box.
20. Click **OK**.
21. Close the Computer Management console.

2.1.3 Mandatory user profiles

This is a roaming profile (stored server side) that will only allow the Administrator the ability to make changes. If a user makes changes to this profile, they will be lost once the computer has been rebooted. This profile can be applied to entire groups of users or individually. Use the steps below to create a mandatory profile.

1. Before you begin, make certain you are logged onto the machine as an Administrator.
2. Click on **Start,** choose **Administrative Tools** and select **Computer Management**.
3. Click on **Local Users and Groups** then select **Users**.
4. Right-click on **Users** then choose **New User.** Enter a name and password for the user.
5. Use the mouse to clear the **User must change password at next logon** box.
6. Select the **Create** option and then choose **Close.**
7. **Log off** of the Computer and then log back on as the user name that was previously created in this step. A local user profile has now been created and the next steps are to configure the environment (desktop settings, shortcuts, appearance) and then copy to the network server.
8. From the server that will store the network profiles, create a folder such as the following: \\network_server\profiles\username.
9. Click on **Start,** choose **Control Panel** and select **System**.
10. Choose the **Advanced** tab and select **Settings** (located in **System Properties** under **User Profiles**).
11. Choose the **Profile** under the **Profiles Stored on this computer** option and select the **Copy To** option.
12. Enter the **Path** to the profile, which was created in Step 8.
13. Select the **Change** under the **Permitted to Use** option.
14. Enter the **Name** of the user account created in step 4, then select **OK**.
15. Click **OK**, **OK**, **OK**.
16. Open the **Computer Management** console by clicking on **Start** then choosing **Administrative Tools**.
17. Open the **Local Users and Groups** console and double-click on the **Users** button.
18. Find the **user account** that was created in Step 4 and select the **Profile** option.
19. Enter the **Network Profile Path** in the profile path box.
20. Click **OK**.
21. Close the Computer Management console.
22. Open the user profile folder and find the **Ntuser.dat** file.
23. To make this a mandatory profile, simply rename the **Ntuser.dat** file to **Ntuser.man**.

Temporary user profiles

The Temporary User Profile is only used in the event that the local user profile or server-side profile cannot be loaded on the client machine. This profile behaves much like the mandatory user profile in that all changes that are made to a machine are lost after the client has logged off. The temporary profile is also deleted once the client has logged off of the machine.

Troubleshooting Damaged Profiles

There are times when you would need to troubleshoot a user profile for problems to see if the profile has been damaged use the following steps:

1. **Create** a new **User account** and give it the exact same rights as the profile you are troubleshooting.
2. You now need to **copy** the user settings from the "damaged" profile to the profile of the new user account you created in step 1.
3. Open the **Control Panel** and choose the **System** option. Select the **Advanced** option and then choose **Settings** from **User Profiles**.
4. Select the "damaged" user profile from the **Profiles Stored on this computer** and choose the **copy to** option.
5. Choose **Browse and** locate the newly created user profile, then click on **OK**.
6. Click **OK** again and select **Yes** to overwrite the contents of the folder.
7. Click **OK** again and then once more.
8. Login using the newly created user account. If the same error occurs that was occurring before you made these changes then the user profile is damaged. If the problems disappear then the user account is damaged.

Deleting and Recreating a User Profile that has been damaged

In the above scenario, if the user profile has been damaged, you will need to delete the damaged profile and then create a new one.

1. Login to the computer that contains the damaged user profile.
2. Do a search for the folder that contains the name of the damaged user profile.
3. Once the folder has been found press the **Delete** key.
4. Choose **Yes** to confirm then logoff the computer.
5. Logon to the machine with the user account that the damaged profile belonged.
6. A new profile will be automatically created for the user.

Creating a Custom Default User Profile

To create a Custom Default user profile use the following steps:

1. Make certain you are logged onto the computer as an **Administrator**.
2. Create a **new** local user account.
3. Log off as **Administrator** and then log back on as the **local user account** you just created.
4. Configure the **desktop settings** you wish to use as a default (display, mapped drives, etc.).
5. Log off as the **local user** and log back on as the **Administrator**.
6. Open **Windows Explorer**.
7. From the **Tools** menu select the **Folder Options** menu item.
8. Select the **View** tab.
9. Choose the **Show hidden files and folders** option and click **OK**. This step will unhide the default user profile so it can be replaced.
10. To replace the default user profile with the newly customized profile click on **Start** choose **Control Panel** and select **System**.
11. Choose the **Advanced** tab and select **Settings** under the **User Profiles** option.
12. Choose the newly created **user profile** and click **Copy to** from the **Profiles stored on this computer**.
13. Select **Browse** from the **Copy Profile to** item and find the **Default User** folder under the **Windows directory** and **Documents and Settings** folder and click **OK**.
14. Under the **Permitted to use** option select **Change**.
15. Type **Everyone** in the **Select user or Group** option then click **OK**, then **OK** again.
16. Click on the **Yes** button to continue with the procedure.

Windows will now replace the default local user profile with the newly created user profile. You could also run into issues when dealing with user profiles, such as the time it can take for a profile to load. Try not to copy large folders such as **My Documents** in the profile especially when using Roaming Profiles. Consider using Folder Redirection via Group Policy to keep large folders on a network share, instead of locally on the client machine.

2.2 Create/Manage Computer Accounts in Active Directory Environments

Computer accounts are unique in the Windows Server 2003 domain and are used by Windows Server 2003 to allow users to login to the domain and authenticate as well as auditing the use of network resources and devices. Computer accounts are not assigned to older legacy operating systems such as Windows 95 or Windows 98 machines. Administrators can add, delete, reset or disable computer accounts by using the Active Directory Users and Computers console. The Active Directory Users and Computers console can be accessed on a Windows Server 2003 machine running Active Directory by using the following steps:

1. Click on **Start**.
2. Click on **Administrative Tools**.
3. Select **Active Directory Users and Computers**.
4. Open the Organizational unit or domain you wish to manage.
5. To create a new computer account just right-click in the OU or Domain and select the **New**.

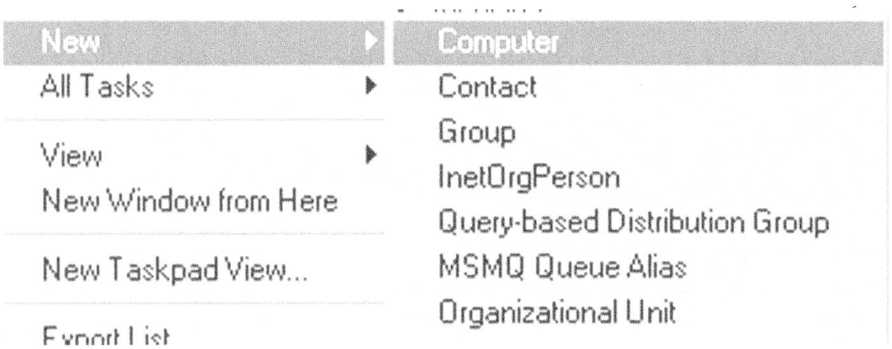

Figure 2-1: Creating a new computer account using the Active Directory Users and Computers console.

After this you will have the option to enter a computer name for the new computer shown in Figure 2.2.

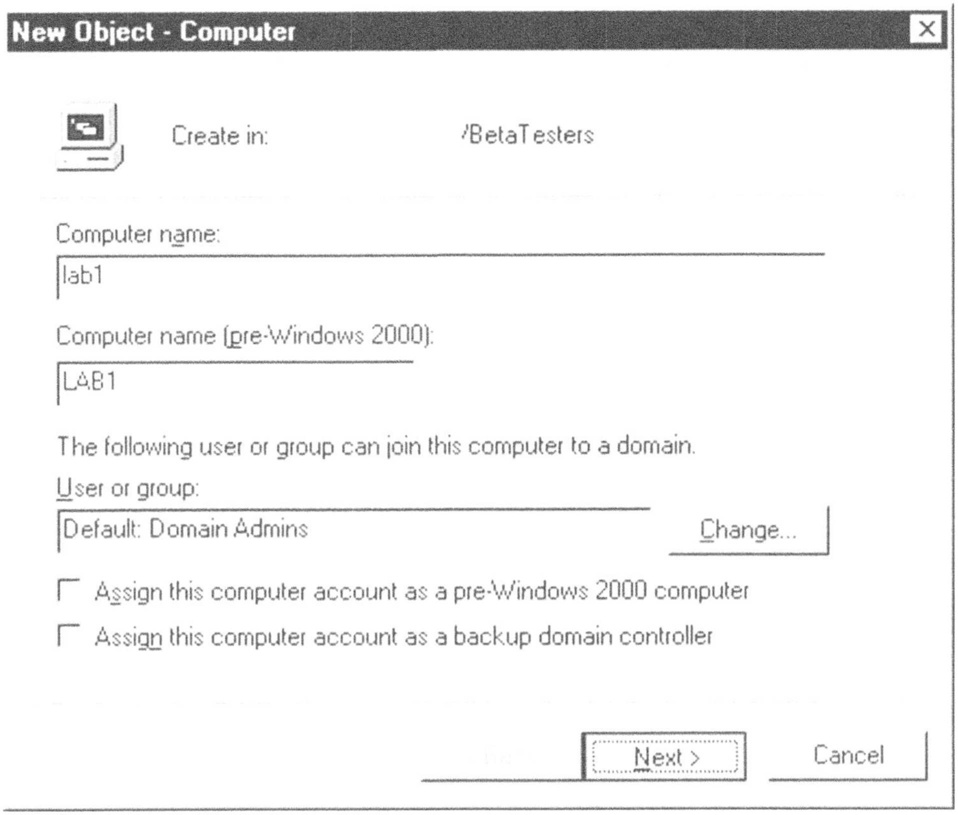

Figure 2-2: Give the Computer a name.

Enter a name for the computer and, if needed, change the default user or group that is required to add the computer to the domain by selecting the **Change** option. Select the **Next** option and a screen like the one shown in Figure 2.3 is shown. It gives you the option of entering managed information, if the computer is a managed computer.

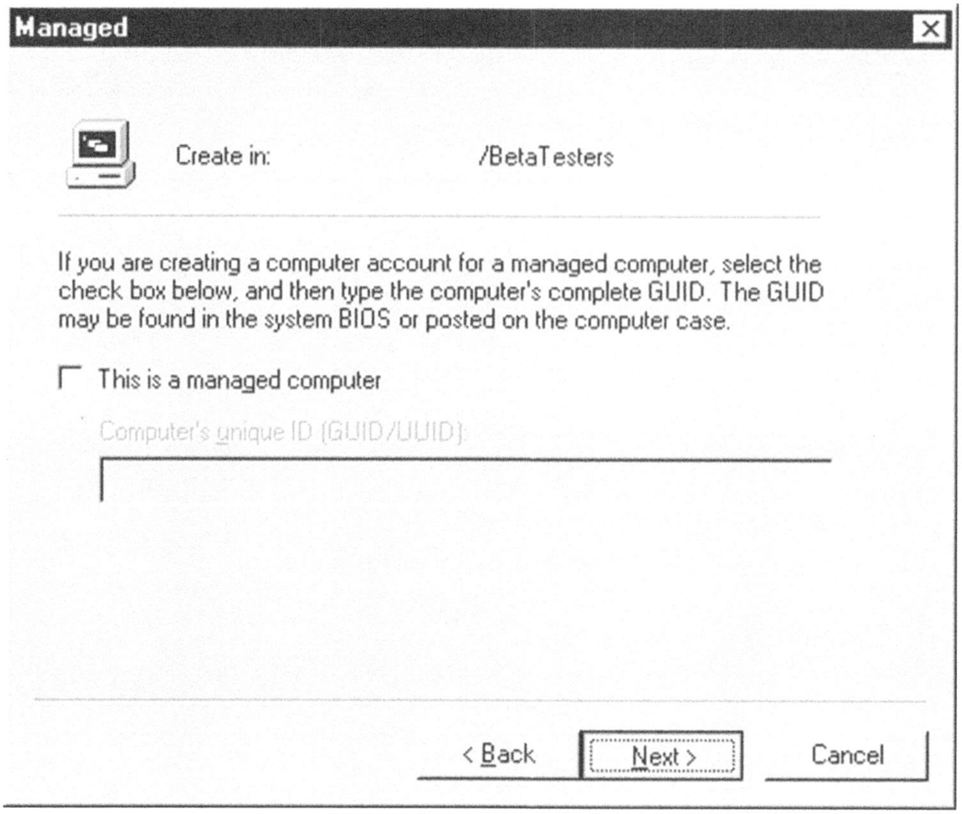

Figure 2-3: Entering information for Managed Computers.

Select **Next** and the computer will be added to the OU or domain you selected in Step 1.

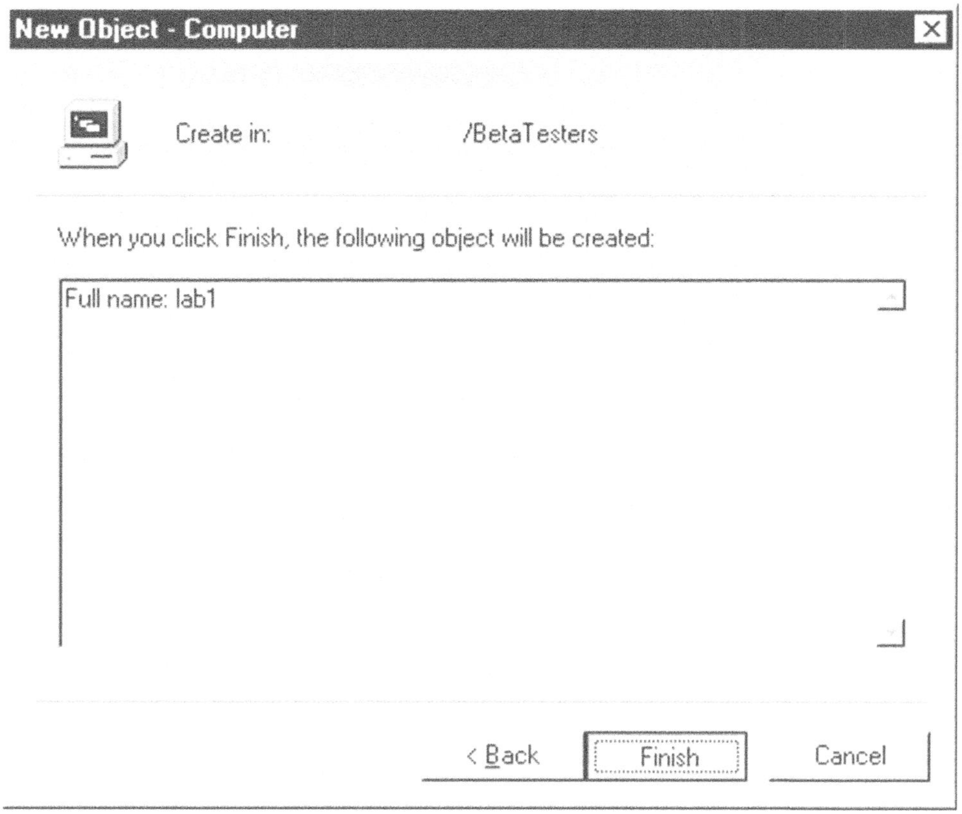

Figure 2-4: Finishing adding a new Computer using the Active Directory Users and Groups console.

Pop Quiz 2.1

Pop Quiz 2.1 *Questions*

1. How do you change a profile from normal to mandatory?
2. What is the difference between a local profile and a roaming profile?
3. What is a temporary profile and when is it used?
4. You are running a Windows 98 machine on a Server 2003 network. Does it have a computer account?
5. What tool does an Administrator use to add or disable computer accounts?

Pop Quiz 2.1 *Answers*

1. To change a profile from normal to mandatory, simply rename the Ntuser.dat to Ntuser.man.
2. A local profile is stored locally on the machine, and is applied only when the user logs onto that machine. A roaming profile is stored on a server and "follows" the user; no matter what machine the user logs onto, the profile is applied.
3. A Temporary User Profile is only used in the event that the local user profile or server-side profile cannot be loaded on the client machine. This profile behaves much like the mandatory user profile in that all changes that are made to a machine are lost after the client has logged off. The temporary profile is also deleted once the client has logged off of the machine.
4. No. Computer accounts are not assigned to older legacy operating systems such as Windows 95 or Windows 98 machines.
5. Administrators can add, delete, reset or disable computer accounts by using the Active Directory Users and Computers console.

2.3 Create and manage groups

Creating and managing groups in Group Scopes in Windows Server 2003 and Active Directory

- Active Directory group types
- Active Directory group scopes
- How to modify the scope of a group.

In the old days of NT4 domain administration, there were two group scopes that could be created in User Manager for Domains. You could either make a global group or a local group, and that local group was essentially a shared local group—it could be used on any domain controller, but only on a domain controller.

2.3.1 Identify and modify the scope of a group

With Active Directory, we now have two types of groups and three different scopes of groups, each with their own advantages and limitations. Figure 2.5 shows the New Object dialog box.

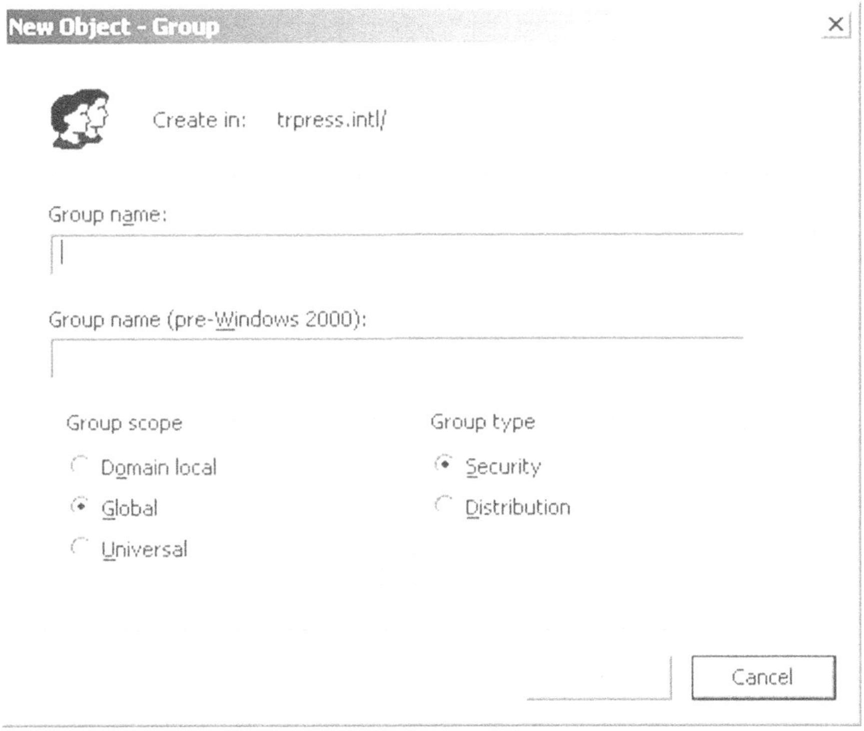

Figure 2-5: Creating a User Group using the Active Directory console.

There are three scopes of groups. Each scope has its advantages, as well as having limitations. Again, for the purpose of this article, we will only be discussing group scopes in Active Directory, rather than also discussing the groups that can be created on any non-domain controller.

The three group scopes in Active Directory are:

- Universal
- Global
- Domain.

The scopes apply to both security and distribution type groups.

The two types of group are security and distribution. Distribution groups are used in the same way distribution lists are, while security groups are what we use for managing resource access and other security related functions. This article will focus on security groups, as distribution groups are more appropriately covered in an article on Exchange Server 2000.

There are two ways of identifying the scope of a group in Active Directory Users and Computers. One is to find the group in its container, where you will see the following detail as illustrated in Figure 2.6:

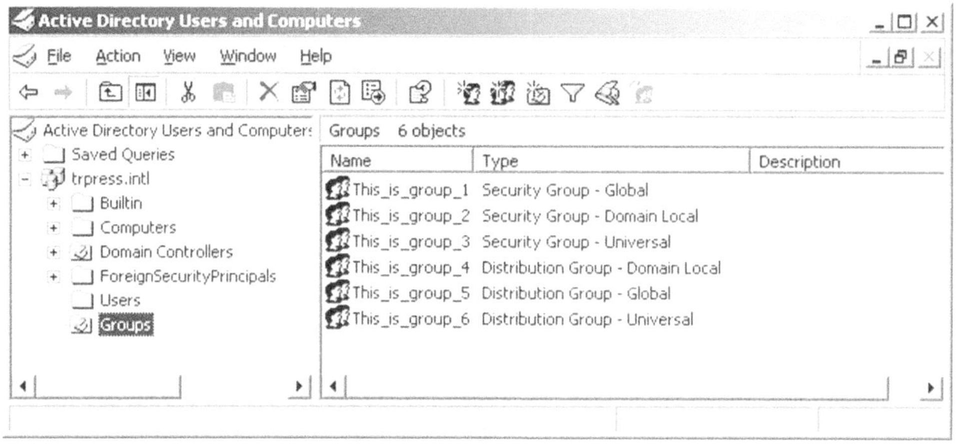

Figure 2-6: Identifying image scopes using the Active Directory User and Computers console.

Note that the *type* column lists both the type and scope for the group. You can also open the properties for the group. Using this method you can also perform various management tasks. Figure 2.7 shows the general tab of the properties.

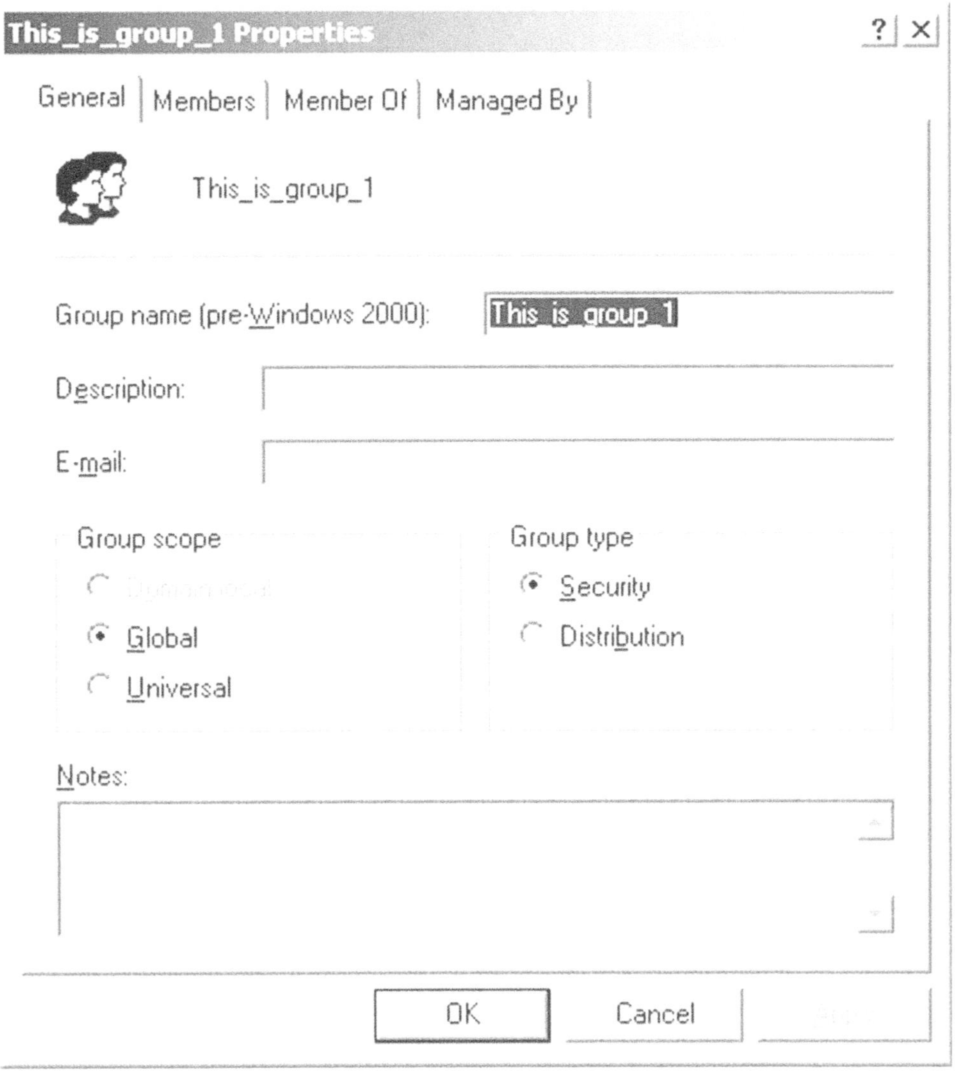

Figure 2-7: Entering the Group Properties.

Note that the radio buttons are on the scope and type for the group, but that you can change both scope and type. If the scope of the group is Universal, then you will be able to immediately change to any of the three scopes. But, if the scope you wish to change is either Domain Local or Global, then you will at first only be able to change to Universal.

In addition to changing the scope, you can also change the type. If you change from Security to Distribution, however, you will see the dialog box shown in Figure 2.8.

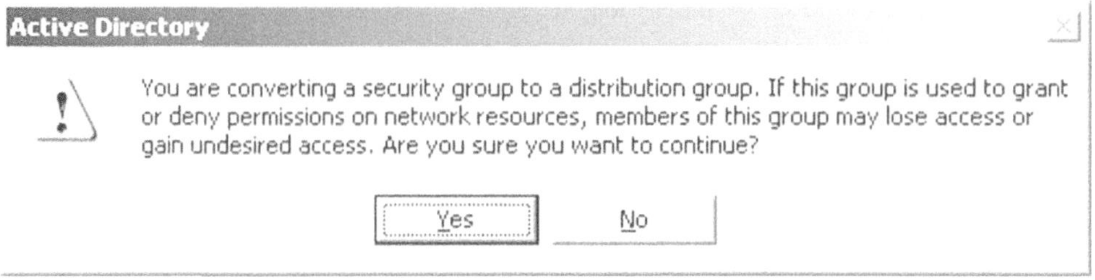

Figure 2-8: Setting the Description Property for the new group.

Now that we have looked at the scopes in Active Directory Users and Computers, let's take a look at how they can be used, and how it is recommended that they be used.

Let's start by looking at the Universal group scope, in terms of when and how it can be used. To do this, however, you need to remember that an Active Directory domain can be in one of three *functional modes*; mixed, Windows 2000 Native or Windows Server 2003 Native. It is important to remember, as well, that the only difference between the modes is whether there are legacy domain controllers—the operating system running on computers in a domain that are not domain controllers is of no importance in determining whether a domain can operate in native mode.

Universal scope security type groups are only available when an Active Directory domain is in native mode, though Universal scope *distribution* groups are available in either mode. Universal groups are very flexible, because a universal group can contain members from any domain in the forest, and can be used in any domain in the forest. There is an important thing to remember about universal groups, however—information on the membership of a Universal group is stored on every domain controller in the forest, and any change to the **direct** membership of a Universal group will be replicated to every domain controller in the forest. I emphasize direct, because one recommended practice with regard to Universal groups is that their membership is only global groups, and not individual user accounts. So, while a user or computer account can be a member of a Universal group, it should not be a direct member. Universal groups are most useful in a multi-domain forest, because it is there that you will most likely have business units in each domain that need common access to enterprise resources. In a single domain model, it is less likely that the need for Universal scope security groups will present itself—though distribution groups are another matter entirely.

2.3.2 Find domain groups in which a user is a member

You can use the Properties tab to find which group a user is a member of by using the following instructions.

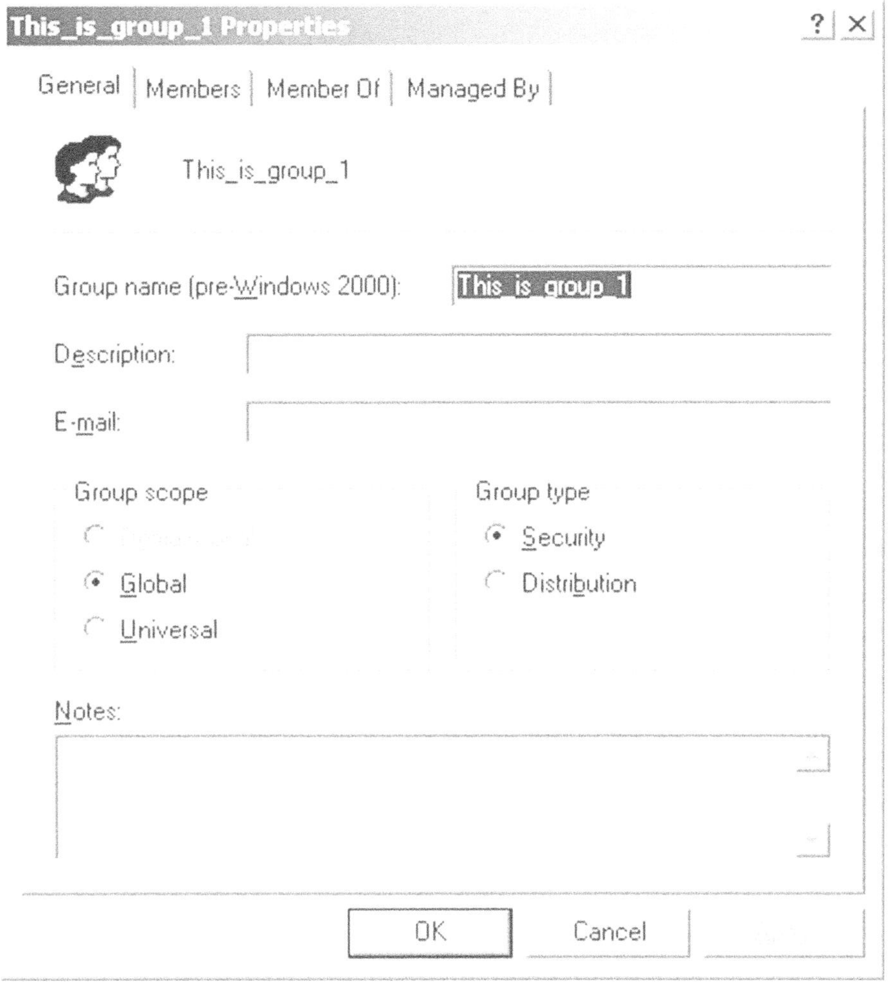

Figure 2-9: Setting the Description Property for the new group.

As you can see in Figure 2.9, there are four tabs that you can access in the properties for a group. You can find the direct members of a group on the *Members* tab, and you can find the groups that a group or account is a direct member of on the *Member of* tab. Note that these are strictly the direct membership, however. If a user is a member of a global group that is a member of a domain local group, the *Members* and *Member of* tabs still only show the direct membership.

2.3.3 Manage group membership

Before we dig into Global and Domain Local groups, let's review the recommended practice for granting resource access permissions. There are many ways to express the acronym we use (yeah, another one of those acronyms!) to remember what goes where. Since this article is discussing Universal groups, I will use the longest of the bunch, AGGUDLP. This acronym stands for:

- ***A***ccounts are members of
- ***G***lobal groups, which in native mode can be members of other
- ***G***lobal groups, which in native mode can be members of
- ***U***niversal groups, which are in turn members of
- ***D***omain ***L***ocal groups, which are the group scope that is granted resource access
- ***P***ermissions.

Now, if you don't have nested Global groups or use Universal groups, you can trim out some of those letters—but only the second G and the U!

The workhorse of Active Directory groups is the Global group. Global groups are limited in that they can only contain members from the domain where they were created, but they can be used in any trusting domain—whether in the forest or not. If the domain is in native mode, global groups can be a member of other global groups (but still in the domain!). User and computer accounts should only be direct members of global groups. All of the direct and indirect members of a group inherit permissions granted to a group. When naming global groups, as with any group, you want to use a name that will make sense 6 months or 3 years from now. Note, too, that while resource access permissions should only be granted to Domain Local groups, you can use Global groups for other purposes such as delegation of authority and GPO filtering.

Now we come to the Domain Local group, which I like to call the Permission group—since it is the group that we use for granting resource access permissions. Domain Local groups have essentially the opposite restriction of Global groups. They can have members from any trusted domain, but can only be used in the domain where they were created. When naming Domain Local groups, I recommend that you use a combination of the resource that the Domain Local group will be used for, and the permission being granted. One significant advantage to using Domain Local groups over local groups that only exist on a non-domain controller is that you use the same interface—Active Directory Users and Computers—to manage them as you use for Global and Universal groups.

2.3.4 Modify groups by using the Active Directory Users and Computers Microsoft Management Console (MMC) snap-in

Modifying a Group using the Active Directory Users and Computer console is a simple task and can be done by click on **Start** click **Administrative Tools** select **Active Directory Users and Computers** choose the Domain or OU which contains the Group you wish to modify and right-click the **Group** shown in Figure 2.10

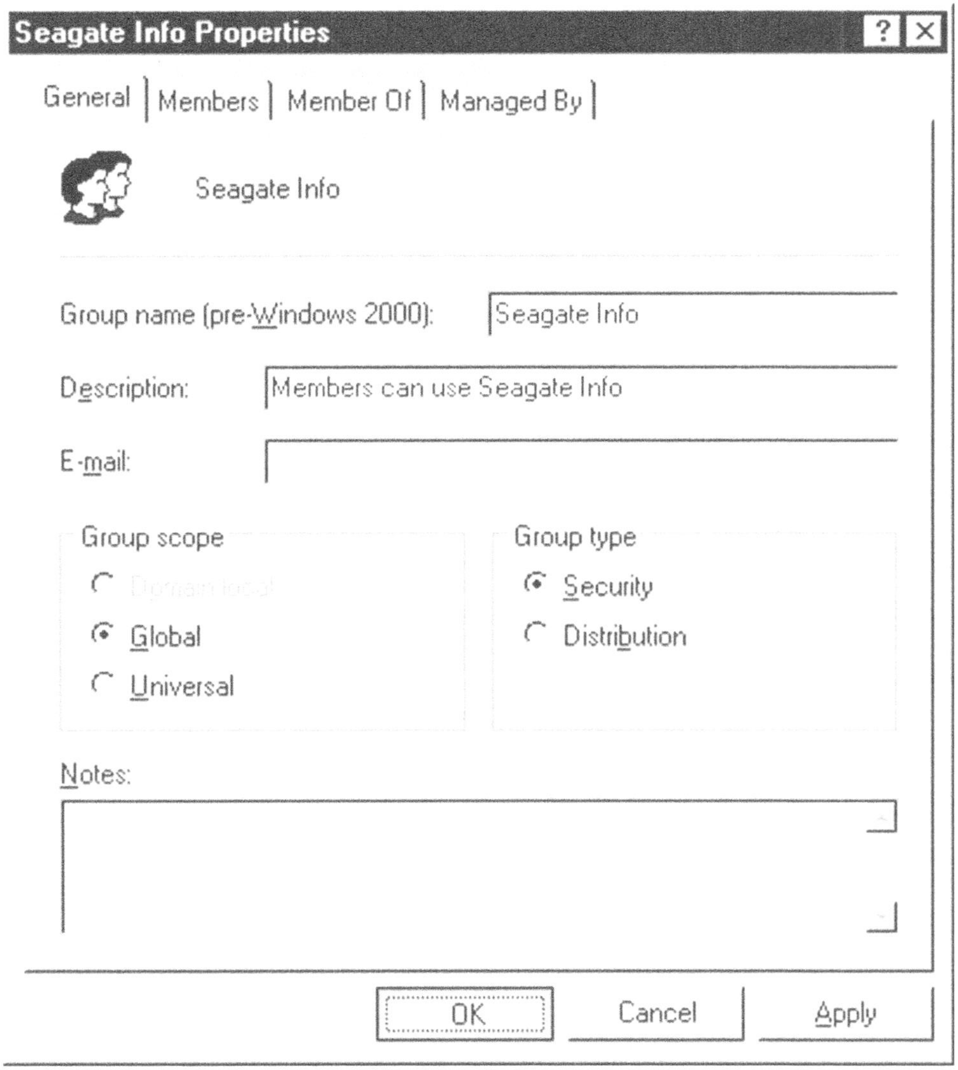

Figure 2-10: Entering General information for Group settings.

This tab allows you to enter and select information for Groups such as Group Name, Description and E-mail information. It also will allow you to enter the Group Scope and Type and Notes pertaining to the group. Figure 2.11 shows the member information for the group.

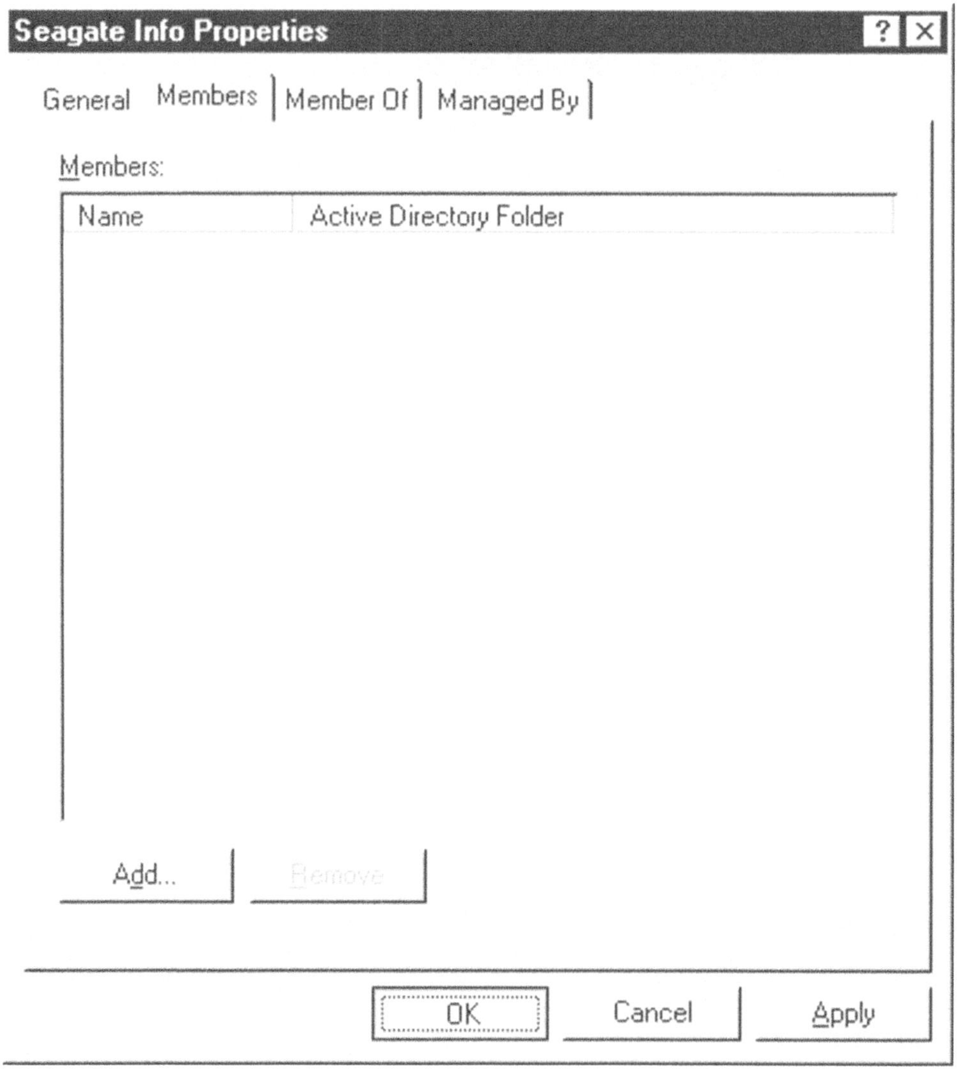

Figure 2-11: Member information for the Group.

Click the **Add** button to add additional members to this group then select **Apply.** Figure 2.12 shows the **Member of** which shows which users or computers belong to this group.

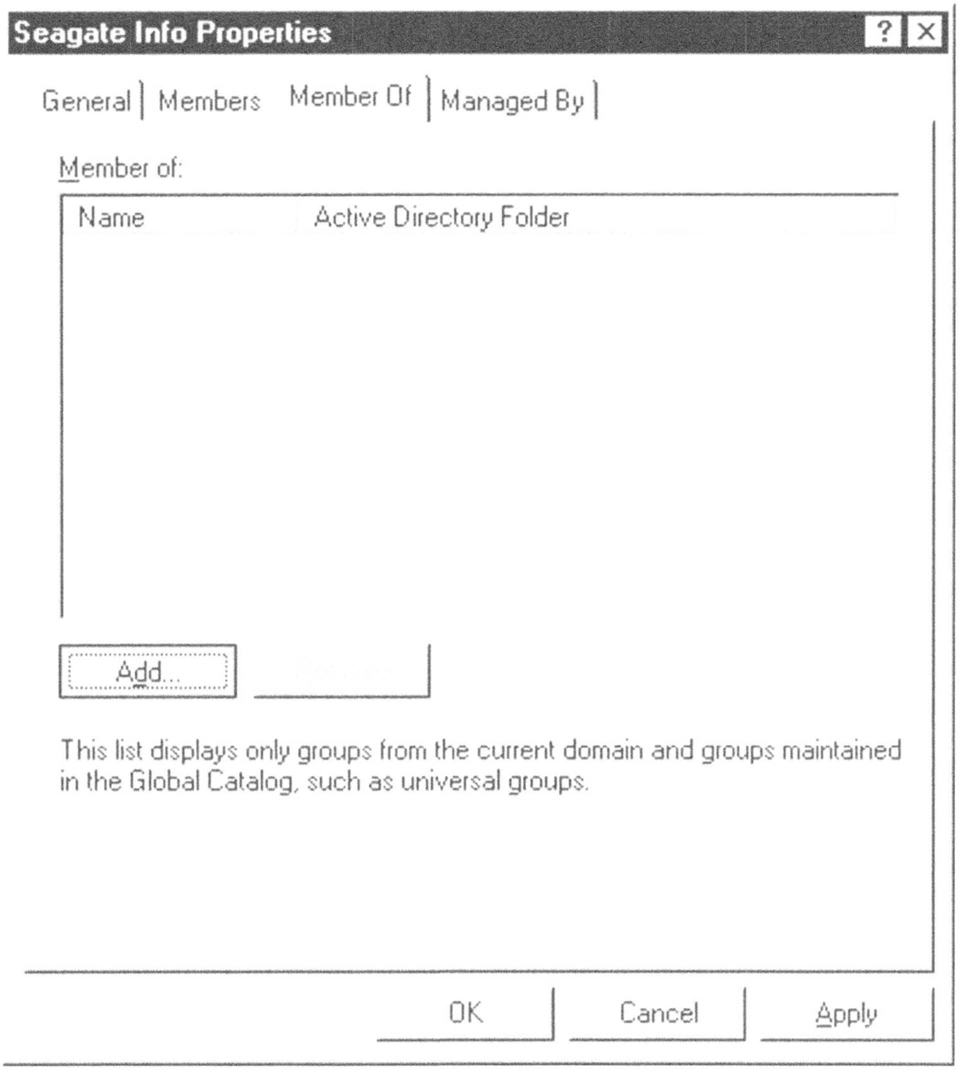

Figure 2-12: The Member of tab for Group settings.

The last tab is the **Managed by** tab shown in Figure 2.13.

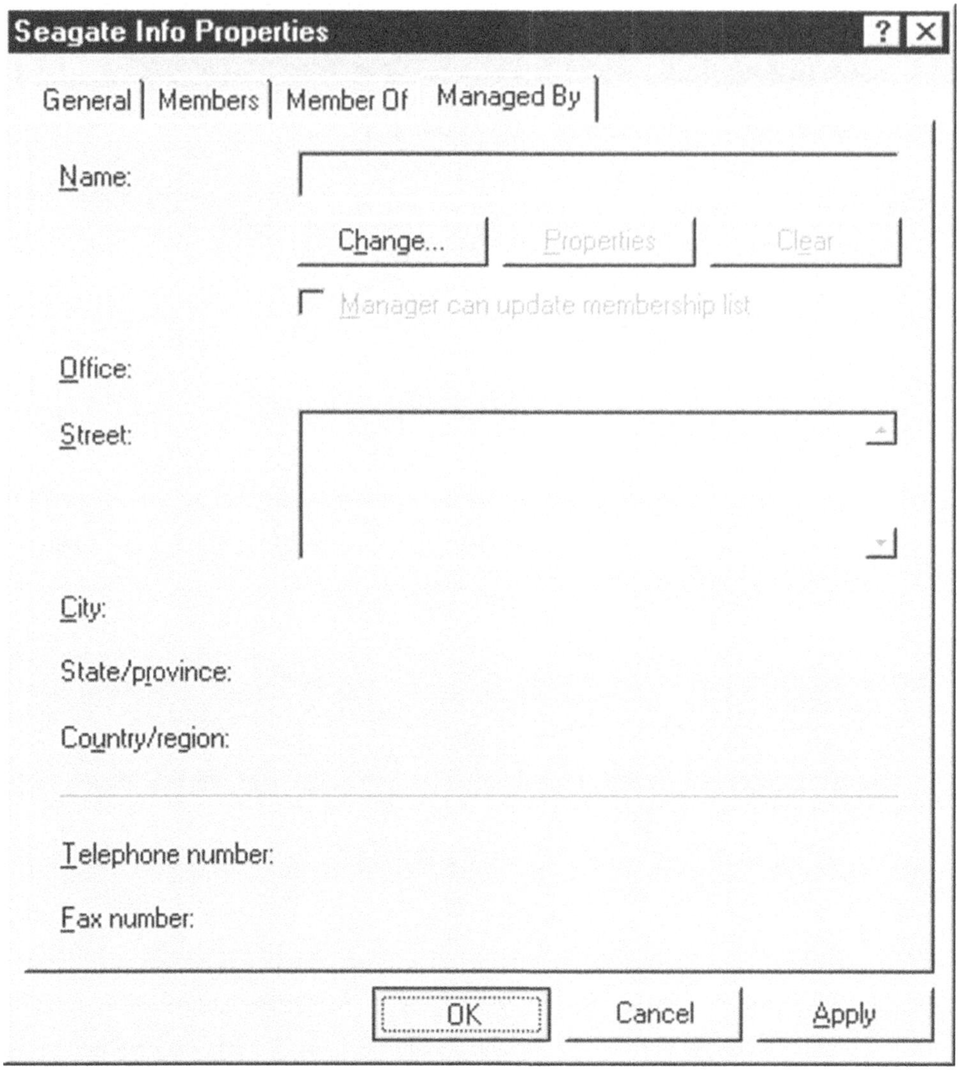

Figure 2-13: Managed By tab for Groups.

This screen allows you to enter the name of the manager for this group, office information and can also allow you to enable the manager of the group to have the ability to update the membership list of the group.

2.3.5 Create and modify groups by using automation

If you have a very large network to control with numerous domain controllers, computers, users, etc., you will be interested to know that you can use a method other than the Active Directory Users and Computers console to control these large environments. With the advent of Windows 2000, a new method became available for network administrators—scripting using Active Directory Service Interface (ADSI). ADSI is a set of COM interfaces that confronts the challenges in a distributed computing environment. ADSI can be used to access directory services' features and present a single set of directory service interfaces to the administrator for the management of resources on the network. Network Administrators can now use ADSI to automate many of the more common tasks, such as adding and removing both users and groups, setting permissions, and even managing printers across a distributed network.

While using the GUI interface remains an available option, being able to develop automated solutions for time consuming and repetitive tasks such as adding users to a new group has given the network administrator the ability to use their time in a cost-efficient fashion.

Active Directory was introduced with Windows 2000, and runs on Windows 2000 and Windows Server 2003 domain controllers. It is important to note that ADSI client applications can run not only on Windows 2000 and Windows XP clients, but also on Windows 95, Windows 98 and Windows NT4.0 (SP6a), if you have the Active Directory Client Extensions installed.

This section will examine the ways that you can automate some of the group management tasks faced by network administrators. Before you begin to work with ADSI there are a few basic concepts you should learn such as: Binding, Containers and Children, Getting and Setting Properties.

Binding

Objects must be bound to a computer, domain controller, printer, user or any other object in the directory structure in order to use ADSI properties and methods. After these objects have been bound object properties can be read or changed, and methods can be called that are applicable to the object type.

An ADSI ADsPath (or binding string) consists of a provider and a path. The provider is the part of the string that specifies what type of namespace is being bound to. With ADSI, there are four different types of providers:

- WinNT – Windows NT 4.0 PDCs and BDCs, Windows XP and Windows 2000/2003 not running Active Directory
- LDAP – LDAP servers, including Exchange 5.x, Windows 2000/2003 Active Directory
- NDS – Novell Directory Services servers
- NWCOMPAT – Novell Netware servers.

These provider names are case sensitive, and should be written exactly as noted above.

The path is exactly that—the path to a computer, object or user.

Look at the following example of a binding string:

```
Set objTarget =
GetObject("WinNT://TotalRecall/TRPublicComputer/Deborah,use
r")
```

Script 2–1: The Set objTarget script.

Notice that "WinNT:" is the provider; "//TotalRecall" is the domain; "/TRPublicComputer" is the computer; "/Deborah" is the object; and ", user" is the class identifier.

While the provider is mandatory, one can list all, some or none of the path. If no path is provided, ADSI will bind to the root of the namespace, and access will be allowed to all objects in the enterprise. Listing only the domain will bind to the root of the specified domain. Listing just the computer, or computer and class identifier, will bind to the local computer accounts.

Containers and Children

A container is an object that holds a collection of similar objects. For example, a domain is a container because it holds computers as members. A group is a container that holds users as members. All objects in a container have the same Class attribute, although they may not have associated ADsPath attributes.

A child of an object is an item one level below that object in the directory structure. A child is, in a sense, the flipside to a member. While an object's member must have the same class, but not necessarily a related ADsPath, an object's child does not need to have the same Class attribute as another child of the same object. It does, however, have a directly related ADsPath attribute. A domain's children are objects directly beneath the domain, such as users, global groups or computers.

These two relationships—container and member, object and child—define the two basic ways objects relate to each other in ADSI.

Two common administrative tasks are creating and deleting groups. It is through the IADs Container interface, used by all ADSI container objects, that we will accomplish the automation of these tasks. The properties of the IADs Container interface that are supported are:

- Filter – When enumerating a container's contents, the filter restricts the return to objects who's Class matches the classes listed in the property of the filter.
- Count – the number of objects in the container, or if a filter has been specified, the number of the objects of classes listed in the filter.

There are some methods that we will be using when working with groups that are specifically tied to the IADs Container interface:

- GetObject – Binds the directory item with the specified ADsPath to a named variable.
- Create – Creates a new object in the current container. The class must be specified.
- Delete – Removes an object from the current container. Again, the class must be specified.
- Movehere – Moves the object from its original location to the current container. The object MUST be in the same directory namespace; for example, you cannot move an object from a WinNT: namespace to a LDAP: namespace.
- Copyhere – Creates a copy of the object in the current container. The same namespace restrictions apply.

Getting and Setting Attributes

When looking at the ability to automate common network tasks, aside from creation and deletion, the most common use for any ADSI object is to be able to read data from it or modify the data contained in it. The data is contained in the object properties. Any ADSI object (except for the Namespaces object) employs the six properties of the IADs interface. These properties are:

- Name – the name of the object
- Class – the schema class name of the object
- GUID – the GUID (Globally Unique Identifier) that gives the object a unique identity
- ADsPath – a case-sensitive string used to uniquely identify the object's path in directory services
- Parent – the ADsPath name of the object's parent container
- Schema – the ADsPath of the object's schema class object.

Some of the methods we will be using on these properties are:

- Get – Retrieves the value of the property
- Put – Sets the value of the property
- GetInfo – Retrieves the values of the object's properties from directory services and places them in the local property cache
- SetInfo – Saves the changes made to the object's properties to directory services.

With that information, let's look at some ways to automate group tasks.

Creating a Local Group

To create a local group, we are going to use two IADs methods: "Create" and "SetInfo."

When we call the Create method, it is actually the method of the group parent object—in this case, the object representing the computer. The syntax is shown in the following example:

```
Set objGroup = objComputer.Create("group", "GroupName")
```

Script 2–2: The Create GroupName script.

As you can see, the Create method takes two arguments: the type of object to create ("group"), and the name for the new object ("GroupName").

The SetInfo method, on the other hand, is the method of the newly created group. It must be called to commit the change.

```
objGroup.SetInfo
```

Script 2–3 The script used to SetInfo.

We are going to take a working piece of code—a Windows Script command line utility—to illustrate how a local group can be created on a machine named "TRPublicComputer". This code requires two arguments at runtime: the name of the group to create, and the new group description. The presumption is made in this sample that TRPublicComputer is the only computer on which local groups are being created. With a little modification, a third argument could be passed using the declared variable strADspath, a binding string (such as WinNT://computername) of the object to which you want to add the group.

We will call the script "CreateLocalGroup.vbs". In this case, we are going to create a group called "Visitors" with a description of "Area 51." To call the script, at the command line, the following syntax would be used:

```
wscript CreateLocalGroup.vbs “Visitors” “Area 51”
```

Script 2–4: Creating a local group called Visitors with a description of Area 51.

Note that while quotes are not necessary for the first parameter, Visitors, they are for the second parameter, Area 51, because of the space. It is always good practice to use quotation marks, even when not necessary.

Prior to running the script, the Groups on the machine appeared as in the following illustration:

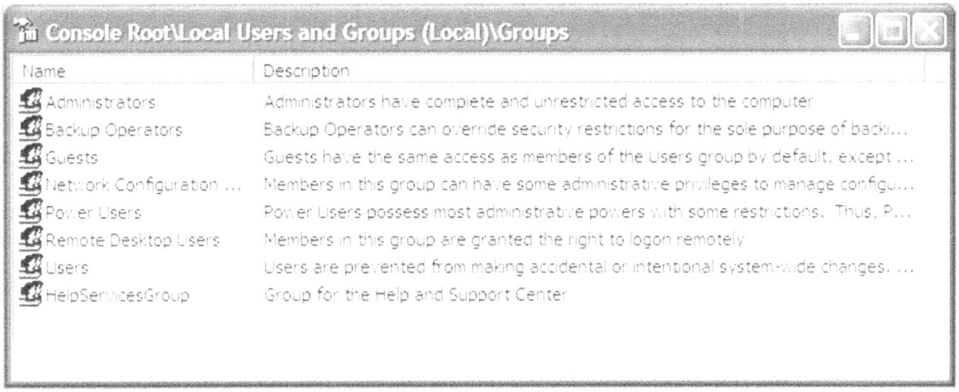

Figure 2-14: Pre-existing local groups on TRPublicComputer.

To start declare the variables that will be needed in the script. The first three variables are string variables.

a. **strADsPath" is a set variable pointing to the computer "TRPublicComputer".**
b. **The other two string variables "strGroupName" and "strDescription" are set to the arguments stated at runtime.**
c. **The second set of variables are object variables. The first "objTarget" will contain the object to which you wish to add the group (TRPublicComputer) and the second "objNewGroup" will contain the new group with the description property set.**

The script will look as the one does in Script 2.5:

```
Dim strADsPath
Dim strGroupName
Dim strDescription

Dim objTarget
Dim objNewGroup
```

Script 2–5: The script used to declare string variables.

On Error Resume Next has been used to trap expected errors in the input arguments. As we will be passing two arguments, the group name and group description, error trapping has been coded to ensure that both arguments, and no more, have been passed. If the correct information has not been passed at runtime, messages will be passed to the administrator.

The error resume script is shown in Script 2.6.

```
On Error Resume Next
If WScript.Arguments.Count <> 2 Then
    WScript.Echo "Wrong number of arguments."
    WScript.Echo "Syntax:  CreateLocalGroup.vbs <name>
<description>"
    WScript.Echo "name         Name for the new group."
    WScript.Echo "description  Description of the new
Group."
    WScript.Quit(1)
End If
```

Script 2–6 The script to resume to the next script On Error.

Values are then assigned to the string variables previously declared as shown in Script 2.7.

```
strADsPath = "WinNT://TRPublicComputer"
strGroupName = WScript.Arguments(0)
strDescription = WScript.Arguments(1)
```

Script 2–7: Assigned Values to the string values previously declared.

We then bind to the computer object. The error subroutine "AdsiErr()" is outlined later in the code Script 2.8 shows this.

```
Set objTarget = GetObject(strADsPath)
If Err Then AdsiErr()
```

Script 2–8: The error subroutine "AdsiErr".

The user object is now created and SetInfo is used to commit the change, the new group, to the directory shown in Script 2.9.

```
Set objNewGroup = objTarget.Create("group", strGroupName)
objNewGroup.SetInfo
If Err Then AdsiErr()
```

Script 2–9: The SetInfo command commits the change for the user object.

The description property is set for the new group, and once again SetInfo is called to commit the description to the directory shown below in Script 2.10.

```
objNewGroup.Description = strDescription
objNewGroup.SetInfo
If Err Then AdsiErr()
```

Script 2–10: Setting the Description Property for the new group.

This code will notify the user that the group has been successfully created, and display the name and description of the new group.

Script 2.11 shows the GetInfo command that is called to ensure that the actual values of Name and Description exist.

```
objNewGroup.GetInfo
strGroupName = objNewGroup.Name
strDescription = objNewGroup.Description
WScript.Echo "New group " & strGroupName & " created."
WScript.Echo "Description: " & strDescription
```

Script 2–11: The GetInfo command.

The administrator would then be displayed the following message boxes shown in Figure 2.15 and Figure 2.16.

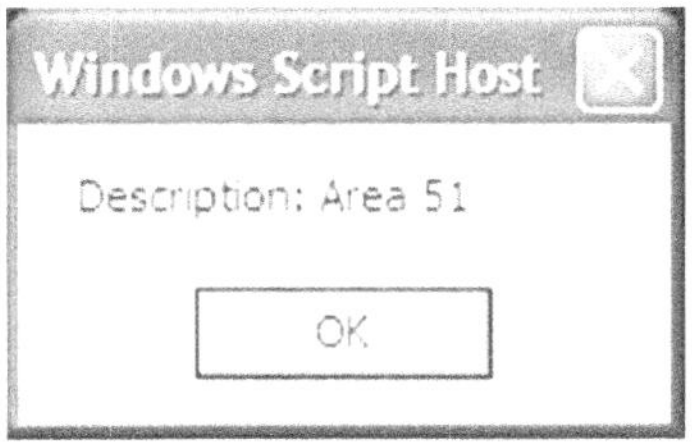

Figure 2-15: and Figure 2-16: Dialog boxes displayed for administrators.

The last part of the script is the AdsiErr() subroutine. It handles two errors that might occur while creating the new group—if a group of the specified name already exists or if the specified group name is invalid.

Any other error is reported as an unexpected error then exits the AdsiErr() subroutine is shown in Script 2.12.

```
Sub AdsiErr()
    Dim scriptoutput
    Dim errornumber

'if the group name exists
If Err.Number = &H80070563 Then
        scriptoutput = "The group " & strGroupName & "
already exists."
'if the group name is invalid
ElseIf Err.Number = &H800A0408 Then
        scriptoutput = "The name '" & strGroupName & "' is
invalid as a group Name."

   'other error
   Else
        errornumber = Hex(Err.Number)
        scriptoutput = "Unexpected Error " & errornumber &
"(" & Err.Number & ")"
    End If
    WScript.Echo scriptoutput
    WScript.Quit(1)

End Sub
```

Script 2–12: The Subroutine AdsiErr.

Figure 2.17 shows what appears after running this script—the Groups on the computer TRPublicComputer:

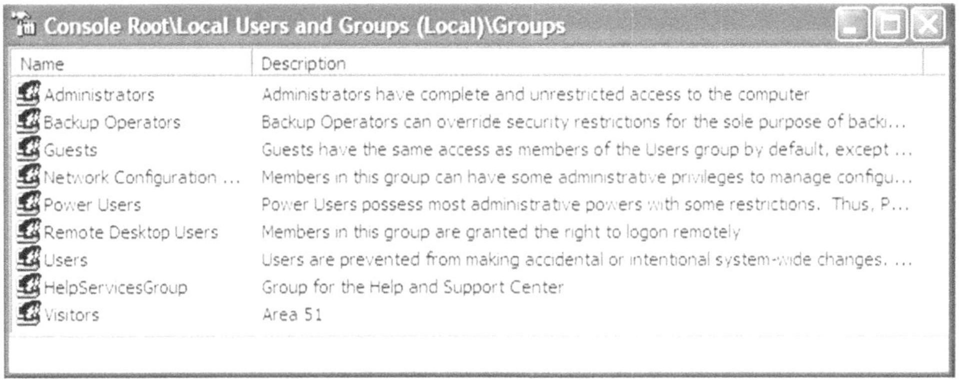

Figure 2-17: The output in the console after running the script.

Most of the samples below are specific to the task at hand; however, each could be modified to hold arguments that are passed at runtime, rather than the identified group or ADsPath.

Creating a Global Group

The following simple script segment demonstrates how you could modify the script previously described to create a global, rather than a local, groups.

We are working with two variables:

- **objOU**, which is the OU in which the group will be contained; and
- **objGroup**, which is the new group.

We are also using Name Properties to specify the path in the binding string for Active Directory. A few of the name properties with which you should be familiar are:

- CN – common name
- DC – domain component
- OU – organizational unit.

For example, in the ADsPath in the script sample below, we are using OU to specify that the organizational unit is named "management", and that the domain components are "TotalRecallPress" and "com". The common name for the group is "visitors".

Script 2.13 shows the Set objOU script.

```
Set objOU = _

GetObject("LDAP://OU=management,dc=totalrecallpublications,
dc=com")
Set objGroup = objOU.Create("Group", "cn=visitors")
objGroup.Put "sAMAccountName", "visitors"
objGroup.SetInfo
```

Script 2–13: The Set objOU script.

Listing Group Members

Let's say that you need to modify the access permissions of a particular group. One of the things that must be considered is the effect this will have on each of the members, based on membership in other groups in the domain.

Listing the members of a particular group can be easily automated, using the ADsPath and a simple "for" loop as shown in Script 2.14.

```
Set objGroup = GetObject _

("LDAP://cn=visitors,ou=public,dc=totalrecallpublications,d
c=com")
For each objMember in objGroup.Members
Wscript.Echo objMember.Name
Next
```

Script 2–14: Script to list Group Members.

Enumerating Groups and their Membership

It is almost as simple to enumerate all the groups on a specific computer as well as their membership. The script below demonstrates the way to enumerate the local groups and their membership on a specific computer, TRPublicComputer. The filter property of the IADsContainer interface was used to specify the Class of group shown in Script 2.15.

```
strComputer = "TRPublicComputer"
Set colGroups = GetObject("WinNT://" & strComputer & "")
colGroups.Filter = Array("group")
For Each objGroup In colGroups
    Wscript.Echo objGroup.Name
    For Each objUser in objGroup.Members
        Wscript.Echo vbTab & objUser.Name
    Next
Next
```

Script 2–15: Enumerating Groups and their Memberships.

Moving a Group within a Domain

Script 2.16 shows an example of the "MoveHere" method in action is below. In this code sample, the group account is being moved from the IT OU to the Visitors container. You should note that the namespace remains the same.

```
Set objOU = _

GetObject("LDAP://cn=Visitors,dc=totalrecallpublications,dc
=com")
objOU.MoveHere _

"LDAP://cn=Visitors,ou=IT,dc=totalrecallpublications,dc=com
", _
 vbNullString
```

Script 2–16: The MoveHere method script.

When dealing with MoveHere, it is important to remember the information given in the Microsoft Knowledge Base Article 326978 **Error When Executing the MoveHere Method of an IADSContainer Object**. A portion of this article is replicated below.

SYMPTOMS

When you run the MoveHere method of the IADsContainer object, you may receive the following

Error Message:

The server is unwilling to process the request. 0x80072035

CAUSE

You receive this error when you try to move a user object that is a member of a global group from a parent domain to a child domain. Global groups can only contain members from the domain where the global group was made.

RESOLUTION

Remove the user from all global groups except the user's primary group. In this way, you can move the user from the child domain to the parent domain.

The user's old security identifier (SID) is added to the new user object's SidHistory attribute, and the user is given a new SID. Additionally, by default, the user's primary group is set to the parent domain's Domain Users group, and the password of the object is preserved.

STATUS

This behavior is by design.

MORE INFORMATION

You may also receive this error message if you try to add a global group with security group type in the same kind of global group in Pre-Windows 2000 mode of your domain. You can successfully add a global group in native mode domain of this group.

This is by design.

Pop Quiz 2.2

Pop Quiz 2.2 *Questions*

1. What are the three group scopes in Active Directory?
2. What are the two types of groups?
3. What does AGGUDLP stand for?
4. On what platforms can ADSI client applications run?
5. What are the four different types of providers with ADSI?

Pop Quiz 2.2 *Answers*

1. The three group scopes in Active Directory are Universal, Global and Domain.
2. The two group types are distribution and security.
3. This acronym stands for:
   - Accounts are members of
   - Global groups, which in native mode can be members of other
   - Global groups, which in native mode can be members of
   - Universal groups, which are in turn members of
   - Domain Local groups, which are the group scope that is granted resource access
   - Permissions.
4. ADSI client applications can run not only on Windows 2000 and Windows XP clients, but also on Windows 95, Windows 98 and Windows NT4.0 (SP6a), if you have the Active Directory Client Extensions installed.
5. With ADSI, there are four different types of providers:
   - WinNT – Windows NT 4.0 PDCs and BDCs, Windows XP and Windows 2000/2003 not running Active Directory
   - LDAP – LDAP servers, including Exchange 5.x, Windows 2000/2003 Active Directory
   - NDS – Novell Directory Services servers
   - NWCOMPAT – Novell Netware servers

2.4 Create and manage user accounts

There are a number of containers with Windows Server 2003. These include:

- Built-in – Container that includes all of the built-in accounts such as Administrator,
- Computers – Holds all computer names in the domain
- Domain Controllers – Lists all domain controllers in domain
- Foreign Security – Allows domain users able to access resources in a different resources
- Users – Container for all users accounts.

For this section we will only be using the **Users** container.

2.4.1 Create and modify user accounts by using the Active Directory Users and Computers MMC snap-in

Using the MMC snap-in, Active Directory Users and Computers, you can add a user three ways:

- Right-click **Domain** in the left pane, choose **New** and choose **User**.
- Right-click **Users** in the left pane, choose **New**, choose **User** as shown in Figure 2.18.
- Under the File menu, choose **New** and the **User** option.

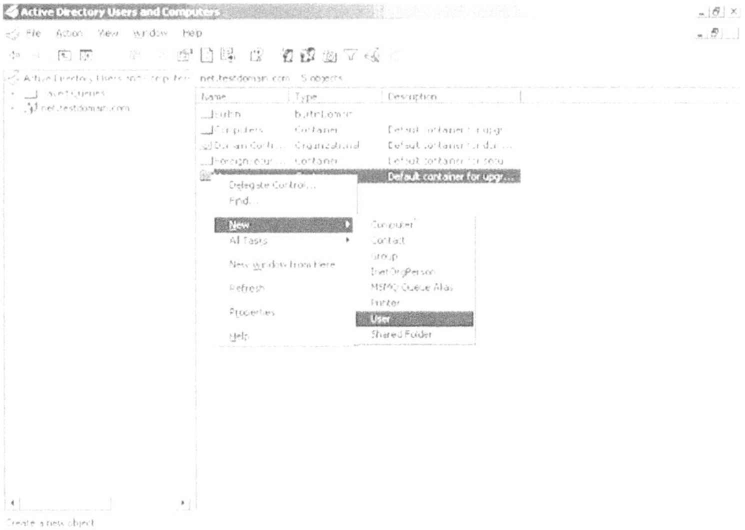

Figure 2-18: Creating a New user by right-clicking on the User object in the Active Directory Users and Computers console.

Once the new user option has been selected, a dialog box will appear (Figure 2. 19).

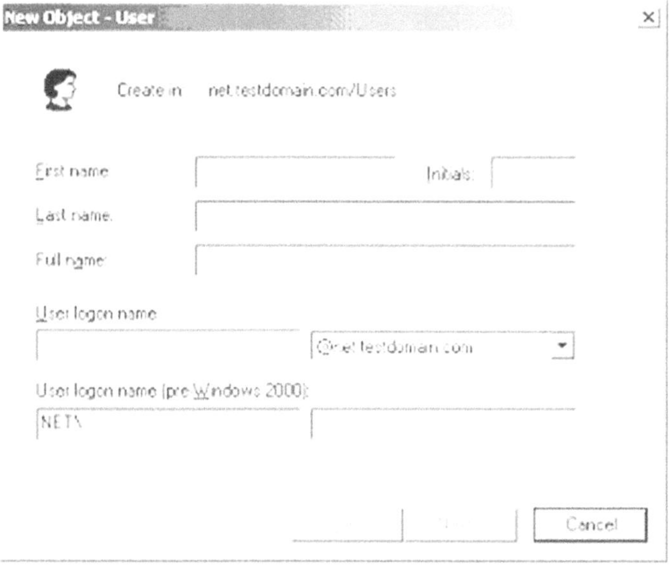

Figure 2-19: The New User Dialog Box in the Active Directory Users and Computers console.

It shows the **Create in:** *domain/group* that you already defined, and allows you to enter the user's first name, initials, last name, and full name, user login name (with "@*domainname* already provided), as well as the pre-Windows 2000 login name. When creating user names remember these important rules, as outlined in Table 2.1:

Username	Rule
Character Type	Up to 20 characters, uppercase, lowercase or a combination of the two.
Special Characters	No " / \ [ ] : ; | = , + * ? < > characters may be used in the user name.
Other special characters	User name may include periods and spaces. However it cannot entirely consist of spaces or periods. Try not to use spaces in user names because if you use command-line utilities or scripting these names have to be enclosed with quotations.
Local Account user names	User Name must be unique to the machine for local accounts.
Domain Account user names	These can be the same name as a local user account name on a non-domain controller that is a member of the same domain. This is because they are entirely separate.

Table 2-1: User Name and Rules.

Now that we have covered the basics for username creation, let's create a user account in our domain. The first name of the user is **myuser**. As you fill in the first name of the user you will notice that the Full Name box and the user logon name box begin to fill as well with what you are typing.

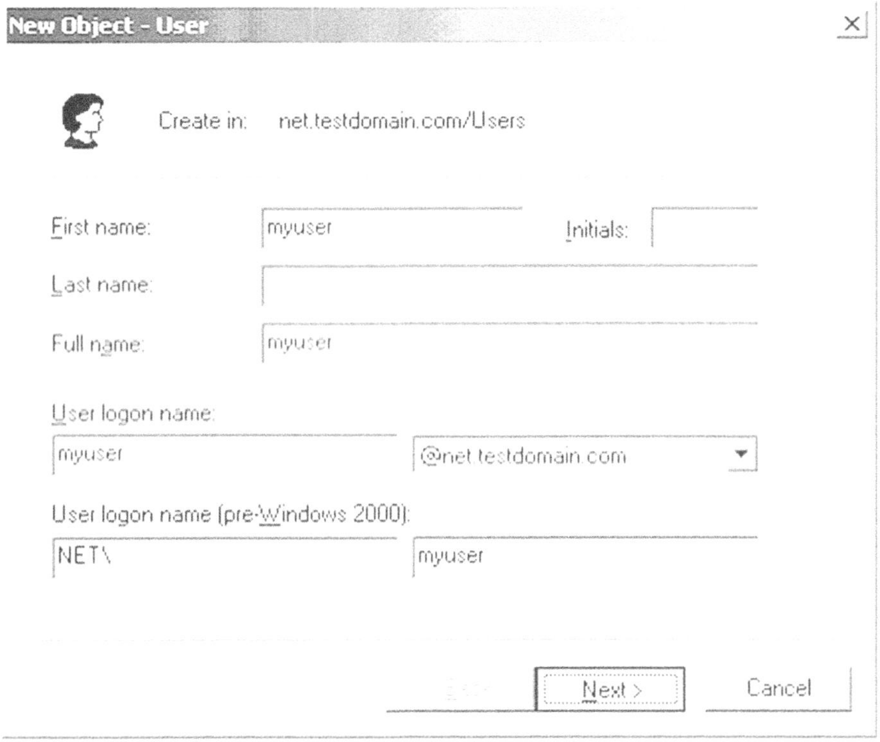

Figure 2-20: Entering the New User information.

Once all of the information has been entered, choose the **Next** button and the dialog box shown in Figure 2.21 will be displayed, allowing you to create a temporary user password for the new user.

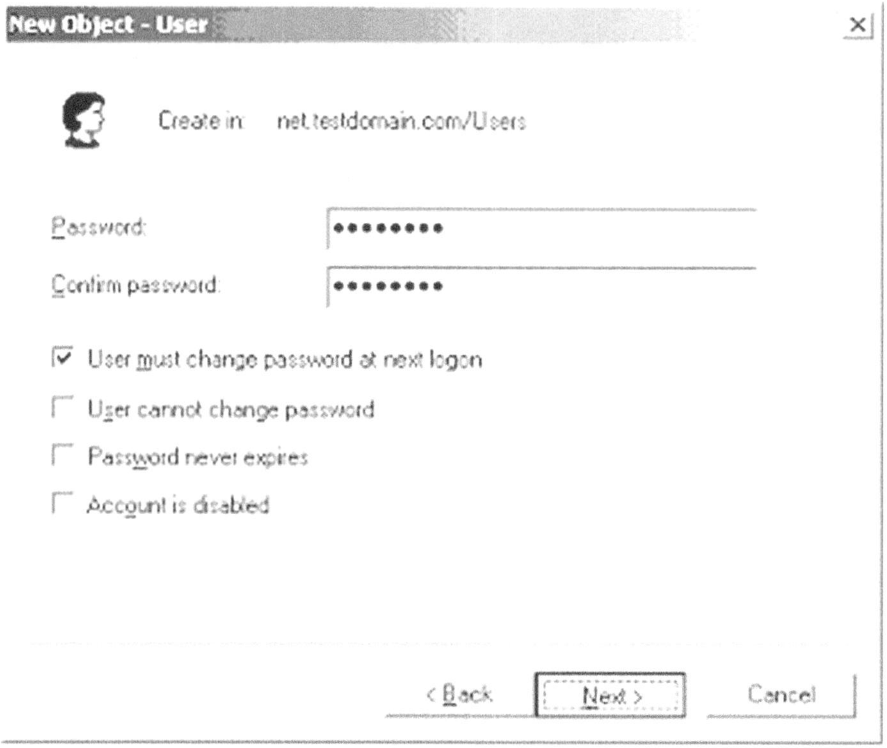

Figure 2-21: Entering a Password and choosing the password options for the new user.

Enter a password for the new user and then choose from the following options:

- User must change password at logon. This will force the user to change their password at the next logon.
- User cannot change password – This is helpful to use when you have user accounts that run server services like SQL Server or Exchange Server. When this option is chosen the user cannot change the password.
- Password never expires – When this option is chosen the user account ignores any password policy that is in place. The password will never expire. Useful for IUSR_(servername) type accounts.
- Account is disabled – This is used in a couple of scenarios. Maybe your company has interns or temporary employees that come back between semesters or every few months. Instead of deleting and reading the user account each time they leave and return you can just disable the account and enable the account as needed.

Note: There have been some rather legendary, humorous outcomes with password options, particularly when combined with Group Policy. One Group Policy option states "User must logon to change password". If this is combined with "User must change password at next logon", a conundrum arises. The user is obliged to change the password as he or she logs onto the network; however, Group Policy prohibits the password from being changed UNTIL the user has logged on. Make sure you know what the outcome will be, before you select particular password options.

Once you have selected the Password option, click the **Next** button. The object will now be created, as illustrated in Figure 2.22.

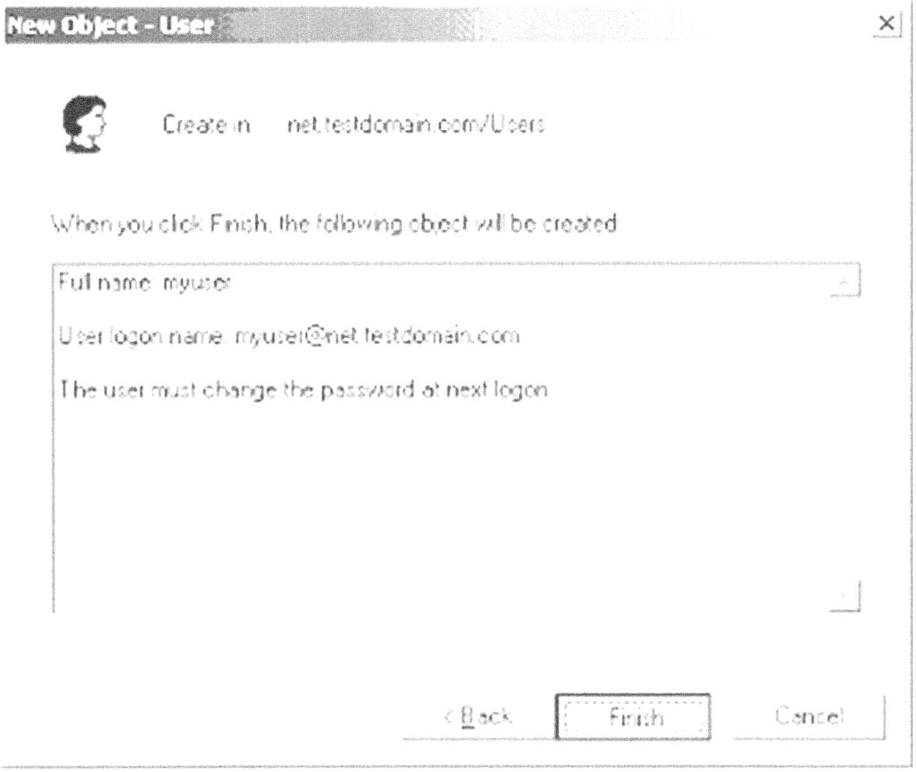

Figure 2-22: New user account object.

The account will now be viewable in the user account container in the Active Directory Users and Computers console. You can view the user account by double clicking on the user container in the right side of the console (Figure 2.23).

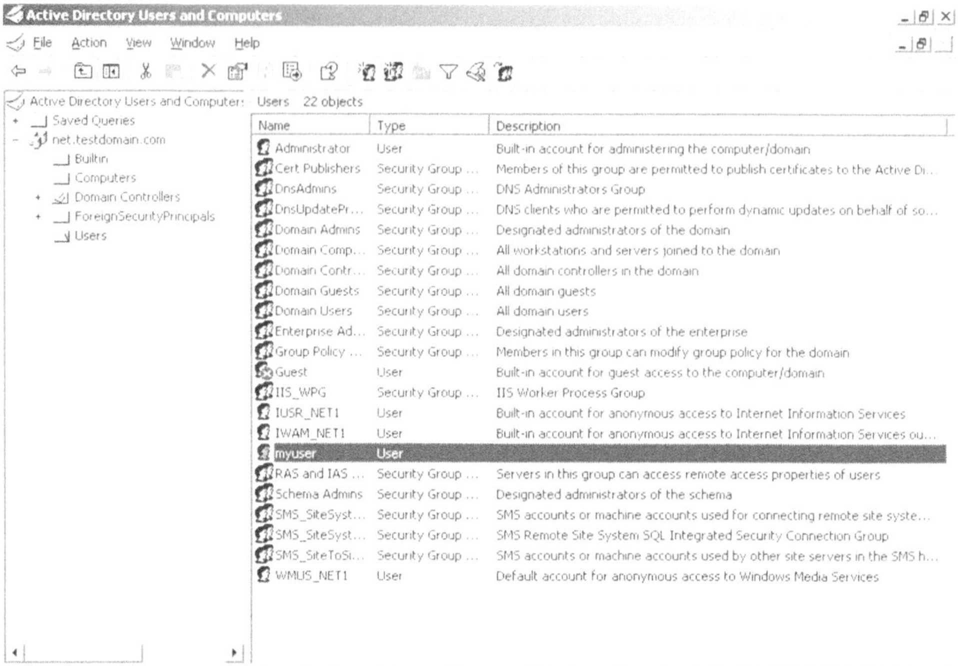

Figure 2-23: The newly added user in the User Container.

As you can see, the new user is listed along with the user accounts that come built-in with Windows Server 2003. Depending on the additional software you install (such as Active Directory, IIS, SMS Server and Exchange Server), you could see a variety of additional user accounts that are not listed in this user container.

2.4.2 Create and modify user accounts by using automation

We already covered the basics of automation in section 2.3.5—Create and modify groups by using automation. Let's just take a quick look at how automation can be used to create and modify user accounts.

The following simple script segment demonstrates how you could modify the script previously described to create a user, rather than a group.

We are working with two variables:

- objOU, which is the OU in which the group will be contained; and
- objUser, which is the new user.

We are also using Name Properties to specify the path in the binding string for Active Directory. A few of the name properties with which you should be familiar are:

- CN – common name
- DC – domain component
- OU – organizational unit.

For example, in the ADsPath in the script sample below, we are using OU to specify that the organizational unit is named "management", and that the domain components are "totalrecallpublications" and "com". The common name for the user is "TimmonsD".

```
Set objOU =
GetObject("LDAP://OU=management,dc=totalrecallpublications,
dc=com")
Set objUser = objOU.Create("User", "cn=TimmonsD")
objUser.Put "sAMAccountName", "timmonsd"
objUser.SetInfo
```

Script 2—17: Creating a New User by Script.

Please note that this script will only create the user account in Active Directory. It will NOT enable it. In order to enable the account, an additional step must be taken.

```
Set objUser = GetObject _
("LDAP://cn=timmonsd,ou=management,dc=totalrecallpubliation
s,dc=com")
objUser.AccountDisabled = FALSE
objUser.SetInfo
```

Script 2—18: Enabling a User, by Script.

Now that we have created the user TimmonsD and enabled the account, let's add the account to two different security groups—ITAdmins and ITExecs.

```
Const ADS_PROPERTY_APPEND = 3

Set objGroup = GetObject _
    ("LDAP://cn=ITAdmins,cn=IT,
dc=totalrecallpress,dc=com")
objGroup.PutEx ADS_PROPERTY_APPEND, _
    "member",
Array("cn=TimmonsD,ou=Management,dc=totalrecallpress,dc=com
")
objGroup.SetInfo

Set objGroup = GetObject _
    ("LDAP://cn=ITExecs,cn=IT,dc=totalrecallpress,dc=com")
objGroup.PutEx ADS_PROPERTY_APPEND, _
    "member", Array("cn=
TimmonsD,ou=Management,dc=totalrecallpress,dc=com ")
objGroup.SetInfo
```

Script 2—19: Adding a user account to two different security groups.

There are a number of other things you can do with user accounts, using scripting. For example, let's say that the password for TimmonsD has been "hacked". You can change the password by using a piece of script. (Note that this particular script requires you know the original password.)

```
Set objUser = GetObject _
("LDAP://cn=timmonsd,ou=management,dc=totalrecallpress,dc=c
om")
objUser.ChangePassword "wh0Ru?", "V4ni114"
```

Script 2—20: Changing a user's password.

Finally, let's delete the TimmonsD user account. (Remember that deleting an account is permanent. In order to reactivate the account, the account will need to be recreated and all group memberships, rights and permissions reassigned to the account.)

```
Set objOU =
GetObject("LDAP://ou=management,dc=totalrecallpress,dc=com"
)
objOU.Delete "User", "cn=timmonsd"
```

Script 2—21: Deleting a user account.

This section has merely scratched the surface of what can be done using ADSI and automation. With Windows 2003, many of these tasks can be automated and placed on an internal Web site that network administrators could access. With a simple click, and the addition of the necessary arguments, users and groups can be created, deleted, and moved across a distributed network. As well, users can be added or removed from groups, groups and membership can be enumerated, and membership lists for each group produced.

It is well worth your time to spend a little time on the MSDN site, learning more about scripting in VBScript, C#, WMI, WSH and ADSI.

2.4.3 Import user accounts

The LDAP Data Interchange Format Directory Exchange or **`ldifde`** command line utility allows Administrators to create, modify, and delete directory objects on Window Server 2003 and Windows XP Professional machines. This utility also allows administrators to extend their Active Directory schema, populate, import and export user and/or group information from within Active Directory to additional applications and services.

Table 2.9 below shows some general import parameters that can be used with the **`ldifde`** command utility.

Switch Definition	Switches
Replace occurrence of FromDN to ToDN	-c From DN ToDN
Input or Output filename	-f
Turn on Import Mode (Export mode is the default mode)	-i
Log File location	-j
Server to bind to	-s
Port Number if you wish to change from default of 389	-t
Use Unicode Format	-u
Turn on Verbose Mode	-v
-?	Help

Table 2-2: Syntax to use with the LDIFDE utility.

To import user accounts from one Active Directory controller to another, you must be logged in as the Administrator. If you log on using an account that does not have administrative privileges, you may not be able to perform export and import operations against the Active Directory. In the following steps we will import a user account named John Doe using the **ldifde** command.

a. Click on Start | Run and type Notepad
b. Name the blank notepad file **myimport.ldf**

On the first line of the Notepad file type the following exactly as it is shown in Figure 2.24.

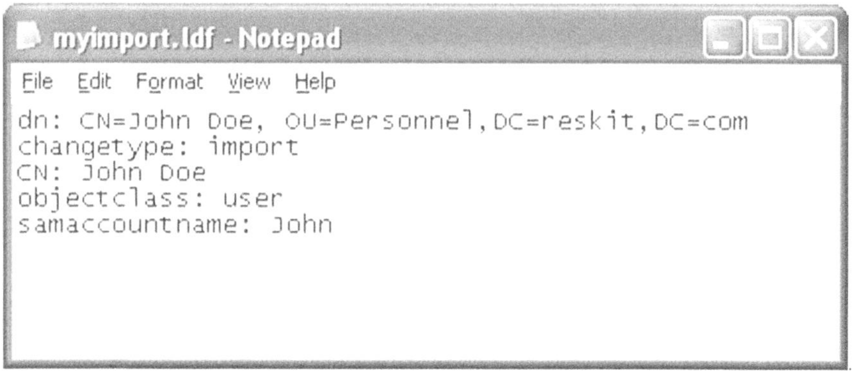

Figure 2-24: Myimport.ldf using Notepad.

Creating the import file to use with ldifde.

1. Click on the **Start** button, click **Run** and type **cmd**
2. Once at the command prompt use the following command:
   `ldifde -v -i -s 2003svr -f myimport.ldf`

To break it down bit by bit, look at the command closely. The –**v** displays the output in the verbose mode, **-i** is the import mode (you must use this to import because the command uses export by default), the **–s** command is the name of the server we are importing from and the –f is the name of the import file we created with notepad.

CSVDE

The CSVDE utility is much like the **ldifde** command but it uses a comma-separated format (CSV). This means that applications such as Microsoft Excel can read the output of the file. This is a great tool to use if you have a large number of accounts to import and you would like to view the output of the import file. However, this utility does has its limitations — it can only be used to import and export from Active Directory, not to create and delete objects like the **ldifde** command.

The command switches are just like the ones that were used in the **ldifde** command in the previous section so we are not going to list those here. An example of how to use this function is listed below. We will use this utility to create an LDAP search filter to import users with the surname smith. The import will be viewable in a filename we create called **myimport.csv.**

1. Click on **Start | Run |** type **cmd**
2. Type in the following command
   ```
   Csvde -r -f -v -i -s 2003svr
   (and(objectClass=User)(sn=smith))
   ```

The –**r** command creates an LDAP search filter for the data export. The –**f** command identifies the name of the import file. The –**v** command displays the information in verbose mode. The –**i** command must be used for importing (exporting is also used by default). The –**s** command specifies the server name. The object class specifies the type of object, which in this case is the user, and the **sn** syntax represents the surname we are importing.

These are a few of the many tools that are available for use with the Windows Server 2003 network operating server. Enhancements to this network operating system allow administrators much more flexibility and control over their environment using command line utilities such as the ones listed in this section.

2.5 Troubleshoot computer accounts

The Active Directory snap-in can be used to assist you with computer account problems.

2.5.1 Diagnose and resolve issues related to computer accounts by using the Active Directory Users and Computers MMC snap-in

Open the **Active Directory Users and Computers** console, drill down to the computer account you wish to troubleshoot and right-click on the computer. A shortcut menu, as shown in Figure 2.25, will appear.

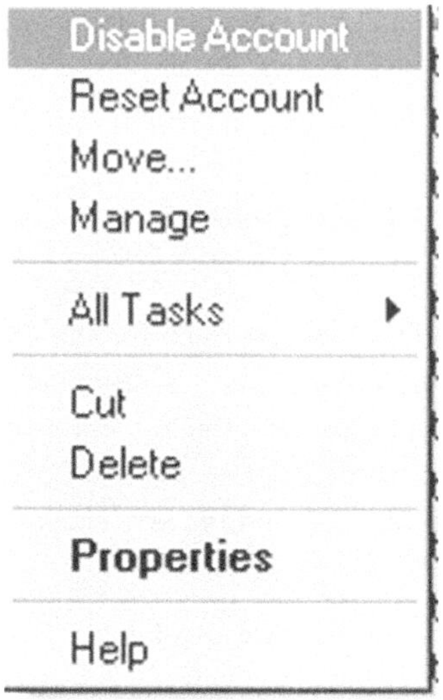

Figure 2-25: Troubleshooting a Computer Account using the Active Directory Users and Computer console.

As you can see from the menu you have options available to:

- **Disable Account** – which would render it unusable, but keeps all rights, permissions and group memberships intact if you choose to re-enable it at a later date.
- **Reset Account** – For each workstation or server that is a member of a domain, there is a secure channel with a domain controller. The secure channel's password is stored along with the computer account on all domain controllers. If, for some reason, the computer account's password and the LSA secret are not synchronized, the Netlogon service will log an error. It is then that the computer account must be reset.
- **Move** – Move the account to another location, for example, a different OU container.

- **All Tasks** – Allows you to do the Disable Account, Reset Account, Move, Manage as well as run the Resultant Set of Policy on the computer, as illustrated in Figure 2.26.

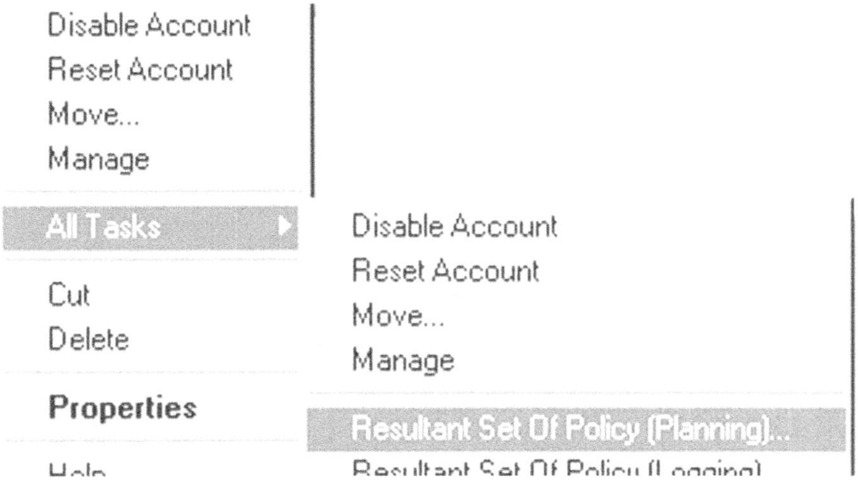

Figure 2-26: The All tasks option for troubleshooting.

- **Resultant Set of Policy** – Can be used to troubleshoot Group Policy problems on an account.

A disabled account will appear, as shown in Figure 2.27.

Figure 2-27: A disabled computer account.

To re-enable a computer account, just right-click the computer and select the Enable option as shown in Figure 2.28.

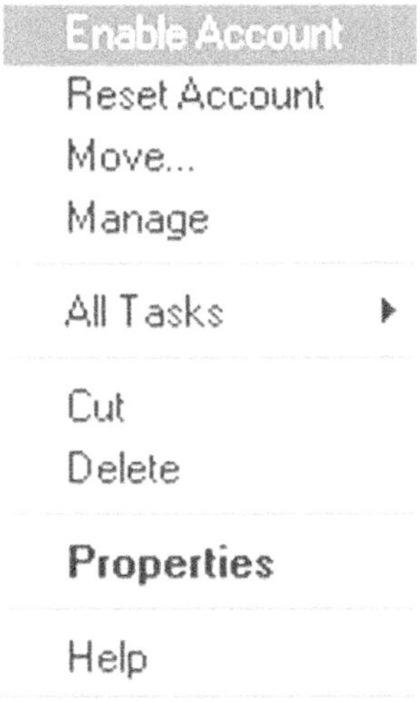

Figure 2-28: Re-enabling a computer account.

After you have re-enabled the account, a dialog box (shown in Figure 2.29) will appear stating the computer account has been re-enabled.

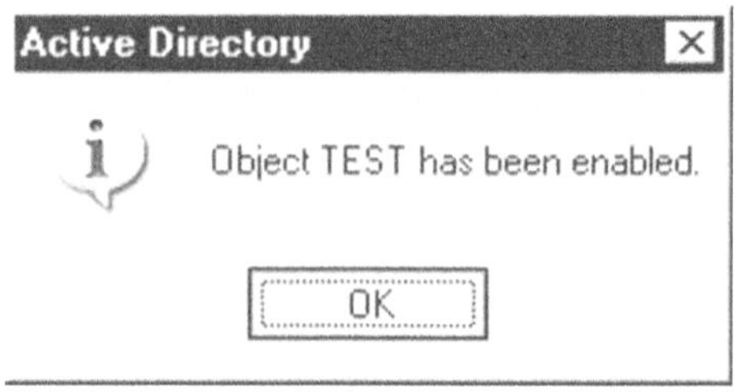

Figure 2-29: The re-enabled computer account verification.

The account will appear in the list of computer accounts and be accessible for use.

2.5.2 Reset computer accounts

Resetting a computer account is done in the same manner as disabling and re-enabling a computer account. Just open the Active Directory Users and Computers console and select the Computer Account you wish to reset. Right-click the computer account and select **Reset**. The dialog box shown in Figure 2.30 will prompt you to make certain you wish to complete this procedure.

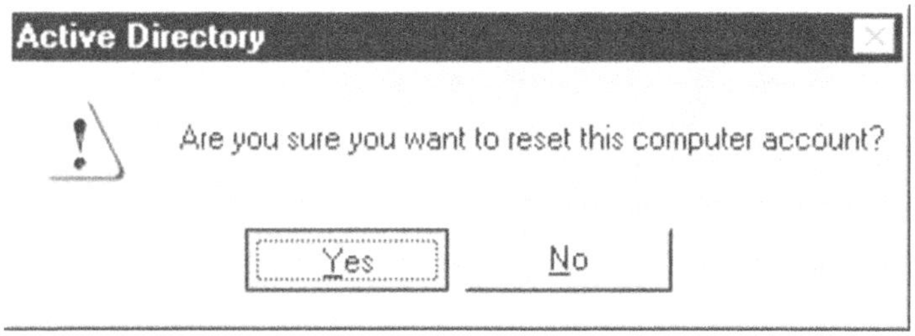

Figure 2-30: Resetting a Computer Account using Active Directory Users and Computers.

Click **Yes** to reset the account. Figure 2.31 shows the successful dialog box that appears once the account has been reset.

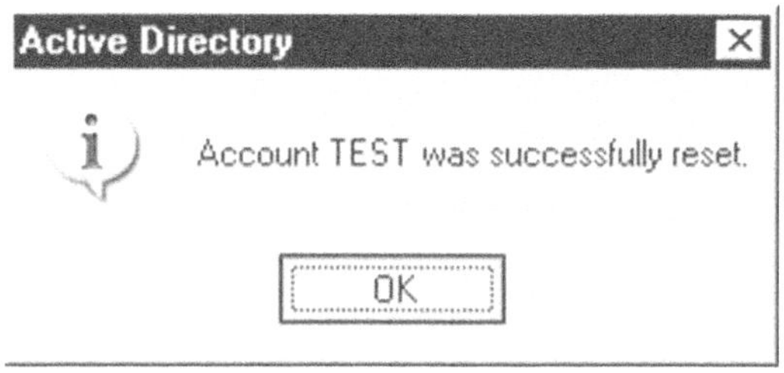

Figure 2-31: Successful completion of a computer account reset.

2.6 Troubleshoot user accounts.

User Account issues can be caused by a number of factors. The following section explains some of the issues and ways to diagnose and solve user account problems.

2.6.1 Diagnose and resolve account lockouts

When a user's account is locked out, it is because it has breached the password policy implemented in Group Policy. When designing a password policy for a domain or OU, remember that you have to maintain a balance between the security needs of the network, and the administrative load on the personnel responsible for unlocking accounts that have breached the policy.

Creating a Password Policy for a Domain

Administrators can create password policies to enforce restrictions on domain and member server passwords. In order to create Group Policy , the Group Policy Object Editor snap-in must first be added. This is done from within an MMC.

Open an MMC by clicking on **Start | Run | MMC**. When the MMC opens, select **File** from the menu, then select **Add/Remove snap-in**. Click **Add** to open the list of available snap-ins, and then choose **Group Policy Object Editor**. Click OK to confirm your selection.

Password Policy is located under **Computer Configuration | Windows Settings | Security Settings | Account Policies**.

The available settings for **Password Policy** are as follows:

- **Enforce Password History** – determines the number of unique new passwords that have to be linked with a user account before an old password can be reused. The value must be between 0 and 24 passwords. This policy allows administrators to increase security by guaranteeing that old passwords are not reused continually. The setting, by default, is 24 on domain controllers and 0 on stand-alone servers. As well, by default, member computers follow the configuration of their domain controllers.
- **Maximum Password Age** – determines the period of time (in days) that a password can be used before the system forces the user to change it. Passwords can expire after a number of days set between 1 and 999. Specifying 0 will mean that passwords never expire. If the maximum password age is greater than 0, the minimum password age must be less than the specified maximum password age; however, if the maximum password age is set to 0, the minimum password age can be set to any value between 0 and 998. Microsoft's security best practice is to have passwords expire every 30 to 90 days, depending on your environment. This way, an intruder has a limited amount of time in which to crack a password and have access to your network resources. The default setting is 42 days.

- **Minimum Password Age** – determines the period of time (in days) that a password must be used before the user can change it. As mentioned above, a value can be chosen between 1 and 998 days, provided it is less than the Maximum Password Age (unless that setting is 0). Setting the minimum password age value to 0 allows the user to immediately change their password. Configure the minimum password age to be more than 0 if you want **Enforce password history** to be effective; without setting a minimum password age, users can cycle through passwords until they get back to the one that just expired. The default setting is 1 on domain controllers and 0 on stand-alone servers. Again, by default, member computers follow the configuration of their domain controllers.
- **Minimum Password Length** – determines the least number of characters that a password for a user account may contain. A value of between 1 and 14 characters can be set. Setting the number to 0 means that no password is required. By default, this setting is 7 on domain controllers, and 0 on stand-alone servers. Again, member computers follow the domain controller configuration by default.
- **Passwords must meet complexity requirements** – determines whether passwords must meet complexity requirements. If this policy is enabled, passwords must meet the following minimum requirements:
  - Not contain all or any part of the user's account name
  - Be at least six characters in length
  - Contain characters from three of the following four categories:
    - English uppercase characters (A through Z)
    - English lowercase characters (a through z)
    - Base 10 digits (0 through 9)
    - Non-alphabetic characters (for example, !, $, #, %).

Complexity requirements are enforced when passwords are changed or created. By default, this setting is enabled on domain controllers and disabled on stand-alone servers. Careful planning should take place before implementing a password policy; however, once it has been in put into place, it should allow for a more controlled and secure domain. Educate end-users on the basics of password use and security. Some Account Password Policy troubleshooting scenarios are listed in Table 2.3 below.

The password policy has been changed but it has not gone into effect.	Click **Start** | **Run** | **gpupdate** | **OK**. The **gpupdate** command is used to refresh group policy settings.
Cannot login to Windows 95, Windows 98, and other passwords are not functioning.	Is the password more than 14 characters? Windows 95 and Windows 98 cannot recognize passwords over 14 characters. Change the password so it is less than 14 characters.
Cannot login to Windows 95, Windows 98, and other passwords are not functioning.	The system you are logging into does not support unusual characters. Change the password.

Table 2–3: Troubleshooting Account Password Policies.

Some topics to remember when implementing security is to think through how your organization functions and how you can use these to assist you with implementing greater security with less administrative overhead.

Table 2.4 below shows some common problems and troubleshooting information.

Issue	Cause	Correction
Computer connects to computers with the incorrect access level or account.	A user name and password was stored for this account that has either too much or too little access to resources.	Delete the stored user name and password.
Computer has incorrect access when using a shared user account.	The user account stored a user name and password for this resource.	Delete the stored user name and password.
When I logon I cannot access resources that were currently available to me.	Either a user name and/or a password which was stored for this account has expired or the password has been changed without updating stored information.	Correct the stored user name and password.

Table 2–4: Issues, Causes and corrections for user account problems.

Passwords

Not enough can be written regarding password security. Some best recommended guidelines are listed below to help you implement strong passwords and account policies.

- Explain to end-users how to protect their accounts, lock their desktops and turn off their computers when they are away. Put a policy in place and enforce it.
- Force the use of strong passwords by setting up Group Policy.
- Discourage "sticky note syndrome." Do not allow users to write their passwords down and post them on their monitors. If a password must be written down (for example, the enterprise administrator password), make sure it is stored in a very secure location.
- Never share passwords with anyone.
- Use different passwords for all user accounts.
- Always remember to change passwords immediately if they may have been compromised.
- The **SysKey** utility may be used throughout a network. This utility is used to enable strong password encryption techniques to secure account password information. The utility can be used by clicking on **Start | Run | syskey**. The utility is shown in Figure 2.32.

Figure 2-32: The SysKey utility.

These are just a few common sense guidelines that Administrators can follow when education clients about the importance of passwords.

2.6.2 Diagnose and resolve issues related to user account properties

Creating and managing users in Windows Server 2003 has changed very little from the methodology used in Windows 2000 Server. Accounts may be added using the **Active Directory Users and Computer** console or via the command prompt with a utility called `dsadd`. (Obviously, using this console means that you have Active Directory installed and properly running on the 2003 Server.) Figure 2.33 shows the **`dsadd`** utility as well as the syntax to use with the command.

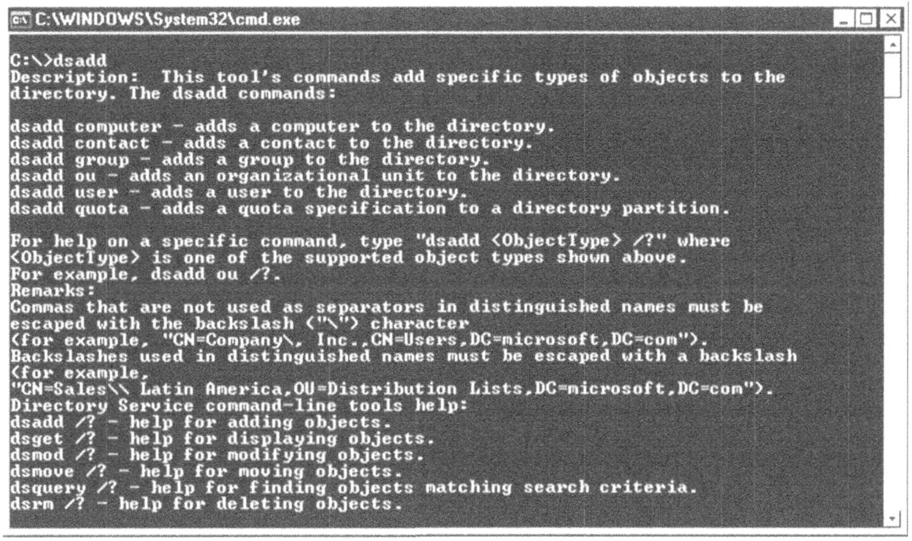

Figure 2-33: DSADD utility.

Pop Quiz 2.3

Pop Quiz 2.3 *Questions*

1. How many characters can be used in a username?
2. What can an administrator do using the "ldifde" command?
3. Can an administrator delete an Active Directory object using the CSVDE command?
4. What happens when you disable a user account?
5. What happens when you reset a computer account?

Pop Quiz 2.3 *Answers*

1. Up to 20 characters, uppercase, lowercase or a combination of the two can be used in a username.
2. The ldifde command line utility allows Administrators to create, modify, and delete directory objects on Window Server 2003 and Windows XP Professional machines.
3. No, CSVDE can only be used to import and export from Active Directory, not to create or delete objects. You must use the ldifde command for those functions.
4. Disabling a user account renders it unusable, but keeps all rights, permissions and group memberships intact if you choose to re-enable it at a later date.
5. Resetting the computer account synchronizes the computer account's password with the LSA.

2.7 Troubleshoot user authentication issues

Microsoft Windows Server 2003 supports various authentication protocols, as well as a key feature known as **Stored User Names and Passwords** for client access to network resources. The topics are discussed in the following pages.

2.7.1 Authentication Process

Authentication is based on two processes in Microsoft Windows Server 2003. The first process is the interactive logon. The interactive logon is used to confirm the user's identity. This verification is done either by a local computer account or a domain account. The process varies for each of these accounts.

- **Local computer account** – A client simply logs onto the computer and the credentials in the local security account database (SAM) are used.
- **Domain Account** – A client logs onto the network with a password or a smart card and the credentials stored in the Active Directory are used to give access to network resources. When a client logs into the domain using a domain account, they can then access any resources in the domain as well as other trusting domains.

2.7.2 Domain User Accounts using Kerberos

Kerberos policies do not exist in local computer policy — only for domain user accounts. Before we jump into the Kerberos policies, you need to know about tickets. Tickets are used as a set of identification and are issued by a domain controller for user authentication. There are two different types of tickets — service tickets and ticket-granting tickets. Kerberos policies may be used to enforce any of the following security features:

- **Enforce User logon restrictions** – Open the Policy and expand the console tree **Computer Configuration | Windows Settings**
Security Settings | Account Policies | then choose the Kerberos Policy.
- **Maximum tolerance for computer clock synchronization** – This is used by Kerberos V5 as a time stamp to prevent replay attacks. Clocks on Servers and client machines need to be in close time sync. Administrators can use this to set the maximum acceptable difference between the server and client time. If the difference between the client and server time is less than the maximum time specified in this policy, then any time stamp used in a session is considered to be authentic.
- **Set the Maximum lifetime for service ticket** – This policy setting is used to determine the maximum amount of minutes that a granted session ticket can be used to access a particular service. It cannot be more minutes than the setting for the Maximum Lifetime user ticket. It also must be a minimum of 10 minutes.

- **Set the Maximum lifetime for a user ticket** – This policy is used to determine in hours the maximum amount of time that a client's ticket granting ticket (TGT) may be used. If the TGT expires then existing ticket may be either renewed or a new ticket must be requested.
- **Set the Maximum lifetime for user ticket renewal** – This policy is used to determine in days (7 by default) the amount of time that a user's ticket granting ticket (TGT) can be renewed.

2.7.3 Local Computer Account Policy

The local computer account policy can be access via the MMC console. Click on **Start | Administrative Tools** | choose the Local Security Policy. The MMC will open as shown in Figure 2.34

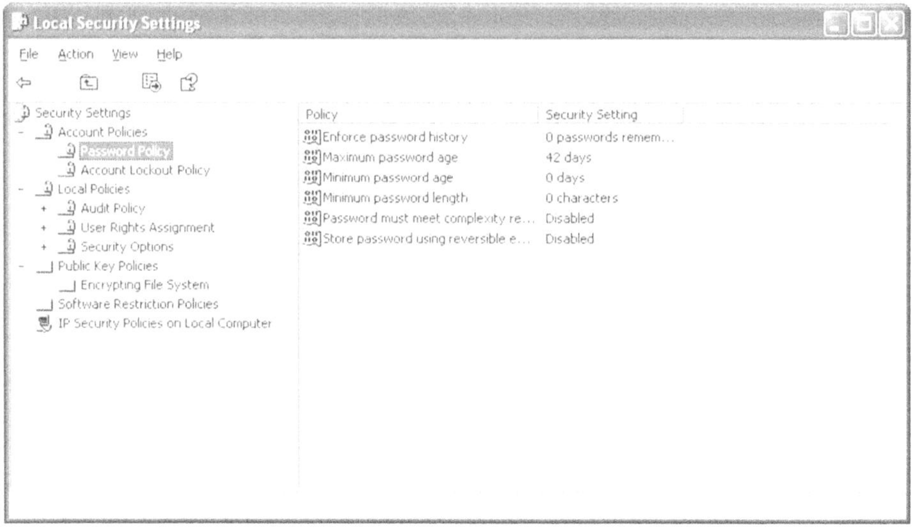

Figure 2-34: The Local Security Policy MMC.

2.7.4 Stored user names and passwords

A new feature in Windows Server 2003, introduced originally with Windows XP, is Stored User Names and Passwords. When a user logs onto their computer, they use their default username and password for authentication. However, there may be occasions when a different name and password is required to connect to a resource. Some examples of this are:

- You need to connect remotely to a server as administrator
- You are working from your home computer and need to connect to work resources
- You are connecting to resources in an untrusted domain
- You are connecting to Web resources using a specific Web identity.

You may also wish to save your username and password for future reuse. It is in these instances that **Stored User Names and Passwords** will come in handy. The benefits of using this feature are:

- User has a single sign-on experience.
- No need for user to log off and on in order to supply multiple user names and passwords for different computers.
- Users can store as many user names and passwords which can in turn be used in the future.
- User names and passwords can be stored in a user's profile to provide privacy and portability of the user names and passwords.
- Various strong passwords can be created and stored for a variety of resources.

Stored User Names and Passwords obtains its information in two ways:

- Explicit creation by the user
- Learning from the user.

When a user logs onto a remote resource, that information is kept and utilized when the users try to log on to an computer. If no information is stored, a user will supply a user name and password. The user can optionally choose to save the information and **Stored User Names and Passwords** collects and stores it.

When Windows XP or a member of the Windows Server 2003 family attempts to connect to a new computer on the network, it provides the current user name and password to the computer. If these credentials do not grant access, **Stored User Names and Passwords** will attempt to supply the necessary user name and password by examining all stored user names and passwords, starting at the most specific for the resource. No more than one particular user name and password can be stored for each individual target, because the credentials are read and applied from most to least specific.

When a user opts to save alternate credentials for a resource, this information is stored in a secure part of the user's profile and cannot be accessed by other users. If the user has a single profile for use across an enterprise environment, the stored user names and passwords will be retained wherever the user logs on to the network.

Because of the power of **Stored User Names and Passwords**, there are some recommended safety precautions:

- **Protect your account** – Remember that anyone that has access to your account also has access to the stored user name and password information attached to your profile. Log off or lock your computer when you leave, even for a short time. Make sure your screensaver is password protected. Most importantly, use strong passwords.
- **Change passwords regularly** – While strong passwords protect against intruders breaking the password, even the strongest password can be stolen eventually. Passwords should be changed periodically to prevent against a patient hacker working against a strong password over a period of time, as well as to minimize the length of time an intruder has access should a stolen password be undetected.
- **Use different passwords for individual accounts** – By having different passwords for different accounts, a stolen password does not substantially weaken security. Think of it this way. Would you really want the same key for your house, your car and your safety deposit box?
- **Store user names and passwords only when appropriate** – Obviously, extremely sensitive resources must be protected carefully. Store user names and passwords only for specific logon sessions, and choose the appropriate options in the Logon Information Properties.

Chapter 2: Summary

In this chapter, we have discussed the many issues surrounding users and groups in a Windows Server 2003 environment. Now that you have completed this chapter, you should feel familiar with the following subjects:

- Managing user profiles, both local and in a domain environment
- Creating and managing computer accounts in an Active Directory environment
- Creating and managing groups, through the GUI interface provided in Windows Server 2003, and through command prompt and scripting tools
- Creating and managing user accounts, through the GUI interface and through command prompt and scripting tools
- Troubleshooting computer account, user account and user authentication issues.

The final part of this chapter is a section with review questions that will help you in confirming your expertise in this subject area.

Chapter 2: Review Questions

1. You suspect that a user's profile or their account might be corrupted. What actions can you take to figure out which is the case?

A. Create a new user account and give it the same rights and group memberships or associations as the account that has the profile that you suspect may be damaged.

B. Copy the user settings in the suspect profile to the profile of the newly created user account. Click Start, point to Control Panel, and then click the System applet.

C. Create an administrative account and give it the same rights and group memberships or associations as the account that has the profile that you suspect may be damaged.

D. Click Advanced, and then under User Profiles, click Settings. Under Profiles stored on this computer, click the suspect user profile, and then click Copy To. In the Copy To dialog box, click Browse. Locate the drive:\Documents and Settings\user_profile folder, where drive is the drive where Windows is installed, and where user_profile is the name of the newly created user profile, and then click OK. Click OK, click Yes to overwrite the folder contents, and then click OK two times. Use the newly-created user account to log on.

2. How can you configure a user account so that it can be trusted for delegation in Windows Server 2003?

A. Double-click the user that you want to configure.

B. Right-click the user that you want to configure, and then click Properties.

C. Click the Delegation tab, click Trust this user for delegation to any service (Kerberos only) , and then click OK.

D. In Active Directory Sites and Services, click Users.

E. In Active Directory Users and Computers, click Users.

---

3. Which of the following options gives you the ability to log on even with a disabled local Administrator account on a 2003 Server?

A. Run the Defragment Tool

B. Use Recovery Console

C. Start Windows 2003 in Safe Mode

D. Boot from a network card that is PXE compliant

4. Which of the following does a remote administrator have control over by using regedit?

A. The number of persons who can be denied access

B. How frequently the failed attempts counter is reset

C. The number of failed attempts before future attempts are denied

D. The number of persons who can be allowed access

---

5. What are some of the requirements for installing Microsoft Group Policy Management Console?

A. Either Windows Server 2003 or Windows XP Professional.

B. The QFE Q326469 hotfix, which updates your version of gpedit.dll to 5.1.2600.1186.

C. Windows Advanced Server 2003 and Windows XP Home with Service Pack 1 (SP1) and the Microsoft .NET Framework.

D. Either Windows Server 2003 or Windows XP Professional with Service Pack 1 (SP1) and the Microsoft .NET Framework.

6. Using the dsadd command, which of the following would create an account in the domain domain.com for John Smith with a password of password?

A. dsadd user 'cn=jsmith,cn=users' -samid user -upn jsmith -fn john -ln smith -display 'user' -pwd password.

B. dsadd user 'dc=domain,dc=com' -samid user -upn domain.com -fn john -ln smith -display 'user' -pwd password.

C. dsadd user 'cn=jsmith,cn=users,dc=domain,dc=com' -samid user -upn jsmith@domain.com -fn john -ln smith -display 'user' -pwd password.

D. dsadd user 'cn=jsmith,cn=users,dc=domain,dc=com' -samid user -upn jsmith@domain.com -fn john -ln smith -display 'user' -pwd.

---

7. What steps are necessary in creating a shared mandatory profile to ensure company employees will have the same desktop?

A. Create a temporary user account, configure it, and change the profile from NTUSER.DAT to NTUSER.MAN.

B. Add the path to the profile in the account.

C. Create a local user template.

D. Create a user template in Active Directory.

E. Create a temporary user account, configure it, and change the profile from NTUSER.DAT to NTUSER.MND.

8. Which of the following statements are true about group nesting?

A. Group nesting isn't used to grant permissions to groups.

B. The domain involved has to be in native mode.

C. The domain involved has to be in mixed mode.

D. Group nesting is the placement of a group into another group.

---

9. If you needed to only give a specific group remote access to a number of terminal servers, what would you do?

A. Create a domain and move all the servers into it. Create a GPO and link it to the domain. Configure the GPO to allow the members in the group to log on locally.

B. Create a GPO and move all the servers into it. Create another GPO and link it to the GPO. Configure the GPO to allow the members in the group to log on locally.

C. Create an OU and move all the servers into it. Create a GPO and link it to the domain. Configure the GPO to allow the members in the group to log on locally.

D. Create an OU and move all the servers into it. Create a GPO and link it to the OU. Configure the GPO to allow the members in the group to log on locally.

10. You Windows Server 2003 has a disabled local Administrator account. After starting up in Safe Mode, what steps can you take to reactivate that Administrative account?

A. Click Start, right-click My Computer, and then click Explore.

B. Expand Local Users and Groups, click Users, right-click Administrator in the right pane, and then click Properties.

C. Click to clear the Account is disabled check box, and then click OK.

D. Click Start, right-click My Computer, and then click Manage.

E. Expand Local Users and Groups, click Users, right-click Guest in the right pane, and then click Properties.

---

11. You have just finished editing the default domain policy for your domain, but you do not want this policy to apply to Administrators. What should you do to prevent this?

A. Delete the user or group from the policy.

B. Add the user or group if you need to.

C. Click the administrators group (or other group or user) that you do not want the policy to apply to. In the Permissions windows, click to select the Deny check box for the Apply Group Policy permission.

D. Open Active Directory Users and Computers and right-click the name of the domain where the policy is applied, and then click Properties. Click the Group Policy tab and select the default domain policy. Click Properties, and then click the Security tab.

E. Open Active Directory Domains and Trusts and right-click the name of the domain where the policy is applied, and then click Properties. Click the Group Policy tab and select the default domain policy. Click Properties, and then click the Security tab.

12. What should you do if you want to install support tools on a 2003 domain controller?

A. Right-click the Suptools.msi file in the Support\Tools folder, and then click Install.

B. Right-click the Suptools.mst file in the Support\Tools folder, and then click Open.

C. Right-click the Suptools.msc file in the Support\Tools folder, and then click Run.

D. Right-click the Suptools.asc file in the Tools folder, and then click Run.

---

13. Which of the following is the proper way to format the netdom command if you are attempting to reset the password on a Windows 2003 domain controller named svr12 in a domain called tiger?

A. netdom resetpswd /s:srv12 /ud:domain\User /pd:*

B. netdom resetpwd /s:srv12 /ud:tiger\User /pd:*

C. netdom resetpwd /s:Servertwelve /ud:tgr\User /pd:*

D. netdom resetpwd /s:server /ud:tiger\User /pd:*

14. When nesting global groups, where should they be placed to give them rights locally and avoid unnecessary overhead?

A. In another global group

B. In a universal group

C. In a distribution group

D. In a domain local group

---

15. If you run the command secedit/refreshpolicy user_policy/enforce on a domain controller, what will result?

A. Password policy changes are enforced immediately for users in the domain

B. Password policy changes are enforced immediately for computers in the domain

C. Password policy changes are enforced after five minutes for users in the domain

D. Password policy changes are enforced after five minutes for computers in the domain

Chapter 2: Review Answers

1. You suspect that a user's profile or their account might be corrupted. What actions can you take to figure out which is the case?

***A. Create a new user account and give it the same rights and group memberships or associations as the account that has the profile that you suspect may be damaged.**

***B. Copy the user settings in the suspect profile to the profile of the newly created user account. Click Start, point to Control Panel, and then click the System applet.**

C. Create an administrative account and give it the same rights and group memberships or associations as the account that has the profile that you suspect may be damaged.

***D. Click Advanced, and then under User Profiles, click Settings. Under Profiles stored on this computer, click the suspect user profile, and then click Copy To. In the Copy To dialog box, click Browse. Locate the drive:\Documents and Settings\user_profile folder, where drive is the drive where Windows is installed, and where user_profile is the name of the newly created user profile, and then click OK. Click OK, click Yes to overwrite the folder contents, and then click OK two times. Use the newly-created user account to log on.**

Explanation: If you want to check to see if a user account has a damaged profile, create a new user account. Give it the same rights and group memberships or associations as the account that has the profile that you suspect may be damaged. Copy the user settings in the suspect profile to the profile of the newly created user account. Click Start, point to Control Panel, and then click the System applet. Click Advanced, and then under User Profiles, click Settings. Under Profiles stored on this computer, click the suspect user profile, and then click Copy To.

In the Copy To dialog box, click Browse. Locate the drive:\Documents and Settings\user_profile folder, where drive is the drive where Windows is installed, and where user_profile is the name of the newly created user profile, and then click OK. Click OK, click Yes to overwrite the folder contents, and then click OK two times. Use the newly-created user account to log on. If you experience the same errors that led you to question the suspect user profile, the user profile is damaged. If you do not experience any errors, it is the user account that is damaged.

2. How can you configure a user account so that it can be trusted for delegation in Windows Server 2003?

A. Double-click the user that you want to configure.

***B. Right-click the user that you want to configure, and then click Properties.**

***C. Click the Delegation tab, click Trust this user for delegation to any service (Kerberos only) , and then click OK.**

D. In Active Directory Sites and Services, click Users.

***E. In Active Directory Users and Computers, click Users.**

Explanation: If you want to configure a user account so that it can be trusted for delegation in Windows Server 2003, click Start, click Control Panel, double-click Administrative Tools, and then double-click Active Directory Users and Computers. In the console tree, click Users. Right-click the user that you want to configure, and then click Properties. Click the Delegation tab, click Trust this user for delegation to any service (Kerberos only) , and then click OK.

---

3. Which of the following options gives you the ability to log on even with a disabled local Administrator account on a 2003 Server?

A. Run the Defragment Tool

***B. Use Recovery Console**

***C. Start Windows 2003 in Safe Mode**

D. Boot from a network card that is PXE compliant

Explanation: To log on to Windows 2003 by using the disabled local Administrator account, start Windows in Safe mode. Even when the Administrator account is disabled, you are not prevented from logging on as Administrator in Safe mode. When you have logged on successfully in Safe mode, re-enable the Administrator account, and then log on again. Start the computer, and then press the F8 key when the Power On Self Test (POST) is complete. From the Windows Advanced Options menu, select Safe Mode. Log on to Windows as Administrator.

If you are prompted to do so, click to select an item in the Why did the computer shut down unexpectedly list, and then click OK. On the message that states Windows is running in safe mode, click OK. Click Start, right-click My Computer, and then click Manage. Expand Local Users and Groups, click Users, right-click Administrator in the right pane, and then click Properties. Click to clear the Account is disabled check box, and then click OK. You can also use the recovery console to access the computer even if the local Administrator account is disabled. Disabling the local Administrator account does not prevent you from logging on to the recovery console as Administrator.

4. Which of the following does a remote administrator have control over by using regedit?

A. The number of persons who can be denied access

***B. How frequently the failed attempts counter is reset**

***C. The number of failed attempts before future attempts are denied**

D. The number of persons who can be allowed access

Explanation: Remote access server administrators can adjust the number of failed attempts before future attempts are denied as well as how frequently the failed attempts counter is reset.

---

5. What are some of the requirements for installing Microsoft Group Policy Management Console?

A. Either Windows Server 2003 or Windows XP Professional.

***B. The QFE Q326469 hotfix, which updates your version of gpedit.dll to 5.1.2600.1186.**

C. Windows Advanced Server 2003 and Windows XP Home with Service Pack 1 (SP1) and the Microsoft .NET Framework.

***D. Either Windows Server 2003 or Windows XP Professional with Service Pack 1 (SP1) and the Microsoft .NET Framework.**

Explanation: Microsoft Group Policy Management Console (GPMC) is a new tool in 2003 Server for Group Policy management. It provides a user interface for ease of use, backups/restores GPOs, imports/exports GPOs and Windows Management Instrumentation filters. it simplifies management of Group Policy security. The requirements to install GPMC aren't that demanding. You need either Windows Server 2003 or Windows XP Professional with Service Pack 1 (SP1) and the Microsoft .NET Framework. You also need the QFE Q326469 hotfix, which updates your version of gpedit.dll to 5.1.2600.1186. This QFE is included with GPMC, and GPMC setup will prompt you to install it.

6. Using the dsadd command, which of the following would create an account in the domain domain.com for John Smith with a password of password?

A. dsadd user 'cn=jsmith,cn=users' -samid user -upn jsmith -fn john -ln smith -display 'user' -pwd password.

B. dsadd user 'dc=domain,dc=com' -samid user -upn domain.com -fn john -ln smith -display 'user' -pwd password.

***C. dsadd user 'cn=jsmith,cn=users,dc=domain,dc=com' -samid user -upn jsmith@domain.com -fn john -ln smith -display 'user' -pwd password.**

D. dsadd user 'cn=jsmith,cn=users,dc=domain,dc=com' -samid user -upn jsmith@domain.com -fn john -ln smith -display 'user' -pwd.

Explanation: To create a user account by using dsadd user, from a command prompt, type dsadd user UserDomainName [-samid SAMName] [-upn UPN] [-fn FirstName] [-ln LastName] [-display DisplayName] [-pwd {Password|*}] Use ' ' if there is a space in any variable. For example, dsadd user 'cn=jsmith,cn=users,dc=domain,dc=com' -samid user -upn jsmith@domain.com -fn john -ln smith -display 'user' -pwd password.

---

7. What steps are necessary in creating a shared mandatory profile to ensure company employees will have the same desktop?

***A. Create a temporary user account, configure it, and change the profile from NTUSER.DAT to NTUSER.MAN**

***B. Add the path to the profile in the account**

C. Create a local user template

***D. Create a user template in Active Directory**

E. Create a temporary user account, configure it, and change the profile from NTUSER.DAT to NTUSER.MND

Explanation: First, create a temporary user account, configure it, and change the profile from NTUSER.DAT to NTUSER.MAN. Then create a user template in Active Directory, and add the path to the profile in the account.

8. Which of the following statements are true about group nesting?
A. Group nesting isn't used to grant permissions to groups
***B. The domain involved has be in native mode**
C. The domain involved has be in mixed mode
***D. Group nesting is the placement of a group into another group**

Explanation: Group nesting is the placement of a group or groups into another group. Generally, you would do this to grant permissions to the groups nested. For example, a global group would be nested in a domain local group to give the global group the permissions of the domain local group. Native mode has to be set for the domain or domains involved.

---

9. If you needed to only give a specific group remote access to a number of terminal servers, what would you do?
A. Create a domain and move all the servers into it. Create a GPO and link it to the domain. Configure the GPO to allow the members in the group to log on locally.
B. Create a GPO and move all the servers into it. Create another GPO and link it to the GPO. Configure the GPO to allow the members in the group to log on locally.
C. Create an OU and move all the servers into it. Create a GPO and link it to the domain. Configure the GPO to allow the members in the group to log on locally.
***D. Create an OU and move all the servers into it. Create a GPO and link it to the OU. Configure the GPO to allow the members in the group to log on locally.**

Explanation: Creating an OU and moving all the servers into it will keep access restricted to just those servers. Creating a GPO, linking it to the OU, configuring the GPO to allow the members in the group to log on locally provides the proper permissions for them to gain access to the terminal servers.

10. You Windows Server 2003 has a disabled local Administrator account. After starting up in Safe Mode, what steps can you take to reactivate that Administrative account?
A. Click Start, right-click My Computer, and then click Explore.
***B. Expand Local Users and Groups, click Users, right-click Administrator in the right pane, and then click Properties.**
***C. Click to clear the Account is disabled check box, and then click OK.**
***D. Click Start, right-click My Computer, and then click Manage.**
E. Expand Local Users and Groups, click Users, right-click Guest in the right pane, and then click Properties.

Explanation: To log on to Windows 2003 by using the disabled local Administrator account, start Windows in Safe mode. Even when the Administrator account is disabled, you are not prevented from logging on as Administrator in Safe mode. When you have logged on successfully in Safe mode, re-enable the Administrator account, and then log on again. Start the computer, and then press the F8 key when the Power On Self Test (POST) is complete. From the Windows Advanced Options menu, select Safe Mode. Log on to Windows as Administrator.

If you are prompted to do so, click to select an item in the Why did the computer shut down unexpectedly list, and then click OK. On the message that states Windows is running in safe mode, click OK. Click Start, right-click My Computer, and then click Manage. Expand Local Users and Groups, click Users, right-click Administrator in the right pane, and then click Properties. Click to clear the Account is disabled check box, and then click OK. You can also use the recovery console to access the computer even if the local Administrator account is disabled. Disabling the local Administrator account does not prevent you from logging on to the recovery console as Administrator.

11. You have just finished editing the default domain policy for your domain, but you do not want this policy to apply to Administrators. What should you do to prevent this?
A. Delete the user or group from the policy.

***B. Add the user or group if you need to.**

***C. Click the administrators group (or other group or user) that you do not want the policy to apply to. In the Permissions windows, click to select the Deny check box for the Apply Group Policy permission.**

***D. Open Active Directory Users and Computers and right-click the name of the domain where the policy is applied, and then click Properties. Click the Group Policy tab and select the default domain policy. Click Properties, and then click the Security tab.**

E. Open Active Directory Domains and Trusts and right-click the name of the domain where the policy is applied, and then click Properties. Click the Group Policy tab and select the default domain policy. Click Properties, and then click the Security tab.

Explanation: If you want to prevent group policies from applying to Administrator accounts, click Start, point to Administrative Tools, and then click Active Directory Users and Computers. In the left console tree, right-click the name of the domain where the policy is applied, and then click Properties. Click the Group Policy tab. Click the group policy object that you do not want to apply to administrators. By default, the only policy that is listed in the window is the Default Domain Policy. Click Properties, and then click the Security tab. If the group or user who you do not want policies to apply does not appear in the list, click Add. Click the domain where the account resides.

Find the account, and then click it in the list. Click Add, and then click OK. Click the administrators group (or other group or user) to which you do not want the policy to apply. In the Permissions window, click to select the Deny check box for the Apply Group Policy permission. This prevents the group policy object from being accessed and applied to the selected group or user account.

12. What should you do if you want to install support tools on a 2003 domain controller?

***A. Right-click the Suptools.msi file in the Support\Tools folder, and then click Install.**

B. Right-click the Suptools.mst file in the Support\Tools folder, and then click Open.
C. Right-click the Suptools.msc file in the Support\Tools folder, and then click Run.
D. Right-click the Suptools.asc file in the Tools folder, and then click Run.

Explanation: You can use Netdom.exe to reset a machine account password. You will need to install the Support Tools for Windows Server 2003 on the domain controller whose password you want to reset. These tools are located in the Tools folder in the Support folder on the Windows Server 2003 CD-ROM. To install these tools, right-click the Suptools.msi file in the Support\Tools folder, and then click Install. If you want to reset the password for a Windows domain controller, you must stop the Kerberos Key Distribution Center service and set its startup type to Manual. After you restart and verify that the password has been successfully reset, you can restart the Kerberos Key Distribution Center service and set its startup type back to Automatic. This forces the domain controller with the incorrect computer account password to contact another domain controller for a Kerberos ticket. Click Start, Run, and type cmd and click OK.

Now type the following command: netdom resetpwd /s:server /ud:domain\User /pd:* The /s:server is the name of the domain controller to use for setting the machine account password. The /ud:domain\User is the user account that makes the connection with the domain you specified in the /s parameter. This must be in domain\User format. If this parameter is omitted, the current user account is used. The /pd:* specifies the password of the user account that is specified in the /ud parameter. Use an asterisk (*) to be prompted for the password. For example, the local domain controller computer is Server1 and the peer Windows domain controller is Server2. If you run Netdom.exe on Server1 with the following parameters, the password is changed locally and is simultaneously written on Server2, and replication propagates the change to other domain controllers: netdom resetpwd /s:server2 /ud:mydomain\administrator /pd:* Restart the server whose password was changed. In this example, this is Server1.

13. Which of the following is the proper way to format the netdom command if you are attempting to reset the password on a Windows 2003 domain controller named svr12 in a domain called tiger?

A. netdom resetpswd /s:srv12 /ud:domain\User /pd:*

B. netdom resetpwd /s:srv12 /ud:tiger\User /pd:

C. netdom resetpwd /s:Servertwelve /ud:tgr\User /pd:*

D. netdom resetpwd /s:server /ud:tiger\User /pd:*

Explanation: You can use Netdom.exe to reset a machine account password. You will need to install the Support Tools for Windows Server 2003 on the domain controller whose password you want to reset. These tools are located in the Tools folder in the Support folder on the Windows Server 2003 CD-ROM. To install these tools, right-click the Suptools.msi file in the Support\Tools folder, and then click Install. If you want to reset the password for a Windows domain controller, you must stop the Kerberos Key Distribution Center service and set its startup type to Manual. After you restart and verify that the password has been successfully reset, you can restart the Kerberos Key Distribution Center service and set its startup type back to Automatic.

This forces the domain controller with the incorrect computer account password to contact another domain controller for a Kerberos ticket. Click Start, Run, and type cmd and click OK. Now type the following command: netdom resetpwd /s:server /ud:domain\User /pd:* The /s:server is the name of the domain controller to use for setting the machine account password. The /ud:domain\User is the user account that makes the connection with the domain you specified in the /s parameter. This must be in domain\User format. If this parameter is omitted, the current user account is used. The /pd:* specifies the password of the user account that is specified in the /ud parameter. Use an asterisk (*) to be prompted for the password.

For example, the local domain controller computer is Server1 and the peer Windows domain controller is Server2. If you run Netdom.exe on Server1 with the following parameters, the password is changed locally and is simultaneously written on Server2, and replication propagates the change to other domain controllers: netdom resetpwd /s:server2 /ud:mydomain\administrator /pd:* Restart the server whose password was changed. In this example, this is Server1.

15. When nesting global groups, where should they be placed to give them rights locally and avoid unnecessary overhead?

A. In another global group
B. In a universal group
C. In a distribution group
***D. In a domain local group**

Explanation: When nesting, place global and universal groups in domain local groups. This allows the global and universal groups to gain the rights that the domain local group possesses. Global groups can only contain user accounts, computer accounts, and global groups from the same domain. Universal groups could work but would increase overhead. Distribution groups cannot be used for security purposes.

---

15. If you run the command secedit/refreshpolicy user_policy/enforce on a domain controller, what will result?

***A. Password policy changes are enforced immediately for users in the domain**
B. Password policy changes are enforced immediately for computers in the domain
C. Password policy changes are enforced after five minutes for users in the domain
D. Password policy changes are enforced after five minutes for computers in the domain

Explanation: The command secedit/refreshpolicy user_policy/enforce, when run on a domain controller, will enforce password policy changes immediately for users in the domain. To accomplish the same thing for computers in the domain, run the secedit/refreshpolicy machine_policy/enforce command. Secedit is used to immediately refresh policy; Windows 2000 domain controllers will refresh after five minutes without any extra administrative action.

Managing and Maintaining Access to Resources

The objective of this chapter is to provide the reader with an understanding of the following:

3.1 Configure access to shared folders

3.1.1 Manage shared folder permissions

3.2 Troubleshoot Terminal Services

3.2.1 Diagnose and resolve issues related to Terminal Services security

3.2.2 Diagnose and resolve issues related to client access to Terminal Services

3.3 Configure file system permissions

3.3.1 Verify effective permissions when granting permissions

3.3.2 Change ownership of files and folders

3.4 Troubleshoot access to files and shared folders

Chapter 3: Access to Resources

Introduction:

Information Technology personnel working with Windows Server 2003 networks always face the task of assigning and maintaining access to network files and folders. The following chapter will show you how to configure shared folder access, manage shared folder permissions, troubleshoot Terminal Service error messages and configure File system permissions. Make certain you do not get user rights confused with permissions. User rights define capabilities at the local level and permissions are used to grant access to objects such as files, folders, printers and additional Active Directory objects.

Getting Ready Questions

1. What is the default permission for shares on Windows Server 2003?
2. Do share permissions apply to terminal service clients?
3. What are the two types of security modes when Terminal Services has been installed in Application mode?
4. What net command can be used to view open sessions on a computer?
5. Can an administrator give ownership of a file to a user?

Getting Ready Answers

1. READ the default permission given to shares created on Windows Server 2003.
2. Share Permissions do not apply to terminal service clients. The NTFS file system or access control should be used to set share permissions instead.
3. Terminal server has two separate security modes they are when Terminal Server has been installed in the Application mode:
   - Full Security – This mode will provide the most security in the Windows Server 2003 environment.
   - Relaxed Security – This mode is commonly used to allow legacy applications (pre-Windows 2000) to run. It allows the system registry to be edited.
4. The net session command can be used to view open sessions on a computer.
5. No. An administrator can give Take Ownership permission to a user. However, the user must assume ownership. Ownership itself cannot be given.

User Right Administration

When a user account is created, specific capabilities can be granted to the user. To keep administration simplified, generally these capabilities are assigned by making the user account a member of a group or groups. When the account is assigned to a group, the account gains all the capabilities assigned to the group. Capabilities can be assigned to user accounts individually, or to a group so that all members gain the capability through their group membership.

There are four different types of capabilities that can be assigned to an account:

- **Privileges** – a type of user right that gives permission for a user account to perform specific administrative tasks, such as the right to shut down a server.
- **Logon rights** – a type of user right that gives logon permission to a user account. An example of this is the ability to logon to a system locally, or remotely.
- **Built-in** – this type of user right is assigned to groups and is included in the automatic capabilities of the group. These capabilities are predefined and unchangeable, but they can be delegated to users who manage objects, OUs or other containers within Active Directory. An example of this is the capability to create, delete and manage user accounts which is assigned by default to members of the built-in Administrator or Account Operator groups.
- **Access permissions** – Most normally referred to as permissions, rather than rights, it is a specific type of user right that specifies what action can be performed on a particular network resource. Access permissions can be

assigned to users, computer and groups, and include such actions as the ability to read a file or the ability to create a folder.

There are many different types of built-in groups:

- **Account Operators –** Members can administer domain user and group accounts.
- **Administrators** – Members have complete and unrestricted access to computer/domain.

> **NOTE:** Local accounts that are created on the local computer are created without passwords and are added to the Administrators group by default. If this is a concern, Security Configuration Manager allows you to control membership of the Administrators (or any other group) with the Restricted Groups policy.

- **Backup Operators** can back-up as well as restore any file on a computer or server. Members of this group cannot change any security setting on the machine, although they can override any security restrictions for the sole purpose of backing up or restoring files.
- **Guests** have the same access as members of the Users Group (see below) by default, except for the Guest Account which is restricted further.
- **Incoming Forest Trust Builders** can create incoming, one-way trusts to the forest.
- **Interactive** – Contains users who are currently logged on locally to the computer. If this server was upgraded from a previous Windows operating system (such as Windows NT 4.0), then this group is added to the Power Users group to allow access to legacy software.
- **Network** holds all users who access the system remotely. This is a system group; membership is assigned and removed dynamically.
- **Network Configuration Operators** have some administrative privileges to manage configuration of networking features.
- **Performance Log Users** have remote access to enable them to schedule logging of performance counters on the computer.
- **Power Users** – Member of this group have higher permissions than those of the User Group. They can perform elevated tasks, except tasks explicitly given to Network Administrators. Power Users can make printer changes, have Control Panel access, can stop and restart services and install software.

> **NOTE:** To allow applications to run that may have backward compatibility issues after the upgrade process from NT 4.0 to Windows Server 2003 the Restricted Users group is by default put into the Power Users Group.

- **Pre-Windows 2000 Compatible Access** allows read access on all users and groups in the domain (for backward compatibility).
- **Print Operators** can administer domain printers.

- **Remote Desktop Users** are granted the right to logon remotely.
- **Replicator** supports file replication in a domain.
- **Server Operators** can administer domain servers.
- **Terminal Server User** – Any user in this group can access applications that are installed and running on the Terminal Server in Application mode (not remote Administration Mode). Any program that a user can run in WindowsNT 4.0 will run for a Terminal Server User in Windows 2000, Windows XP Professional, or a member of the Windows Server 2003 family.
- **Users** – The most secure by default and lowest level of security. Clients belonging to this group cannot, by default, change any operating system setting. The only software members of the User Group can use is administrator-installed Windows logo software such as Windows XP, Windows 2000, Windows Server 2000, Windows Server 2003 or Microsoft Office 2000. Legacy software cannot, by default, be run by members of this group, nor can the operating systems Windows 95 or Windows 98. The members of this group would have to be given Power User rights or the User Group would have to have its privileges elevated to a higher level.

  - The User Group members also have control over their local profile folder, and their own portion of the registry key HKEY_CURRENT_USER, and locally created groups.

NOTE: Legacy Applications that run on the network may need the anonymous access permission applied in order to function. Alternately, you may change the Network Access to allow the Everyone Group permissions to apply to anonymous users. This is because, in the Windows Server 2003 and Windows XP Professional software operating systems the Anonymous group is no longer a member of the Everyone group.

3.1 Configure access to shared folders

Administrators always face the arduous task of assigning access to folders that are on the network. There are three basic ways that you can assign permissions to folders in Windows Server 2003. Using the Windows Explorer, using the Shared Folders Microsoft Management Console (MMC) or using the command line. If you use the Command line or Windows Explorer to configure permissions, you can only do this locally. If you use the **Share Folders MMC,** you can set permissions both locally and on remote computers. In order to assign permissions to folders, you must be logged on as a user that is a member of the Power Users Group, Administrators Group or Server Operator Group. Use the steps below to configure sharing on folders.

3.1.1 Sharing Folders using Windows Explorer

To share folders using Windows Explorer, open Windows Explorer on a Windows Server 2003 by clicking on **Start**, select **All Programs**, click on Accessories and then choose **Windows Explorer**. Locate the folder you wish to share and right-click on it. A shortcut menu appears (Figure 3.1).

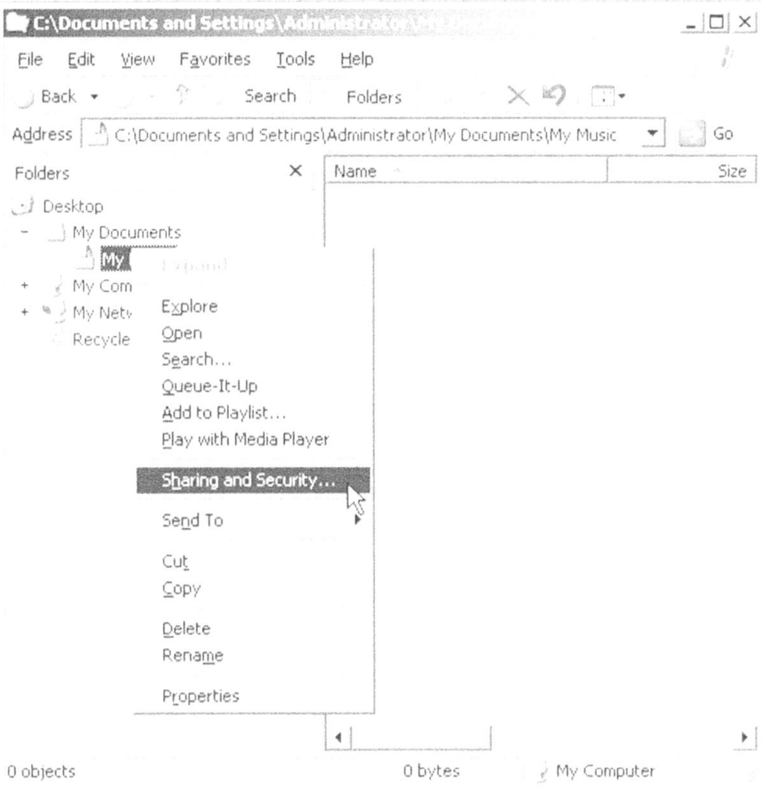

Figure 3–1: Sharing and Security Shortcut Menu.

Select the **Sharing and Security...** option. By default, the **Sharing** tab should appear (Figure 3.2). Choose the **Share this Folder** option. Enter a name for the share and then enter a description for the share if you wish. Next, you can set the **User limit** and **Permissions** for clients who will need to access this folder over the network.

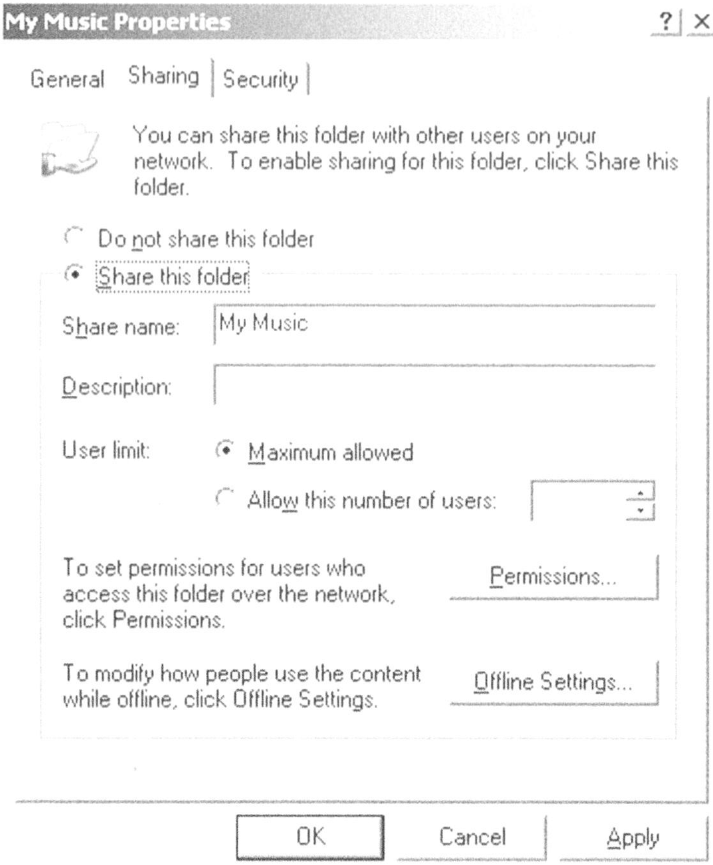

Figure 3–2: Sharing the Folder.

The Permissions tab will open (Figure 3.3). Here you can add Groups or Users that need access to this folder. The default Group is the **Everyone** group and the default permissions are **Read**.

> **NOTE:** The Read permission, the most restrictive permission of the three available, is the default permission given to shares created on Windows Server 2003.

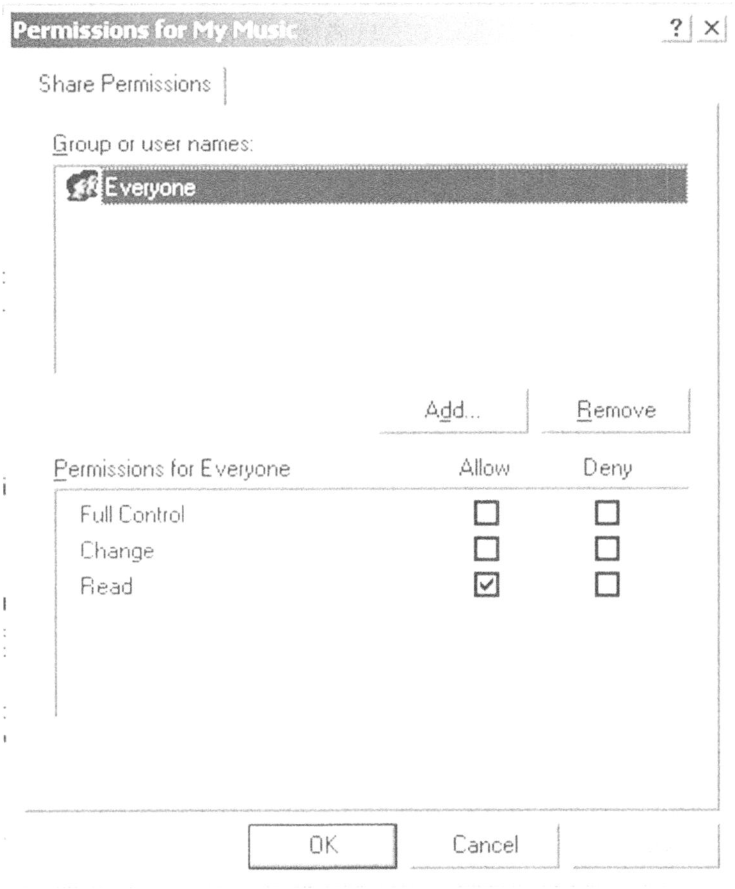

Figure 3–3: Assigning Share Permissions.

The **Read** option, by default allows everyone the ability to read the contents of the shared folder, which means they can view file names, subfolders and programs that are running and the data in each file. Other options are **Change** and **Full Control**. The **Change** option gives clients the ability to delete files and subfolders in the share, modify files by changing data in the file and add subfolders and files to the shared folder, as well as all the permission granted by the **Read** permission. The **Full Control** permission allows the group to have complete control over the shared folder, which means that they can read, write, delete and make any modification to the contents of the folder by default. Just click the **Add** or **Remove** button to change these settings. Click **OK** once the changes have been made and then click **Apply** and **OK** for the settings to take effect.

You also have the option of setting **Offline Settings** (Figure 3.4) for the folders and files. Offline settings are used by Administrators to make the contents of the share available offline. You can choose to allow the users to specify which files or folders are offline, allow all files and/or programs in the share are available offline or allow none of the files or programs inside the share to be available offline.

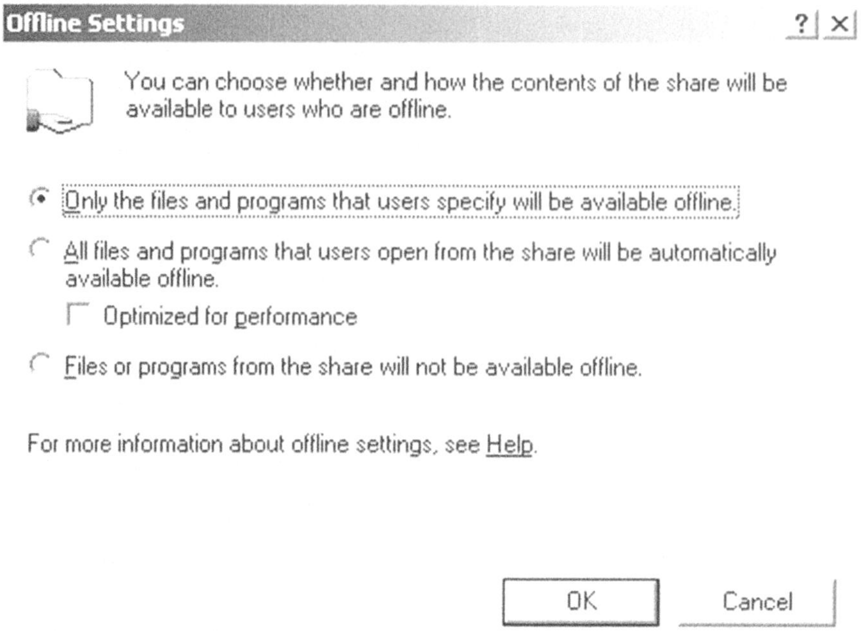

Figure 3–4: Specifying Offline Files.

3.1.2 Sharing Folders using Shared Folder Console

The Shared Folders Console can be opened by clicking on **Start**, selecting **Administrative Tools** and then choosing **Computer Management**.

Alternately, you can click on **Start** then select **Run** and then type **MMC**. Select **File** then **Add/Remove Snap-in**. Clicking the **Add** button brings up a list of available snap-ins. Select **Computer Management** from the list then select **Add**. The option to manage a local computer or another computer is available, as well as the option to have the selected computer to be changed when launching from the command line if you choose to save the console. Select the computer you wish to manage then click the **Finish** button. Choose **Close** then **OK** and the Computer Management console will be added in the Console Root.

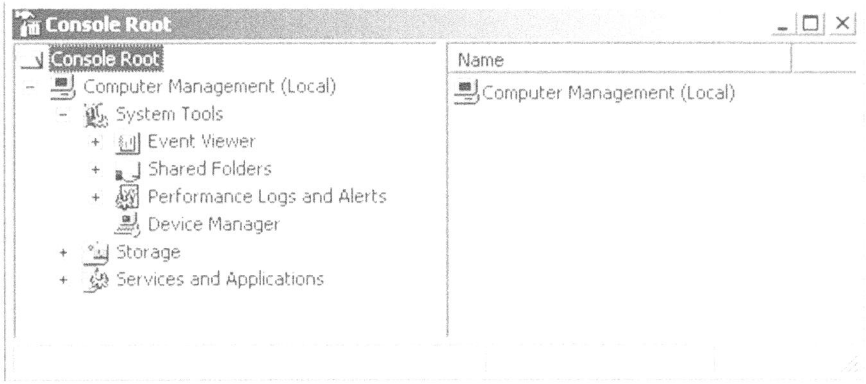

Figure 3–5: Shared Folders (MMC).

Shared Folders is located under **Computer Management | System Tools** (Figure 3.5). Select the **Shares** option from the **Shared Folders** list and open the **Action** menu then select the **New Share** button. If you do not do this, the **New Share** option is not available, so make certain you are on the **Shares** option under **Shared Folders**. The **Share a Folder Wizard** opens (Figure 3.6). The wizard is very self-explanatory, so we will quickly browse through the dialog screens just so you are familiar with them.

Figure 3–6: Share a Folder Wizard.

Clicking the **Next** button brings up the dialog box shown in Figure 3.7.

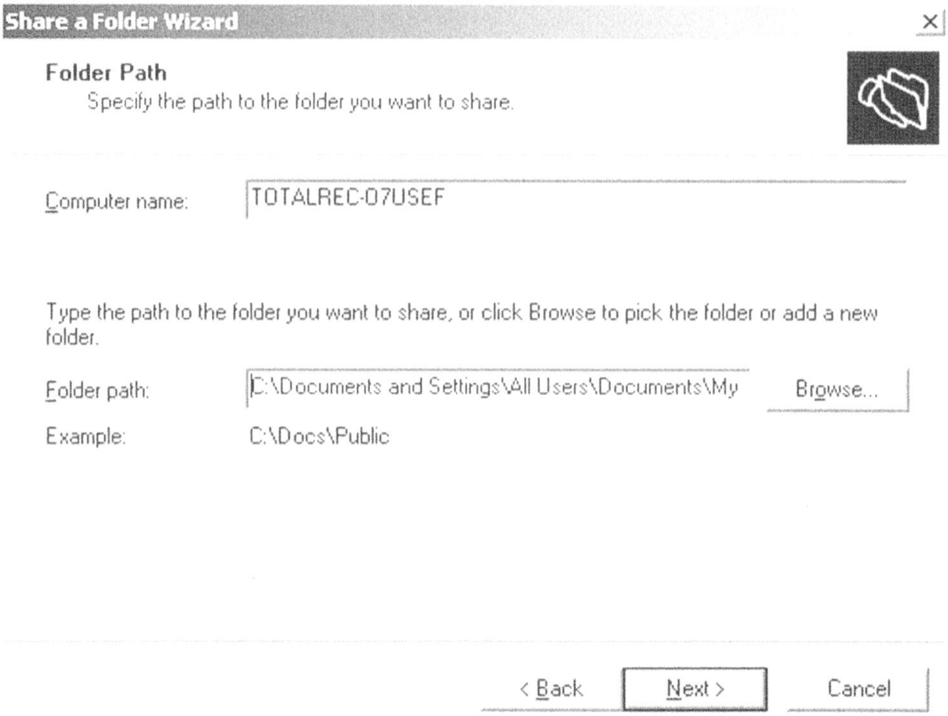

Figure 3–7: Specifying the folder to share.

As you can see, the computer name is preset and cannot be changed. You can select the folder you wish to share either by manually entering the name, or by clicking the **Browse** button and finding the folder from within its natural file structure.

Once these settings have been entered, click the **Next** button. A dialog screen appears (Figure 3.8) that allows you to give the share a user-friendly name.

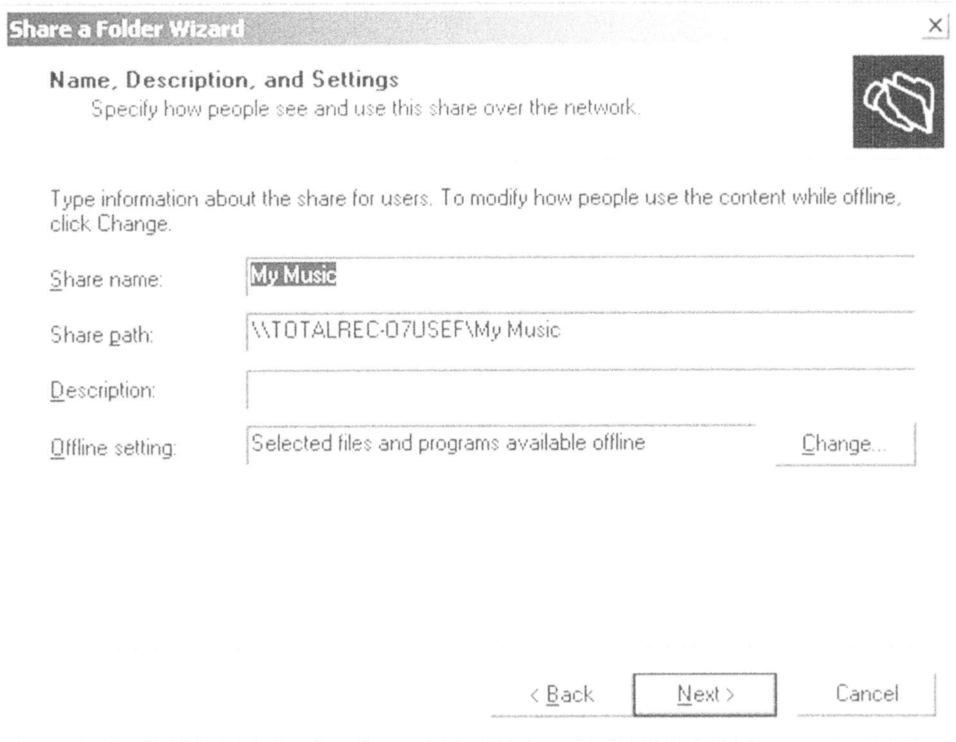

Figure 3–8: Naming the Share.

It is important to give the new shared folder a name that will be easily recognizable by your users. In our example, we are sharing the My Music folder. If, for example, the "My Music" folder contained the theme music used in television commercials for your company, you might want to give it the share name "Corporate Theme Music." As well, you have the option of supplying a more detailed description of contents in the **Description** text box. An example would be "Music used in television spots in Spring 2004."

Clicking the **Next** button brings up the dialog screen that will allow you to set the permissions to the shared folder (Figure 3.9).

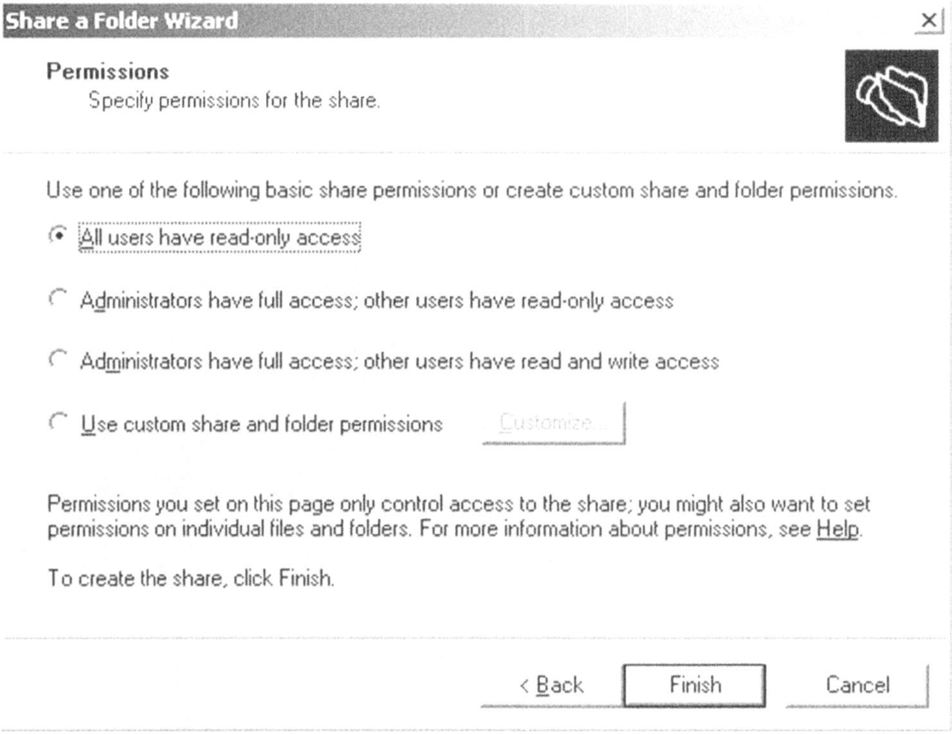

Figure 3–9: Share Permissions.

The default option is to allow all users (the **Everyone** group) the ability to have read-only access, the default setting for Windows Server 2003. The wizard allows you some other preset choices — you can chose to allow Administrators to have full access and all others to have read-only access or Administrators can have full access and all others can have read and write access. As well, you can set custom share and folder permissions by choosing the **Customize** option. If you select the **Customize** option then a small screen will appear that is identical to the one that is used in the Windows Explorer permission option (Figure 3.3). As mentioned earlier, this screen shows the default **Everyone** group with **Read** access. This can be changed by adding the Groups or Users you wish to give access to and then selecting the appropriate permissions. Once this has been completed just select the **OK** button and then **Finish**. The final dialog screen (Figure 3.10) appears.

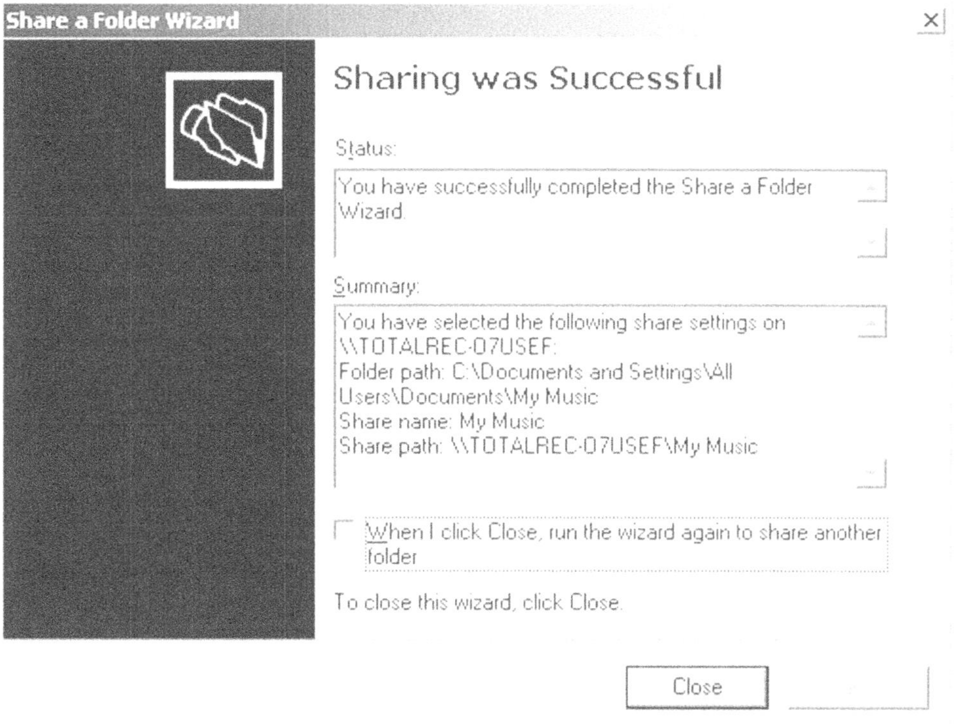

Figure 3–10: Completing the Sharing Wizard.

The last screen will appear stating that **Sharing was Successful** displays the status of the share and the summary of the share properties. The option to add another share is also available. If you select this option, then **Close**, the Share Wizard will start over again giving you the option to add more shares. Once you have completed your sharing tasks, the new share or shares will be shown in the left pane of the Shared Folders console.

3.1.3 Sharing Folders using the Command Line

To share a folder using the command line just open the command line by clicking on **Start | Run** | and entering **cmd**. Alternately, you can use **Start | All Programs | Accessories** then choose the **Command Prompt** option.

Once you are in the Command Prompt window, the syntax to use is the **net share** command. The net share command has numerous switches available, which allow advanced settings to be configured. Make sure you know your path to the folder you need to share before you type this command. To share a simple folder just type the following:

net share ***sharename=drive:path*** then press the **enter** key.

Additional **net share** switches are:

- **net share** ***sharename*** ***/USERS:number*** *or/* ***unlimited*** – This allows you to select the number of users who have access to this share or give unlimited users access to this share in numbers only.
- **net share** ***sharename*** **/grant:user [*****Read, Change*** **or** ***Full*****] permissions –** This syntax allows you to grant users access permissions.

To view all syntax available for the Net share command just type **net help share** at the command prompt. Once this command has completed successfully, you can close the command prompt.

Security Settings on Files and Folders

One of the things that always seems to confuse people when facing the exam is the different between Share Security and NTFS Security. If you look at Figure 3.2, you will note that there are two tabs—Sharing and Security. The permissions we have just assigned are the security permissions assigned to shared folders; in other words, they apply ONLY when data is accessed through a network connection (remotely). If the same folder is accessed locally, no restrictions apply.

The Security tab enforces NTFS Security. When a hard disk is formatted NTFS, specific access permissions can then be applied to folders AND files. It doesn't matter if the folder or the file is accessed via the network (through a share) or locally—the NTFS permissions are applied.

If a disk is formatted FAT (or FAT32), NTFS permissions do not exist. The Security tab will not appear in the Properties dialog box. As well, if a file or folder is copied or moved from an NTFS partition, where it has been assigned NTFS security permissions, to a partition formatted FAT or FAT32, the file (or copy of the file) will no longer have NTFS permissions assigned.

One last thing to note is the combination of the two permissions when accessing a shared folder across the network. Share permissions apply ONLY when the information is accessed remotely. NTFS permissions apply when the information is accessed locally or remotely. All explicitly allowed permissions are tallied and then the permissions explicitly denied permissions are removed. Because the permissions are combined, a user can find themselves in the unique permission of being able to modify a document when accessing it locally, but only being able to read it when accessing it across the network. This would happen when a user or group has been assigned the NTFS permission Change, but the Share permission Read.

As mentioned, NTFS permissions are assigned on the Security tab of the Properties dialog box (Figure 3.11).

The full list of NTFS Permissions are outlined in Table 3.1.

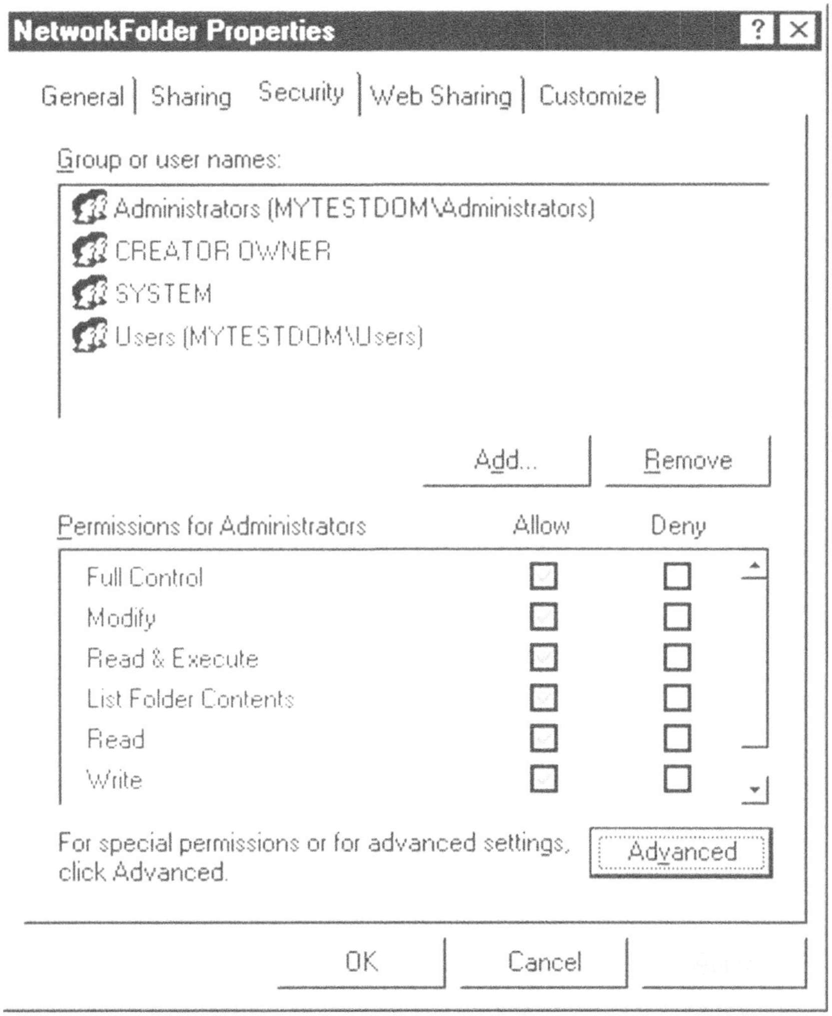

Figure 3–11: Assigning Access to Network Folders.

Permission	Description
Traverse Folder/Execute File	For folders: Traverse Folder allows or denies moving through folders to reach other files or folders, even if the user has no permissions for the traversed folders. (Applies to folders only.) Traverse folder takes effect only when the group or user is not granted the Bypass traverse checking user right in the Group Policy snap-in. (By default, the Everyone group is given the Bypass traverse checking user right.) For files: Execute File allows or denies running program files. (Applies to files only.) Setting the Traverse Folder permission on a folder does not automatically set the Execute File permission on all files within that folder.
List Folder/Read Data	List Folder allows or denies viewing file names and subfolder names within the folder. List Folder only affects the contents of that folder and does not affect whether the folder you are setting the permission on will be listed. (Applies to folders only.) Read Data allows or denies viewing data in files. (Applies to files only.)
Read Attributes	Allows or denies viewing the attributes of a file or folder, such as read-only and hidden. Attributes are defined by NTFS.
Read Extended Attributes	Allows or denies viewing the extended attributes of a file or folder. Extended attributes are defined by programs and may vary by program.
Create Files/Write Data	Create Files allows or denies creating files within the folder. (Applies to folders only). Write Data allows or denies making changes to the file and overwriting existing content. (Applies to files only.)
Create Folders/Append Data	Create Folders allows or denies creating folders within the folder. (Applies to folders only.) Append Data allows or denies making changes to the end of the file but not changing, deleting, or overwriting existing data. (Applies to files only.)
Write Attributes	Allows or denies changing the attributes of a file or folder, such as read-only or hidden. Attributes are defined by NTFS. The Write Attributes permission does not imply creating or deleting files or folders, it only includes the permission to make changes to the attributes of a file or folder. In order to allow (or deny) create or delete operations, see Create Files/Write Data, Create Folders/Append Data, Delete Subfolders and Files, and Delete.

Permission	Description
Write Extended Attributes	Allows or denies changing the extended attributes of a file or folder. Extended attributes are defined by programs and may vary by program. The Write Extended Attributes permission does not imply creating or deleting files or folders, it only includes the permission to make changes to the attributes of a file or folder. In order to allow (or deny) create or delete operations, see Create Files/Write Data, Create Folders/Append Data, Delete Subfolders and Files, and Delete.
Delete Subfolders and Files	Allows or denies deleting subfolders and files, even if the Delete permission has not been granted on the subfolder or file. (Applies to folders.)
Delete	Allows or denies deleting the file or folder. If you do not have Delete permission on a file or folder, you can still delete it if you have been granted Delete Subfolders and Files on the parent folder.
Read Permissions	Allows or denies reading permissions of the file or folder, such as Full Control, Read, and Write.
Change Permissions	Allows or denies changing permissions of the file or folder, such as Full Control, Read, and Write.
Take Ownership	Allows or denies taking ownership of the file or folder. The owner of a file or folder can always change permissions on it, regardless of any existing permissions that protect the file or folder.
Synchronize	Allows or denies different threads to wait on the handle for the file or folder and synchronize with another thread that may signal it. This permission applies only to multithreaded, multiprocess programs.

Table 3-1: Permissions.

As you are assigning permissions to a folder remember:

- If a folder is within a folder and you assign permissions to a parent folder, the child folder will inherit the parent folders permissions by default.
- If you choose to not allow the child folder the ability to inherit the parent folder permissions you can choose the **This folder only** in **Apply onto** settings as you are setting up the folder permissions. To access the shared folder permissions **right-click on the folder | Select Security | Select the Advanced option**. This is shown below in Figure 3.12.

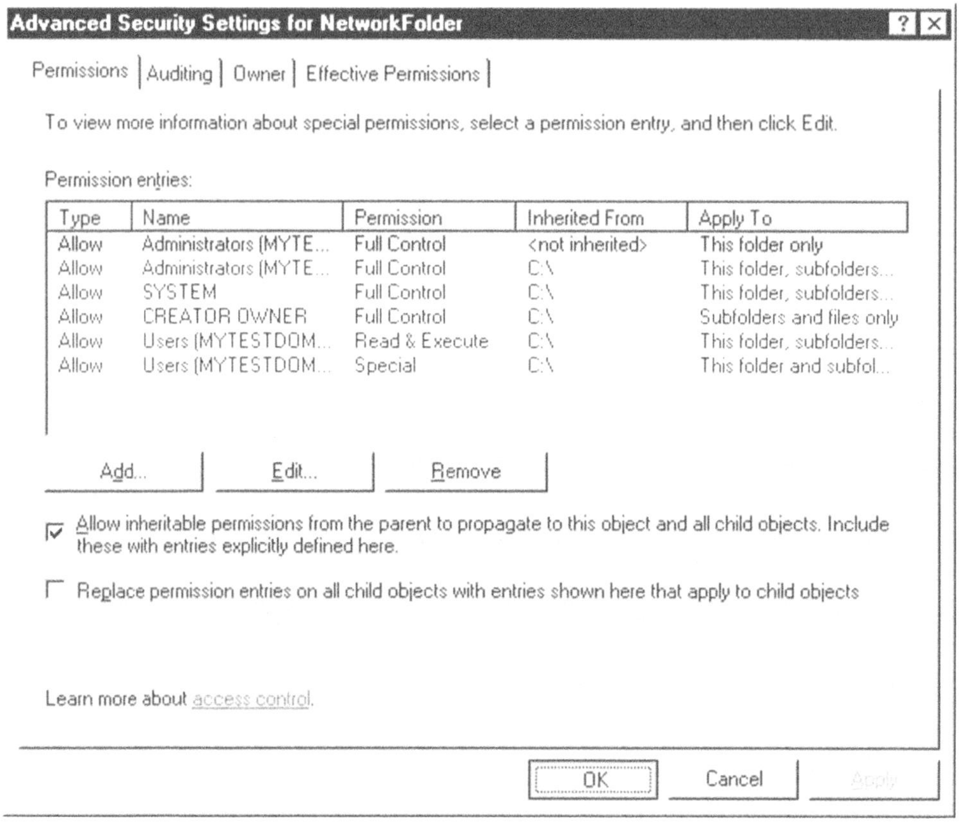

Figure 3–12: The Advanced Option (Folder Security).

> **NOTE:** Typically the **Allow** permission will always be overridden by the **Deny** permission unless the folder or file inherits conflicting settings from different parents. When this occurs, the setting inherited from the parent closest to the object in the subtree will have priority.

In cases where you want to prevent only certain files or subfolders from inheriting permissions you can use the following steps to stop the rights from being applied to the folders or files. Just right-click on the folder or file and click the **Properties** button | Click **Security** then choose the **Advanced** option. If you are unable to make changes to the boxes because they are shaded this means that the folder or file already has inherited permissions from the parent folder. Inherited permissions on folders or files can be changed in three various ways:

1. If you change the parent folder then the child folder will inherit the permissions.
2. Take the check mark out of the **Inherit from parent the permission entries that apply to child objects**.
3. Override the inherited permissions by choosing either **Allow** or **Deny**.

Clear the button that reads **Inherit from parent the permission entries that applies to the child objects. Include these with entries explicitly defined here** option. A dialog box like the one shown in Figure 3.13 below will appear and explain to you that once you have selected this option for this particular file or folder, none of the parent permission entries applied will be applied to this file or folder. If you are certain that you want to prevent this folder or file from inheriting permissions from the parent, click the **Remove** option.

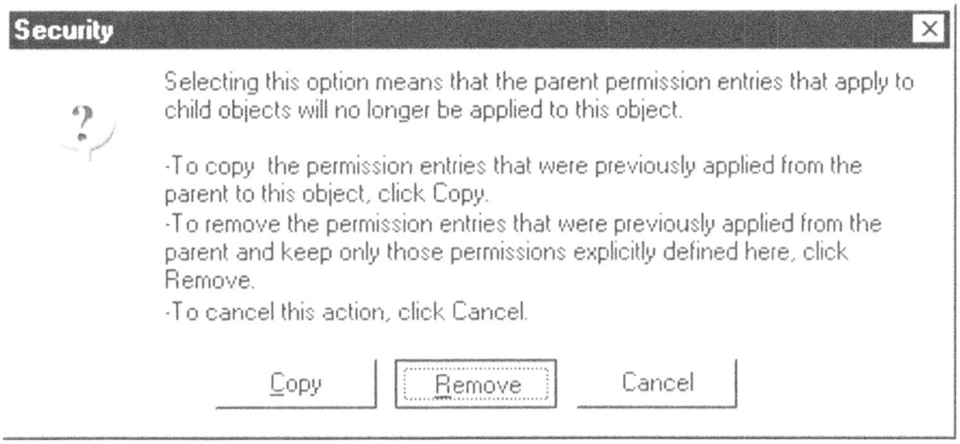

Figure 3–13: Removing the Parent Permission entries from a child object.

After the **Remove** option has been selected, the file or folder will not inherit permissions from the parent folder. The following screen will appear as shown in Figure 3.14.

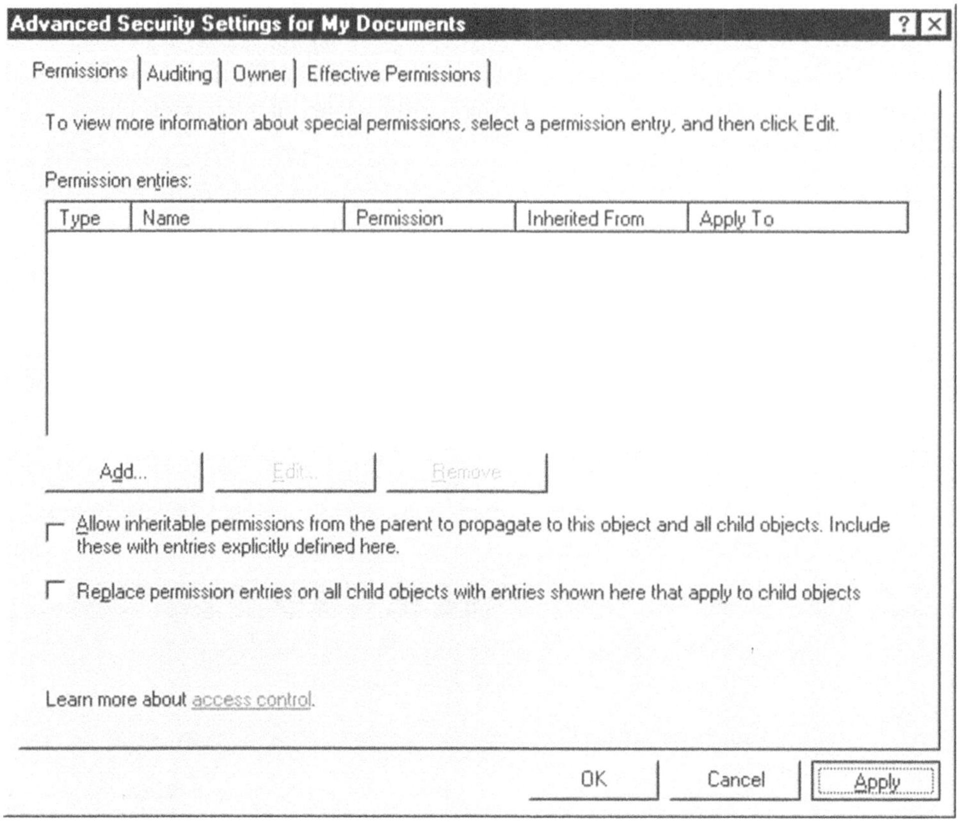

Figure 3–14: Permissions that have been removed from a file or folder.

After this screen has appeared and you select the **Apply** button, another dialog box will appear that makes you confirm that this is REALLY what you want to do (Figure 3.15). This is to prevent accidental removal of permissions from files and folders.

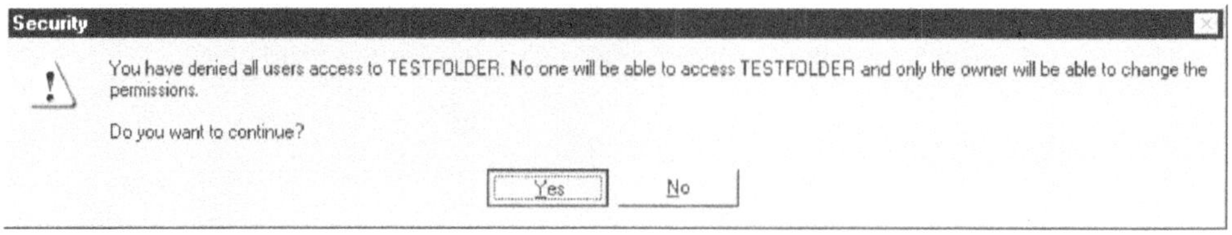

Figure 3–15: Final dialog box — Removing permissions from a file or folder.

Click **Yes** to remove the permissions from the folder or file. In this example, we removed all permissions from the folder named TestFolder so that the owner is the only user who can access the folder.

To reapply the permissions that had previously been removed from the file or folder, just right-click the file or folder, then click the **Advanced** option. In the **Permissions** tab, select the checkbox **Allow inheritable permissions from the parent to propagate to this object and all child objects**. **Include these with entries explicitly defined here** option. Then choose **Apply**. The permissions from the parent folder will reappear in the dialog box. After selecting **Apply**, click the **OK** button.

Security descriptors are used by Active Directory to store access controls permissions. These security descriptors are made up of two access control lists: the System access control list (SACLS) which is used to identify the groups and users that can be audited for object access, and the Discretionary access control list (DACLS) which is used to identify users and groups that try to access an object and are denied access.

To view this information, open **Active Directory Users and Computers**, click on the **View** menu, then select **Advanced Features** option. The **Security** tab will display this information.

Shared Folders

If you have forgotten which folders are being shared on a server or computer you can easily view the folders by using the **Shared Folders** console. This does not show you all folders on the computer, but it will help you out if you need information on shared folders.

> **NOTE:** Share Permissions do not apply to terminal service clients or users who log on locally. The NTFS file system or access control should be used to set share permissions instead.

To access this console, you will need to add the **Shared Folders** snap-in to an MMC console. If you need to refresh your memory on how to do this, we covered these steps in the section entitled "**Sharing Folders using Shared Folder Console**" under section 3.1.

A screen like the one shown in Figure 3.16 below will appear allowing you to select a Computer you wish to view shared folders.

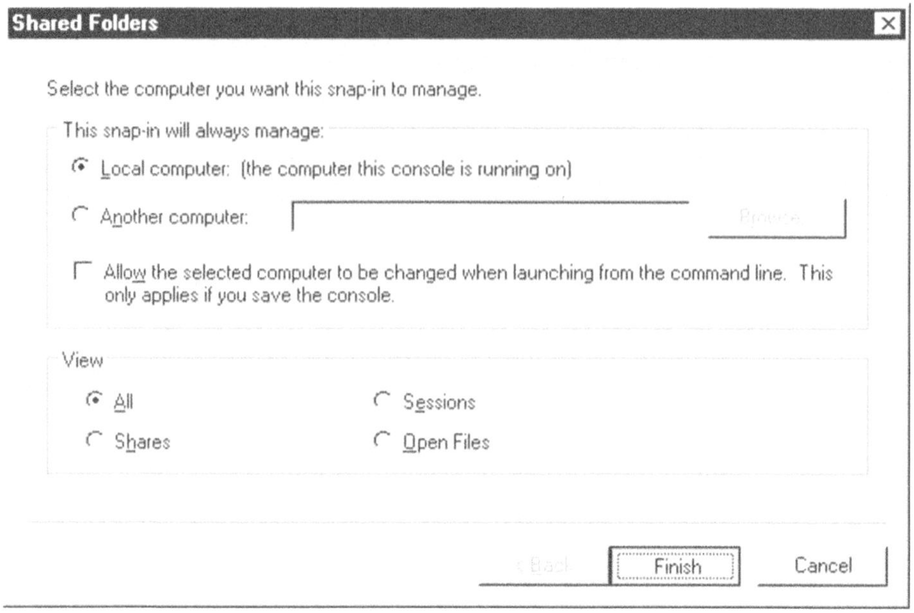

Figure 3–16: Viewing the Shared Folder Management Console.

Once the computer has been chosen, just click the **Finish** option and **Close** then **select OK**. The console will open and show the shared folder information as in Figure 3.17.

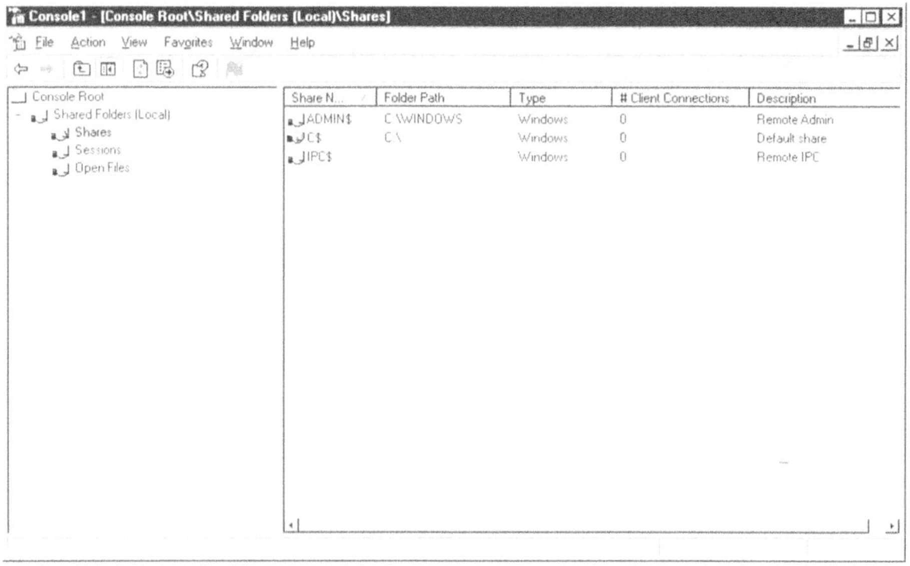

Figure 3–17: Viewing Shared Folders using the Shared Folders console.

The folder with the blue-sleeved arm under it lets me know that this folder is on my local computer and is being shared. To view the settings and permissions on the folders just go to the folder in Windows Explorer and right-click it. From the shortcut menu, select **Properties**.

> **NOTE**: Some folders are shared by default and it is not advisable to change the share permissions on folders without knowing in advance what repercussions the change will cause to the system.

Auditing Folders and Files

Files and folders may be audited by Network Administrators to enhance and secure network information. This is a great option to implement when you need to make certain documents and folders (let's say, Human Resource information stored in a folder on the network) remain secure. Group Policy can be used to audit files and folders. As well, auditing can be set up on files and folders by manually right-clicking the file or folder and selecting **Advanced** from the menu. The Auditing tab is shown in Figure 3.18.

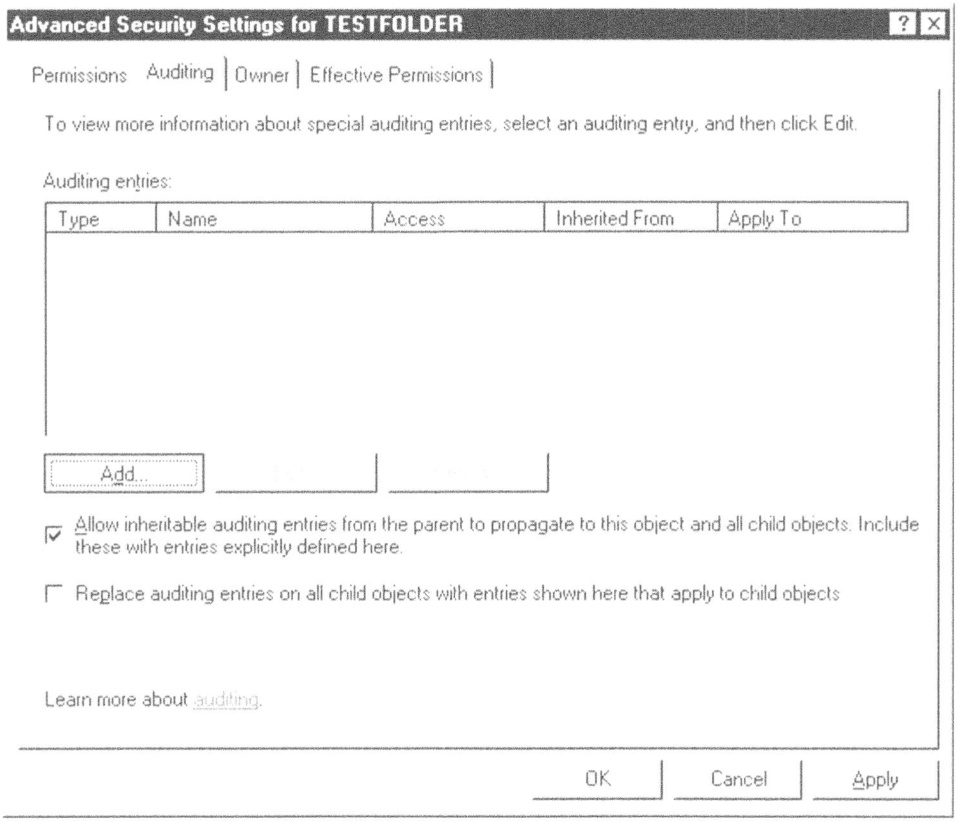

Figure 3–18: Auditing Files and Folders.

Before you turn auditing on for a domain or OU, you need to make sure you have your Security Logs settings in the Event Viewer set up properly. Security Logs fill up amazingly fast, even on a small network, so make sure you have them set to grow to a reasonable size. Figure 3.19 shows the Security Log. To access the Security Logs click on **Start** select **Administrative Tools** and choose **Event Viewer**. Select the **Security Log** from the list.

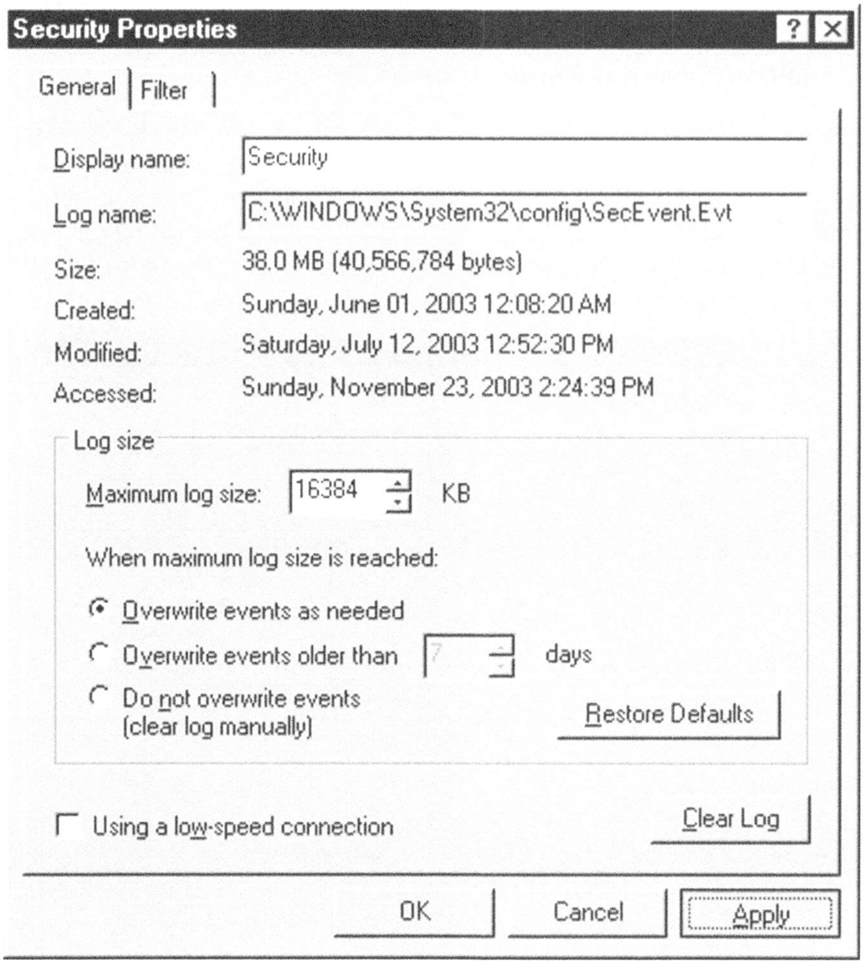

Figure 3–19: The Default Security Log settings in Windows Server 2003.

The default options on the Security Log are:

- **Display Name** – The default display name is Security. You do have the option to change this if you wish.
- **Log Name** – The name and location that the log is saved to on the server, %systemroot%\config\SecEvent.evt.
- **Log Size** – By default the log size is set to 16,384 KB.
    - The size can be increased if the server is particularly busy.
    - The log file can also be set to overwrite itself when it reaches it maximum size.
    - Events can also be overwritten if they are older than a certain number of days.
    - Events can also be set not to clear by being overwritten or if they are a certain age. The log would have to be cleared manually by the Administrator. Be cautious when using this setting if Auditing is enabled.
- **Using a low-speed connection** – This setting is helpful if you need to view the security logs over a low speed connection such as dial-up.

To change the default properties of the Security Log, just choose the option you wish to change and enter the new settings. Click the **Apply** button once the entries have been entered. Take special consideration when dealing with the Security Log. If this is an e-mail or database server, your security log will fill up quickly. If you are auditing files that are accessed often and the server is a Domain Controller, your security log will also fill up rather quickly.

Implementing an Audit Policy

Once changes have been made to the Event Viewer Security Log, you can choose what functions you wish to audit. Deciding on what to audit can be a difficult task for Administrators. Some questions you may wish to ask yourself are:

- What information am I trying to obtain?
- Am I trying to audit for forensics, detecting unauthorized access to files and folders?
- Am I auditing for typical day-to-day events?

Knowing the answers to these questions will help you decide on the auditing of success and failure events. It should also help you not to "over-audit" events on the system. As a word of precaution, always archive copies of Security Logs for future use. Personally, I save my events around the same time of day with the date and the word security in a single location. As time progresses, I will purge old events (after I have made certain that my backups have retained them AND if I note nothing odd within the events). Table 3.2 shows some events that may be audited, as well as the console that is used to audit the event.

> **NOTE**: Remember that auditing uses extensive resources and can adversely affect the ongoing performance of a server. Use auditing wisely.

Event	Description	Default Setting	Configuration container
System Event	This is used to audit any Successful or Failed entries in the Event Viewer Security log or the security of the system.	Success events on Domain Controllers and auditing are not turned on for Member Servers.	Computer Configuration\Windows Settings\Security Settings\Local Policies\Audit Policy
Logon Events	If enabled will audit each attempt that a user makes to log onto or off of a computer. The account must be a domain user account.	Success only events are audited by default.	Computer Configuration\Windows Settings\Security Settings\Local Policies\Audit Policy.
Object Access	If this is enabled, a file, printer, folder, registry, etc. will be audited. Only object that have their own System Access Control List are audited.	Auditing is Turned off by default.	Computer Configuration\Windows Settings\Security Settings\Local Policies\Audit Policy
Privilege Use	This audit property will audit any instance of a user exercising any user right. The following rights are not audited by default even with this turned on: Bypass traverse checking Debug programs, Create token objects Generate security audits Back-up and Restore files and directories	No auditing is enabled by default. Not all rights are audited because if they were the computer's performance could be degraded. To enable the auditing of all rights navigate to the Registry using regedt32 and enable the key **FullPrivilegeAuditing**.	Computer Configuration\Windows Settings\Security Settings\Local Policies\Audit Policy
Policy Change	This will audit any changes to user rights assignment policies, audit policies or trust policies.	Enabled on Domain Controller only.	Computer Configuration\Windows Settings\Security Settings\Local Policies\Audit Policy

Table 3-2: Audit Events available for tracking on Windows Server 2003.

> **NOTE**: When viewing the Security Log in the Event Viewer, if you notice a Policy Change Event category it means that the Local Security Authority LSA policy has been changed by someone.

Security Auditing

Security Auditing is turned off by default. To configure security auditing, you need to open the policy. Select the Domain or OU on which you wish to enable security events. After the Domain or OU has been selected, drill to the following policy: **Computer Configuration\Windows Settings\Security Settings\Local Policies\Security Options choose enabled**. The computer will have to be rebooted for the changes to take effect.

Security Configuration and Analysis

This tool is used to configure security settings on local files, folders, services on the local system and registry settings that are local to the computer. It does **not** require Administrative Privileges. Only use this tool for local computer security settings. Remember that Group Policy settings will always override settings made from this tool to the local computer. To access this tool, you will need to add the **Security Configuration and Analysis** snap-in to an MMC console.

> **NOTE**: Do not use the Security Configuration and Analysis MMC to configure security for a domain or organizational unit. If you do then each client would have to be configured one by one. Use Security Templates and then apply to the Domain or Organizational Unit.

Editing the Security Settings on Group Policy Objects

There are different ways to edit the GPO security settings, depending on whether you are at a local computer, a domain controller or somewhere else. Table 3.3 below shows the settings to use based on where you are located.

Setting	Procedure
Local computer	Open your Local Security Settings by clicking on Start then Run type MMC. File then Add/Remove Snap-in. Add the Local Security Policy. To change the security settings click on Local Policies. Then double-click the policy you wish to change. When finished click OK.
Workstation or Domain controller using Administratio n Tools Pack	Open Active Directory Users and Computers. In the console select the Group Policy object you wish to edit and right-click on the object. Choose Properties and click the Group Policy tab. You can either create a new Group Policy Object by clicking on New and Edit or you can edit an existing object by clicking on Edit. Click the Security Settings option from the Computer configuration\Windows Settings\Security Settings console. Select Local Policies to edit the Audit Policy, User Rights or Security settings.
Workstation or Server joined to the domain	Click Start and Run then type MMC. Add/Remove Snap-in and select Add then choose Group Policy Object Editor. Select Browse to obtain the object you wish to edit. Click Finish, Close and OK. Computer configuration\Windows Settings\Security Settings console. Select Local Policies. To edit the Audit Policy, User Rights or Security settings.
Domain Controller for the Domain	Click on Start then Administrative Tools then select the Domain Controller Security Policy. Select the GroupPolicy Object\ Computer configuration\Windows Settings\Security Settings console. Select Account Policies. To edit the Audit Policy, User Rights or Security settings.

Table 3-3: Computer Settings.

If you choose to audit numerous objects, events or accesses, make certain the Security log settings will meet the needs of the Audit Policy. Use extreme caution when changing any settings for a domain or OU that is in a live environment. Here are a few best practices to use when implementing changes via Security templates.

- Do not change the default template of the console, but make changes and save the template under a different name, such as the date and template name. This way if you find you have made an error, the default template will be available with pristine settings.
- Always test the changes first on a test lab before going "live."
- Do not edit the default security template named **security.inf**. It has a built-in option to reapply default security settings in the event that security errors are made on the Domain, OU or local computer.
- Never use Group Policy to apply the **Setup Security.inf** template, which is a local computer template. This template is typically applied using either the Security Configuration and Analysis console or the command prompt file `secedit.exe`.

If the Security Settings are enabled and are not properly implemented, and the system cannot log security events, it will shut down. The most regular occurrence of this is when the Security event log reaches its size limit and either **the Overwrite Events by days** or the **Do not Overwrite Events** are enabled. A STOP error will generate that states the following:

`STOP: C0000244 {Audit Failed} An attempt to generate a security audit failed.`

The Administrator will have to logon to the Server and clear the Security logs. Until the log settings have been changed to appropriate settings, only members of the Administrators Group will be able to access the server. The Server will also have to be rebooted after the changes have been made.

Pop Quiz 3.1

Pop Quiz 3.1 *Questions*

1. What can members of the Incoming Forest Trust Builder built-in group do?
2. What is the default share permission in Windows Server 2003?
3. What are the steps involved in adding a new snap-in to an MMC Console?
4. What is the difference in how the security is applied between the options available on the Sharing tab and the options available on the Security tab?
5. You are viewing the Security Log in Event Viewer and notice a Policy Change event. What does that mean?

Pop Quiz 3.1 *Answers*

1. Members can create incoming, one-way trusts to the forest.
2. The default share permission is **Everyone**, **Read**.
3. Click on **Start**, then select **Run** and then type **MMC**. Select **File**, then **Add/Remove Snap-in**. Clicking the **Add** button brings up a list of available snap-ins. Select the appropriate snap-in from the list provided then select **Add**.
4. The Share tab allows you to set up Share Security. Share Security is applicable only for folders and only when accessed remotely (through a network connection). The Security tab allows you to set up NTFS Permissions, which are available only when a partition is formatted with the NTFS file system. NTFS Security is applicable to files and folders, for both local and remote access.
5. When viewing the Security Log in the Event Viewer, if you notice a Policy Change Event category it means that the Local Security Authority LSA policy has been changed by someone.

3.2 Troubleshoot Terminal Services

Terminal Services allow Administrators the ability to gain remote access to a Windows Client computer. Terminal Server Services can also be used by Network Administrators to run applications from a single server. Multiple client machines can access the application on the Terminal Server instead of having the application loaded individually on each machine. Clients can run programs, save files, and use network resources as if they were sitting at that machine. Administrators will typically have to troubleshoot issues pertaining to Terminal Server such as client connectivity and error messages.

3.2.1 Diagnose/Resolve issues on Terminal Services Security

Administrators have various settings that may be applied to enhance security while using Terminal Server in the Application mode on Windows Server 2003. Terminal Server has two separate security modes when Terminal Server has been installed in the Application mode (not Remote Administration mode):

- **Full Security** – This mode will provide the most security in the Windows Server 2003 environment.
- **Relaxed Security** – This mode is commonly used to allow legacy applications (pre-Windows 2000) to run. It allows the system registry to be edited.

Which security mode is selected will have a large impact on the security of the Windows Server 2003. A security descriptor is written to the user group in the **Relaxed** mode to allow legacy applications the ability to run properly. The **Full Security** mode does not apply a security descriptor to the user group. If the Relaxed mode was chosen and it has been decided to be changed to the Full Security mode, it can be done by opening the Terminal Services Configuration console. Use the **Run As** command or make sure you are a member of the Domain Administrators (for computers joined to a domain) or Administrators group (for local computers).

To open the consoled click on **Start** then select **Administrative Tools** and choose the **Terminal Services Configuration** option from the menu. Choose the **Server Settings** option and then on the left select the **Permissions Compatibility** option. Choose **Full Security** and click **OK**.

NOTE: If you attempt to upgrade a Windows NT 4.0 Terminal Server Edition computer to Windows Server 2003 you could receive an error stating:
You need Whistler Advanced Server or higher for Terminal Server. Microsoft Windows XP Setup has detected that the computer you are upgrading is running Terminal Server (formerly "Terminal Services in Application Server mode"). Terminal Server is not supported on Windows XP Server. To upgrade this computer and continue to run Terminal Server, you must cancel this upgrade and install Windows XP Advanced Server. Terminal Server is also included as part of Windows XP Datacenter Server.
This error means that you need to use Microsoft Windows Server 2003 Advanced Server.

Administrators also have the ability to set time-out settings for clients who are active, idle or disconnected. Open the **Terminal Services Configuration Console** by clicking on **Start**, selecting **Administrative Tools**, then choosing the **Terminal Services Configuration** option. **Right-click** the connection that needs modifying and choose **Properties**.

- Select the **Sessions** tab and choose the **Override user settings** box. Enter the maximum amount of time that a client disconnected session can remain on the server in the **End a disconnected session** option. Once this time has been reached, the session will end. The session will permanently be removed from the server unless you select the **Never** option, which allows the session to remain on the server for an indefinite amount of time.
- The **Active Session Limit** option can be used to enter the maximum amount of time a session can be active on the Terminal Server. The user will be disconnected once the time limit has been reached or the session will end and the session is permanently removed from the Terminal server.
- The **Idle session limit** is used to set a maximum amount of time a session can remain without client activity. Once the session ends, it is deleted from the server and the **Never** option may be used to allow an idle session to remain on the server forever.

3.2.2 Diagnose/Resolve issues on Terminal Services Client Access

Before the Terminal Server computer can give clients licenses, it must be activated. The activation process is used to validate the server ownership and identity and is provided by Microsoft. The license can be activated by a Telephone, Web Browser or Automatic Activation. Review the process below for the procedures to use for Terminal Server Activation:

Telephone Activation – Click **Start** select **Administrative Tools** choose **Terminal Server Licensing**. Open **All Servers** and choose the server that needs activation and **right-click** on the server. Select the **Activate Server** option then click **Next** on the Activation Wizard. Choose the **Telephone** option for the **Activation method** and then choose **Next**. Select your **Country** or **Region** then choose **Next.** The telephone number will appear for you to call. Have the **Product ID** for the product available, name, organization name and the licensing you need to activate. A unique ID will then be created and given to you to enter by the Microsoft support representative. Enter the **ID** and then select **Next**. The license will then be activated. You will now have the option to install the client license key packs on the server by choosing the **Next** button or you may uncheck the **Start Terminal Server Client Licensing Wizard Now** and choose the **Finish** button to complete this step at a later time.

- **Web Browser** – Click **Start** select **Administrative Tools** choose **Terminal Server Licensing**. Open **All Servers** and choose the server that needs activation and **right-click** on the server. Select the **Activate Server** option then click **Next** on the Activation Wizard. Choose the **Web Browser** activation method and choose **Next**. Click on the **hyperlink** given to activate the license and choose the **Select Option** and select **Activate a License Server** then click on **Next**. Enter your **Product ID**, **Name**, **Organization Name**, **Country** or **Region** then choose the **Next** button. The License server ID will then be given to you and you can go to the **License Activation Page** and enter the **License ID** and select the **Next** button. You will now have the option to install the client license key packs on the server by choosing the **Next** button or you may uncheck the **Start Terminal Server Client Licensing Wizard Now** and choose the **Finish** button to complete this step at a later time.
- **Automatically** – Click **Start** select **Administrative Tools** choose **Terminal Server Licensing**. Open **All Servers** and choose the server that needs activation and **right-click** on the server. Select the **Activate Server** option then click **Next** on the Activation Wizard. Choose the **Automatic connection (recommended)** and then select **Next**. Enter your **name**, **organization**, **country** or **region** and click on **Next**. The option is also available for you to enter the e-mail address of the company or yourself and company address. Select **Next** after this optional information has been entered. You will now have the option to install the client license key packs on the server by choosing the **Next** button or you may uncheck the **Start Terminal Server Client Licensing Wizard Now** and choose the **Finish** button to complete this step at a later time.

3.3.1 Verify effective permissions when granting permissions

There are some very specific "best practices" that should be considered when granting permissions for Terminal Services:

1. Deny permissions should be used for certain special cases—to exclude a subset of a group that has Allowed permissions or to exclude one special permission when you have already granted full control to a user or group.
2. Rather than set individual permissions, use security templates whenever possible.
3. If possible, avoid changing the default permission entries on file system objects, particularly on system folders and root folders. Changing default permissions can cause unexpected access problems or reduce security.
4. Never deny the Everyone group access to an object. If you deny everyone permission to an object, that includes administrators. A better solution would be to remove the Everyone group, as long as you give other users, groups or computers permissions to that object.
5. Assign permissions to an object as high on the tree as possible and then apply inheritance to propagate the security settings through the tree. You can quickly and effectively apply access control settings to all children or a subtree of a parent object. By doing this, you gain the greatest breadth of effect with the least effort. The permission settings you establish should be adequate for the majority of users, groups and computers.
6. Privileges can sometimes override permissions. Privileges and permissions may disagree and you should know what happens if they do. Active Directory has its own set of best practices regarding permissions.
7. Inherited Deny permissions do not prevent access to an object if the object has an explicit Allow permission entry. Explicit permissions take precedence over inherited permissions, even inherited Deny permissions.

3.3.2 Change ownership of files and folders

On Windows Server 2003, Administrators need to know how to take ownership of files and folders in order to repair or change them.

All Active Directory objects, files and folders have an owner. Owners have the right to control access permissions on the object. Ownership cannot be transferred by current owners to other users; however the user who current has ownership rights can give another user the right to take ownership.

In simple terms—you cannot force ownership of a document, folder or printer onto another person. All you can do is offer ownership. The other user must be the one to take ownership.

NOTE: The exception to this rule is if the owner of the file or folder has the **Restore Files and Directories** privilege. A user who has that can double-click **Other users and groups** and choose any user or group to assign ownership to. Assigning this user right can be a security risk. Since users with this user right can overwrite registry settings, hide data and gain ownership of system objects, only assign this user right to trusted users. Backup Operators, Server Operators and Administrators are groups that have this right by default.

The Windows Server 2003 Administrators have the built-in ability to take ownership of a file from the **Take Ownership of files or other objects** right You can take ownership from within Windows Explorer. Find the file or folder you wish to take ownership of and **right-click** on the file, choose **Properties**, then select **Security** from the security tab. Select the **Advanced** tab then choose the **Ownership** tab as shown on Figure 3.20.

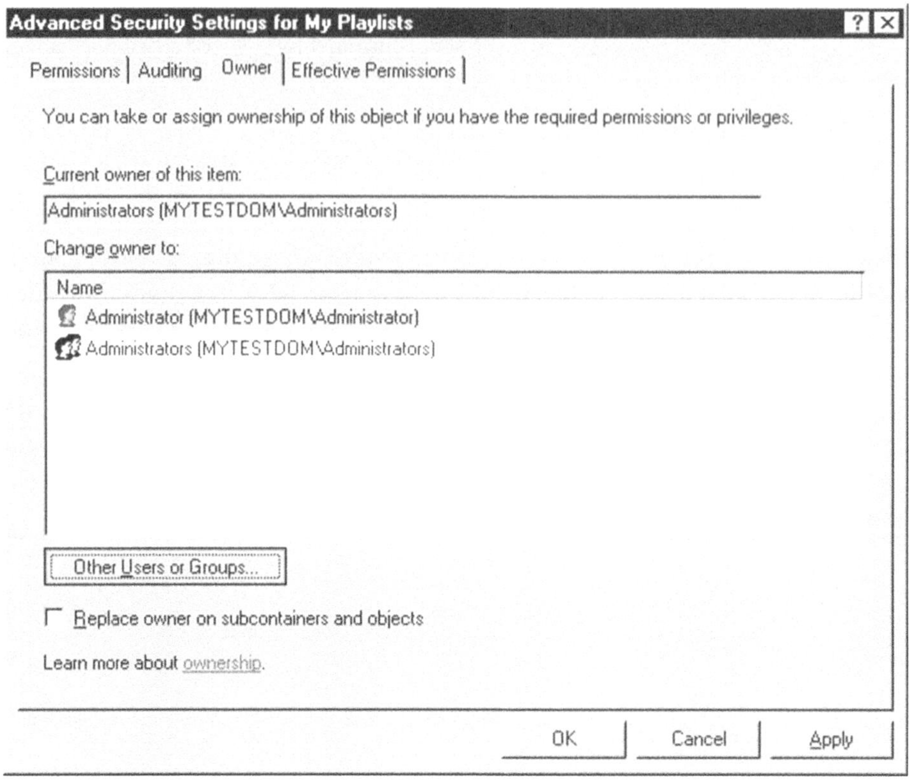

Figure 3–20: Taking Ownership of a file using the Ownership tab in the Advanced properties of the object.

The screen will show the current owner of the file or folder. To give **Take Ownership** rights to a user or group just click on the **Other Users or Groups** button and type the user or group name in the **Enter the object name to select (examples)**. To change the owner to a user or group that is listed, click the new owner. All subfolders (if applicable) and objects in the tree can have their ownership changed by selecting the **Replace owner on subcontainers and objects** check box. Ownership can also be transferred by clients with the **Restore files and Directories** privilege by double-clicking the **Other users and groups** and then selecting a user or group to assign ownership. Or the **Take ownership** permission can be applied to clients.

Pop Quiz 3.2

Pop Quiz 3.2 *Questions*

1. When Terminal Server has been installed in Application mode, what are the two separate security modes available?
2. What are the three ways you can activate a license for Terminal Server?
3. What is an unwelcome side-effect if you assign Deny access to the Everyone group?
4. Which will take precedence—an inherited Deny permission or an explicit Allow permission?
5. What privilege must a user or group have in order to explicitly assign ownership to another user?

Pop Quiz 3.2 *Answers*

1. The two modes are **Full Security** which will provide the most security in the Windows Server 2003 environment, and **Relaxed Security** which is commonly used to allow legacy applications (pre-Windows 2000) to run. It allows the system registry to be edited.
2. The license can be activated by a Telephone, Web Browser or Automatic Activation.
3. By denying the Everyone group, you do, indeed, deny everyone—even the Administrators. A better choice is to remove the Everyone group from the permissions list and then specifically assign permissions to other users and groups.
4. Explicit permissions take precedence over inherited permissions, even inherited Deny permissions.
5. If the owner of a file or folder has the "Restore Files and Directories" privilege, they can assign ownership to another user. Backup Operators, Server Operators and Administrators, by default, have that privilege.

3.4 Troubleshoot access to files and shared folders

Troubleshooting access to files and folders that are shared on Windows Server 2003 can sometimes be daunting. Table 3.4 shows some common problems, causes and solutions that uses could experience when accessing shared resources on a Windows Server 2003.

Problem	Cause	Solution
Shared Folders that are shared cannot be accessed by any client.	Shared folder permissions are set incorrectly.	Check the permissions to the folder for accuracy.
Folders that are shared cannot be accessed by any client.	Possible network connection has been lost.	Check and verify network connectivity on server and client machines.
Shared Files that are shared cannot be accessed by any client.	Shared folder permissions are set incorrectly.	Check the permissions to the file for accuracy.

Table 3-4: Troubleshooting Shared Resources.

Usually you want to also make certain the Everyone Group has not been denied access to files or folders.

The **`net share`** command, the **`net file`** (for machines running the server service only) command (which shows all open files on a machine) or the **`net session`** command may also be used at the command prompt to view information on shares or files. You must be a member of the local Administrators group for local computers or the Domain Administrators group for computers joined to the domain before these commands may be used. To view syntax for these commands open the command prompt and type:

- **net share –** *net help share* – this command will show the net share command syntax that can be used to troubleshoot shares**.**
- **net file –** net help file – *share* this command will show the net share command syntax that can be used to troubleshoot files as shown in Figure 3.21.
- **net session –** *net help session* this will show the net session command syntax that can be used to show all open sessions on a computer as shown in Figure 3.22.

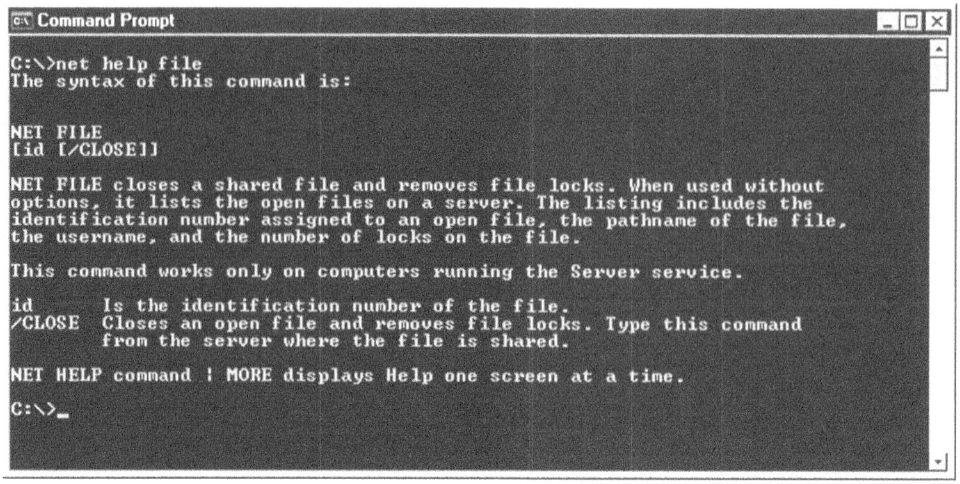

Figure 3–21: The net file command syntax.

The net session command shown in Figure 3.22 can be used to view open sessions on a computer.

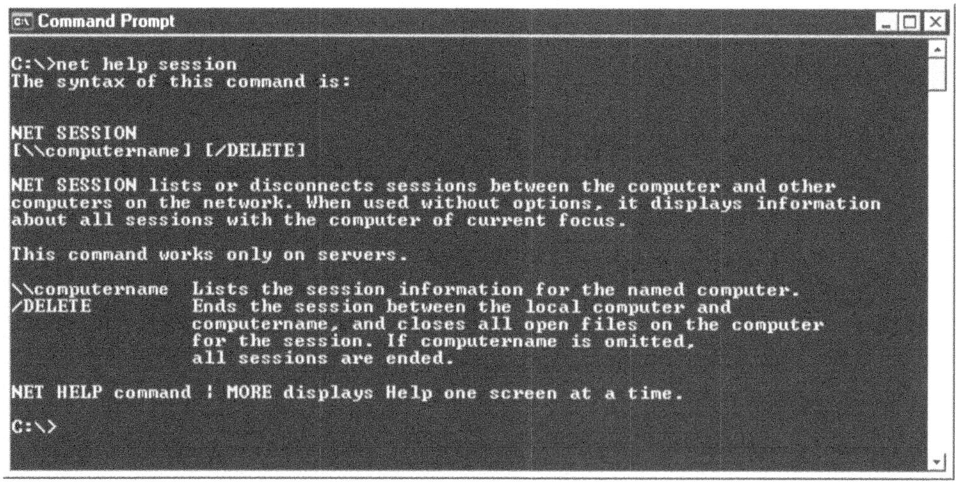

Figure 3–22: The net session command syntax.

Using any or all of the methods above can typically assist you with troubleshooting client access to files and shared folders.

Chapter 3: Review Questions

1. You want to ensure that your clients respond to your Terminal Server's requests for security. What steps do you need to take?

A. Click Start, click Run, type gpedit.msc and then click OK.

B. Click Start, click Run, type gpmod.moc and then click OK.

C. Expand Security Settings in the left pane, right-click the Client (respond only) policy and then click Assign.

D. Expand Security Settings in the left pane, right-click the Server (respond only) policy and then click Distribute.

---

2. Which of the following are ways that a shared folder can be accessed in Windows 2003?

A. By its IP address

B. By its Universal Naming Convention (UNC)

C. By a mapped network drive

D. Through My Network Places

3. Users are able to do more in the Backup folder when they log onto the Windows 2003 member server you have made available to users. What might be the problem?

A. Inherited permissions that are incorrect for the shared resource

B. The member server doesn't have an NTFS partition

C. Group memberships that may grant different levels of permissions

D. The users are in the Everyone group

---

4. Edward has permissions assigned to his account specifically, as well as permissions assigned to groups of which he is a member on the Accounts folder. Some of these permissions are shared permissions and some are NTFS permissions. What permissions will apply to Edward when he connects to the Accounts folder?

A. His user permissions

B. His user permissions, group permissions in which he is a member, NTFS permissions, and shared folder permissions

C. His user permissions and group permissions in which he is a member

D. His user permissions, group permissions in which he is a member, and NTFS permissions

5. Which of the following security templates are default security templates?

A. Setup security.inf

B. DC security.inf

C. Compatws.inf

D. Secure*.inf

E. hisec*.inf

---

6. Which of the following security templates is the most secure?

A. DC security.inf

B. Compatws.inf

C. Secure*.inf

D. hisec*.inf

7. Which of the following might be the cause of network connectivity issues?

A. Insufficient rights (i.e.—the proxy server only allows access to certain persons or sites)

B. Bad IP information (incorrect IP, subnet mask, default gateway)

C. Physical connectivity is down (the server may be down or the cable could have failed)

D. No Answer is Correct

---

8. Which of the following audit events should you enable to monitor misuse of privileges?

A. Success and Failure audit for file-access and object-access events

B. Failure audit for logon/logoff

C. Success audit for logon/logoff

D. Success audit for user rights, user and group management, security change policies, restart, shutdown and system events

9. You want to set up Software Update Services. What steps do you have to take to accomplish this?

A. Download Software Update Services from http://www.technet.com/windows2000/windowsupdate/sus/default.asp

B. Double-click the SUS101SP1.exe file to begin the installation process and follow the prompts in the wizard

C. Download Software Update Services from http://www.microsoft.com/windows2000/windowsupdate/sus/default.asp

D. Double-click the SU.exe file to begin the installation process and follow the prompts in the wizard

---

10. Which of the following audit events should you enable to monitor access to sensitive files?

A. Success audit for logon/logoff

B. Failure audit for logon/logoff

C. Success and Failure audit for file-access and object-access events

D. Success audit for user rights, user and group management, security change policies, restart, shutdown and system events

11. Which of the following directories contains the Remote Desktop Client program?

A. %windir%\system32\clients\sclient\drivers

B. %windir%\system32\clients\tsclient

C. %windir%\system32\clients

D. %windir%\system32\tsclient\win32

E. %windir%\system32\clients\tsclient\win32

---

12. Which of the following operating systems can have the Remote Desktop Client program installed on them by using the installation program in the %windir%\system32\clients\tsclient\win32 directory?

A. Windows NT 4.0, Windows 2000, Windows XP

B. Windows 95 and 98

C. Windows XP Home and Professional

D. Windows XP and Server 2003

E. All Answers are Correct

13. Which of the following HTTP error messages would indicate that the file for which you are looking isn't found?

A. 400

B. 401

C. 402

D. 404

E. 405

---

14. Which of the following is the default user account that IIS uses when you specify anonymous access?

A. IUSR_SERVERNAME

B. USER_SERVERNAME

C. IUSR_SERVERNAME

D. R_SERVERNAME

E. USR_SERVERNAME

15. You want to remove the administrative shares on your Windows Server 2003. How can this be accomplished using the registry?

A. Click Start, and then click Run. In the Open box, type regedit, and then click OK.

B. Locate, and then click the following registry key: HKEY_LOCAL_MACHINE\SYSTEM\CurrentControlSet\Services\LanmanServer\Parameters\AutoShareServer. On the Edit menu, click Modify. In the Value data box, type 0, and then click OK.

C. Click Start, and then click Run. In the Open box, type cmd, and then click OK. Type the following: net stop server (Press Enter) net start server (Press Enter). Type exit to quit Command Prompt.

D. Locate, and then click the following registry key: HKEY_LOCAL_MACHINE\SYSTEM\CurrentControlSet\Services\LanmanServer\Parameters\AutoShareServer. On the Edit menu, click Modify. In the Value data box, type 1, and then click OK.

E. Locate, and then click the following registry key: HKEY_LOCAL_MACHINE\SYSTEM\CurrentControlSet\Services\LanmanServer\Parameters\AutoShareServer. On the Edit menu, click Modify. In the Value data box, type 2, and then click OK.

Chapter 3: Review Answers

1. You want to ensure that your clients respond to your Terminal Server's requests for security. What steps do you need to take?

***A. Click Start, click Run, type gpedit.msc and then click OK.**

B. Click Start, click Run, type gpmod.moc and then click OK.

***C. Expand Security Settings in the left pane, right-click the Client (respond only) policy and then click Assign.**

D. Expand Security Settings in the left pane, right-click the Server (respond only) policy and then click Distribute.

Explanation: To ensure that your clients respond to your Terminal Server's requests for security, click Start, click Run, type gpedit.msc and then click OK. Expand Security Settings in the left pane, right-click the Client (respond only) policy and then click Assign.

---

2. Which of the following are ways that a shared folder can be accessed in Windows 2003?

A. By its IP address

***B. By its Universal Naming Convention (UNC)**

***C. By a mapped network drive**

***D. Through My Network Places**

Explanation: In Windows 2003, a shared folder can be accessed in My Network Places, by its Universal Naming Convention (UNC) or by a mapped network drive.

3. Users are able to do more in the Backup folder when they log onto the Windows 2003 member server you have made available to users. What might be the problem?

***A. Inherited permissions that are incorrect for the shared resource**

B. The member server doesn't have an NTFS partition

***C. Group memberships that may grant different levels of permissions**

D. The users are in the Everyone group

Explanation: By default, permissions are inherited from the folder that contains the object. If users have permissions that they shouldn't have when they log on locally, look for both inherited permissions that are incorrect for the shared resource and for group memberships that may grant different levels of permissions.

---

4. Edward has permissions assigned to his account specifically, as well as permissions assigned to groups of which he is a member on the Accounts folder. Some of these permissions are shared permissions and some are NTFS permissions. What permissions will apply to Edward when he connects to the Accounts folder?

A. His user permissions

***B. His user permissions, group permissions in which he is a member, NTFS permissions, and shared folder permissions**

C. His user permissions and group permissions in which he is a member

D. His user permissions, group permissions in which he is a member, and NTFS permissions

Explanation: When you access data over the network, both share permissions and file and folder permissions apply. Share access permissions are combined with any permissions that are assigned directly to the user and those that are assigned to any groups of which the user is a member.

5. Which of the following security templates are default security templates?

***A. Setup security.inf**

***B. DC security.inf**

C. Compatws.inf
D. Secure*.inf
E. hisec*.inf

Explanation: The Setup security.inf template is created during installation of the operating system for each computer and represents default security settings that are applied during installation, including the file permissions for the root of the system drive. The DC security.inf template is created when a server is promoted to a domain controller. It reflects default security settings on files, registry keys and system services. The Compatws.inf template changes the default file and registry permissions that are granted to the Users group. The Secure templates (Secure*.inf) define stronger password, lockout, and audit settings. The Highly Secure templates (hisec*.inf) are supersets of the Secure templates and they impose further restrictions on the levels of encryption and signing that are required for authentication and for the data that flows over secure channels and between server message block (SMB) clients and servers. Rootsec.inf defines the permissions for the root of the system drive.

---

6. Which of the following security templates is the most secure?

A. DC security.inf
B. Compatws.inf
C. Secure*.inf

***D. hisec*.inf**

Explanation: The Setup security.inf template is created during installation of the operating system for each computer and represents default security settings that are applied during installation, including the file permissions for the root of the system drive. The DC security.inf template is created when a server is promoted to a domain controller. It reflects default security settings on files, registry keys and system services. The Compatws.inf template changes the default file and registry permissions that are granted to the Users group. The Secure templates (Secure*.inf) define stronger password, lockout and audit settings. The Highly Secure templates (hisec*.inf) are supersets of the Secure templates and they impose further restrictions on the levels of encryption and signing that are required for authentication and for the data that flows over secure channels and between server message block (SMB) clients and servers. Rootsec.inf defines the permissions for the root of the system drive.

7. Which of the following might be the cause of network connectivity issues?

***A. Insufficient rights (i.e.—the proxy server only allows access to certain persons or sites)**

***B. Bad IP information (incorrect IP, subnet mask, default gateway)**

***C. Physical connectivity is down (the server may be down or the cable could have failed)**

D. No Answer is Correct

Explanation: If the IP information is wrong or dated (incorrect IP, subnet mask, default gateway), it could stop a client from getting to the Internet. DNS issues (a bad DNS server address, whether it is manually entered or cached) could also be the problem. Insufficient rights or restrictions could the problem, if the client is trying to access the Internet in an improper way. If the issue is physical in nature, which is possible, test the connectivity with ping, tracert and pathping.

---

8. Which of the following audit events should you enable to monitor misuse of privileges?

A. Success and Failure audit for file-access and object-access events
B. Failure audit for logon/logoff
C. Success audit for logon/logoff

***D. Success audit for user rights, user and group management, security change policies, restart, shutdown, and system events**

Explanation: Use the 'Failure audit for logon/logoff' audit event when you want to monitor random password hacking or brute force attacks. Use the 'Success audit for logon/logoff' audit event when you want to monitor for stolen or unsecured passwords. Use the 'Success audit for user rights, user and group management, security change policies, restart, shutdown, and system events' audit event when you want to monitor misuse of privileges. Use the 'Success and Failure audit for file-access and object-access events' audit event when you want to monitor access to sensitive files.

9. You want to set up Software Update Services. What steps do you have to take to accomplish this?

A. Download Software Update Services from http://www.technet.com/windows2000/windowsupdate/sus/default.asp.

***B. Double-click the SUS101SP1.exe file to begin the installation process and follow the prompts in the wizard.**

***C. Download Software Update Services from http://www.microsoft.com/windows2000/windowsupdate/sus/default.asp.**

D. Double-click the SU.exe file to begin the installation process and follow the prompts in the wizard.

Explanation: If you want to set up Software Update Services on your Windows Server 2003, download Software Update Services from http://www.microsoft.com/windows2000/windowsupdate/sus/default.asp. Double-click the SUS101SP1.exe file to begin the installation process. In the Setup Wizard, on the Welcome page, click Next. Read and accept the End User License Agreement. Select the Typical check box. Click Install, and then click Finish in the Setup Wizard to open the Software Update Services administration Web site in Internet Explorer.

---

10. Which of the following audit events should you enable to monitor access to sensitive files?

A. Success audit for logon/logoff

B. Failure audit for logon/logoff

***C. Success and Failure audit for file-access and object-access events**

D. Success audit for user rights, user and group management, security change policies, restart, shutdown, and system events

Explanation: Use the 'Failure audit for logon/logoff' audit event when you want to monitor random password hacking or brute force attacks. Use the 'Success audit for logon/logoff' audit event when you want to monitor for stolen or unsecured passwords. Use the 'Success audit for user rights, user and group management, security change policies, restart, shutdown, and system events' audit event when you want to monitor misuse of privileges. Use the 'Success and Failure audit for file-access and object-access events' audit event when you want to monitor access to sensitive files.

11. Which of the following directories contains the Remote Desktop Client program?
    A. %windir%\system32\clients\sclient\drivers
    B. %windir%\system32\clients\tsclient
    C. %windir%\system32\clients
    D. %windir%\system32\tsclient\win32

***E. %windir%\system32\clients\tsclient\win32**

Explanation: The %windir%\system32\clients\tsclient\win32 directory contains the Remote Desktop Client program. This program can be used to install Remote Desktop client on Windows 9x, Me, NT 4.0, 2000, as well as XP and 2003.

---

12. Which of the following operating systems can have the Remote Desktop Client program installed on them by using the installation program in the %windir%\system32\clients\tsclient\win32 directory?
    A. Windows NT 4.0, Windows 2000, Windows XP
    B. Windows 95 and 98
    C. Windows XP Home and Professional
    D. Windows XP and Server 2003

***E. All Answers are Correct**

Explanation: The %windir%\system32\clients\tsclient\win32 directory contains the Remote Desktop Client program. This can install Remote Desktop client on Windows 9x, Me, NT 4.0, 2000, as well as XP and 2003.

13. Which of the following HTTP error messages would indicate that the file for which you are looking isn't found?

A. 400
B. 401
C. 402
***D. 404**
E. 405

Explanation: The 404 HTTP error message would indicate that the file for which you are looking isn't found.

---

14 Which of the following is the default user account that IIS uses when you specify anonymous access?

A. IUSR_SERVERNAME
B. USER_SERVERNAME
***C. IUSR_SERVERNAME**
D. R_SERVERNAME
E. USR_SERVERNAME

Explanation: IUSR_SERVERNAME is the default user account that IIS uses when you specify anonymous access.

15. You want to remove the administrative shares on your Windows Server 2003. How can this be accomplished using the registry?

***A. click Start, and then click Run. In the Open box, type regedit, and then click OK.**

***B. Locate, and then click the following registry key: HKEY_LOCAL_MACHINE\SYSTEM\CurrentControlSet\Services\LanmanServer \Parameters\AutoShareServer. On the Edit menu, click Modify. In the Value data box, type 0, and then click OK.**

***C. Click Start, and then click Run. In the Open box, type cmd, and then click OK. Type the following: net stop server (Press Enter) net start server (Press Enter). Type exit to quit Command Prompt.**

D. Locate, and then click the following registry key: HKEY_LOCAL_MACHINE\SYSTEM\CurrentControlSet\Services\LanmanServer\Parameters\AutoShareServer. On the Edit menu, click Modify. In the Value data box, type 1, and then click OK.

E. Locate, and then click the following registry key: HKEY_LOCAL_MACHINE\SYSTEM\CurrentControlSet\Services\LanmanServer\Parameters\AutoShareServer. On the Edit menu, click Modify. In the Value data box, type 2, and then click OK.

Explanation: To remove administrative shares and prevent them from being automatically created in Windows, click Start, and then click Run. In the Open box, type regedit, and then click OK. Locate, and then click the following registry key: HKEY_LOCAL_MACHINE\SYSTEM\CurrentControlSet\Services\LanmanServer\Parameters\AutoShareServer. When this value is set to 0 (zero), Windows does not automatically create administrative shares. Note that this does not apply to the IPC$ share or shares that you create manually. On the Edit menu, click Modify. In the Value data box, type 0, and then click OK. Quit Registry Editor. Stop and then start the Server service. Click Start, and then click Run. In the Open box, type cmd, and then click OK. At the command prompt, type the following lines. Press ENTER after each line: net stop server (Press Enter) net start server (Press Enter). Type exit to quit Command Prompt.

Managing and Maintaining a Server Environment

The objective of this chapter is to provide the reader with an understanding of the following:

4.1 Monitor and analyze events.

- **4.1.1 Tools might include:**
  - **4.1.1.1 Event Viewer**
  - **4.1.1.2 System Monitor**

4.2 Manage software update infrastructure

4.3 Manage software site licensing

4.4 Manage servers remotely

- **4.4.1 Manage a server by using Remote Assistance**
- **4.4.2 Manage a server by using Terminal Services remote administration mode**
- **4.4.3 Manage a server by using available support tools**

4.5 Troubleshoot print queues

4.6 Monitor system performance

4.7 Monitor file and print servers. Tools might include:

- **4.7.1 Task Manager**
  - **4.7.1.1 Monitor disk quotas**
  - **4.7.1.2 Monitor print queues**
  - **4.7.1.3 Monitor server hardware for bottlenecks**
- **4.7.2 Event Viewer**
  - **4.7.2.1 Monitor disk quotas**
  - **4.7.2.2 Monitor print queues**
  - **4.7.2.3 Monitor server hardware for bottlenecks**
- **4.7.3 System Monitor**
  - **4.7.3.1 Monitor disk quotas**
  - **4.7.3.2 Monitor print queues**
  - **4.7.3.3 Monitor server hardware for bottlenecks**

4.8 Monitor and optimize a server environment for application performance

- **4.8.1 Monitor memory performance objects**
- **4.8.2 Monitor network performance objects**
- **4.8.3 Monitor process performance objects**
- **4.8.4 Monitor disk performance objects**

4.9 Manage a Web server

- **4.9.1 Manage Internet Information Services (IIS)**
- **4.9.2 Manage security for IIS**

Chapter 4: The Server Environment

Introduction:

Let's be honest. When it comes to monitoring servers, you either love it or you view it with all the enthusiasm of a visit to the dentist. If you fall into the second category, as I do, you pray that you work with someone who falls into the first category. They attack it like a dog munching a t-bone. And you don't have to do it.

However, in reality, most of the time there's only one person to do the job. And it's you.

Getting Ready Questions

1. What are the three basic logs in Event Viewer?
2. What are the three views available to you in System Monitor?
3. What are the four process priority classes?
4. What is SUS?
5. What is Remote Assistance?

Getting Ready Answers

1. The three basic logs in Event Viewer are Application, System and Security. In addition, with Server 2003, you may have logs for DNS Server, Directory Service and File Replication Service.
2. There are three views available to you in System Monitor—Chart, Histogram and Report.
3. The four process priority classes are Idle, Normal, High and Real Time.
4. SUS (Software Update Services) is a server-based distribution system for critical updates, security patches and service packs.
5. Remote Assistance allows the administrator to assist another individual remotely, in real time, when the remote system is running Server 2003 or Windows XP. Remote Assistance requires explicit permission from the individual requesting assistance.

4.1 Monitor and analyze events

This section is designed to point out what is new in monitoring and analysis for Server 2003. It will also help those who view monitoring in a less-than-eager light to understand the necessity of monitoring and how to do it in an expedient and efficient manner.

Monitoring is not only for maintenance. It is vital for predicting future growth, and for identifying those nagging trouble areas in a network before they become migraine headaches. The up-to-date data from a monitoring session will fall under one of three analytical categories, as shown in the table below.

Category	Examples
Maintenance	Consolidating servers Supporting request for new hardware
Troubleshooting Network Problems/Server Bottlenecks	Lack of memory Unbalanced workloads Incorrect configurations Application monopolizing resources
Future Planning	Monitoring trends Planning upgrades

Table 4-1: Reasons for Monitoring/Analysis.

One thing that is necessary for any successful analysis of monitored servers is a baseline. In other words, what is the normal state of the four main subsystems?

- Memory
- Processor
- Disk
- Network.

When considering establishing what baseline performance for a server is, you want to take into consideration your users' habits—during certain times of the day, days of the week or periods during the month. If your performance is poor just during peak periods, you can assume that the poor performance is only temporary. However, if poor performance is occurring during downtime, you may want to do a more thorough analysis of your situation, and what should be done to improve it.

It is helpful to track a baseline. Long term decrease in performance may indicate change in usage patterns that may require additional servers or better load balancing.

Just before we look at the monitoring tools available in Server 2003, let's just review the two types of monitoring you will be performing—real time and logged monitoring. Real time monitoring establishes the current state of the four main subsystems. It is, in essence, a snapshot of what is happening at that moment in time. Logged monitoring, on the other hand, is used to monitor data stored over an extended period of time on the network. You will want to perform analysis on this data to determine how the server is performing on all four subsystems.

4.1.1 Tools might include:

4.1.1.1 Event Viewer

The Event Viewer console (Figure 4.1) uses event logs to gather hardware and software information, system problems and security events (auditing).

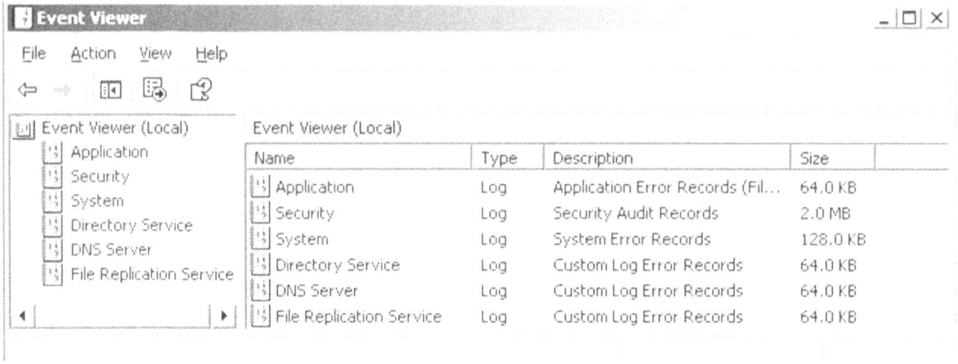

Figure 4-1: Event Viewer.

The Event Log service provides the capabilities for applications and services to log their respective events. Under any configuration of Server 2003, Event Viewer will always record events in three different logs:

- Application Log
- System Log
- Security Log.

Let's discuss these logs in further detail.

- **Application Log**
  contains events logged by programs or applications, such as a file error logged by a database program. These events are determined by the developer of the application as to what events to produce and to what degree of verbosity to implore.

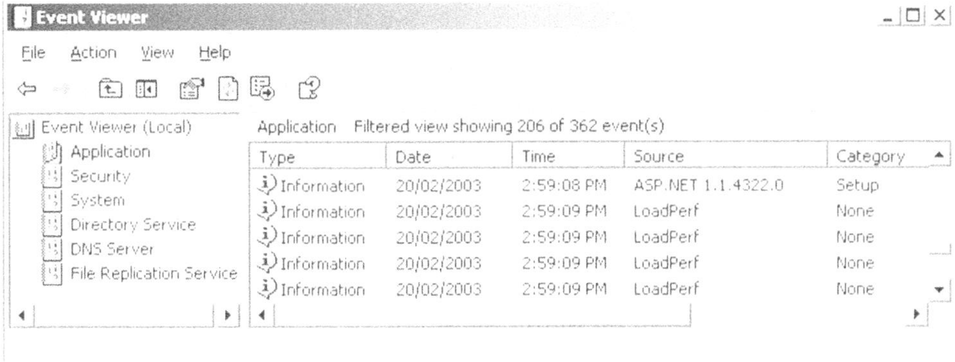

Figure 4-2: Application Log.

Double-clicking on any of the events shown in the console window will display a dialog box with further detail on the particular event.

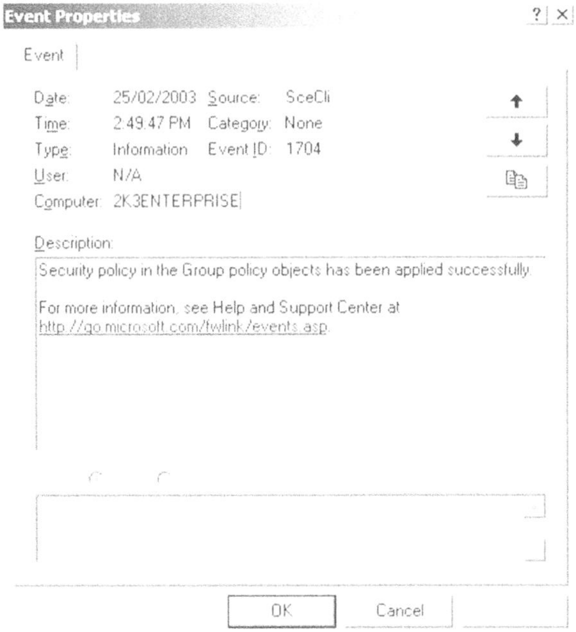

Figure 4-3: Application Log Event.

NOTE: Both the **Application** log and the **System** log can show three different types of events: Error, Warning and Information. Each of these event types shows a degree of severity for the event, with Error being the most critical.
The **Security** log produces two events. The first is the Success Audit, which indicates a successful security access. The second is the Failure Audit, which indicates a failed security access.
For each log you can quickly view the events in the console window. There are eight columns showing information about the event. These columns are Type, Date, Time, Source, Category, Event, User and Computer.

- **System Log**
  contains events, predetermined by the server, logged by system components, such as failure of a driver to load.

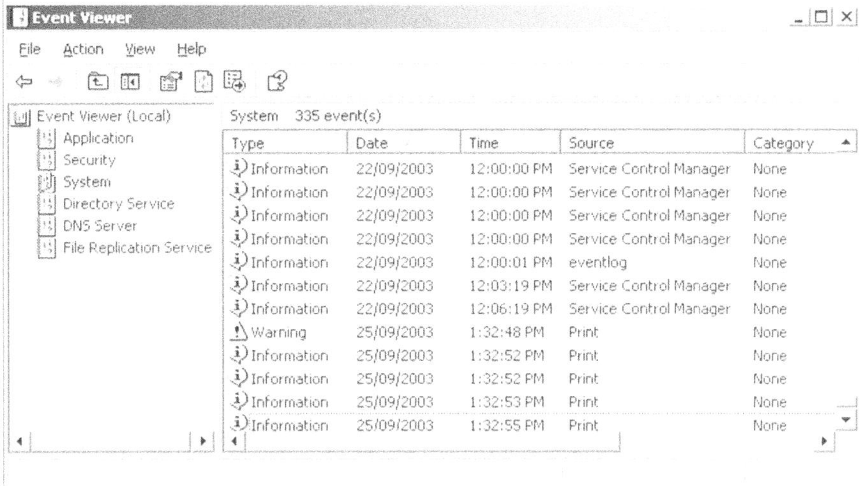

Figure 4-4: System Log.

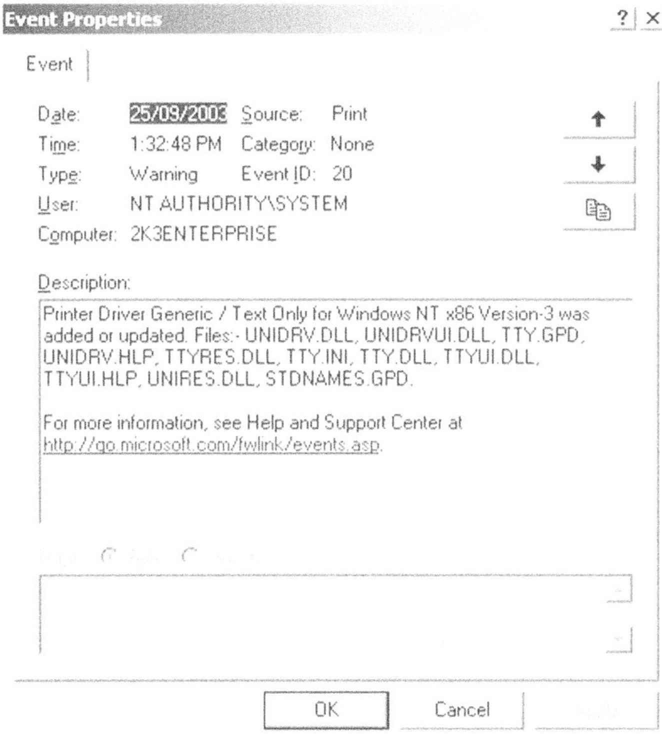

Figure 4-5: System Log Event.

- **Security Log**
  records security events as successful or failed, depending on what was requested to be audited, for example, a failed logon attempt. These events are controlled by the auditing functions of the various resources and subsystems. By default, these events are not recorded. Security logs are only viewable by administrators.

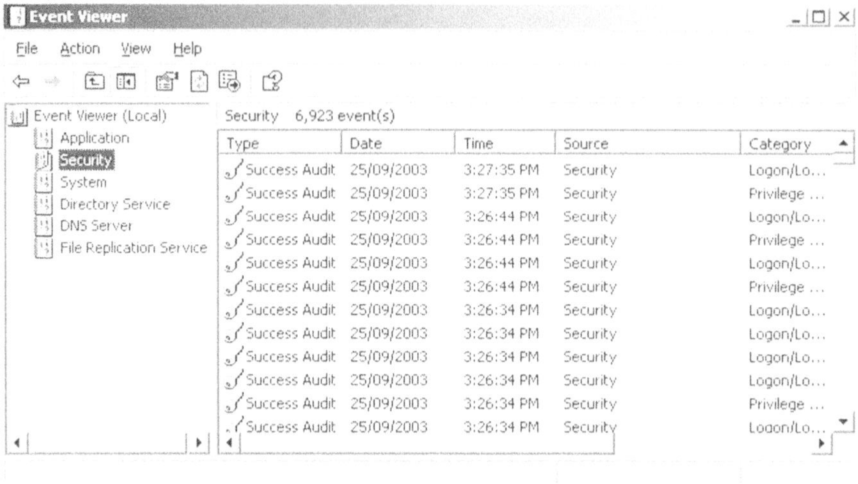

Figure 4-6: Security Log.

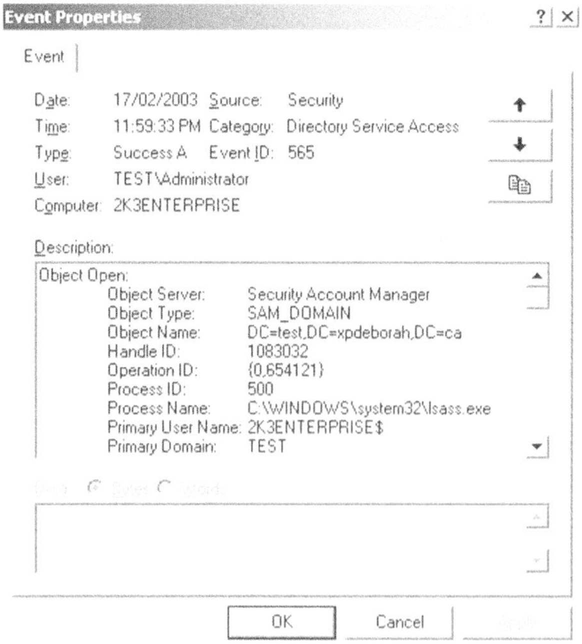

Figure 4-7: Security Log Event.

- **System Log**
  contains events predetermined by the server, logged by system components, such as failure of a driver to load.

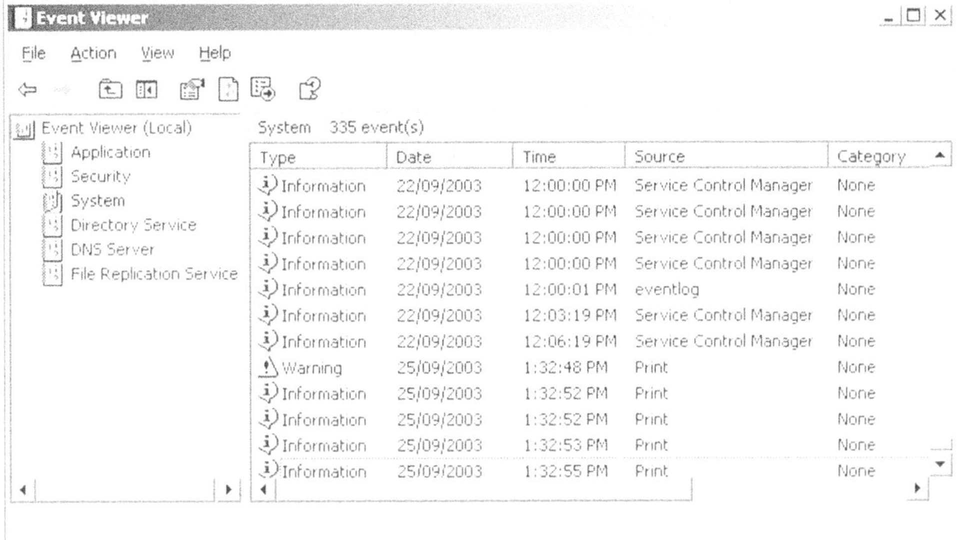

Figure 4-8: System Log.

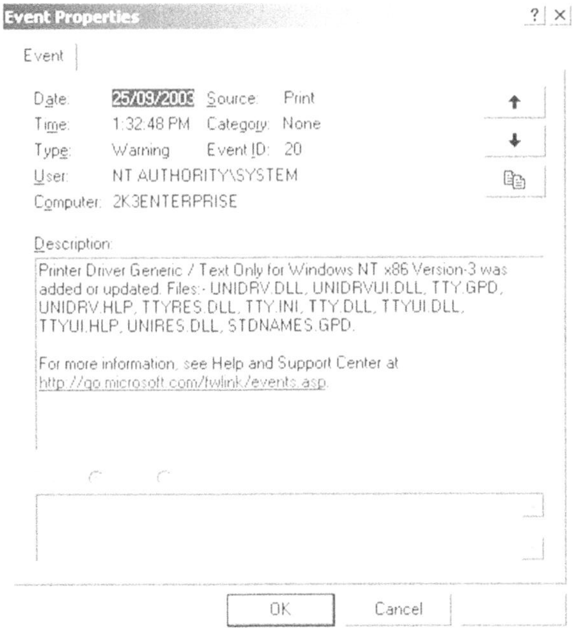

Figure 4-9: System Log Event.

If Server 2003 is configured as a domain controller, there will be two additional logs available:

- **Directory Services Log**
  contains events logged by the Active Directory services, such as connection problems between the global catalog and the server.

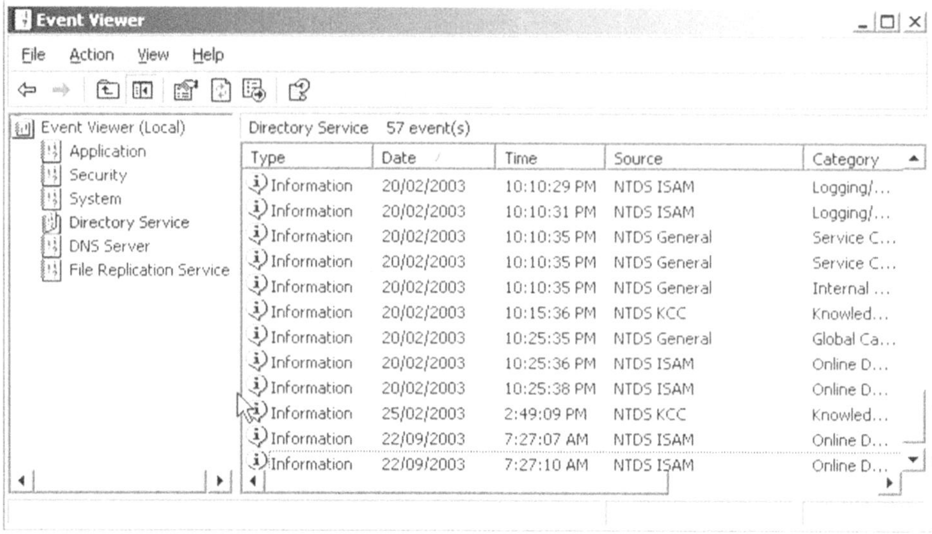

Figure 4-10: Directory Service Log.

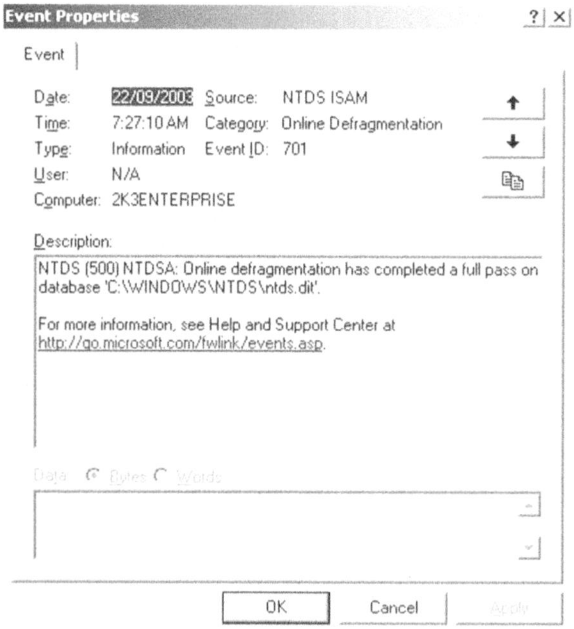

Figure 4-11: Directory Service Log Event.

- **File Replication Service Log**
  contains events logged by the File Replication service, such as file replication failures.

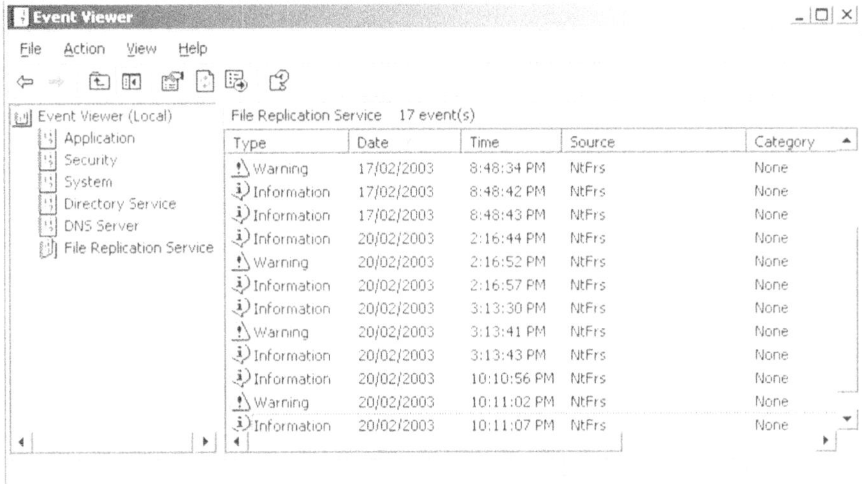

Figure 4-12: File Replication Service Log.

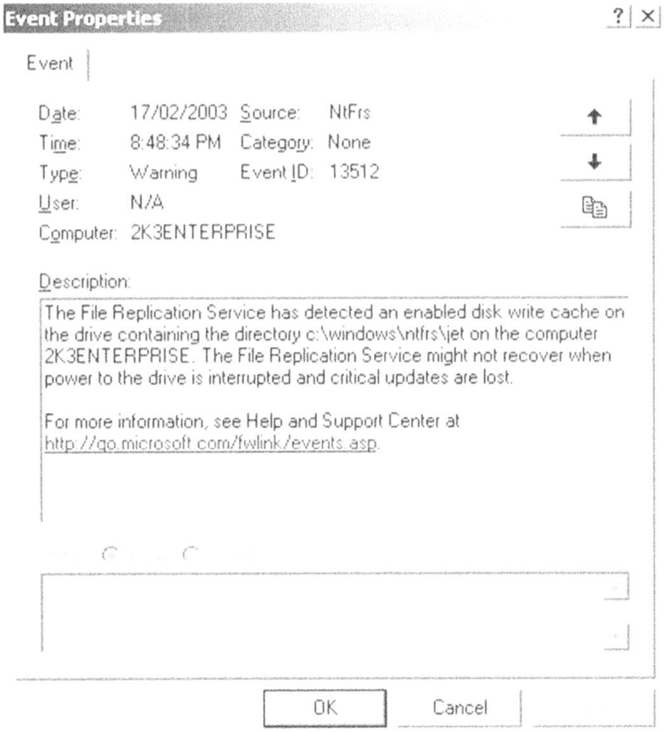

Figure 4-13: File Replication Service Log Event.

If Server 2003 is configured as a DNS Server, an additional log is available:

- **DNS Server Log**
  contains events logged by the DNS Service, such as the start of the DNS service.

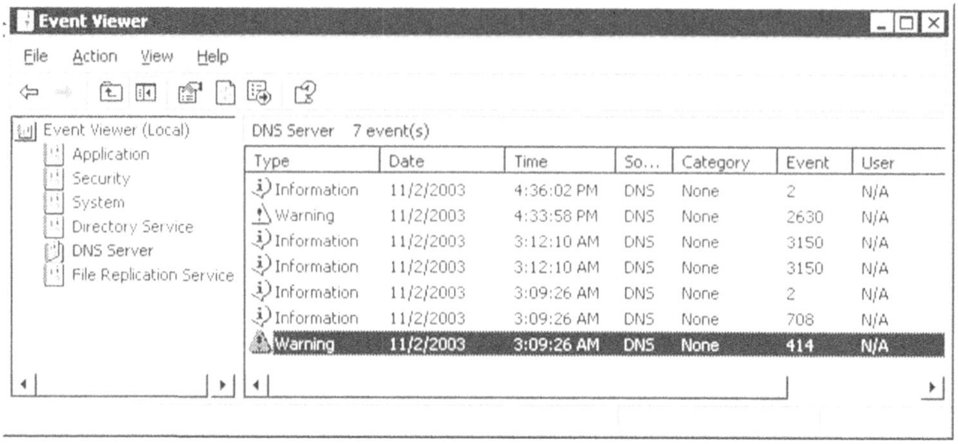

Figure 4-14: DNS Server Log.

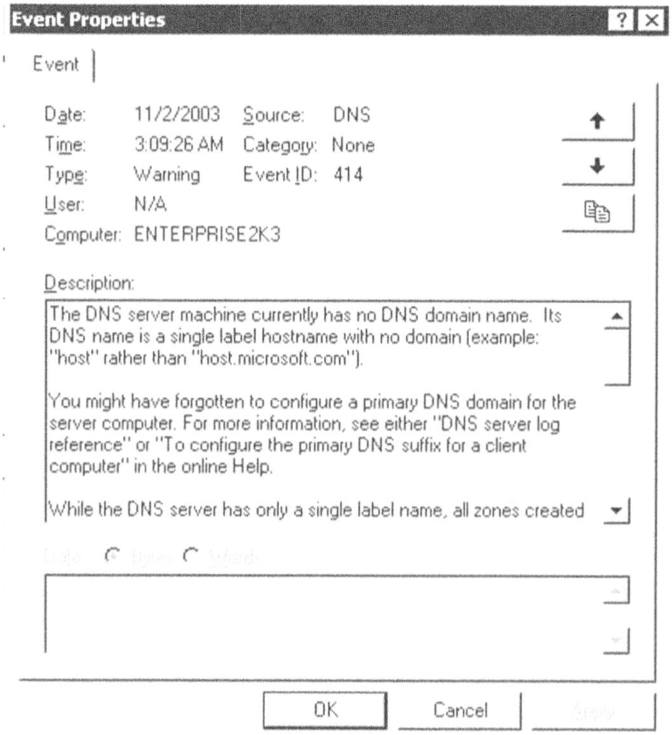

Figure 4-15: DNS Server Log Event.

Event Viewer provides great functionality for monitoring and analysis. Not only can you view events for the local server, but also you can view events for other remote servers, simply by right-clicking on **Event Viewer** at the top of the left pane.

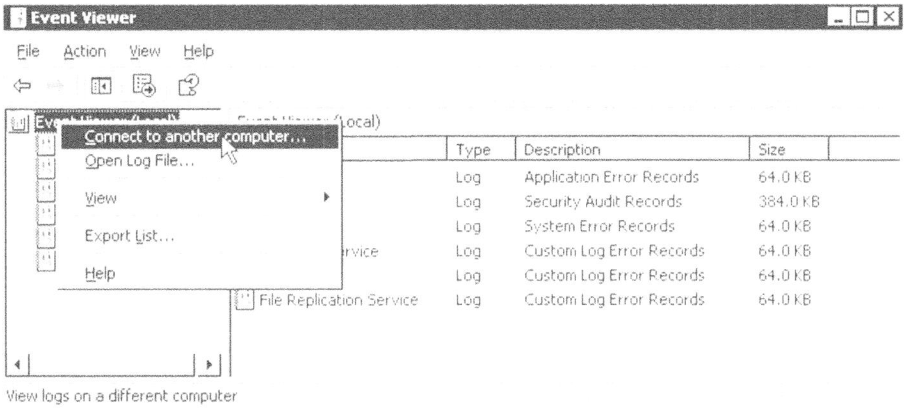

Figure 4-16: Connecting to another computer.

Another feature is the ability to filter the events that are displayed to identify any problem areas quickly. The filters are applied on a per log basis.

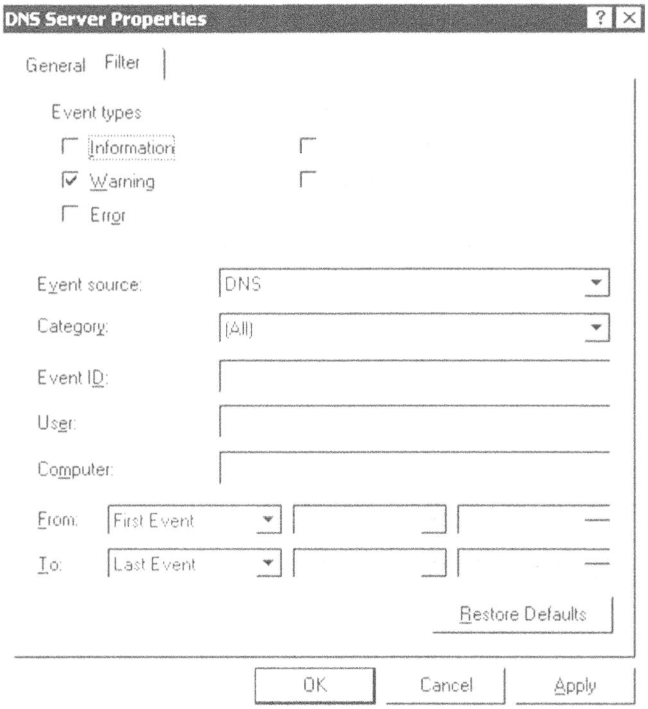

Figure 4-17: Log Filter.

4.1.1.2 System Monitor

System Monitor and Performance Logs and Alerts are both found in the Performance Console in Server 2003. **Performance** can be found under Administrative Tools in Control Panel.

System Monitor allows you to view real time performance of your server. You can capture this data in a log as well, so that you can view it at a later time. When you first open System Monitor, you will notice that nothing is being tracked. This is because you must first set counters to monitor the particular process in which you are interested. These counters will be displayed on the screen.

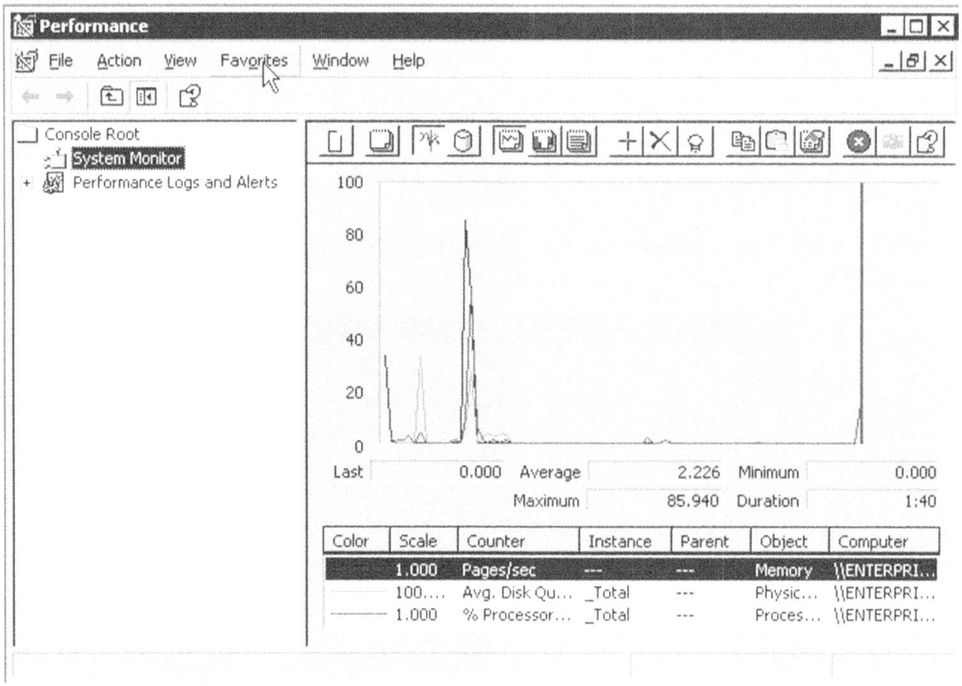

Figure 4-18: System Monitor.

There are three views available to you in System Monitor:

- **Chart**
  (the default view) allows you to view a small number of counters over a set period of time.
- **Histogram**
  (bar chart) allows you to view a large number of counters as a snapshot.
- **Report**
  allows you to view the counters in text format in real time.

Using the Performance Logs and Alerts will allow you to create counter and trace logs, as well as define alerts. You can use this tool to collect logged data, which can be used for detailed analysis and record keeping.

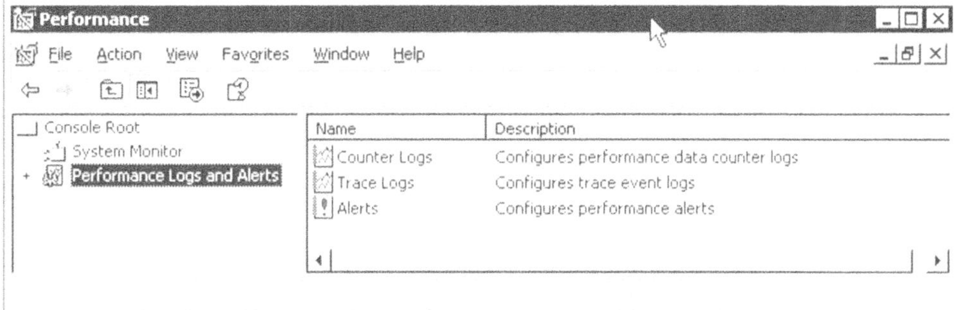

Figure 4-19: Performance Logs and Alerts.

The three logs available to you through Performance Logs and Alerts are:

- **Counter logs**
  record data about hardware usage and activity on a system. You can configure logging to occur on a regular basis, or on-demand. As an administrator, you should plan how often to collect data, based on the type of results you need to obtain.

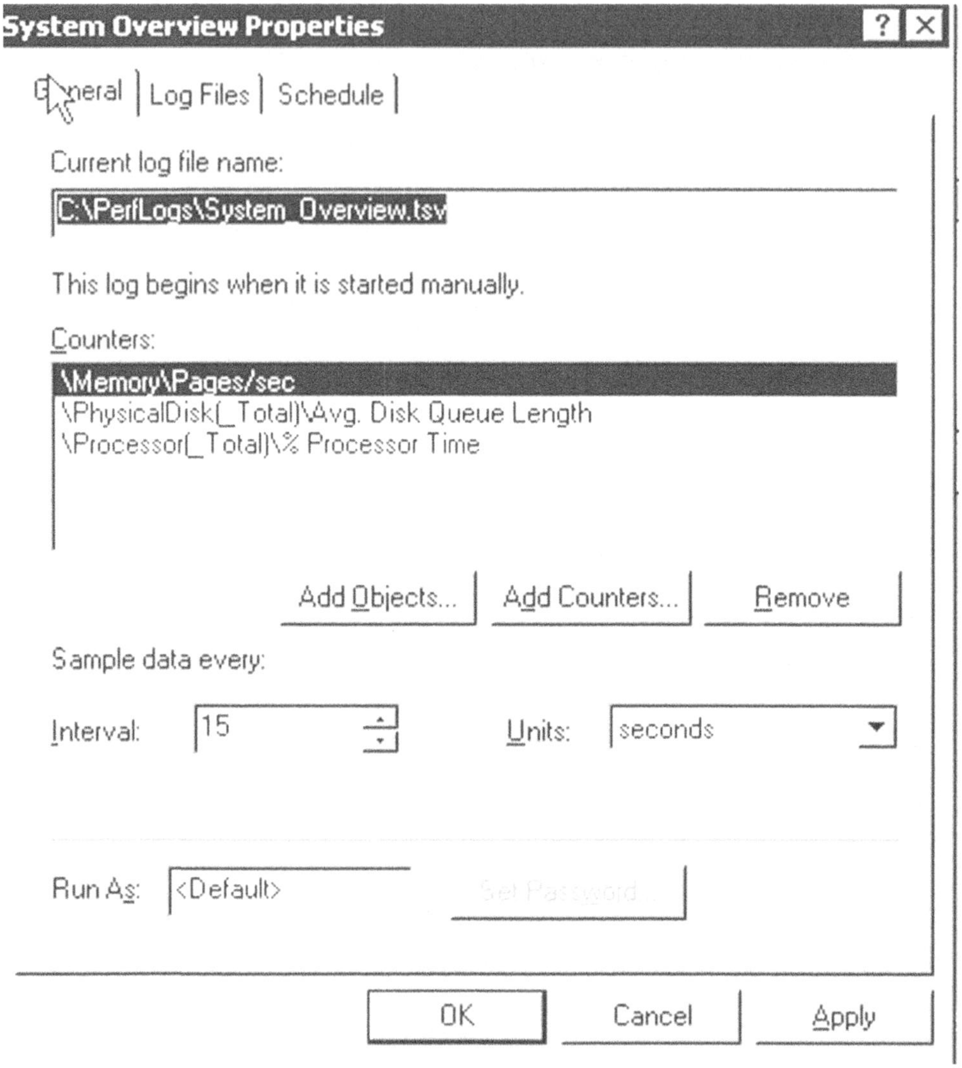

Figure 4-20: Setting Up a Counter Log.

- **Trace logs**
  measure data on a continuous basis.

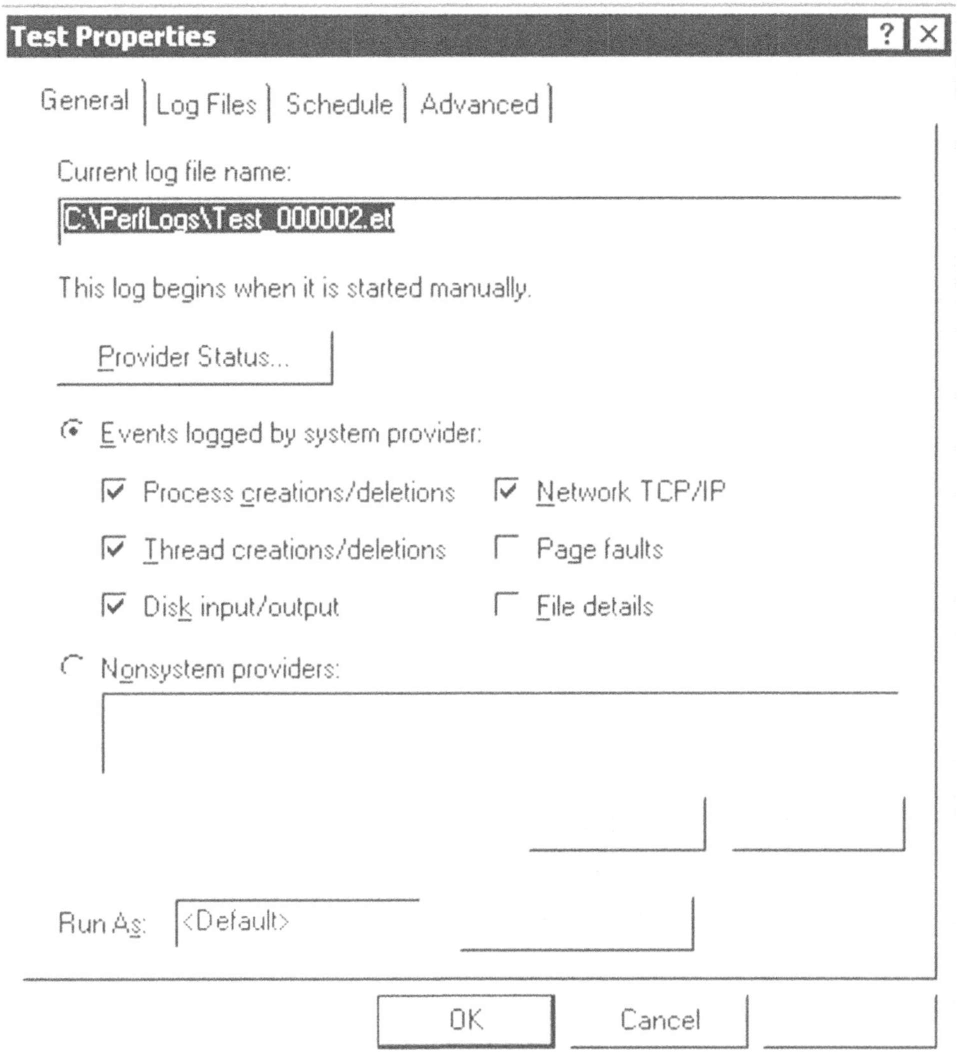

Figure 4-21: Setting Up a Trace Log.

- **Alerts**
  are messages that are sent to the system administrator when a specific counter exceeds, or falls below, a predetermined setting.

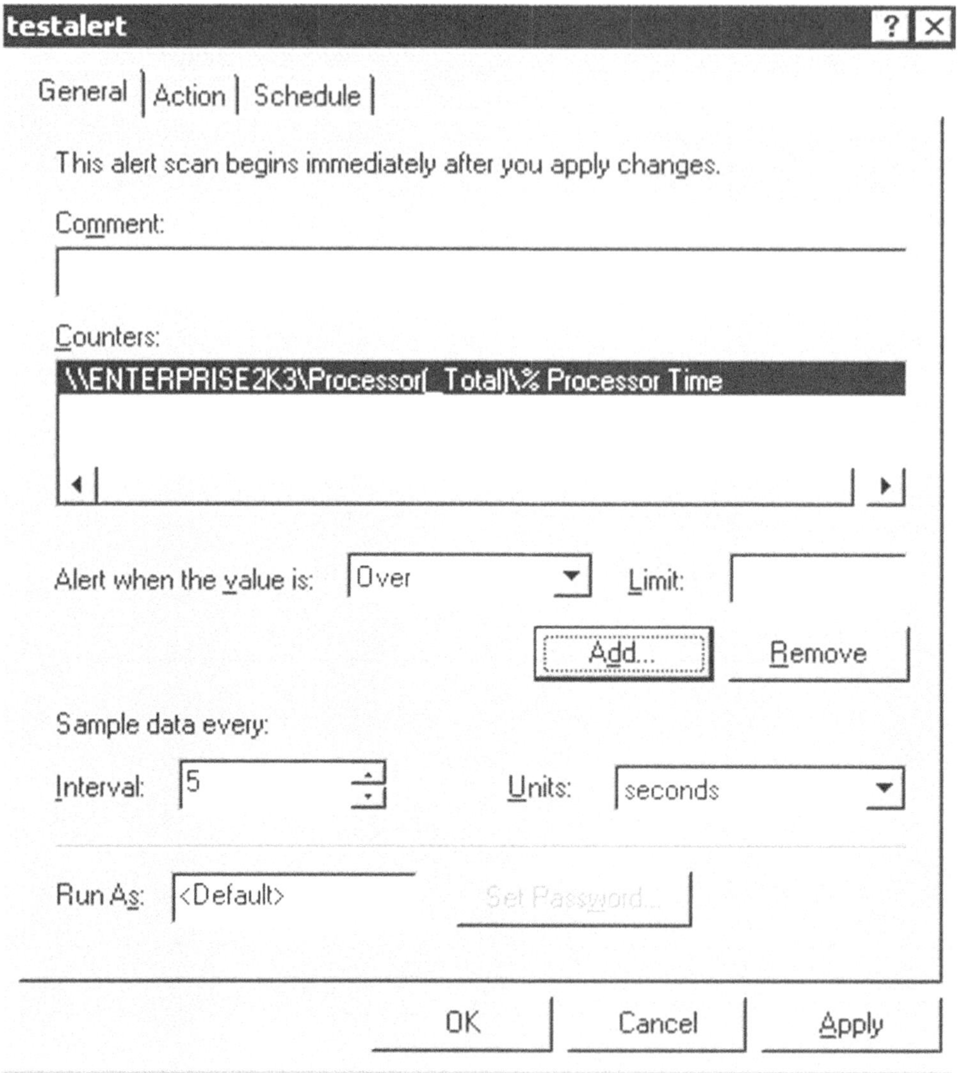

Figure 4-22: Setting Up an Alert.

4.1.1.3 Task Manager

- Task Manager will allow you to view the applications and processes that are currently running on your system. Task Manager provides "real time" monitoring of a server or system. You can access it in a number of ways:
    - Right-click the taskbar
    - Using CTRL|SHIFT|ESC
    - Using CTRL|ALT|DEL.
- There are five tabs available under Task Manager:
    - Applications
    - Processes
    - Performance
    - Networking
    - Users.

When you view the Applications Tab, you will see the applications that are running and their status (running | not responding | stopped). On this tab you can end a task, switch to a task or start a new task.

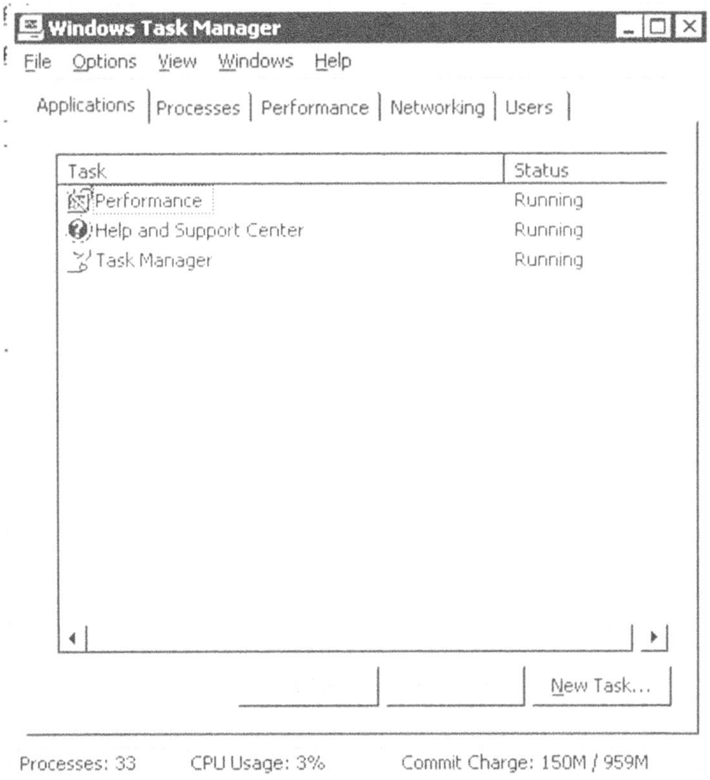

Figure 4-23: Applications Tab (Task Manager).

The **Processes** tab will show you all the processes currently running on your server, including processes used by the operating system. This tab allows you to end a process that has ceased to function or is causing system instability. If you right-click a process, a menu is displayed allowing you to end the process, end the process tree, debug (if a debugger is registered on the system), set the affinity (on multiprocessor systems) or change the priority of the process.

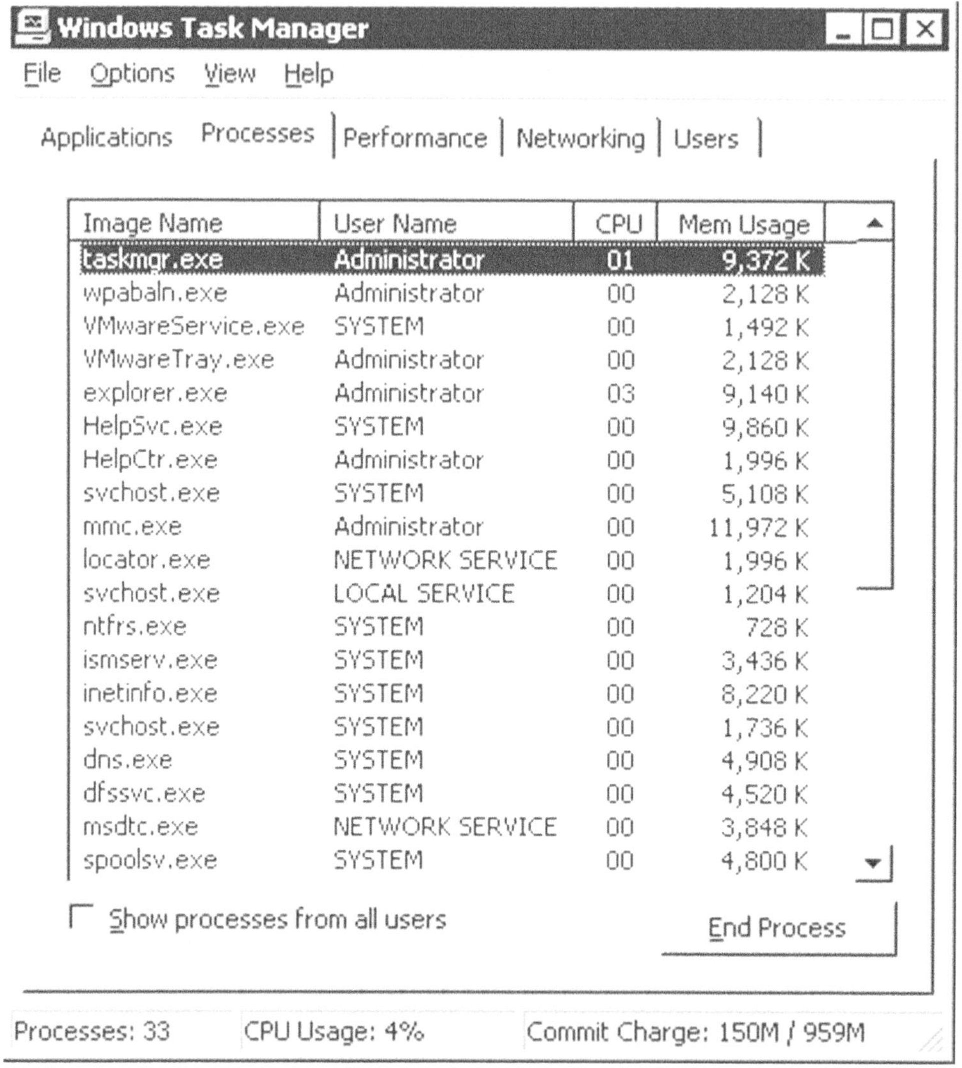

Figure 4-24: Processes Tab (Task Manager).

On multiprocessor systems, the **Set Affinity** command can inform an application or process to use a specific processor or processors. The effect of this can be a double-edged sword. You are essentially removing the ability of the process to benefit from the asymmetrical processing capabilities of Windows 2003. On the other hand, certain applications can gain substantial benefits from it, specifically if they do not use threading.

By changing the priority of a process, you can optimize it to use a specific amount of processor time. This can adversely affect the overall performance of not only the process itself, but of all other processes as well. By raising the priority, you grant the process more processing time, making it run faster. Inversely, by lowering the priority, you limit the amount of processing time, making it run slower.

In order for Windows 2003 to guarantee that every process will get a chance for processing time, a mechanism for scheduling threads is used. This mechanism is the basis for the pre-emptive multitasking strategy in Windows 2003. Each and every thread and process are assigned a priority, which then determines the order in which they are granted processing time. A thread's priority is based on the priority class of its parent process. There are four process priority classes:

- **Idle** – used for processes (such as screen savers) that periodically update the display.
- **Normal** – the default priority class for a process.
- **High** – these processes receive the majority of processor time.
- **Real Time** – used mostly by kernel-mode processes (such as mouse and keyboard input).

Each of these priority classes set a range of priority values between 0 and 31. Priority 0 is reserved for system use. Priorities between 1 and 31 have increasingly higher priorities (with 1 being the lowest). Idle, Normal and High priorities range between 1 and 15, Real Time priorities range between 16 and 31. For processes that are Real Time, the thread's priority cannot change while the thread is running. For all other priorities, the threads are considered variable (they can change thread priority while running). For threads running in the Normal or High priority classes, the thread's priority can be raised or lowered by up to a value of 2, but cannot fall below its original, program-defined base priority. The resulting value of changing the base priority for optimized thread scheduling is called the thread's dynamic priority.

A listing of all Windows 2003 process priorities is listed in Table 4.2.

Note: If you have at least one priority 31 thread running, other threads cannot run.

	Process Priority Classes			
Thread Priorities	**Real Time**	**High**	**Normal**	**Idle**
Time Critical	31	15	15	15
Highest	26	15	10	6
Above Normal	25	14	9	5
Normal	24	13	8	4
Below Normal	23	12	7	3
Lowest	22	11	6	2
Idle	16	1	1	1

Table 4-2: Server 2003 Process Priorities.

With Task Manger, you can change the base priority of a process to one of the following:

- Real time (Time Critical)
- High (Highest)
- Above Normal
- Normal
- Below Normal
- Low (Lowest).

Remember that you cannot change the Process Priority Class, just the thread priority. Changes made to the base priority of the process are not permanent; they are effective only as long as the process runs.

Note: You must be an administrator to change a process' priority.

The information on the Processes tab can be modified to gain even more information. By choosing Select Columns... on the View menu will display Figure 4.25. Each of these options are explained in Table 4.3.

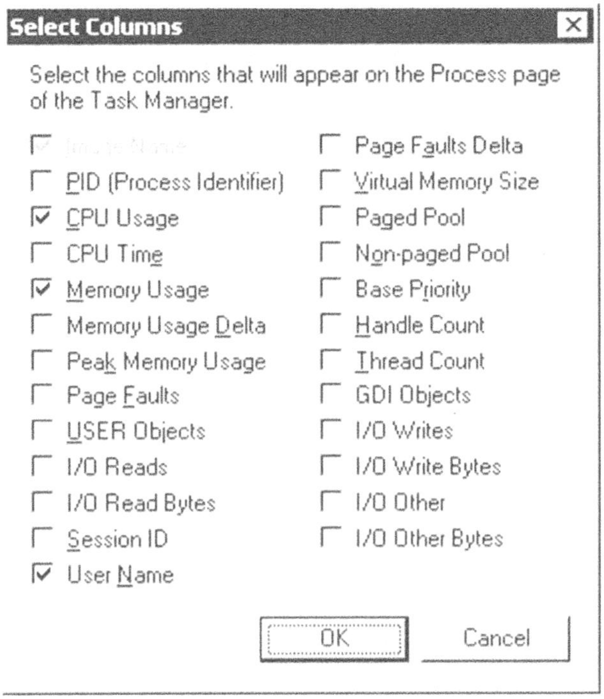

Figure 4-25: Task Manager Processes.

Column	Description
Base Priority	A precedence ranking that determines the order in which the threads of a process are scheduled for the processor.
CPU Time	The total processor time, in seconds, used by a process since it started.
CPU Usage	The percentage of time that a process used the CPU since the last update.
GDI Objects	The number of Graphics Device Interface (GDI) objects currently used by a process.
Handle Count	The number of object handles in a process's object table.
Image Name	The name of a process.
I/O Other	The number of input/output operations generated by a process that are neither a read nor a write, including file, network and device I/Os.
I/O Other Bytes	The number of bytes transferred in input/output operations generated by a process that are neither a read nor a write, including file, network and device I/Os.
I/O Reads	The number of read input/output operations generated by a process, including file, network and device I/Os. I/O Reads directed to CONSOLE (console input object) handles are not counted.
I/O Read Bytes	The number of bytes read in input/output operations generated by a process, including file, network and device I/Os. I/O Read Bytes directed to CONSOLE (console input object) handles are not counted.
I/O Writes	The number of write input/output operations generated by a process, including file, network and device I/Os. I/O Writes directed to CONSOLE (console input object) handles are not counted.
I/O Write Bytes	The number of bytes written in input/output operations generated by a process, including file, network, and device I/Os. I/O Write Bytes directed to CONSOLE (console input object) handles are not counted.
Memory Usage	The current working set of a process, in kilobytes. The current working set is the number of pages currently resident in memory.
Memory Usage Delta	The change in memory, in kilobytes, used since the last update.
Non-paged Pool	The amount of memory used by a process, in kilobytes, that is not paged to disk.
Page Faults	The number of times data has to be retrieved from disk for a process because it was not found in memory. The page fault value accumulates from the time the process started.

Column	Description
Page Faults Delta	The change in the number of page faults since the last update.
Paged Pool	The amount of system allocated virtual memory, in kilobytes, used by a process.
Peak Memory Usage	The peak amount of physical memory resident in a process since it started.
PID (Process Identifier)	A numerical identifier that uniquely distinguishes a process while it runs.
Thread Count	The number of threads running in a process.
USER Objects	The number of USER objects (windows, menus, cursors, icons, etc.) currently being used by a process.
Virtual Memory Size	The amount of virtual memory, or address space, committed to a process.
Session ID (Terminal Services Only)	The Terminal Services session ID that owns the process.
User Name (Terminal Services Only)	The name of the user whose Terminal Services session owns the process.

Table 4-3: Process Definitions.

The **Performance** Tab will give you a quick glance at CPU and memory usage. This tab provides you with a quick version of the System Monitor tool.

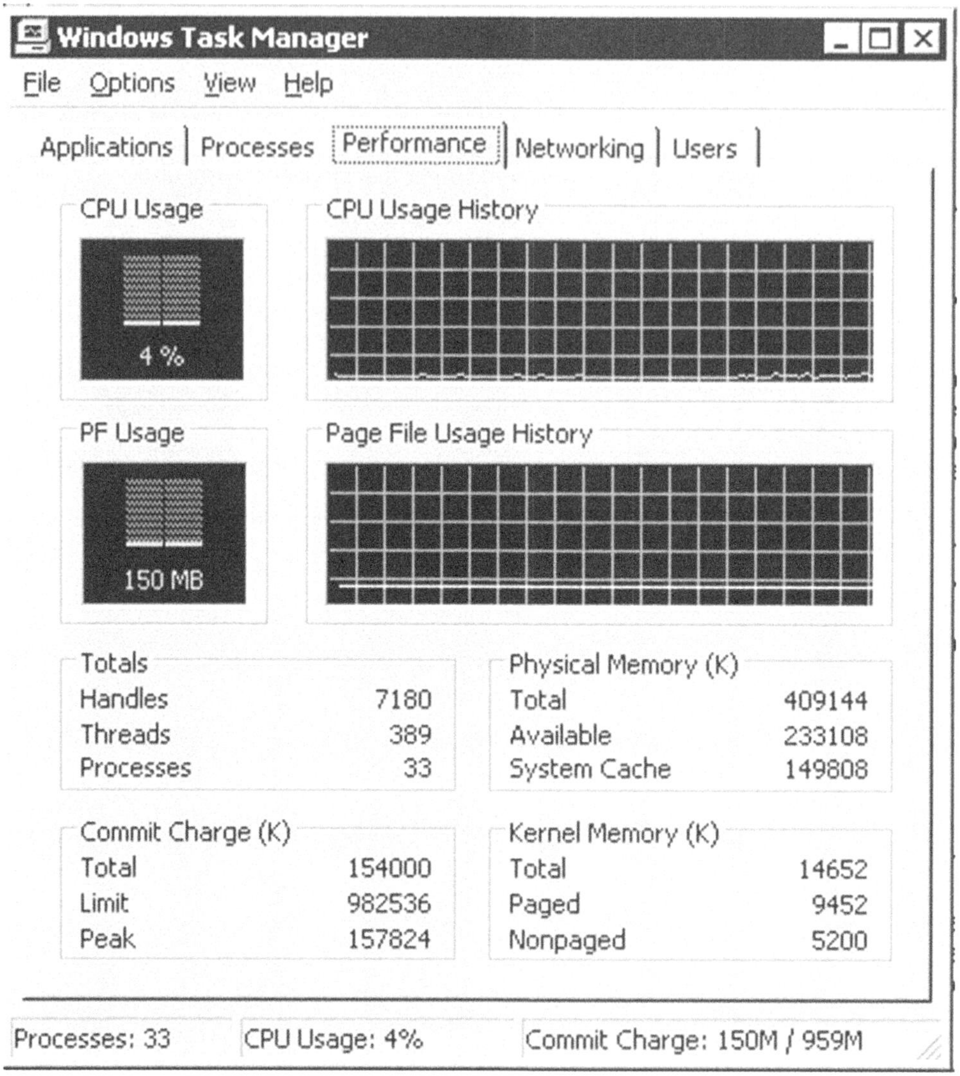

Figure 4-26: Performance Tab (Task Manager).

By clicking **Show Kernel Times** on the **View** menu, red lines are added to the CPU Usage gauge and CPU Usage History graph. These red lines indicate the percentage of processor time consumed in privileged or kernel mode.

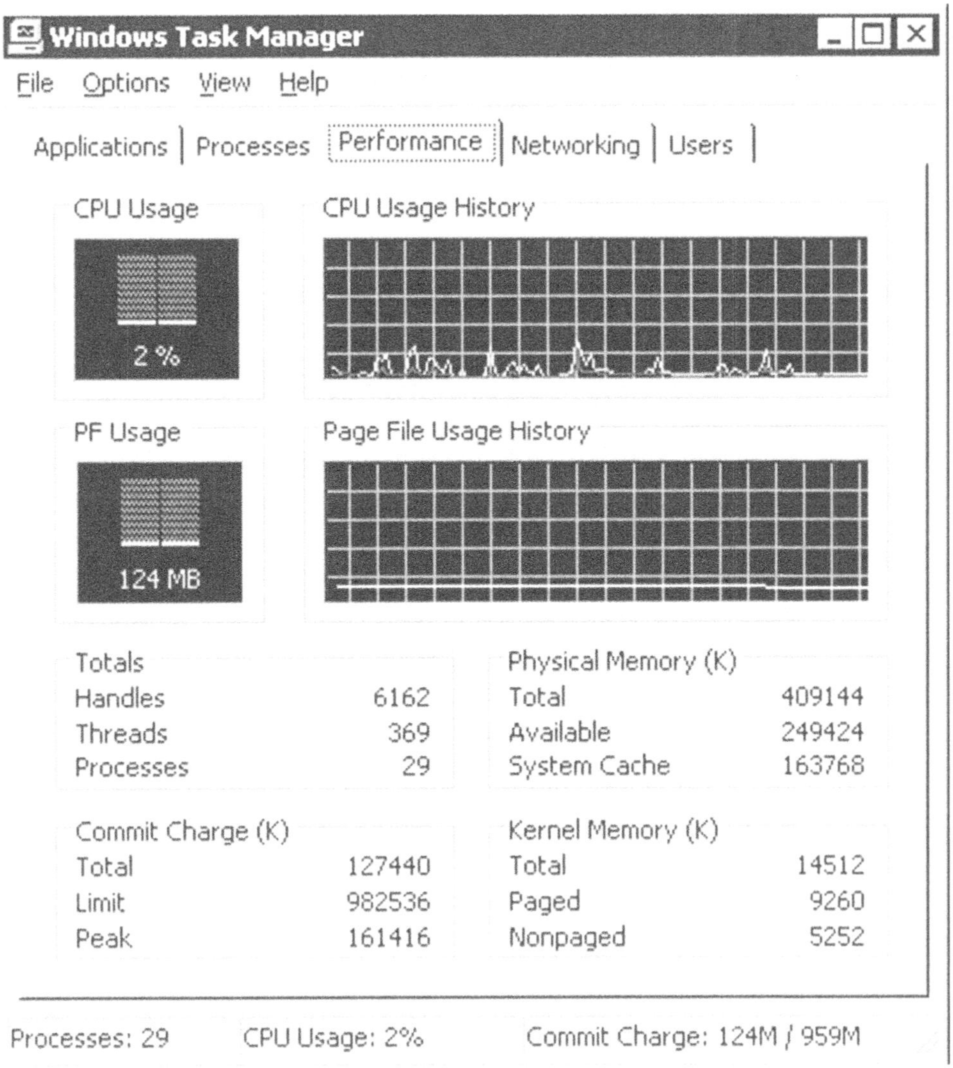

Figure 4-27: Performance View with Kernel Times.

On multiprocessor systems, you can change the graph to display each processor in a single graph, or in separate graphs. Clicking **CPU History** on the **View** menu achieves this functionality.

New to Server 2003 is the Networking Tab. Introduced with Windows XP, with this view, you can see bytes sent, received and total. The Networking tab provides a quick indication of the network traffic on the server. A quick reference for determining the amount of network bandwidth being consumed, when there are multiple network connections;it allows easy comparison of the traffic for each connection.

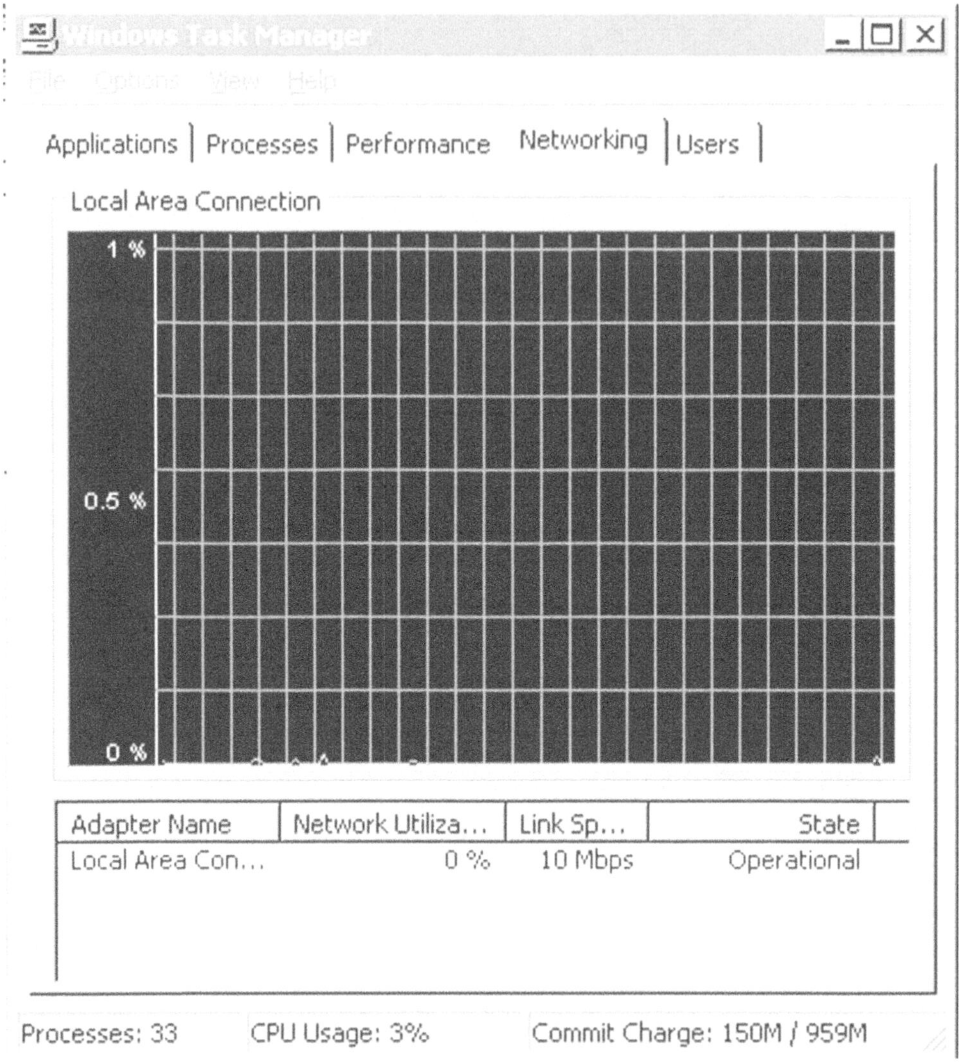

Figure 4-28: Networking Tab (Task Manager).

Note: If there is no network card connected to the server, this tab will not appear.

Also new to Server 2003 is the **Users** tab, which was introduced in Windows XP with Fast User Switching enabled. When there is more than one user connected to the server, you can see who is connected, what they are working on and you can send them a message. As well, you can disconnect users if necessary.

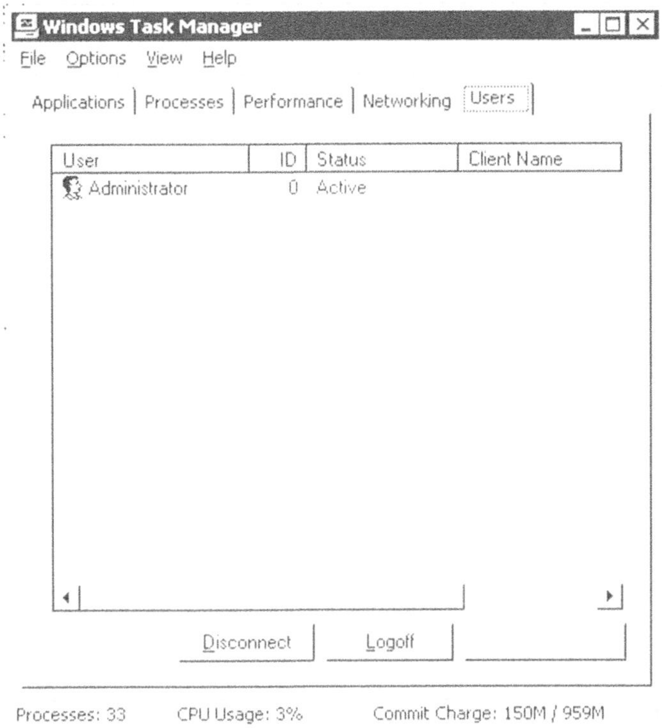

Figure 4-29: User Tab (Task Manager).

Pop Quiz 4.1

Pop Quiz 4.1 *Questions*

1. What are the four main subsystems?
2. In any configuration of Server 2003, what are the three logs that will appear in Event Viewer?
3. What events will show in the System Log?
4. If Server 2003 is a domain controller, what two additional logs become available?
5. What three views are available to you in System Monitor?

Pop Quiz 4.1 *Answers*

1. The four main subsystems are memory, processor, disk and network.
2. No matter what the configuration, Event Viewer will always record events in the Application Log, the System Log and the Security Log.
3. The System Log (and the Application Log) will show three events—Error, Warning and Information.
4. In Windows Server 2003 domain controllers, there will also be a Directory Services log and a File Replication Service log.
5. The three views in System Monitor are Chart, Histogram and Report.

4.2 Manage software update infrastructure

Most people who are running Windows 2000 Professional or Windows XP are familiar with the new innovation, Windows Update. With Windows Server 2003, Software Update Services (SUS) is introduced as a server-based distribution system for critical updates, security patches and service packs.

SUS is, essentially, a server-based Windows Update that provides updates for Server and Professional 2000 SP3, Windows XP SP1 and Server 2003. Running as a service on an internal server, SUS connects through the corporate firewall to the Windows Update site and allows administrators to collect the patches, updates and service packs needed for their network via a Web-based application.

In the past, network administrators had to set up a schedule to check for critical updates, service packs and security patches that had been released since the last check. After verifying and testing these "fixes." the administrator would have to distribute them to the desktop PCs and servers in their network using a distribution methodology.

The Network Administrator must first sign up for e-mail notification. This can be done at http://www.microsoft.com/windows2000/windowsupdate/sus/redir-email.asp (Figure 4.30).

Using SUS, network administrators will receive an e-mail notification (Figure 4.31) when updates are added to their SUS channel. The updates can be downloaded from the live Windows Update servers and saved on the SUS Server on the network. Administrators are then able to verify, test and install critical updates quickly without disruption to the network, using the Automatic Update feature on client machines and servers.

Note: All non-security-related patches, such as patches for applications or device drivers cannot be managed through SUS. SUS is designed for distribution of critical patches, service packs and security updates.

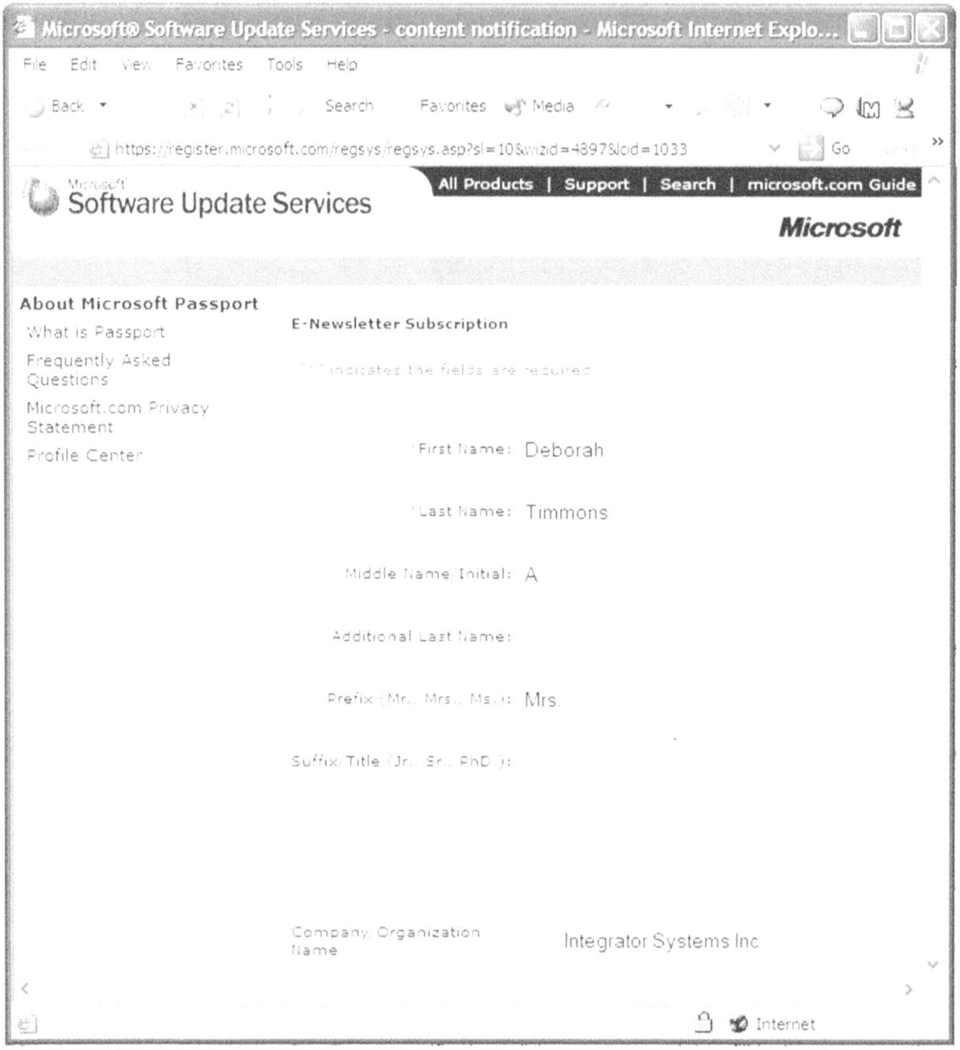

Figure 4-30: E-Newsletter Subscription.

Figure 4-31: SUS Content Notification Email.

4.2.1 Components

SUS is comprised of three components that can be downloaded from the Microsoft site:

- **Server Component –** the service to be installed on the SUS Server (SUS10SP1.exe).

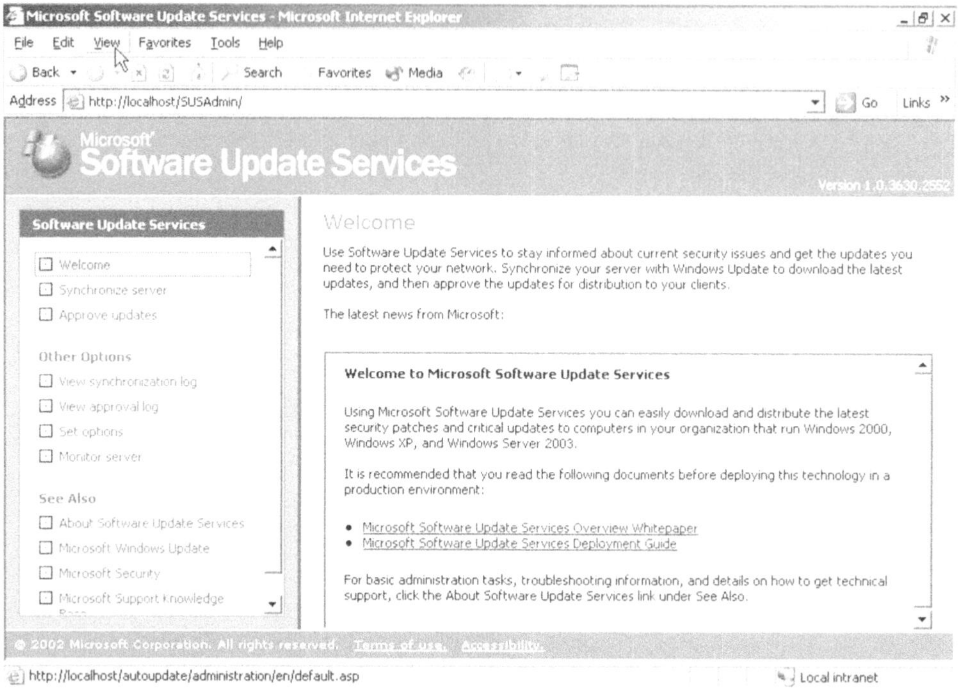

Figure 4-32: SUS Server Component Webpage Interface.

From this interface the administrator can tune the corporate SUS Service to meet the needs of the organization. He or she can synchronize the corporate SUS Server with the main Software Update Services servers at Microsoft, or set up the synchronization schedule. From the list of downloaded patches, the updates can be approved. As well, the synchronization log and approval log can be viewed, and options such as proxy server and storage of updates can be set. Finally, the SUS server can be monitored from this interface.

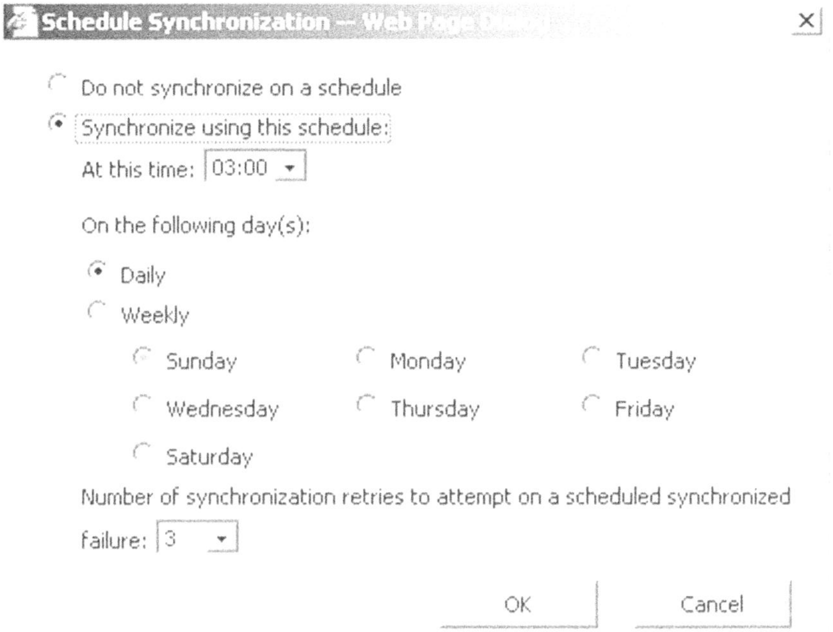

Figure 4-33: Scheduling SUS Server Synchronization.

- **Client Component –** download is only required for systems running Windows 2000 SP2 and Windows XP RTM. Already included in Windows 2000 SP3 or later, Windows XP SP1 or later and Windows Server 2003 (wuau22*.msi).
- **Group Policy Component –** template add-on to configure the Automatic Updates component on client computers (servers and workstations). There are four settings that can be configured (Figure 4.34).

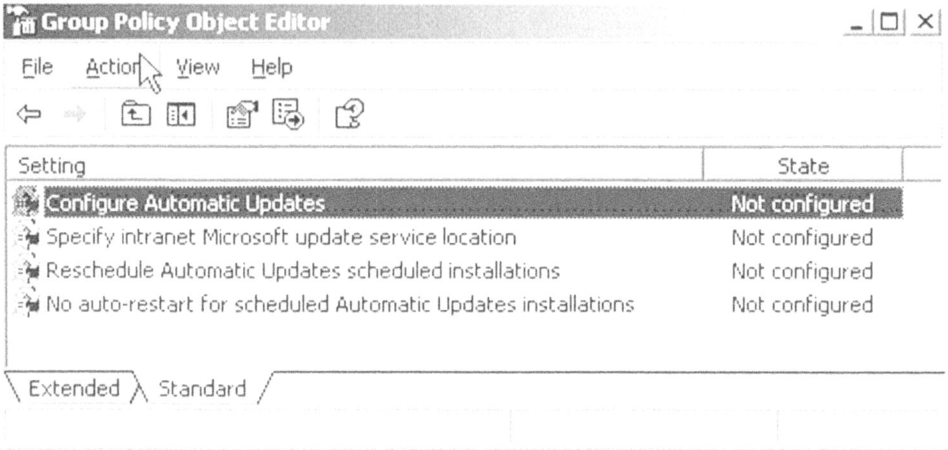

Figure 4-34: SUS Automatic Update GPO.

Configure Automatic Updates (Not Configured | Enabled | Disabled) Under Enabled, there are three options—notify on download and on install, automatic download/notify on install, automatic download and schedule install. With the third option, the administrator can then schedule the install date and time.

- **Specify intranet Microsoft update service location (Not Configured | Enabled | Disabled)**
  Under Enabled, the administrator can then specify both the intranet update service for detecting updates and the intranet statistics server.
- **Reschedule Automatic Updates scheduled installations (Not Configured | Enabled | Disabled)**
  Under Enabled, the administrator can schedule when the Automatic Updates should be applied, if the system is powered off during the specified time. This schedule is "x" number of minutes after system startup.
- **No auto-restart for scheduled Automatic Updates installations**
  This is a specific setting so that Automatic Updates are not rescheduled on system startup.

4.3 Manage software site licensing

Let's review the differences in the licensing options for Server 2003.

- If users frequently access multiple servers on the corporate network, **Per User** or **Per Device** licensing is the best option. This licensing mode enables all network devices or users to access all the servers on a network, with an unlimited number of simultaneous connections to any server. This is the normal licensing mode for Server 2003 installed on multiple servers in a network setting.

> **NOTE:** For the purposes of Windows licensing, any electronic equipment that can access or use the services of Server 2003, including file and print sharing, remote access and authentication, is considered a device. This can include servers, workstations, terminals and handhelds.

- If Server 2003 is installed on only one server, which is accessed by only a certain number of users at any one time, **Per Server** is the best option. Per Server connections are allocated on a first-come, first-serve basis to the server licensed. The numbers of connections are limited to the number of CALs (Client Access Licenses). This type of license is best in a single server environment or in an environment where a designated server is used by only a single group (for example, a server dedicated to the Human Resource Department). There is a one-time conversion available to Per User or Per Device licensing.

> **NOTE:** If you are installing Server 2003 on a single server, and you are unsure which license mode to use, select Per Server, as you are allowed a one-time conversion to Per User or Per Device licensing.

4.3.1 Administering Enterprise Licensing

Administration of licensing in an enterprise environment for Server 2003 is done through the **Licensing** tool, located in **Administrative Tools** in Control Panel. You must be the Administrator, or a member of the Administrators Group, in order to work with this tool. By default, the licensing tool is not enabled. In order to use it, you must enable it under **Services**, located under **Administrative Tools**.

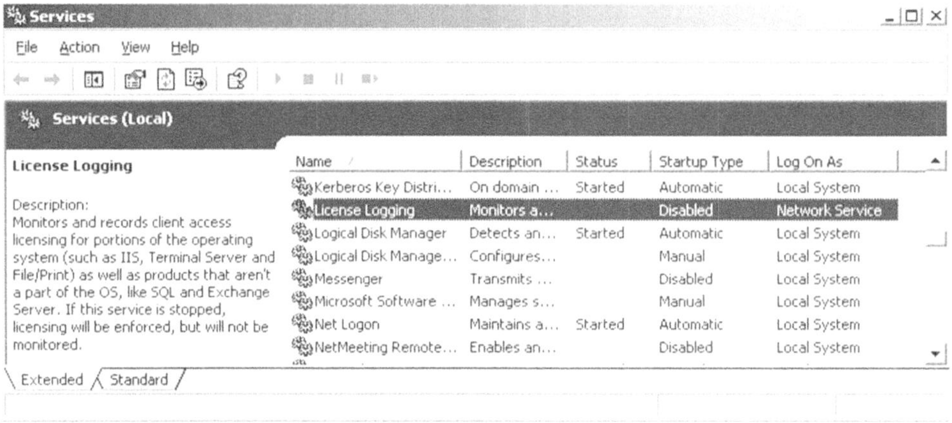

Figure 4-35: Enabling the Licensing Tool.

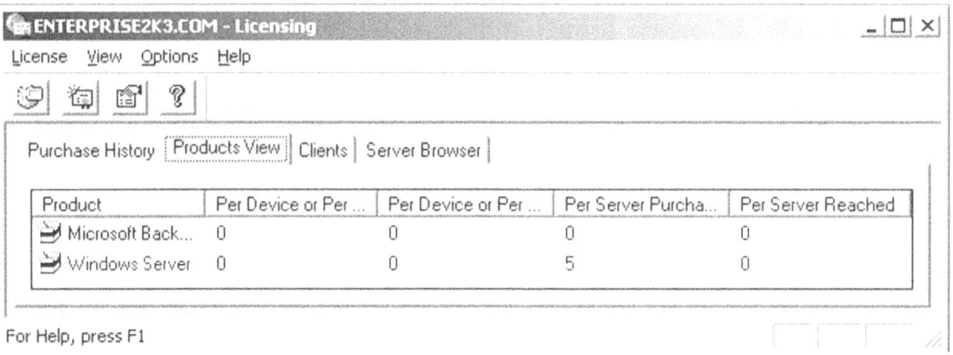

Figure 4-36: Licensing Tool.

The interface for the Licensing Tool in Server 2003 family is similar to that in Windows 2000 or Microsoft Windows NT 4.0. There are four tabs:

- **Purchase History**
  It is under this tab that you will manage the purchase or deletion of licenses for server products on network servers. Here you enter the number of licenses, the type of license and the date of purchase. The **Purchase History** entries are not intuitive—that is, the entries you make are not verified by the system, nor are they entered automatically. It is important that you track your licensing carefully and accurately. When you enter a number of licenses into the **Purchase History** dialog box, the license agreement will appear.

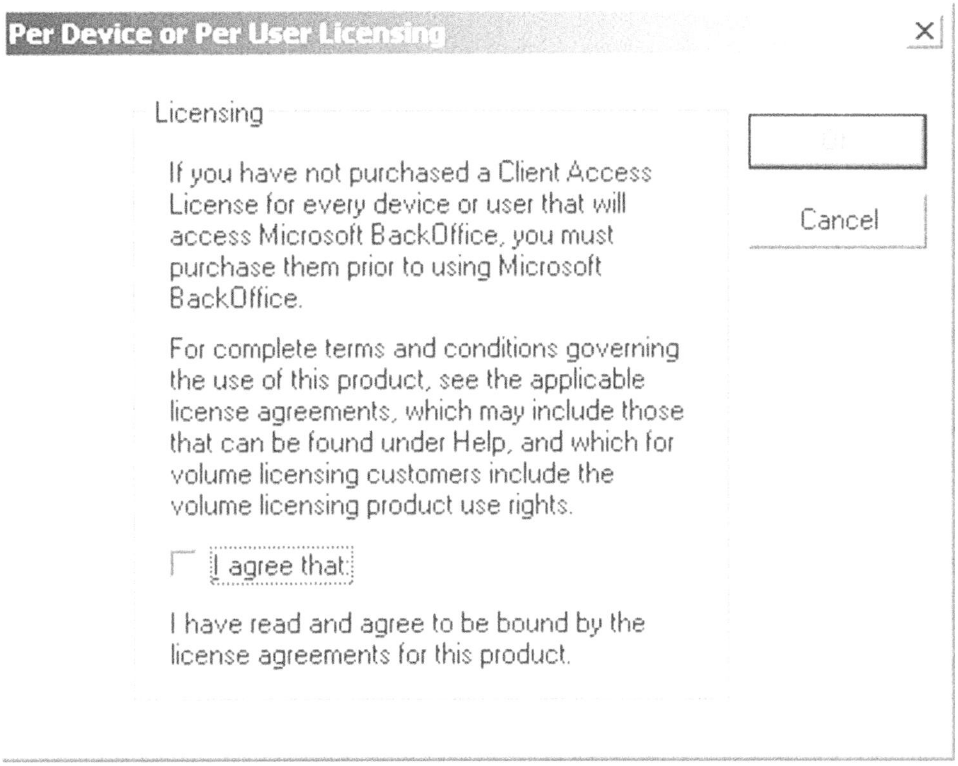

Figure 4-37: Licensing Agreement.

- **Products View**
  Under this tab, you can view Per Server and Per Device or Per User licenses for the site or a particular group in the site.
- **Clients**
  Under this tab, you can view usage statistics for each user, including licensed and unlicensed usage. This tool will allow you to track license usage and ascertain when additional licenses are required.
- **Server Browser**
  Under server browser, you can remotely manage licensing on servers (for server products licensed in Per Server mode). You can also manage replication remotely, by right-clicking the server, select **Properties**, and then using the **Replication** tab.

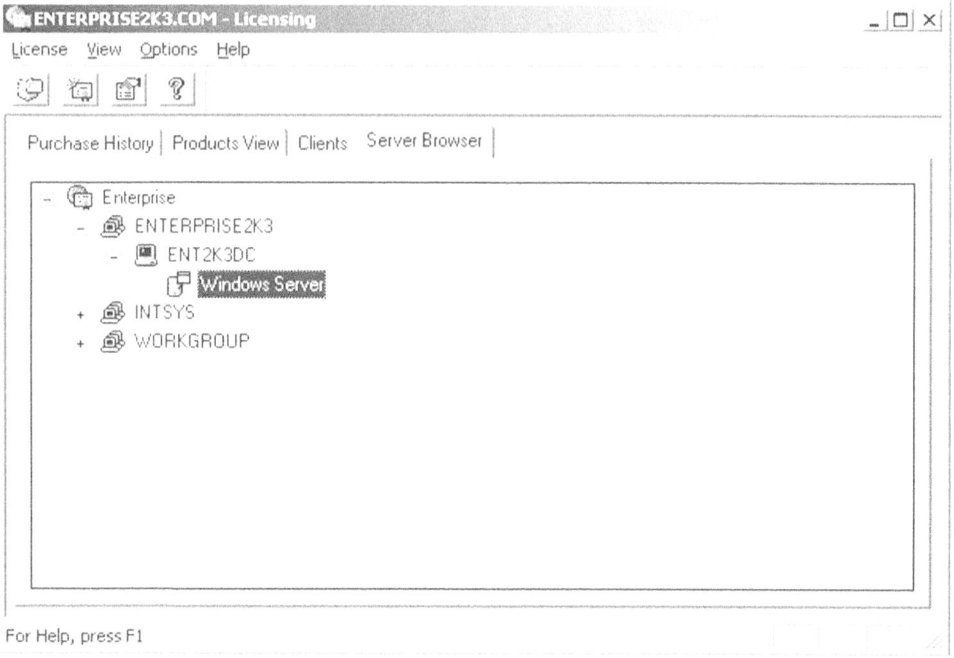

Figure 4-38: Remote Licensing Management.

4.3.2 License Replication

4.3.2.1 Configuring Replication Locally

To record a number of new licenses (that will appear in the **Products View** tab of the Licensing Tool) or to configure replication for the local server, you can use **Licensing** under **Control Panel**.

> **Note:** You can also record local licensing under the **Server Browser** tab of the Licensing Tool, by right-clicking the local server and selecting **Properties.** However, you CANNOT configure replication for a local machine through this process.

To configure the number of licenses, just go to Control Panel and select **Licensing**. The dialog box illustrated in Figure 4.39 will appear.

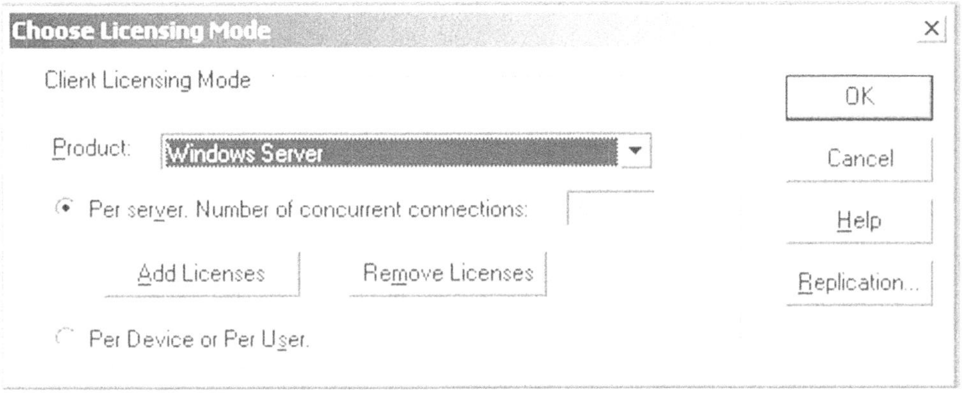

Figure 4-39: Licensing Mode (Control Panel).

It is from this interface that you can add licenses for both Windows Server 2003 and Windows Back Office. You can also switch your licensing, one time only, from Per Server to Per Device or Per User.

If you look at Figure 4.39, you will note the **Replication...** button on the bottom right hand corner. Clicking that button will bring up the dialog box in Figure 4.40 that will allow you to configure replication for the local server.

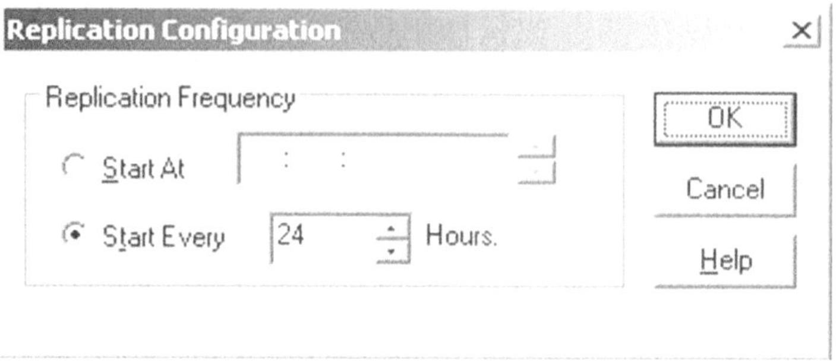

Figure 4-40: Replication (Control Panel).

From here, you can configure when you want the licensing information to replication, either at a specific time, or at a scheduled interval.

4.3.2.2 Configuring Replication for Remote Servers

In order to configure replication for remote servers, the steps are similar to those listed above. From **Administrative** Tools, open **Licensing**. On the **Server Browser** tab, expand the domain, right-click the server to manage and then click **Properties**. Select the **Replication** tab.

Under **Replication Frequency**, specify the interval at which the licensing information should replicated to the site license server. As outlined in the previous section, you have two choices. You can select a specific time for daily replication by clicking **Start At** and entering a time, or you can set a time interval between replication cycles by clicking **Start Every** and entering the desired interval.

Note: It is important to note that under Windows NT 4.0 domains, you can use the **Master Server** options to specify where the server replicates. If it is a stand-alone server in an NT 4.0 domain, it will replicate to the PDC. This has changed with Windows 2000 and 2003 domains. Server 2003 replicates automatically to a domain controller, and domain controllers replicate to the site license server. The option to specify a master server does not exist in a Server 2003 environment.

Pop Quiz 4.2

Pop Quiz 4.2 *Questions*

1. What is the difference between Windows Update and Software Update Services?
2. There are patches for your word processing application. Can you manage these through SUS?
3. What are the three components that comprise SUS?
4. When dealing with Windows licensing, what is a device?
5. To records local licensing, you can use Licensing under Control Panel as well as under the Server Browser tab of the Licensing Tool. Can you configure replication for the local machine as well through both processes?

Pop Quiz 4.2 *Answers*

1. Windows Update is a client-based tool that provides a Windows 2000 or XP client with critical updates, security patches and service packs. SUS is a server-based "Windows Update" that provides updates for Server/Professional 2000 SP3, Windows XP SP1 and Server 2003.
2. No. All non-security-related patches, such as patches for applications or device drivers cannot be managed through SUS. SUS is designed for distribution of critical patches, service packs and security updates.
3. SUS is comprised of three components, which can all be downloaded from Microsoft—the Server component, the Client component and the Group Policy component.
4. For the purposes of Windows licensing, any electronic equipment that can access or use the services of Server 2003, including file and print sharing, remote access and authentication, is considered a device. This can include servers, workstations, terminals and handhelds.
5. You can record local licensing under the Server Browser tab of the Licensing Tool, by right-clicking the local server and selecting Properties. However, you CANNOT configure replication for a local machine through this process.

4.4 Manage servers remotely

Remote Desktop and Remote Assistance are both new to Server 2003. They use the same basic technology, but there are some fundamental differences between these two features.

Remote Desktop allows access to a remote Windows computer. For example, if you are working at home, you can use Remote Desktop to connect to your work computer. Your work computer will appear in a new window, and you can work remotely off your own desktop at work, gaining access to files and applications.

Remote Assistance allows an administrator to use an Internet connection to access a user's computer or remote server to provide help. The administrator can view the remote computer's screen in a window and communicate with the user through a "chat box." This feature is used so that administrators can resolve problems without having to be physically at the user's computer or server.

4.4.1 Manage a server by using Remote Assistance

Remote Assistance was first introduced in Windows XP. It allows the administrator to assist another individual remotely, in real time. The remote system must be running Server 2003 or Windows XP. Remote Assistance requires explicit permission from the individual requesting assistance.

Note: This feature is NOT available under Server 2003 64-bit version.

In order to use Remote Assistance, Group Policy must be enabled. This can be done by:

- Click **Start | Run**, type **gpedit.msc** and click **OK**.
- Under **Computer Configuration**, double-click **Administrative Templates**, double-click **System** and then double-click **Remote Assistance**.

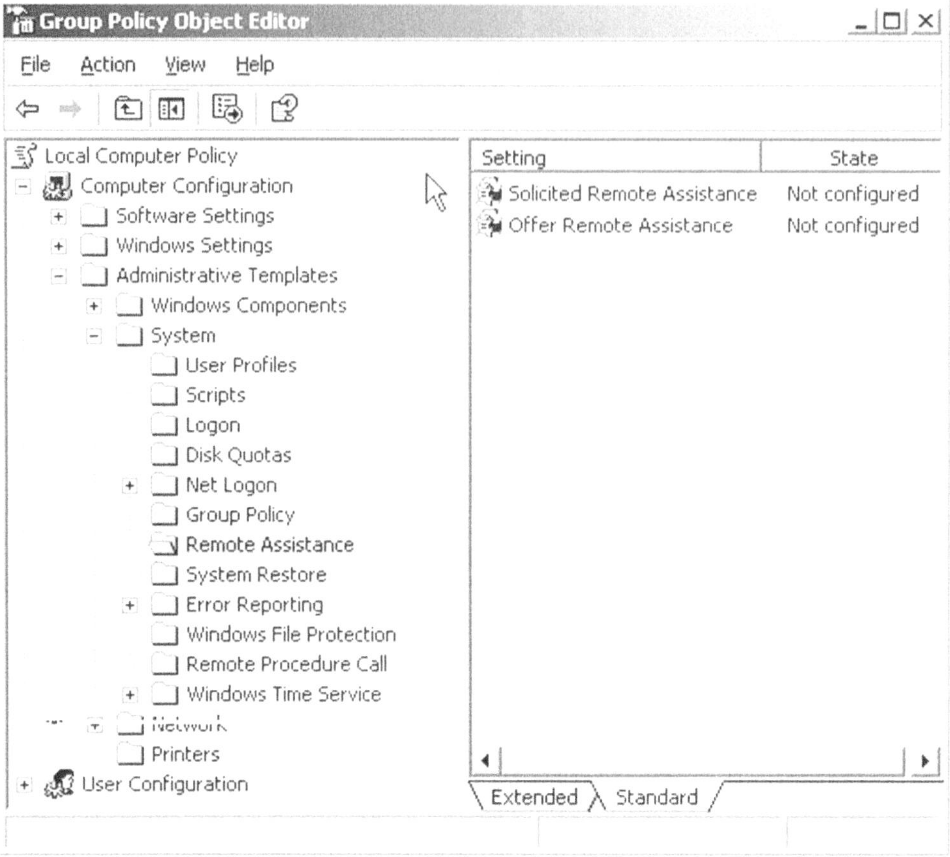

Figure 4-41: Group Policy Object Editor.

As you will note, there are two settings that can be configured under Remote Assistance Group Policy.

Solicited Remote Assistance

This setting specifies whether a user can request (solicit) assistance using Remote Assistance. By default, this setting is set to "Not Configured." When the status is set to Not Configured, a user can enable, disable and configure Remote Assistance in System properties in Control Panel. The default maximum time a Remote Assistance invitation can stay open is determined by this Control Panel setting (Figure 4.42).

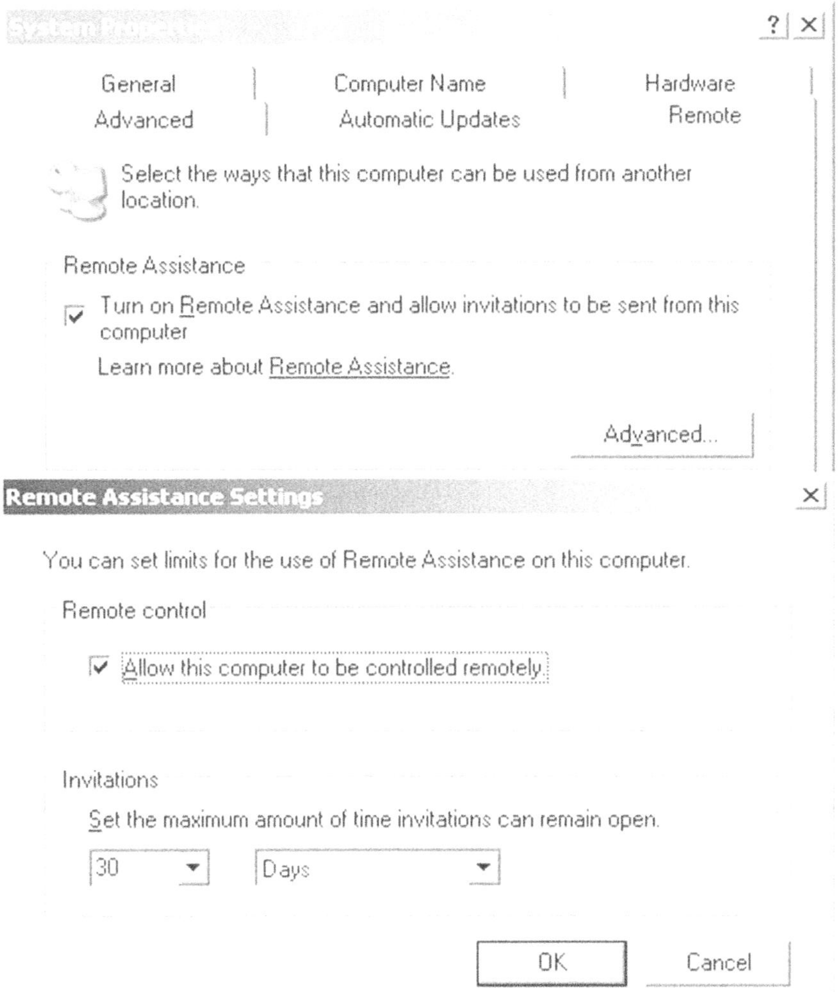

Figure 4-42: Remote Assistance (Control Panel).

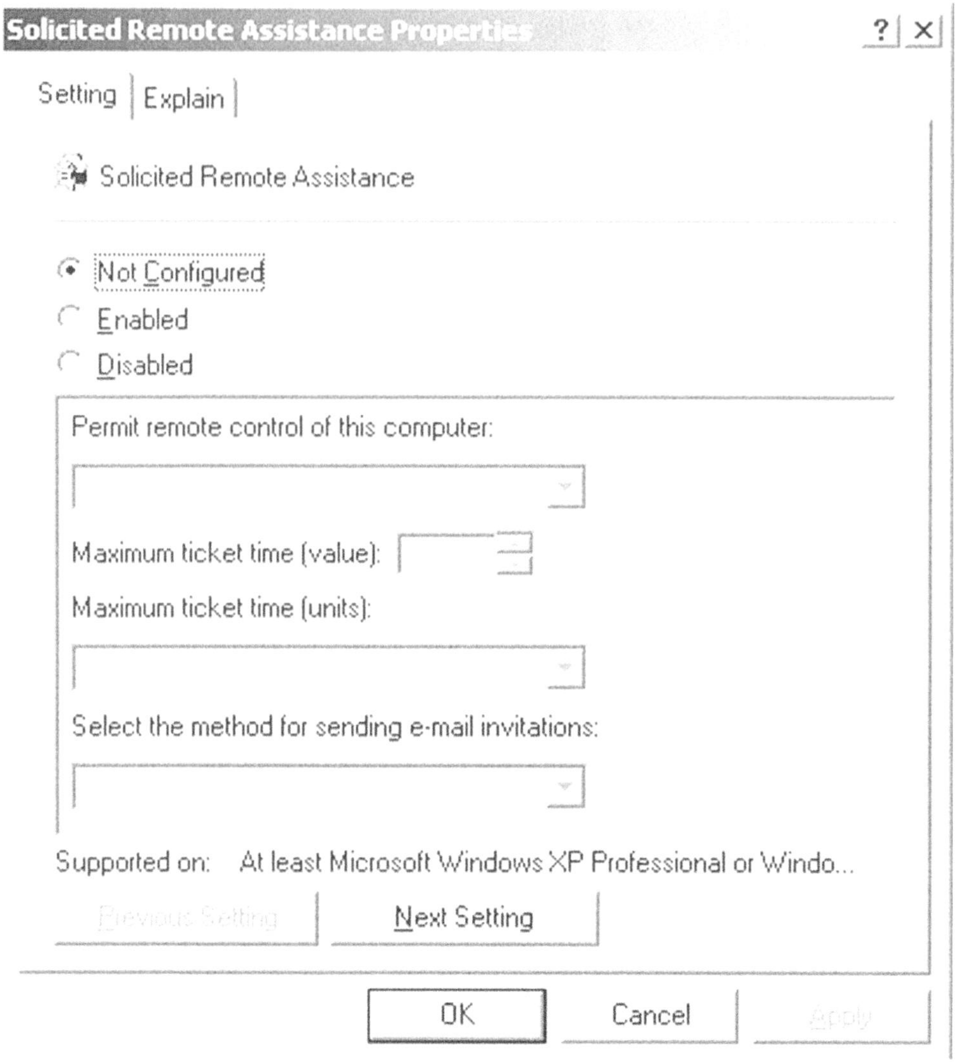

Figure 4-43: Solicited Remote Assistance (Registry).

If you set the status to **Enabled**, a user can create a Remote Assistance invitation that the administrator (or another support person) can use at another computer to connect to the user's computer. When permission is given, the administrator can view the user's screen, mouse and keyboard activity in real time.

The **Permit remote control of this computer** setting specifies whether a user on a different computer can control this computer. When the user invites an administrator to connect to the computer and gives permission, the administrator can then take control of this computer. The user can stop the administrator's control at any time. The expert cannot assume control, but only make a request to take control.

The **Maximum ticket time** setting sets a time limit on the period that a Remote Assistance invitation can remain open. After that period expires, the Remote Assistance invitation is closed and a new one must be generated.

The **Select the method for sending e-mail invitations** setting specifies which e-mail standard to use when sending Remote Assistance calls. You can use either the **Mailto**, in which case the invitation recipient will connect through an Internet link. You can also use the SMAPI standard, in which case the invitation will be attached to an e-mail message. It is important to remember that the email program MUST support the selected e-mail standard.

If the status is set to **Disabled**, users cannot request Remote Assistance and this computer cannot be controlled from another computer.

Offer Remote Assistance

How this setting is configured will determine whether or not the administrator (or a support person) is able to offer remote assistance to this computer without a user first explicitly requesting it. If Remote Assistance is disabled in the previous setting (Solicit Remote Assistance), or if it is set to "Not configured" and disabled in Control Panel, the "Offer Remote Assistance" setting will also be disabled.

If this setting is enabled, you can offer remote assistance. There are two additional choices. You can select either **Allow helpers to only view the computer** or **Allow helpers to remotely control the computer**, both of which are self-explanatory.

As well, you can also specify the list of users or user groups that will be allowed to offer remote assistance. These are termed "helpers." To set up the list of helpers, click **Show**. A new window opens in which you can enter the names of the helpers.

If you disable or do not configure this policy setting, users or groups cannot offer unsolicited remote assistance to this computer.

Note: You cannot connect to the computer unannounced or control it without permission from the user, even under this setting. When you try to connect, the user is given an opportunity to accept or deny the assistance. When it is accepted, the administrator is given view-only privileges to the user's desktop. The user just then clicks a button to give you the ability to remotely control the desktop, if remote control has been enabled.

4.4.2 Using Terminal Services Remote Administration Mode for Remote Desktop

There are some administrative tasks that can be performed by you, the administrator, using Remote Desktop (formerly Terminal Services remote administration mode) along with different tools. These are:

- Logging onto one server remotely, or switching among several servers, and managing them as if you were physically there.
- Managing your servers from any computer on your network.

This certainly makes life easier for any administrator! So, how do we set it up?

The first requirement is that Remote Desktop must be enabled on each remote server. This is done through **Control Panel | System** and then clicking on the **Remote** tab.

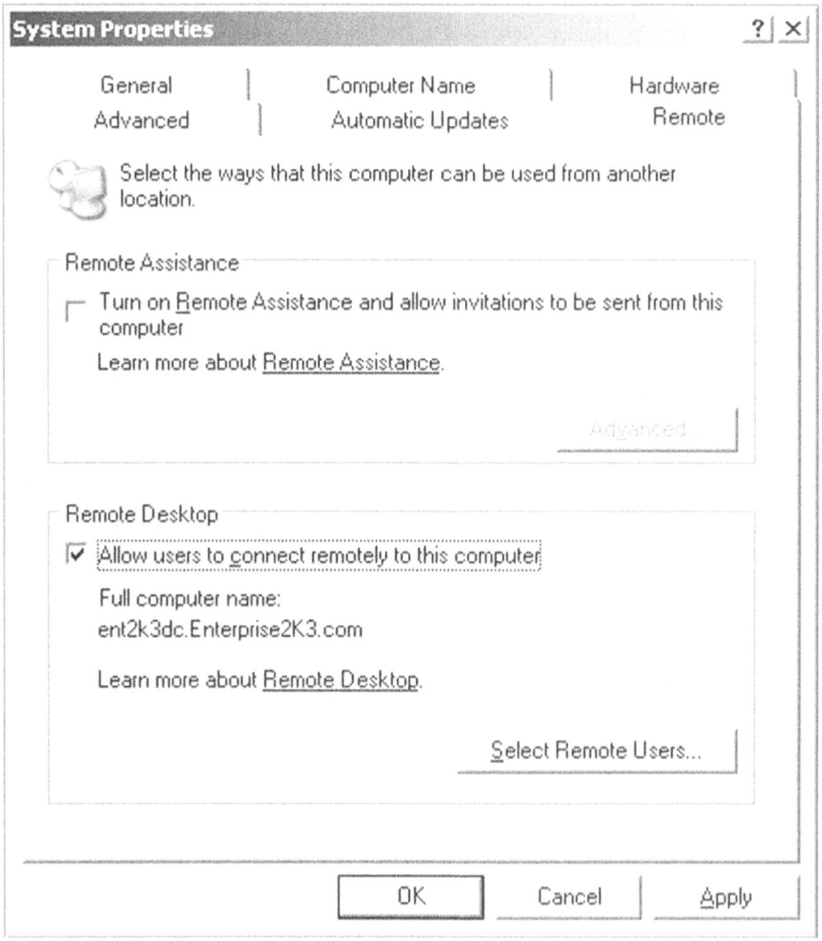

Figure 4-44: Enabling Remote Desktop.

You will note that there is a button **Select Remote Users**. Clicking on the button will display the dialog box shown in Figure 4.45. From that dialog box, you can designate which users, or groups of users, will be allowed to access the server through Remote Desktop.

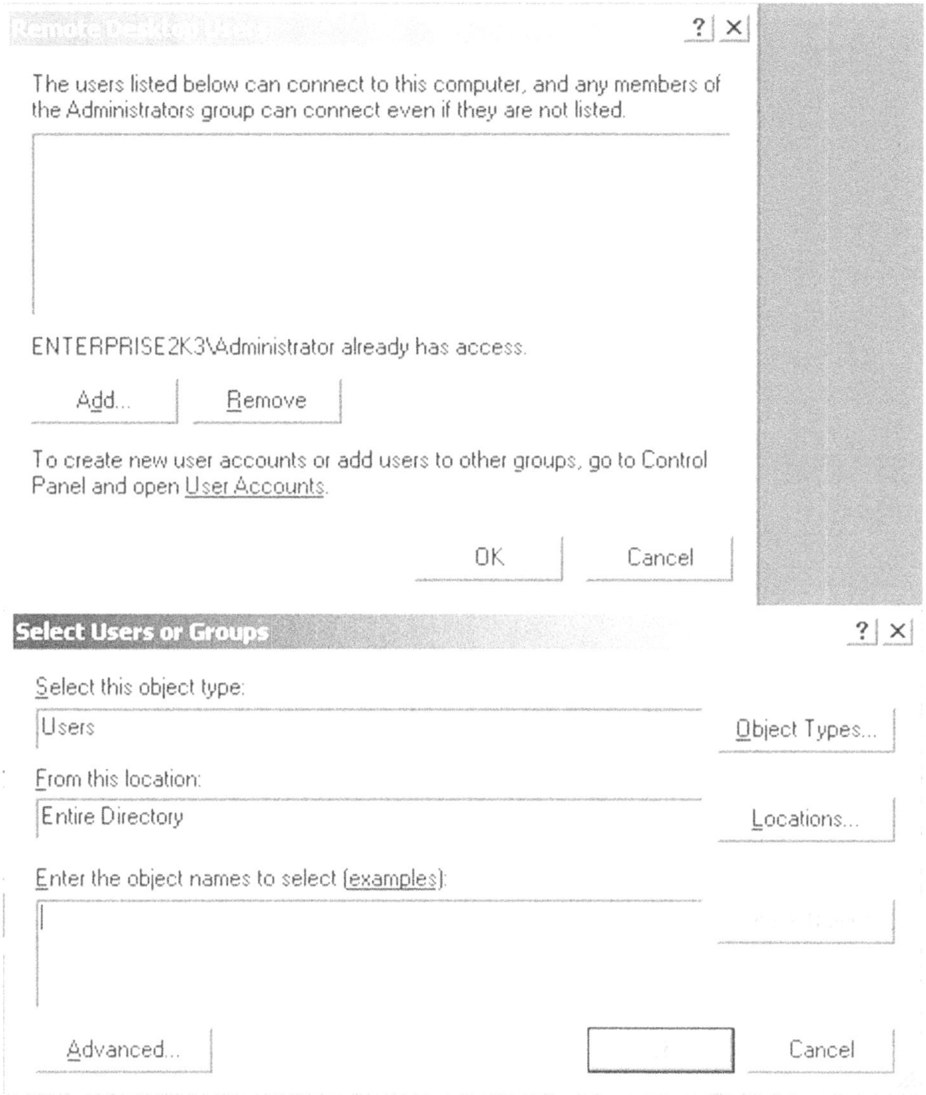

Figure 4-45: Configuring Remote Desktop Users.

Once you have set up all of your servers to allow Remote Desktop access, you should set up the connections to each server. This is done through **Start | Programs | Accessories | Communications | Remote Desktop Connection**.

A Remote Desktop Connection dialog appears. in Figure 4.46.

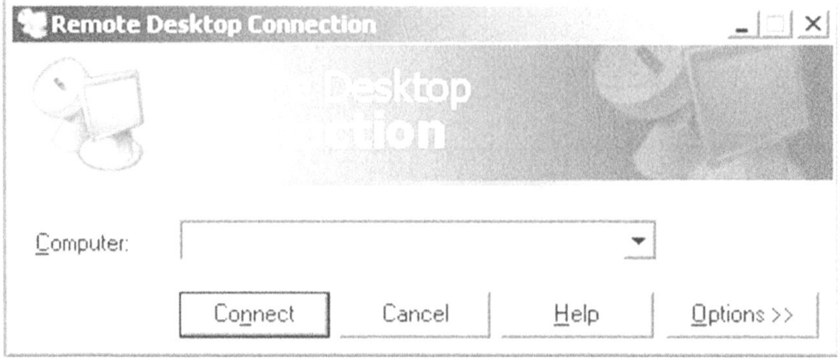

Figure 4-46: Remote Desktop Connection.

You will note the **Options** button in the bottom right hand corner of this dialog box. These options will allow you to set up each connection to suit particular network demands.

We will walk through each of these options, one by one.

When you click options, the dialog box shown in Figure 4.47 will appear, on the first tab, **General**. The General tab allows you to set up certain logon parameters, such as the name of the computer, to which you wish to connect, and the username, password and domain being used to establish the connection. There is an option to save the password, which enables you to reconnect to this remote computer without any input. As well, after configuring all the options, it is from this dialog box that you will save the settings as a .rdp file, so that the settings are saved for the next time you wish to use this connection.

Note: If your network is set up to have passwords expire after a certain preset time period, you will need to remember to modify the password for each .rdp connection after changing the password.

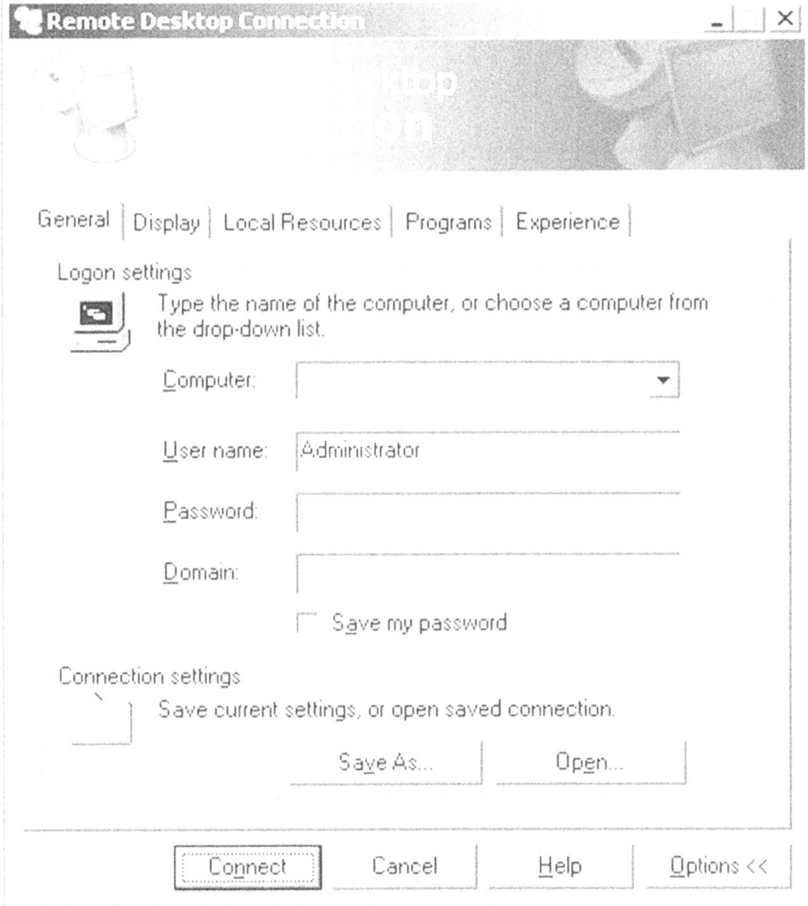

Figure 4-47: Remote Desktop; General Tab.

The second tab (Figure 4.48) is the display tab. From this tab, you are able to configure how you wish the remote desktop to appear on your computer. You can select the default size of the remote desktop window, from a smaller window to full desktop. You are also able to ensure that the connection bar still appears at the top of the screen should you choose to operate the remote desktop in full screen mode.

As well, you can select the color settings for the remote desktop. However, it is important to note that the settings on the remote computer may override the selection you make at this tab.

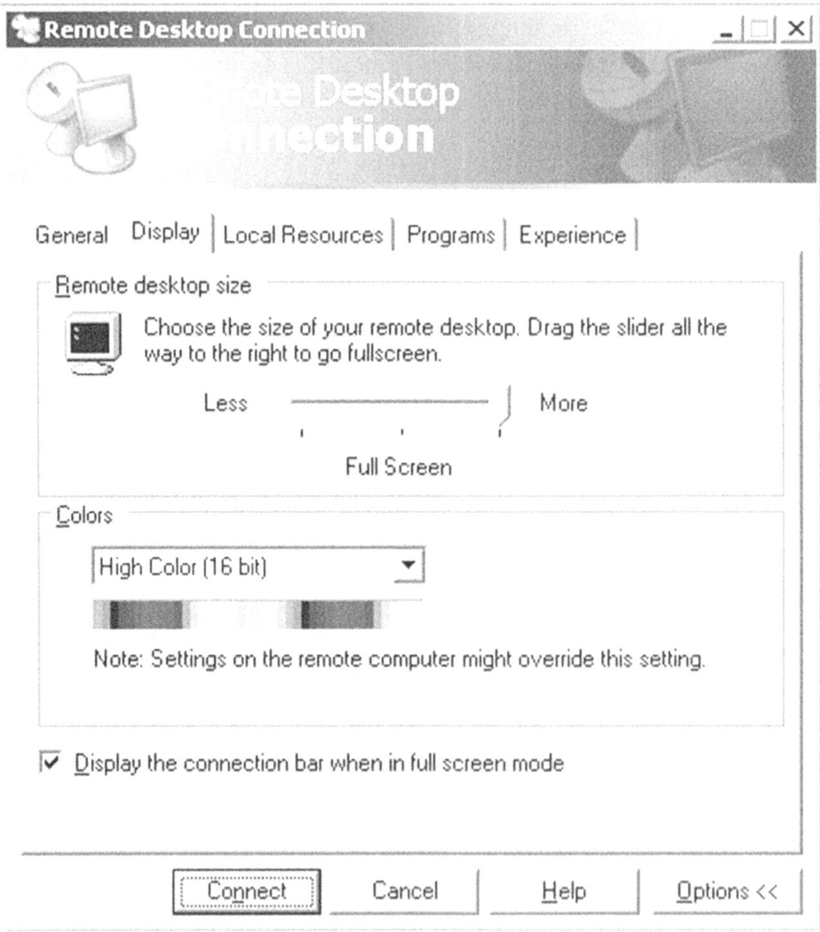

Figure 4-48: Remote Desktop (Display).

The third tab is the **Local Resources** tab. From this dialog box, you can choose whether or not you want the sound from the remote computer to be brought to your desktop. As well, you can select whether you want certain Windows key combinations to work on the remote desktop, or if, perhaps, you only want them to work when you are in full screen mode. Finally, you can select whether the disk drives, serial ports and printers assigned to the remote computer will be automatically connected when you log onto the remote computer.

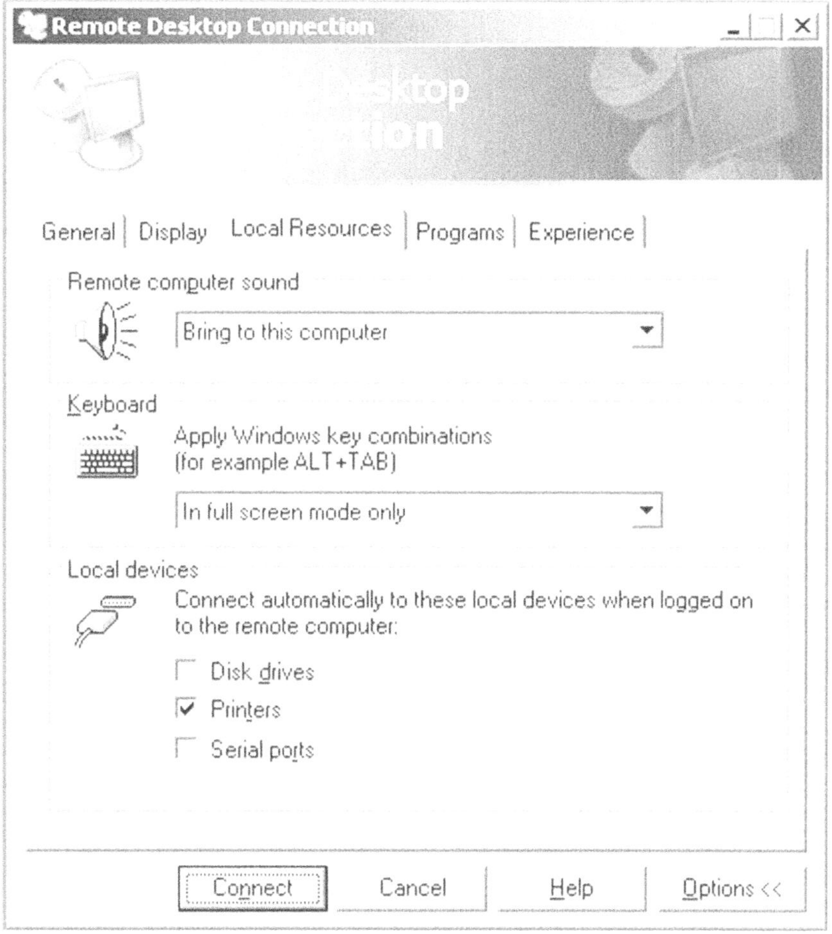

Figure 4-49: Remote Desktop (Local Resources).

From the fourth tab, you can choose to have certain monitoring or maintenance programs run when the connection is established. For example, you may wish to view the Event Viewer on the remote server each time you connect. In that case, you would check the **Start the following program on connection** checkbox, and then put the appropriate path and file name into the text box.

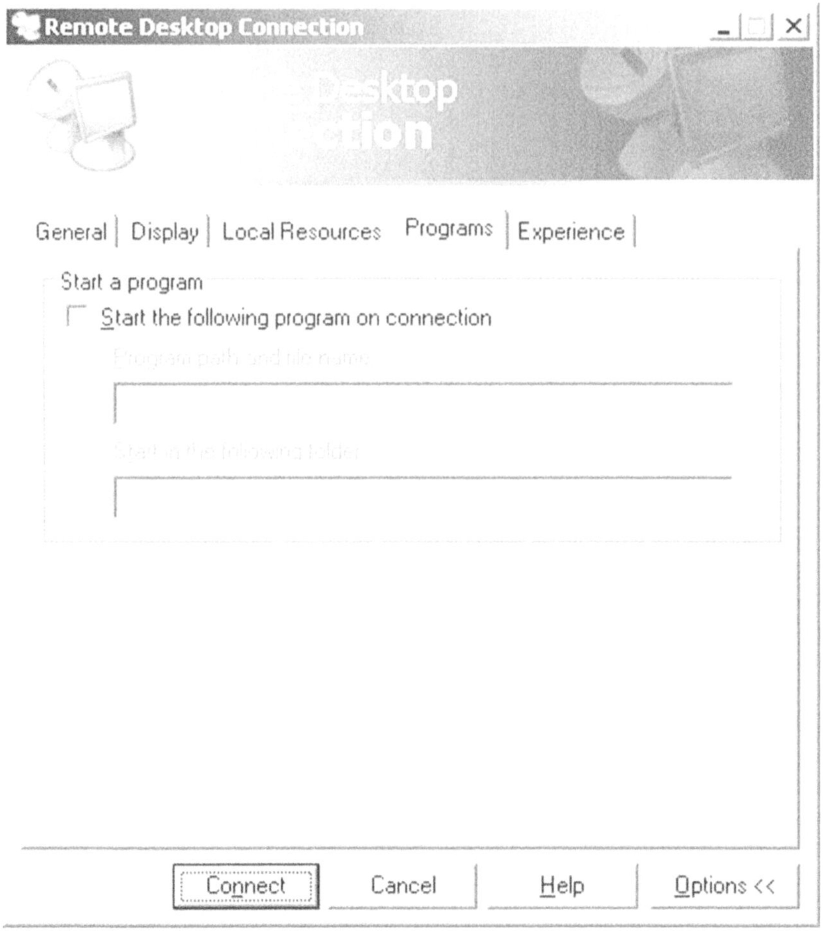

Figure 4-50: Remote Desktop (Programs).

The fifth and final tab for configuration is the **Experience** tab. It is from this dialog box that you can specify what your connection speed is, so that performance can be optimized. By default, certain options will be selected according to your connection speed. By default, 28.8 Kbps Modem is selected. You will note in Figure 4.51, that the only item selected is **Bitmap Caching**. The faster the connection speed, the more options that are selected. You may wish to opt for custom settings. I usually select only Menu and Window animation and Bitmap Caching, leaving the desktop background, windows contents and themes "behind," even on a 100 mbps LAN, for optimal performance.

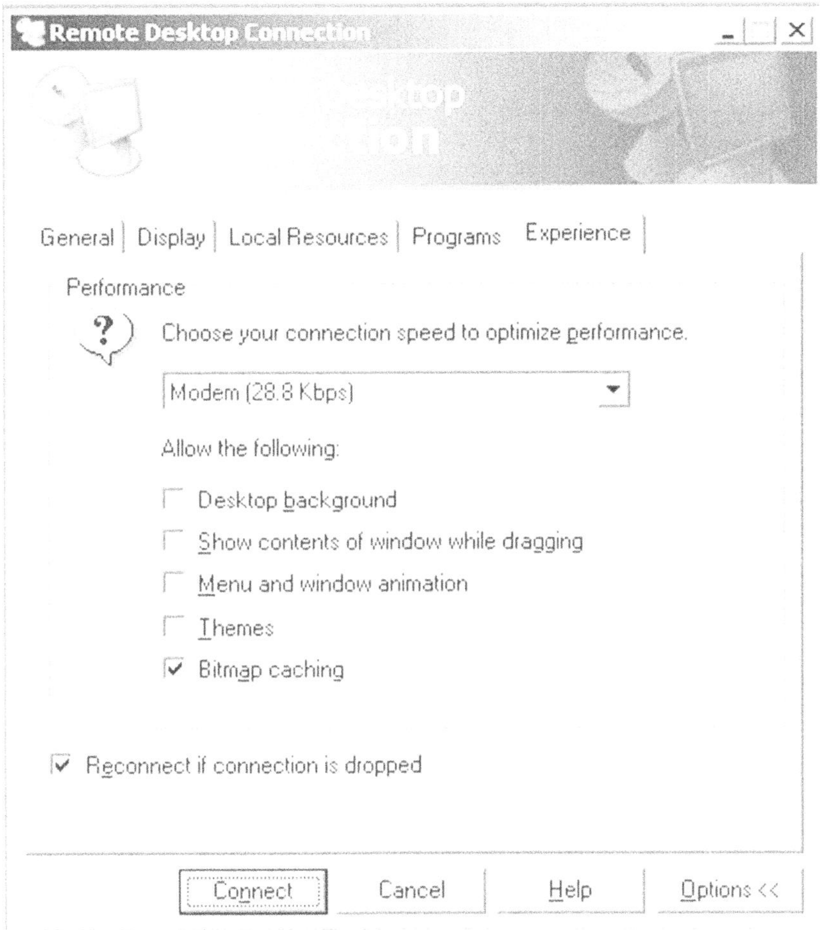

Figure 4-51: Remote Desktop (Experience).

You can also choose to have the remote desktop connection automatically reconnect if, for whatever reason, the connection is unexpectedly dropped.

Remember! Return to the General tab to save your settings, so that the connections to the remote servers are saved for next time.

4.4.3 Manage a server by using available support tools

There are a few other ways of managing your servers remotely. Let's look at them briefly.

- **Manage several servers by performing similar tasks**
  This can be achieved by using the appropriate saved MMC consoles, if available. Alternately, you can create your own custom MMC consoles for tasks you frequently do, or delegate to other members of your team.
- **Connect to a remote computer when that computer cannot access the network or is not in an operational state because of hardware or software failure.**
  This can be accomplished using the old standby—Telnet. Remember—it is command line driven, capabilities are limited and security is minimal at best. However, there are times, such as the situation listed above, when the "old way" is still the "best way."

There is one new remote administration feature with Server 2003 that is worth a closer look—the **Web Interface for Remote Administration**.

NOTE: The feature is, by default, NOT set up on any version of Server 2003, except for the Web Edition.

In order to install this feature on another version of Server 2003, you must utilize the **Windows Components Wizard**, found in **Control Panel | Add/Remove Programs**. The feature is buried quite deep within the Wizard. Select **Application Server | Internet Information Services | World Wide Web Service** and then select the checkbox next to **Remote Administration (HTML)** (Figure 4.52).

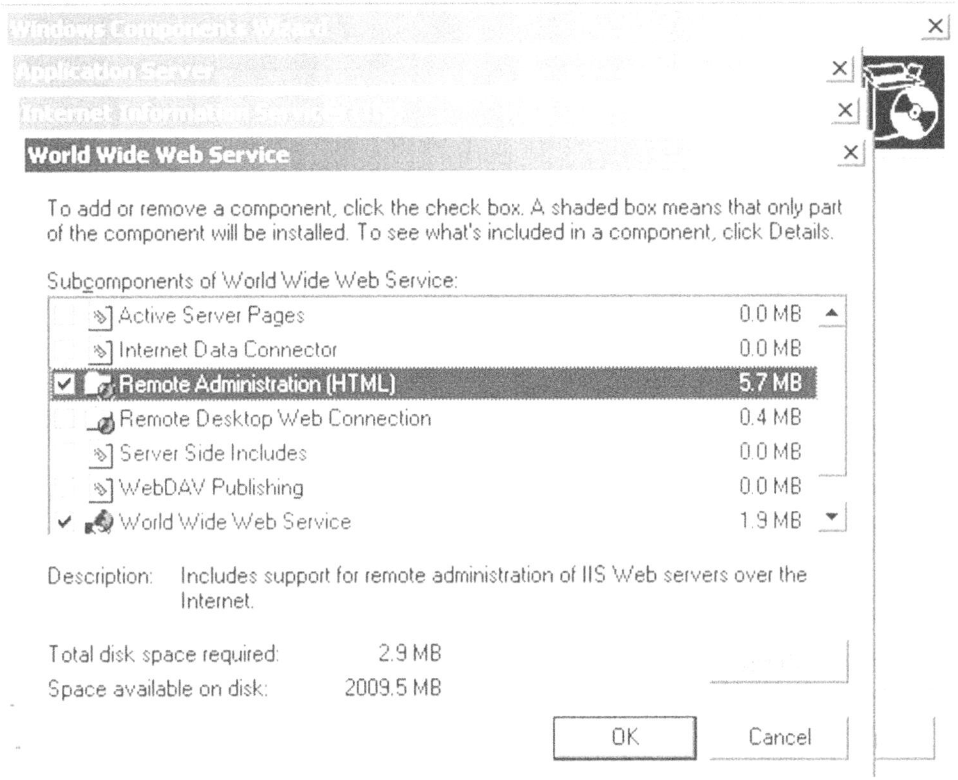

Figure 4-52: Installing the Web Interface for Remote Administration.

Designed specifically for remote administration of Web servers, the Web Interface for Remote Administration is a HTML-based application that you can use to configure and manage the server from a remote client. Individual servers, server farms and multiple sites per server can be remotely managed from your workstation.

The Web Interface for Remote Administration provides a new way of performing common Web server configuration tasks, including:

- Creating and deleting Web sites
- Configuring network settings
- Managing local user accounts
- Restarting the Web server.

The interface is very easy to work with and maneuver through. It is worth your while to take a moment and walk through each page to familiarize yourself.

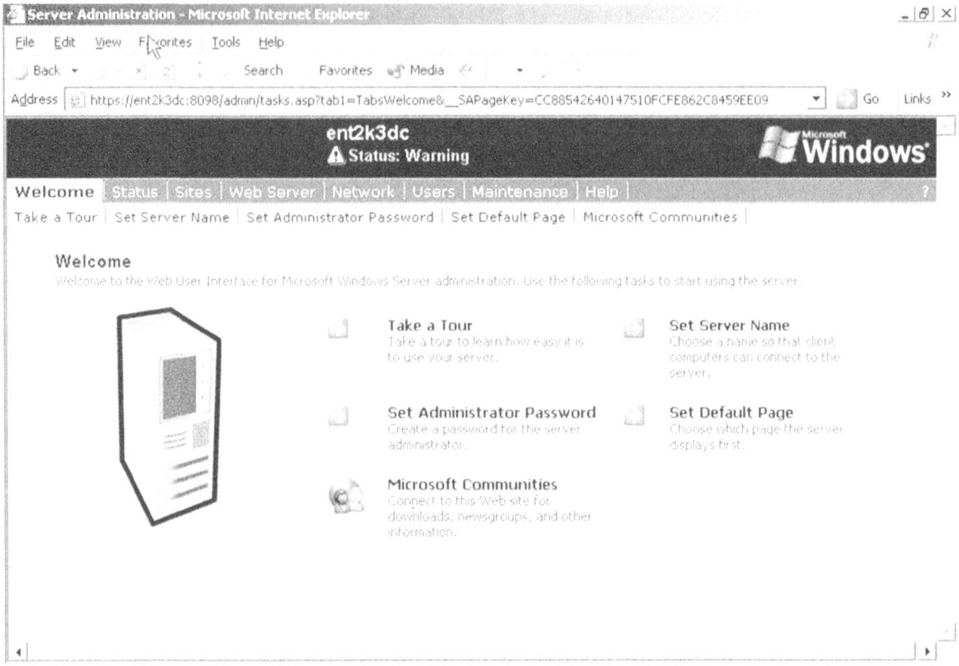

Figure 4-53: Remote Administration Web Interface.

Pop Quiz 4.3

Pop Quiz 4.3 *Questions*

1. As Administrator, you need to use an Internet connection to access a user's computer to provide help. Will you use Remote Desktop or Remote Assistance to accomplish this?
2. You have recently deployed the 64-bit edition of Windows Server 2003 and wish to use Remote Assistance, but you cannot find the feature to install. What is the problem?
3. One of your users is concerned about his computer's security. He feels that, because you have allowed Remote Assistance on his PC, an intruder could use this feature to access his desktop. How do you reassure this user?
4. What are two administrative tasks that can be performed using Remote Desktop (Administration Mode)?
5. There is a new remote administration feature with Server 2003, the Web Interface for Remote Administration. Which version or versions of Windows Server 2003 installs this feature by default?

Pop Quiz 4.3 *Answers*

1. You will be using Remote Assistance. Remote Assistance allows an administrator to use an Internet connection to access a user's computer or remote server to provide assistance. The administrator can view the remote computer's screen in a window and communicate with the user through a "chat box." This feature is used so that administrators can resolve problems without having to be physically at the user's computer or server.
2. The problem is that Remote Assistance feature is NOT available under Server 2003 64-bit version. You will need to move to a server running the 32-bit version of Server 2003 to perform Remote Assistance.
3. Explain to the user that no one can connect to the computer unannounced or control it without explicit permission from him, even under this setting. When someone tries to connect, the user is given an opportunity to accept or deny the assistance. Even when it is accepted, the person connecting is given view-only privileges to the user's desktop, until the user explicitly allows the ability to remotely control the desktop, if remote control has been enabled.
4. Two administrative tasks that can be performed are logging onto one server remotely, or switching among several servers, and managing them as if you were physically there, and two, managing your servers from any computer on your network.
5. This feature is, by default, set up only on the Web Edition of Windows Server 2003.

4.5 Troubleshoot print queues

Normally, when we're talking about printers, we mean the piece of hardware that produces printed copy. In the Windows world, the printer is a software interface between the physical printing device and the Windows operating system. Therefore, before you can access your physical print device, you must first configure a printer.

You can access your printer configuration by using **Control Panel**, or by going **Start | Printers and Faxes**. You must be a member of the Administrators group to create a printer in Windows 2003.

4.5.1 Connect to a local print device

When you run the Add Printer Wizard (Figure 4.54), and create the printer, the computer on which the printer has been created becomes the print server for that print device. If the printer is going to be shared on the network, make sure that the computer has enough processing power to handle the printing requests and enough free disk space to queue the print jobs.

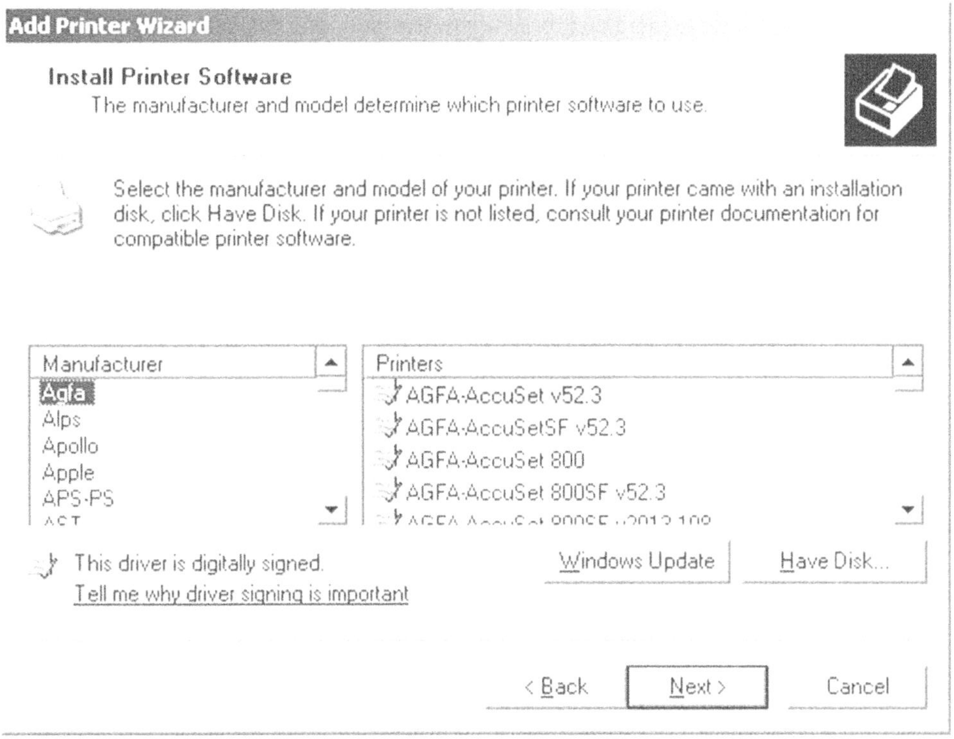

Figure 4-54: Add Printer Wizard.

In order to use the printer, all clients will have to have the appropriate driver installed on their system. Most Microsoft client operating systems will automatically download the driver from the print server the first time the client connects to the printer. If the driver is updated on the server, it will also be automatically updated on Windows NT, 2000, 2003 and XP clients the next time it connects to the print server.

NOTE: One word of caution—Windows 95 and 98 clients will download the driver the first time they connect to the print server only. If you update the driver on the print server, you will have to manually install the updated drivers on the clients.

Other operating systems may require a specific protocol or service to be running on the print server in order to use the shared printer.

4.5.2 Manage printers and print jobs

You manage the printer properties by right-clicking on the printer and selecting **Properties**. The Properties' dialog box has a number of different tabs. Let's look at some of them.

The **General Tab** (Figure 4.55) has the basic information and features of the installed printer, including its model name, the optional location and comment provided at the time of installation, and the features available with the printer.

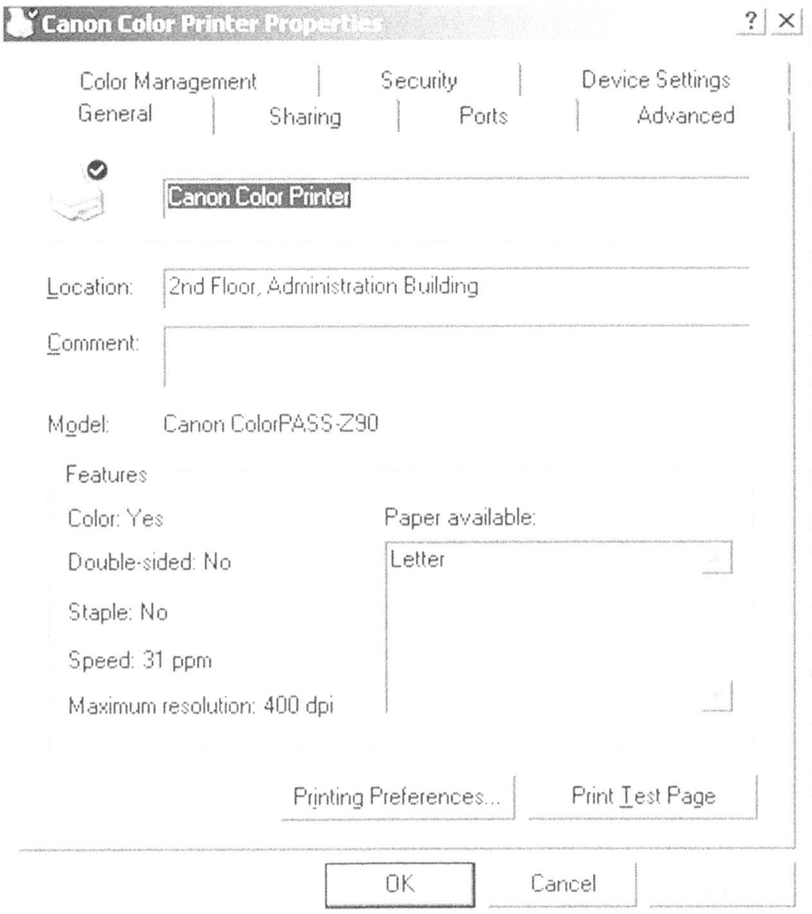

Figure 4-55: Printer Properties General Tab.

It also allows you to configure printing preferences, such as the layout of the paper, the page order and the paper source. You can also print a test page from the General tab of Properties. Printing a test page is frequently used for troubleshooting. You may choose to print a test page when you have installed an updated driver for your printer and want to verify that it is working. If a Windows 2003 driver is not available for the printer, and you wish to try a compatible print driver, you may wish to test the driver by printing a test page.

The **Sharing Tab** (Figure 4.56) in Properties allows you to start or stop sharing the printer with the network. It provides a checkbox if you wish to have the printer listed in the network's Active Directory. The Additional Drivers button allows you to add drivers onto the print server for the Itanium versions of Windows XP and Server 2003, as well as x86 drivers for Windows 95, 98, ME and NT 4.0.

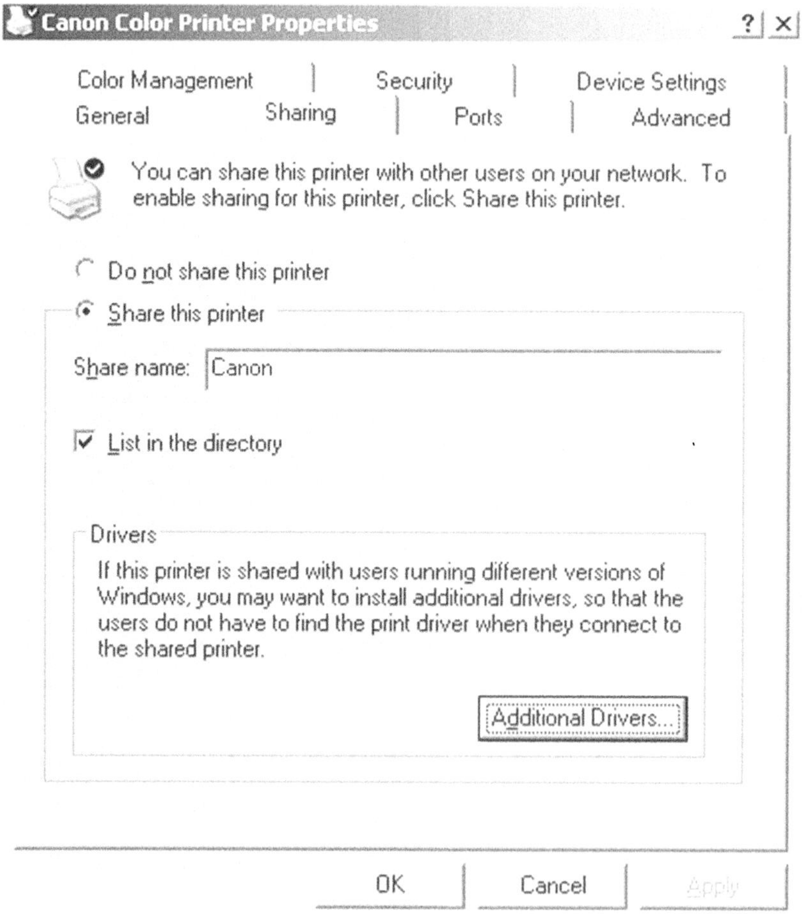

Figure 4-56: Printer Properties Sharing Tab.

Server 2003 supports both physical printing ports (LPT and COM) as well as logical (TCP/IP) ports. A physical (local) port is used when the print device is connected physically to the computer. A logical port is used when the print device has its own network card and IP address, and the computer will be acting as the print server for the network enabled print device.

The **Ports Tab** (Figure 4.57) allows you to add, configure, and delete ports for the printer. It also allows you to set up printer pooling. Printer pooling is when multiple print devices are acting as one printer. The jobs sent to the printer are shared among the print devices. It should go without saying that if you create a printer pool with multiple print devices, the print devices should be located in the same physical workspace. Print devices in a printer pool MUST use the same print driver.

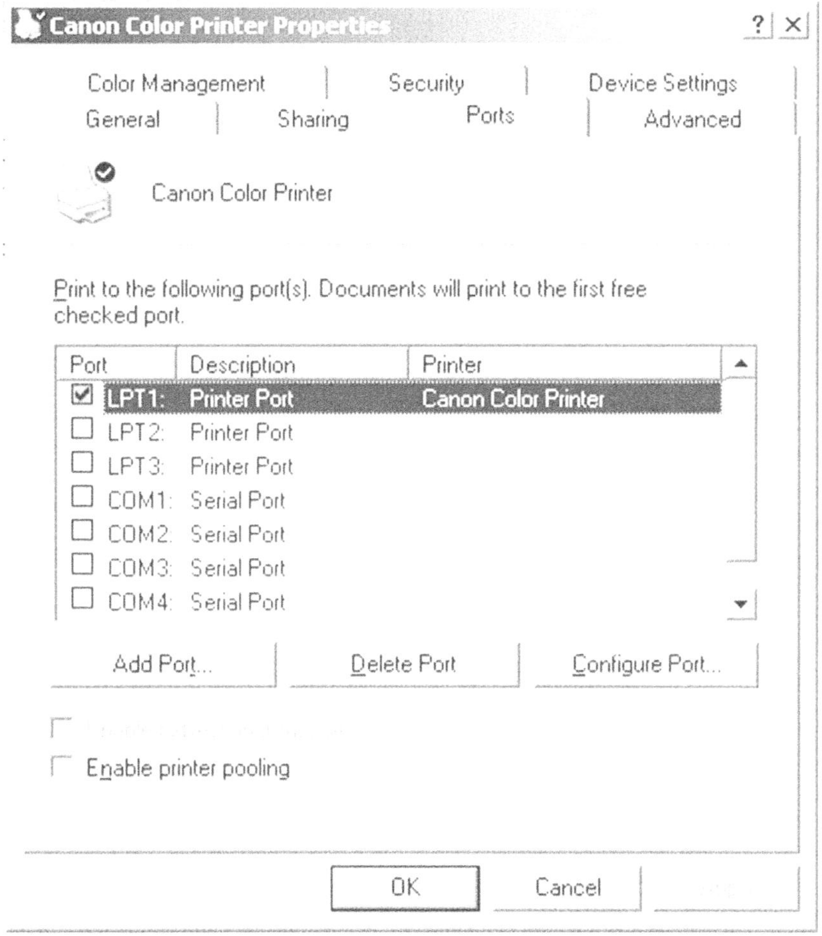

Figure 4-57: Printer Properties Ports Tab.

If your printer device fails, the Ports tab enables you to redirect scheduled print jobs to another print device, provided that print device can use the same driver as the failed print device. To redirect a print job, click the Add Port button, select New Port and choose New Port time. You should use the UNC naming convention to name the printer, that is, ***\\SERVERNAME\SHARENAME***, where ***SERVERNAME*** is the name of the computer acting as the print server for the new print device and ***SHARENAME*** is the name given to the shared printer.

There are a number of options available under the **Advanced Properties tab** (Figure 4.58). The first item on the dialog box allows you to schedule **Hours** when the printer is available. There can be a number of reasons why you might choose to do this.

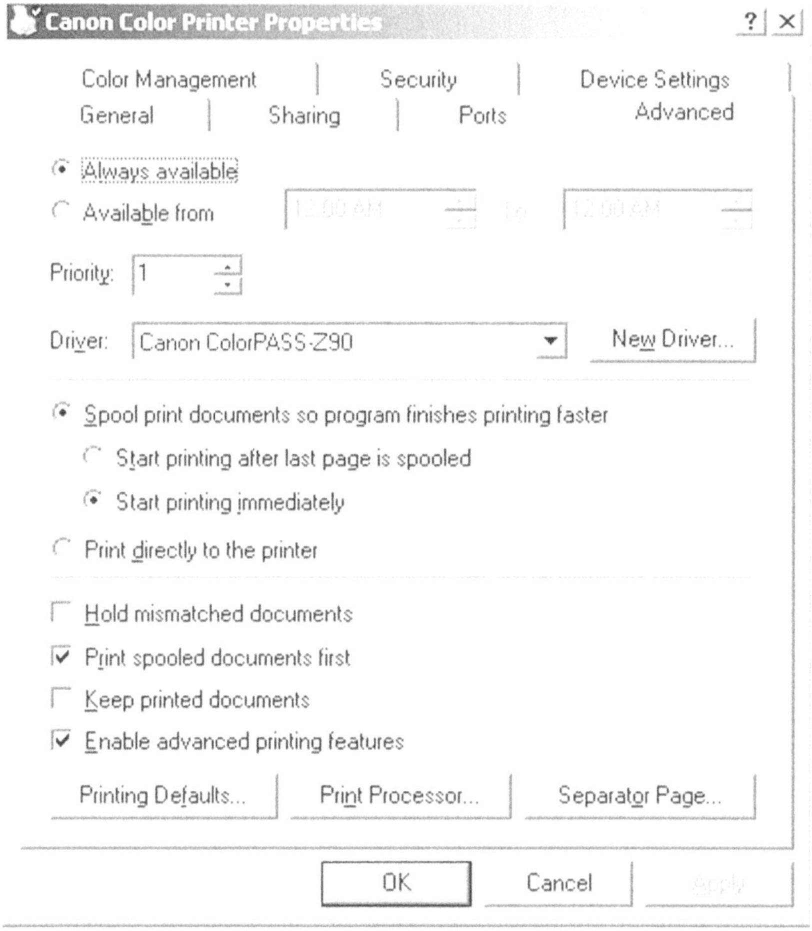

Figure 4-58: Printer Properties Advanced Tab.

Let's say that the print device is in a secure area that is locked at 6:00 p.m. If a user is working late, he or she wouldn't be too happy if they printed out an important job and then discovered that they can't get to it. By scheduling the printer to not be available after 6:00 p.m., this situation can be avoided.

Keep in mind, though, that a printer is NOT a print device. You can create two printers for one physical print device. You could name one "Daytime Printer" and have it scheduled from 7:00 a.m. to 6:00 p.m. You could then create a second printer "Overnight Printer" and have it scheduled from 6:00 p.m. to 7:00 a.m. Large jobs, or jobs that are heavy in graphics that might take a long time to print, can be sent to the "Overnight" printer. Both printers work on the same print device. By default, when a printer is created, it is always available.

The next item on the Advanced Properties dialog box is **Priority**. This is used to ensure that urgent print jobs are produced before less urgent ones. The lowest priority is "1" and the highest priority is "99." You would create two printers for the same print device, and give each a different priority. Make sure that the share names reflect the priority of the printer. Jobs sent to the printer with the higher priority will print first on the print device.

Spooling is the next selection on the Advanced tab. You can choose to have jobs spooled or print directly to the printer. If you choose not to have the job spooled, the application doing the printing will not be free until the job is completed. Printing directly to the printer can be helpful in troubleshooting printer problems. If you can print directly to the printer, but printing fails when you try to print through the spooler, you know that the problem lies with the spooler, not the print device.

Spooling, the normal choice in a multi-user environment, allows jobs to be queued for the printer. The spooler acts as traffic lights—all the jobs do not try to print at the same time.

There are four print options available:

- **Hold Mismatched Documents**
  Used when there are multiple forms associated with the printer. If, for example, you have one paper type, and need to print on both plain paper and a sales form, enabling the "Hold Mismatched Documents" feature will allow all jobs that need to be printed on the special form to be printed first, and then all the documents that need plain paper. By default, this feature is disabled.
- **Print Spooled Documents Firs/Start Printing Immediately**
  A set of radio buttons, the first of which instructs the spooler to print jobs that have completed spooling before printer larger jobs that are still spooling, even if the larger job has a high priority. This option is enabled, by default, because it increases printer efficiency. If Start Printing Immediately is selected, the first job in the queue is printed, whether or not it has completed spooling. A long document will need to complete spooling and printing before a second, shorter document will begin to print.
- **Keep Printed Documents**
  By default, this option is disabled, because it takes up a lot of hard disk space on

the print server. When selected, jobs are kept in the spooler even after printing is completed.

- **Enable Advanced Printing Features**
  Enabled by default, this option specifies that features such as Page Order and Pages Per Sheet, which are supported by your printer, can be used. If problems occur with special features, this option can be disabled.

At the bottom of the dialog box are three buttons—**Printing Defaults**, **Print Processor** and **Separator Pages**. Printing Defaults opens the Print Preferences dialog box, the same one as on the General tab. The Print Processor tab is used when Server 2003 needs to do additional processing to print jobs. Unless specified otherwise by the print device manufacturer, it is best to leave this at the default setting.

Separator pages are used to identify the owner of the print job. To save paper, this is normally disabled; however, when a large number of users share one printer, it can be handy. Server 2003 comes with four separator page files:

- **PCL.SEP**
  Used with HP Printers that have dual printer language capabilities, it sends a separator page when the printer has switched from PostScript to PCL.
- **PSCRIPT.SEP**
  Used to switch the print server to PostScript printing mode (does not send a separator page).
- **SYSPRINT.SEP**
  Used by PostScript printers to send a separator page.
- **SYSPRTJ.SEP**
  Used by PostScript printers to send a separator page, but also has support for Japanese characters.

Another tab on the Properties dialog box is **Color Management** (Figure 4.59).

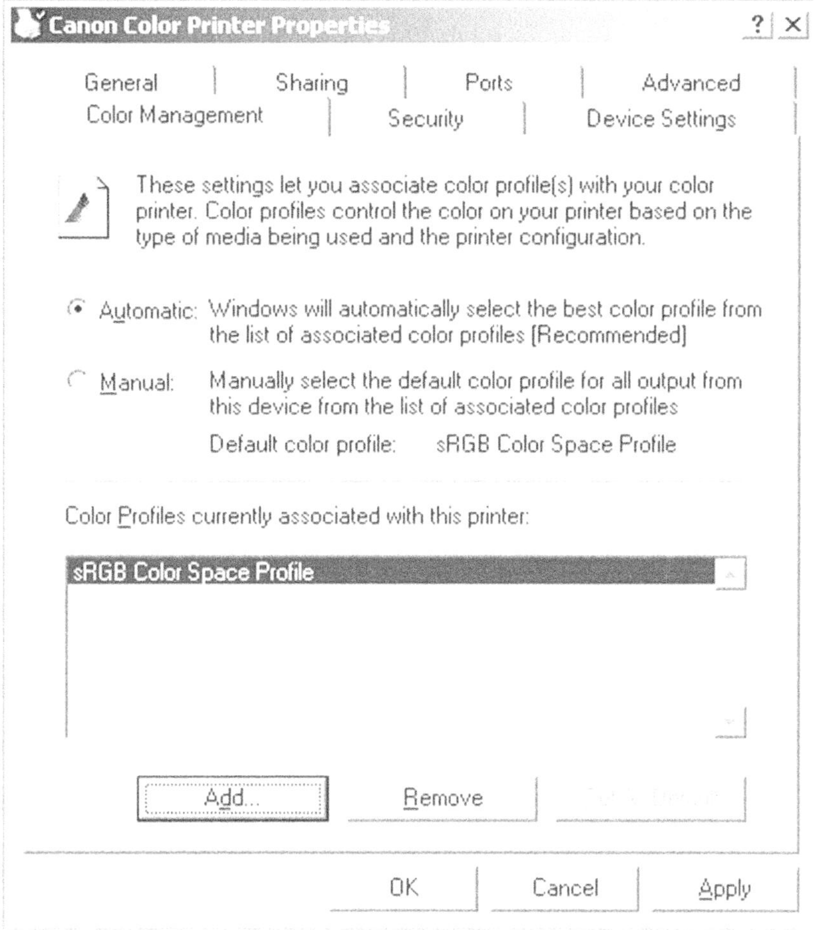

Figure 4-59: Printer Properties Color Management Tab.

This tab with appear only when a color print device has been installed. The Color Management tab allows you to assign a color profile to the printer depending on what medium is being used and how the printer is configured. You can select Automatic, which allows Server 2003 to select the color profile from the associated list. This option is selected by default. You can also choose to select Manual, which allows you to select which color profile will be used by default. You can also add and remove color profiles.

If you have permission to modify printer access and permissions, the **Security Tab** will appear (Figure 4.60). These permissions are covered in detail in the next section. For now, let's just take a look at the tab.

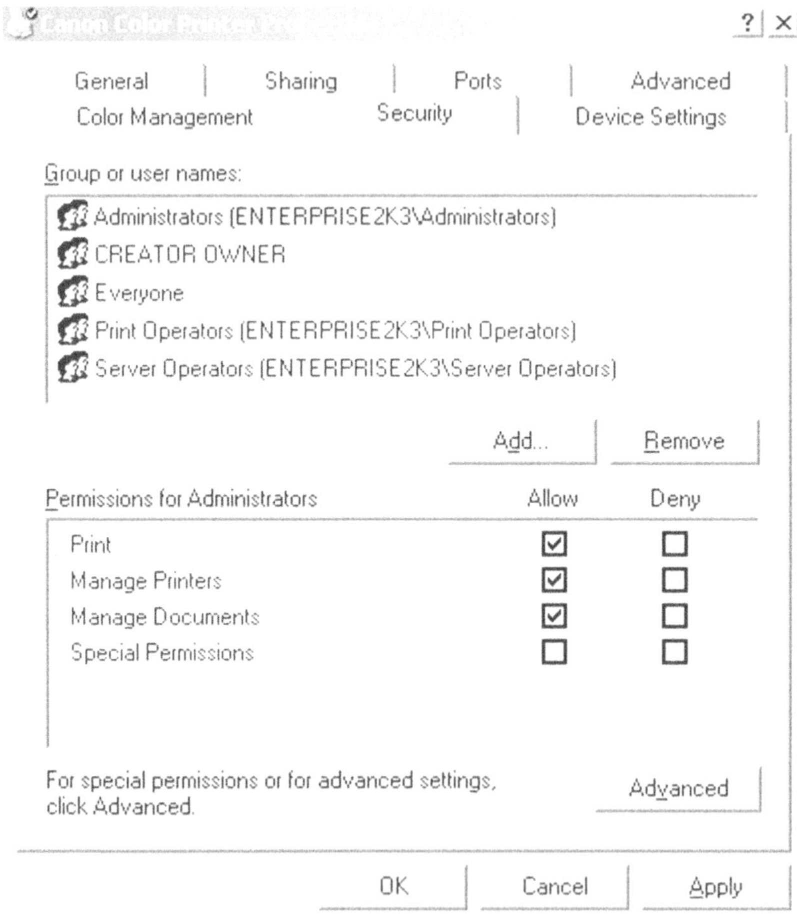

Figure 4-60: Printer Properties Security Tab.

Another tab on the Properties dialog box is the **Device Settings Tab** (Figure 4.61). The properties that are displayed are dependent upon the printer and driver installed on the print server. This tab is useful if, for example, you want to assign different forms to different trays, or assign the Euro currency symbol to postscript fonts.

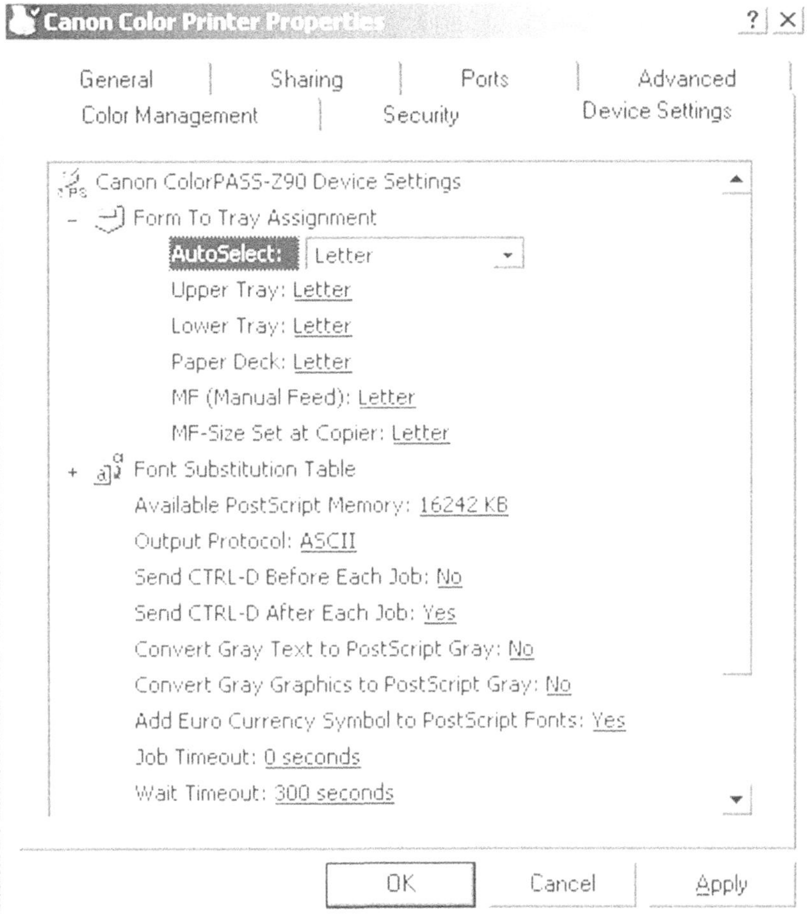

Figure 4-61: Printer Properties Device Settings Tab.

Other tabs may appear with different printers. Some printers will show a tab called **Services**, which allows you to do certain maintenance tasks, such as aligning or cleaning the print cartridges, or printing an ink-level page. Other printers may have an **About** tab.

4.5.3 Control access with permissions

Assigning permissions to users and groups can control access to printers. Access can mean the ability to use the print device, to delete jobs, change permissions, pause, or restart the printer. As with shared folders, shared printers have different levels of access. The three levels of basic printer permissions are:

- **Print**
  Print permission allows the user, or group, to connect to the printer and to send print jobs to the print device. A user with print permission can pause and restart their own print job or delete that job from the queue. The user cannot perform any action on any other print job.
- **Manage Printers**
  Manage Printers permission is a permission you granted to a user or group that needs to have administrative control of the printer. A user with this permission can pause and restart the printer and the spooler, change spooler settings, share the printer, as well as change printer permissions and manage properties.
- **Manage Documents**
  Manage Documents permission is granted to user or group to troubleshoot the day-to-day problems that can occur with printers. A user with this permission can pause, restart and delete queued documents; however he or she cannot control the printer status.

There is now a new permission, Special Permissions (Figure 4.62). This allows:

- **Read Permissions**
  The individual can see what permissions are effective, but cannot make changes to them.
- **Change Permissions**
  The individual can alter permissions.
- **Take Ownership**
  The individual can become the Creator/Owner.

It should be noted that permission can be changed for that printer only, the documents only, or both the printer and the documents.

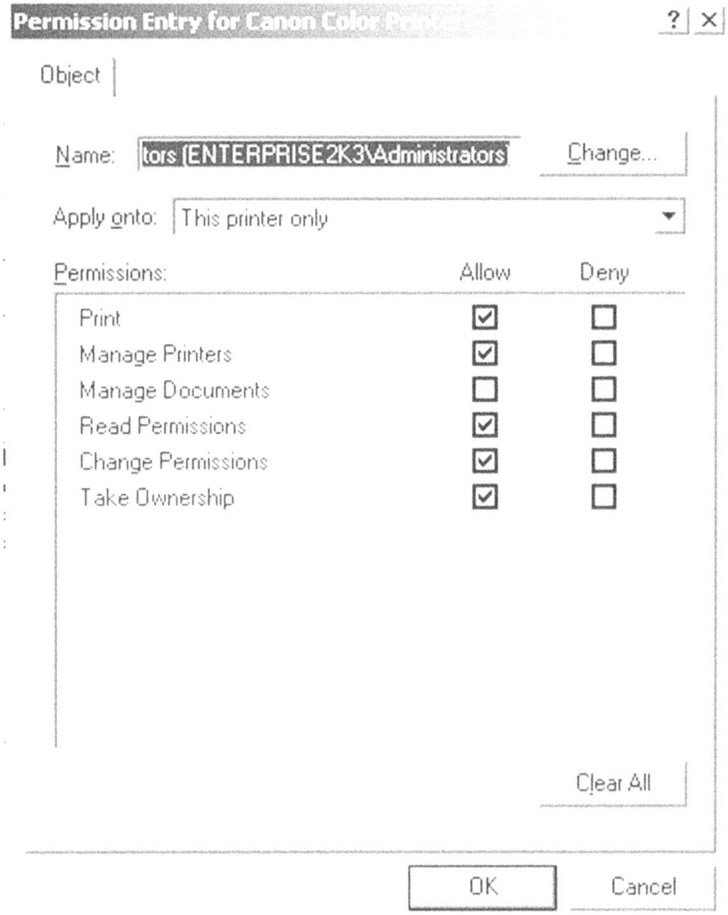

Figure 4-62: Editing Special Permissions.

There are also **Advanced Security Settings** as shown in Figure 4-63. This dialog box allows the management of permissions, the management of auditing, changing the Creator/Owner, and managing the permissions for that printer.

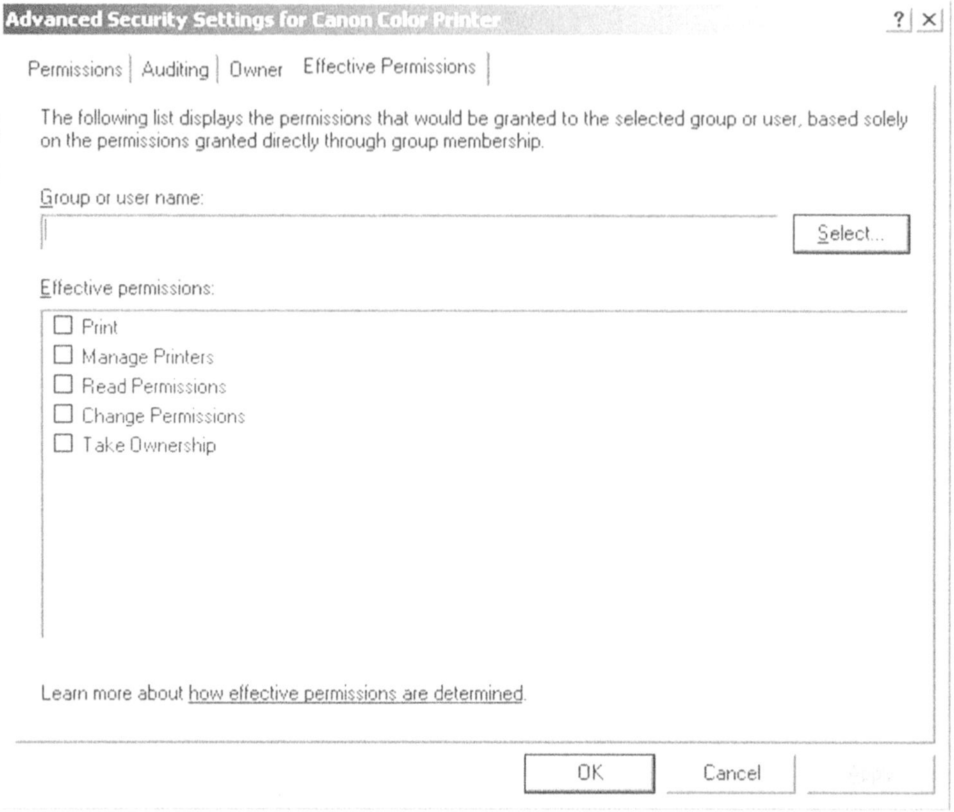

Figure 4-63: Advanced Security Settings.

Printers and documents are managed from the **Printers** folder. The printer administrator (the user with Manage Printers permission) right-clicks the printer to be managed. A shortcut menu appears with the following management choices on a local printer:

- Open
- Set as Default Printer
- Printing Preferences…
- Pause Printing
- Sharing
- Use Printer Offline
- Create Shortcut
- Delete
- Rename (Printer)
- Properties.

Managing documents is done from within the print queue. Double-click the printer that contains the documents that need to be managed. By choosing Document from the menu bar, the following options are available:

- Pause
- Resume
- Restart
- Cancel
- Properties.

Figure 4.60 shows the **Security** tab for the printer. As with share permissions, printer permissions can be explicitly allowed, denied or not specified. The effective permission for any user account is determined in the same fashion as share permissions.

Pop Quiz 4.4

Pop Quiz 4.4 *Questions*

1. Define "printer" as used in a Windows Server 2003 environment.
2. You wish to create a printer. Of what group must you be a member to do this?
3. What is the unique requirement of clients running Windows 95 or 98 when updating drivers in a Windows Server 2003 environment?
4. What is a physical print port? A logical port?
5. What is the difference between the Manage Printers permission and the Manage Documents permission?

Pop Quiz 4.4 *Answers*

1. The printer is a software interface between the physical printing device and the Windows operating system.
2. You must be a member of the Administrators group to create a printer in Windows 2003.
3. Windows 95 and 98 clients will download the driver the first time they connect to the print server only. If a driver is updated on the print server, the updated drivers will have to be manually installed on those clients.
4. A physical (local) port is used when the print device is connected physically to the computer. A logical port is used when the print device has its own network card and IP address, and the computer will be acting as the print server for the network enabled print device.
5. Manage Printers permission is granted to a user or group that needs to have administrative control of the printer. A user with this permission can pause and restart the printer and the spooler, change spooler settings, share the printer, as well as change printer permissions and manage properties. Manage Documents permission is granted to user or group to troubleshoot the day-to-day problems that can occur with printers. A user with this permission can pause, restart and delete queued documents; however he or she cannot control the printer status.

4.6 Monitor system performance

Server 2003 has been designed for high performance immediately upon installation. However, it is always possible to tune the server settings for performance gains, which is why monitoring system performance is a natural part of system administration.

We have already outlined some of the main tools using in monitoring and analyzing system performance earlier in this chapter, and we will be looking at some very specific counters later in the chapter. However, this is a very good opportunity to take quick look at certain TCP parameters that you may want to monitor, as they can affect performance.

Monitoring should always examine the hardware, the network and the workload so that the system can be tuned to meet performance goals.

4.6.1 TCP Parameters

There are certain TCP parameters that can be monitored and adjusted to improve server performance and increase throughput.

Parameter	Description
TCPWindowSize	This value determines the maximum amount of data (in bytes) that can be outstanding on the network at any given time. It can be set to any value from 1 to 65,535 bytes by using the following registry entry: `HKEY_LOCAL_MACHINE\System\CurrentControlSet\Services\Tcpip\Parameters\TcpWindowSize (REG_DWORD)` Default settings: Gigabit interface – 65,535 100 Mbps link – 16,384 Lower speeds – 8,192
Window Scaling	For high bandwidth-delay products, like satellite links, you may need to increase window size over 64K. Modify the following registry entry: `HKEY_LOCAL_MACHINE\System\CurrentControlSet\Services\Tcpip\Parameters\Tcp1323Opts (REG_DWORD)` to 1 to enable window sizes of greater than 65,535. After you do this, you can modify TCPWindowSize to values up to 1GB.
MaxHashTableSize	This value determines the size of the hash table holding the state of TCP connections. Default value is 128 * number of processors[2]. When a large concurrent connection load is expected on the system, set the following registry entry to a higher value: `:HKEY_LOCAL_MACHINE\System\CurrentControlSet\Services\Tcpip\Parameters\MaxHashTableSize (REG_DWORD)` The maximum value is 0x10000 (65,536).
MaxUserPort	A port is used whenever an active connection is used from a computer. Given the default value of available user mode ports (5,000 for each IP address) and TCP time-wait requirements, it may be necessary to make more ports available on the system. You can set the following registry entry to as high as 0xfffe (65534): `HKEY_LOCAL_MACHINE\System\CurrentControlSet\Services\Tcpip\Parameters\MaxUserPort`

Table 4-4: TCP Performance Parameters.

4.7 Monitor file and print servers

The following section will outline some of the key parameters to utilize, specifically when fine-tuning performance on file and print servers under Server 2003.

Parameter	Description
PagedPoolSize	HKLM\System\CurrentControlSet\Control\Session Manager\MemoryManagement\ (REG_DWORD) File cache space and paged pool space share a common area in system virtual address. Limiting the paged pool allows for a larger system cache, which causes more content to be cached and allows faster serving of files.
NtfsDisable8dot3NameCreation	HKLM\System\CurrentControlSet\Control\FileSystem\ (REG_DWORD) Default is 0. This parameter determines whether NTFS generates a short name in the 8.3 (DOS) naming convention for long file names and for file names that contain characters from the extended character set. If the value of this entry is 0, files can potentially have two names: the name that the user specifies and the short name that NTFS generates. If the name the user specifies conforms to the 8.3 naming convention, NTFS does not generate a short name. Changing this value does not change the contents of a file, but it avoids the short-name attribute creation for the file, also changing the way NTFS displays and manages the file.
Disablelastaccess	HKLM\System\CurrentControlSet\Control\FileSystem\. (REG_DWORD) By default, this registry key is not created. If you have an NTFS volume with a high number of folders or files, and a program is running that briefly accesses each of these in turn, the I/O bandwidth used to generate the Last Access Time updates can be a significant percentage of the overall I/O bandwidth. To increase the speed of access to a folder or file, you can set disablelastaccess to disable updating the Last Access Time. After you use this command and restart the computer, the Last Access Time is no longer updated. If you create a new file, the Last Access Time remains the same as the File Creation Time.
NumTcbTable Partitions	HKLM\system\CurrentControlSet\Services\Tcpip\Parameters\. (REG_DWORD) By default this key is not created. This parameter controls the number of TCB table partitions. The TCB table can be partitioned to improve scalability on multiprocessor systems by reducing contention on the TCB table.

Parameter	Description
TcpAckFrequency	Note: TcpAckFrequency applies only to Windows Server 2003. The recommended setting for TcpAckFrequency is between one-third and one-half of TcpWindowSize. **For Gigabit cards**: `HKLM\system\CurrentControlSet\Services\Tcpip\Parameters\Interfaces` For each Gigabit adapter, add: TcpAckFrequency (REG_DWORD) = 13 (decimal) By default this entry is not in the registry. If only acking data and not any control packets, ack once every 13 packets, instead of the default of two. This helps reducing packet processing costs for the Network Stack, in the case of large writes (uploads) from the client into the server. **For FastEthernet cards**: `HKLM\system\CurrentControlSet\Services\Tcpip\Parameters\Interfaces` For each FastEthernet adapter, add: TcpAckFrequency (REG_DWORD) = 5 (decimal) By default this entry is not in the registry. If only acking data and not any control packets, ack once every five packets, instead of the default of two. This helps reducing packet processing costs for the Network Stack, in the case of large writes (uploads) from the client into the server.

Table 4-5: File Server Parameters.

4.8 Monitor & optimize a server environment for application performance

Before you can optimize your system, you will need to monitor all the critical subsystems, such as memory, processor, disk and network, to see if anything needs to be changed or upgraded on your system. Server 2003 comes with two tools: System Monitor and Performance Logs and Alerts. These can be found in the **Performance** console, under **Administrative Tools** in **Control Panel**.

These system tools will allow you to create a baseline, identify system bottlenecks and determine trends.

A baseline is a snapshot of how your system is performing. It is a good idea to take a baseline report at the same time every day for a set period of time. This will allow you to get a real feel for how your system is reacting to different requests.

A bottleneck is a system resource that is causing slowdowns because of inefficient performance. By setting counters (which we will review a little later in this chapter), you will be able to ascertain which, if any, of your systems may be causing degraded performance.

Determining trends, on the other hand, is a proactive approach to optimization. If you monitor your system on a regular basis, you may notice that your page file usage is increasing slowly but steadily. This will indicate that you will need to upgrade the amount of RAM in your system in the future. Determining trends allows you to predict what upgrades your system may need in the future so that you can plan accordingly.

4.8.1 Memory Performance

There was a running joke among IT Professionals using Windows NT. The solution to every performance problem is "Add RAM." Just like NT, Windows 2003 loves RAM. The more RAM available to the system, the less paging (use of virtual memory) has to occur. No matter how fast your hard drive's performance, it is still going to be substantially (up to 1,000 times) slowerthan RAM.

Some counters that you will want to use to monitor memory usage are:

- **Memory >Available Mbytes**
  The amount of physical memory available to run processes—the more, the better!
- **Memory>Pages/Sec**
  The number of times the requested information had to be retrieved from the page file on the hard disk—optimal performance should be around 4.
- **Paging File>% Usage**
  Indicates how much of the page file is currently being used—the lower, the better!

4.8.2 Processor Performance

Unless you are running processor intensive programs, the odds are that your processor is not the cause of your bottleneck. However, you will want to monitor the processor to make sure that it is running efficiently. Otherwise, you may want to upgrade your processor or, if your system supports it, add another processor.

The counters you may wish to monitor are:

- **Processor>%Processor Time**
  The amount of time the processor spends responding to system requests. Optimally, this will not be above 80%.
- **Processor>Interrupts/Sec**
  Shows the number of hardware interrupts the processor receives each second. Lower is better.

4.8.3 Disk Performance

Disk access can be improved by using faster disks and faster disk controllers. As mentioned earlier in the book, using disk striping and volume striping will also improve I/O performance. Adding another disk controller will help with load balancing as well.

There are two important counters for disk performance:

- **PhysicalDisk>%Disk Time**
  The amount of time that the disk is busy processing read and write requests. It is preferable that this counter be below 90%. Keep in mind that paging also takes place on the hard disk; so adding RAM may also help performance in this area.
- **PhysicalDisk>Current Disk Queue Length**
  Indicates the number of disk requests waiting to be processed. You do not want this value above 2.

4.8.4 Network Performance

You can optimize performance on the network card by monitoring the traffic generated on your NIC and by monitoring the network protocols you are using.

To optimize network traffic, use only the network protocols you need. There is no need to install NetBEUI, for example, if you never need to use it. If you do use multiple protocols, place the most commonly used protocols at the top of the binding order. Use faster network cards, and ones that take full advantage of the bus width.

Two counters that are useful for monitoring the network are:

- **Network Interface>Bytes Total/Sec**
  Measures the total number of bytes sent and received by the NIC. This includes traffic from all protocols.
- **TCP>Segments/Sec**
  Measures the number of bytes that are sent or received by the NIC by the TCP protocol only.

4.8.5 Application Performance

The benefit of any Windows operating system is that you can operate a number of applications at the same time. By default, the foreground application (active window) is given a higher priority than any background application. The **Performance Options** dialog box, through the **System Icon**, **Advanced Tab**, will allow you to configure your system so that performance is optimized for either the background applications or for the foreground applications. (By default, the Programs radio button is selected, to give priority to foreground applications.)

Pop Quiz 4.5

Pop Quiz 4.5 *Questions*

1. What two tools are provided with Windows Server 2003 to assist you in monitoring your server?
2. What is a bottleneck?
3. Name three counters you may wish to use to monitor memory usage.
4. What is one of the easiest ways to optimize network traffic?
5. Name two important counters for monitoring disk performance.

Pop Quiz 4.5 *Answers*

1. Server 2003 comes with two tools: System Monitor and Performance Logs and Alerts. These system tools will allow you to create a baseline, identify system bottlenecks, and determine trends.
2. A bottleneck is a system resource that is causing slowdowns because of inefficient performance.
3. Three counters you may wish to use to monitor memory usage are `Memory >Available Mbytes`, `Memory>Pages/Sec`, and `Paging File>% Usage`.
4. To optimize network traffic, use only the network protocols you need. If you use multiple protocols, place the most commonly used protocols at the top of the binding order.
5. Two counters that are important to use when monitoring disk performance are `PhysicalDisk>%Disk Time` and `PhysicalDisk>Current Disk Queue Length`.

4.9 Manage a Web server

4.9.1 Manage Internet Information Services (IIS)

Internet Information Services 6.0 is a book unto itself. What this section will do is try to give you a brief overview of what IIS 6.0 is, and what it can do for your organization.

There are essentially five major areas for IIS administration. They are:

- Web site Administration
- FTP Site Administration
- NNTP Site Administration
- SMTP Site Administration
- Application Administration.

For purposes of this chapter, we will be focusing solely on web site administration.

About Web Site Administration

Quite frequently, Web site Administration becomes an exercise in troubleshooting. A server goes down and users must be redirected. A new job listing has to be posted onto the site. How smoothly these challenges are overcome are directly related to your ability to control your web site.

Getting Started

The very first thing you should do when setting up your web site is to decide which directories have the documents or information that your company wants published up on the "Web." The Web server will only publish documents contained within these directories. Organize your documents into a well-structured directory system and then use IIS to identify these directories as part of your site.

If the site is small and all of your files are on the same physical hard drive as IIS, you can simply copy your documents into the default home directory (`localdrive:\Inetpub\Wwwroot`). Users can access these files on the Intranet by using the following URL: `http://servername/filename`.

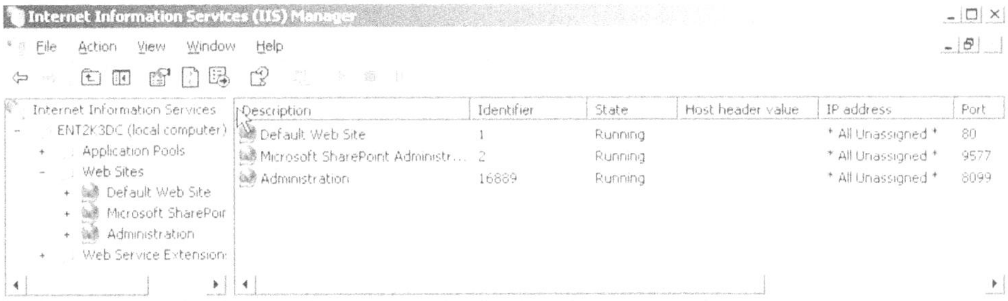

Figure 4-64: IIS Default Installation.

Home Directories

Every web site must have a home directory, the central location for all pages being published on your site. The home directory is the central location for your published pages. The home directory will have the default page or index file that contains the links to other pages on your site and is mapped to your site's domain name or server name.

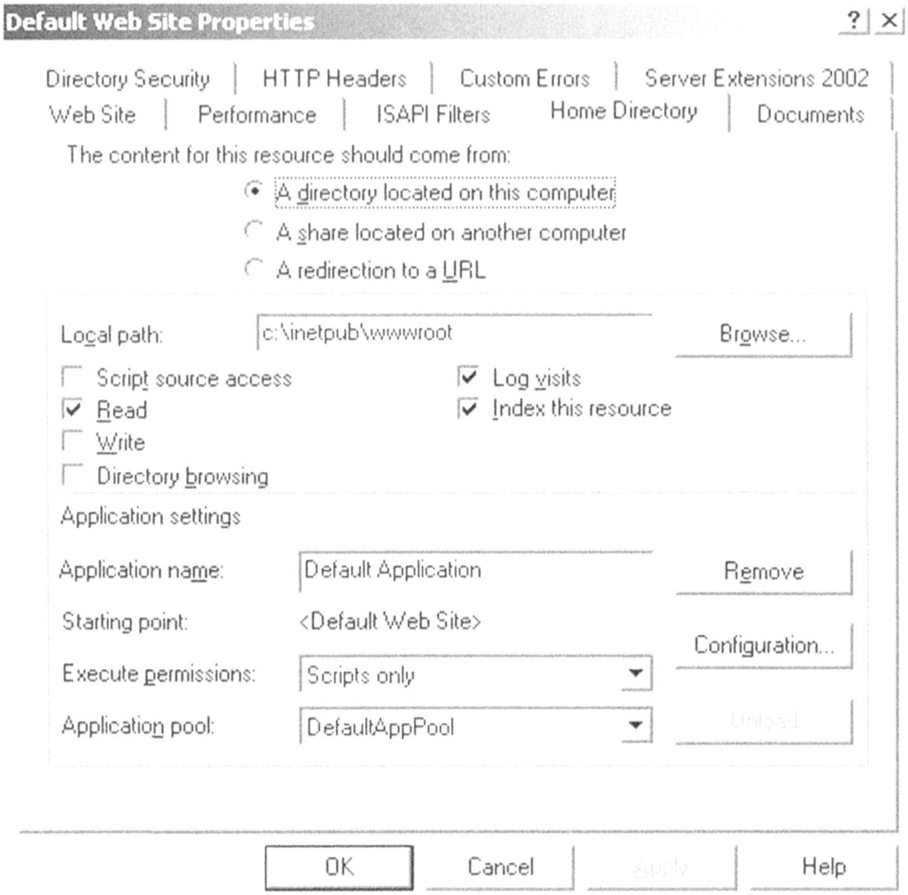

Figure 4-65: Properties: Home Directory.

Virtual Directories

However, in most cases, you are not going to want to have every document on your site contained within your home directory. To be able to publish pages from any directory that is not contained in the home directory, you will need to use virtual directories. A virtual directory appears to be a subdirectory of your home directory to all users, but it can really reside anywhere.

This is done through the use of aliases. An alias is the name that the Web browsers use to access that directory. It is more secure because users do not know where your files are physically located on the server. It also makes it simpler to move directories within the site, for the very reason that you do not need to change the URL. You simply need to change the mapping between the alias and the physical location of the directory.

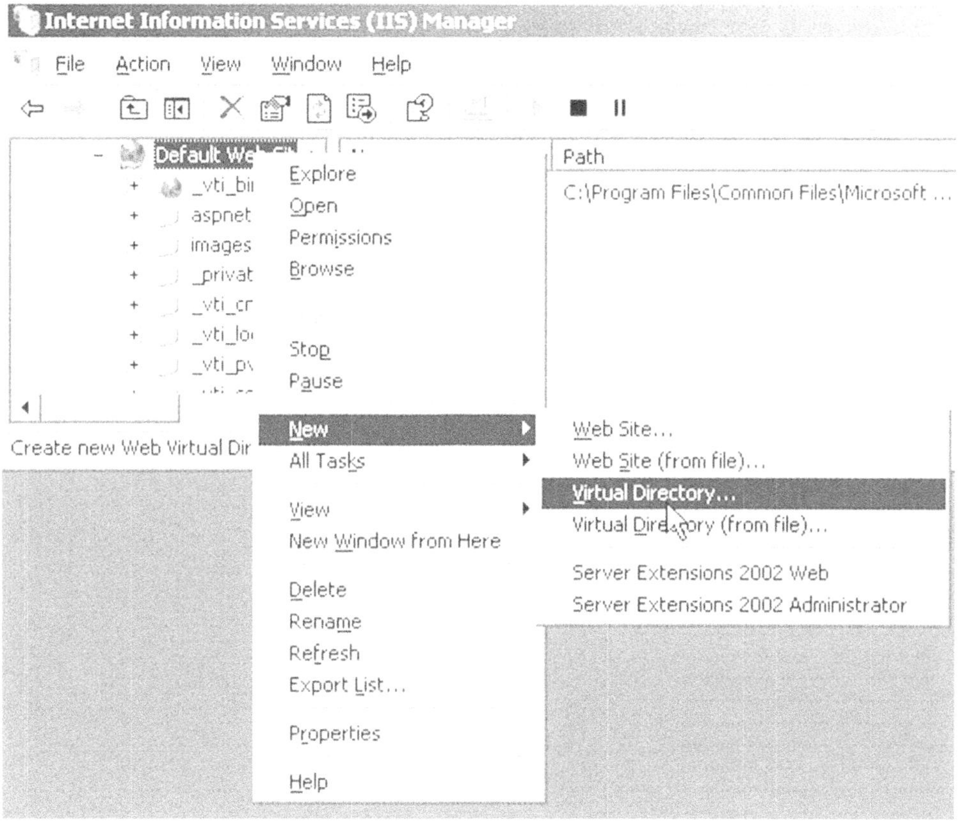

Figure 4-66: New Virtual Directory.

Reroute Requests with Redirects

When you move homes, one of the first things you have to remember to do is to notify the post office of your new address. By doing this, the post office will forward any mail addressed to you from your old address to your new address.

Redirects are the same thing in the web site world. When you move a page on the web site, you want to make sure that browsers can still find the page. By using the process called "redirecting a browser request" or "redirecting a URL," the Web server will provide the browser with an updated URL, so that a new request can be made.

When you are modifying your web site, redirects can be indispensable in terms of time and accuracy. Even if you rename a virtual directory, a redirect can ensure that the links that pointed to the original name still access the files in the newly named directory.

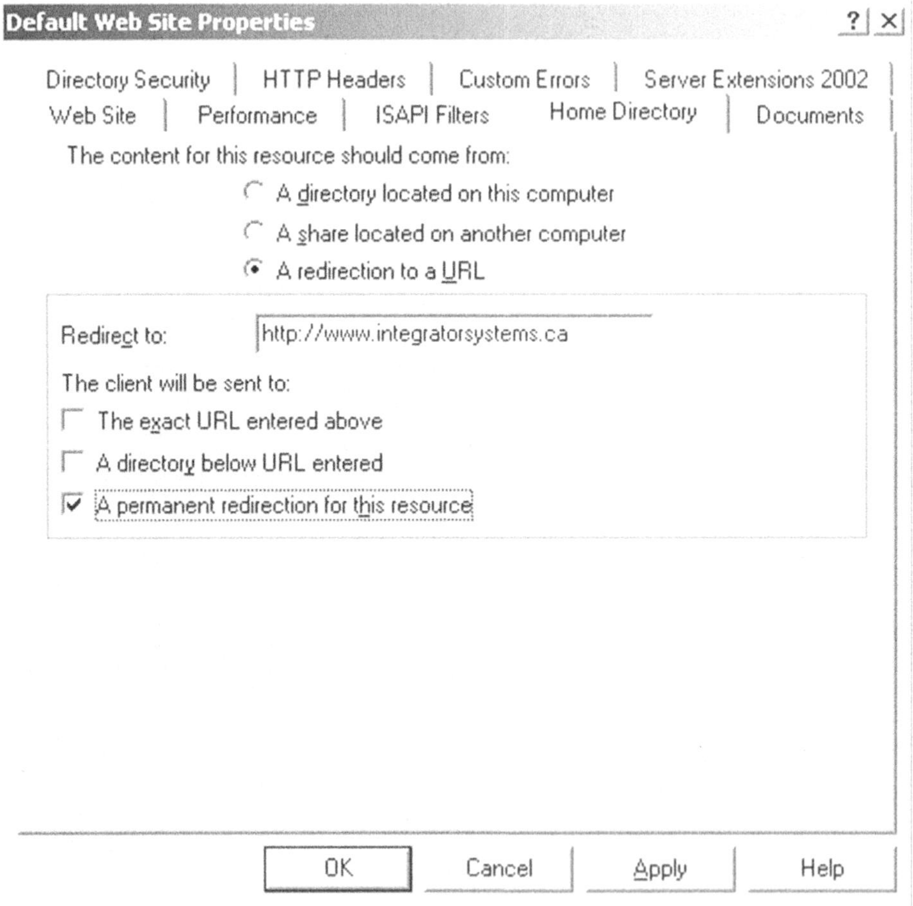

Figure 4-67: Redirection.

4.9.2 Manage security for IIS

There are major risks to the security of your web site. The first risk is the one of which we are all aware—malicious individuals. The second is the one of which we rarely think—well-intentioned users who accidentally alter files without knowing what they have done. Appropriate safeguards on your Web server can reduce, or even eliminate, the danger from both of these risks.

IIS Installed Locked Down

One of the greatest innovations to come about with IIS 6.0 is also one of the simplest. IIS is installed in a fully locked-down mode. Request-handling for static Web pages is enabled. All other request-handling features are disabled. Additional services must be enabled by the administrator. This allows only the necessary services to be enabled, and lowers the risk from intruders from the minute of installation.

Authentication

IIS supports seven methods of authentication, tied in with the basic security features of Server 2003.

- **Anonymous authentication**
  allows anyone access without requesting a user name or password.
- **Basic authentication**
  requests a username and password, which are sent in plain text unencrypted over the network.
- **Digest authentication**
  requests a username and password. Passwords are sent as a hash value. Digest authentication is available only on domains with a Windows domain controller.
- **Advanced Digest authentication**
  improves on the security of Digest authentication, by storing the client credentials as an MD5 hash in the AD Directory Service on the Server 2003 domain controller.
- **Integrated Windows authentication**
  uses hashing technology to identify users without actually sending passwords over the network.
- **Certificates**
  are digital credentials that can be used to establish a Secure Sockets Layer (SSL) connection. They can also be used for authentication.
- **.NET Passport**
  uses the already-existing Microsoft .NET passport to verify the user's identity. You will frequently see this type of authentication when accessing secure sites on the Microsoft web site.

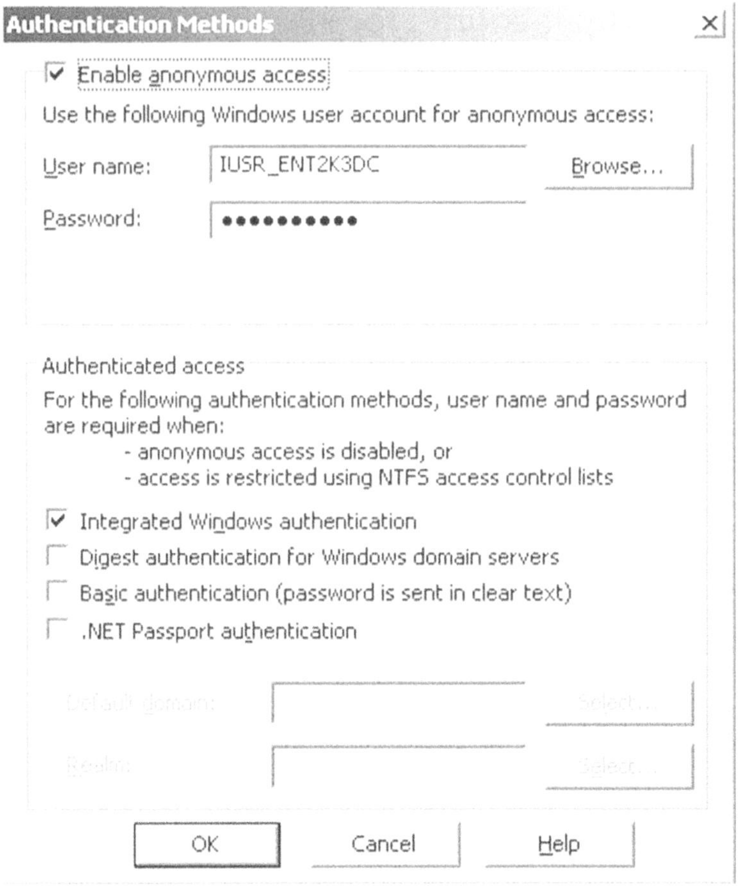

Figure 4-68: Authentication.

Access Control

IIS takes advantage of Server 2003 NTFS permissions to allow the administrator to restrict write access to individuals who have the appropriate assigned permissions. Any individual can view the web site, but only those who have been assigned the appropriate permissions can alter content.

Certificates

Certificates are digital identification documents that allow both clients and servers to authenticate each other. They are required for both the server and client's browser in order that an SSL connection can be set up, so that encrypted information can be dispatched. IIS has certificate-based SSL features that consist of a server certificate, a client certificate and digital keys. These certificates can be created for internal use only with Microsoft Certificate Server. You can also obtain certificates from an external certificate authority, for external use.

What does a server certificate contain? It includes very detailed identification information, and a public key that is used in establishing a secure connection. Essentially, it is a way for any user visiting your site to confirm its identity and be assured of the integrity of the secure connection.

As well, the Web server can optionally authenticate users by checking the contents of their client certificates. Again, it contains detailed information meant to identify the user and the issuing organization, as well as a public key.

Figure 4-69: Certificates.

Encryption

IIS 6.0 uses certificate key pairs (SSL 3.0) to establish a secure encrypted connection. The key pair consists of a public key and a private key. During the exchange of information a session key (or encryption key) is created, which is used by both the Web server and the client browser. The degree of strength of the encryption is measured in bits, with more bits comprising a higher level of security. ISS can go up to 128 bit encryption—however, utilizing this level of encryption depends on the laws of the country in which the server resides. In North America, 128 bit security is allowed.

Server-Gated Cryptography

Server-Gated Cryptography (SGC) is the solution for worldwide secure financial transactions. It uses 128-bit encryption, the highest commercial encryption presently available, to allow financial institutions to provide highly secure connections for their clients.

What is unique about SGC is that it does not require any application to run on the client's browser. While it can be used by any standard of IIS (versions 4.0 and later), a special certificate is required to use SGC.

Auditing

Using the standard Server 2003 utilities, you are able to use auditing techniques to monitor a wide rage of user and Web server security activity. It is strongly recommended that the Web server is regularly audited to monitor for hacking, unauthorized access or tampering.

As well, you can use ASP applications to create your own customized auditing logs.

Chapter 4: Summary

This chapter has reviewed monitoring and analyzing tasks on a Windows Server 2003. We took a look at some of the tools you can use to do these tasks, including Event Viewer, System Monitor and Task Manager, as well as some of the specific counters you might use to gain an in-depth knowledge of what is happening on your servers and your network. We have taken a look SUS and licensing, and discussed the world of remote assistance and remote desktop. Finally, we examined the administration of both printers and what is new in the administration of Web servers.

The next section will provide you with some review questions that may help you get "exam-ready." Take the opportunity to go back and review some of the topics we have discussed if you find you are struggling with some of the concepts. You will find you are ready to tackle the monitoring and analysis environment of Windows Server 2003 in no time at all!

Chapter 4: Review Questions

1. What steps do you need to take after installing DHCP to ensure that it will provide users with IP addresses in your network?

A. Configure a scope

B. Slate a scope

C. Start the DHCP service

D. Authorize the DHCP server

E. Change the IP address of the DHCP server to a dynamic one

---

2. You configure a scope for your newly installed DHCP service. Users are complaining that they aren't receiving IP addresses from the DHCP server. What should you do?

A. Reinstall the DHCP service

B. Authorize the DHCP server

C. Install WINS

D. Install RRAS

3. You need to install the Windows Terminal Services, Remote Desktop Connection client from a Windows Server 2003. You have Terminal Services running on the 2003 Server. What steps do you need to take?

A. Share the Client Setup Folder.

B. Share the Server Setup Folder.

C. Install the 32-Bit Terminal Services Client.

D. Install the 16-Bit Terminal Services Client.

---

4. You have a need to use Terminal Services and subsequently you need to reactivate a License Server. What steps should you take to do this?

A. In the console tree, double-click the license server that you want to reactivate, point to Advanced and then click Reissue Server.

B. In the console tree, right-click the license server that you want to reactivate, point to Advanced and then click Reactivate Server.

C. After the Licensing Wizard starts, confirm that your name, your phone number (optional) and your e-mail address that are listed under Information Needed are correct, and then click Next.

D. Open the Licensing Terminal Services window.

5. Multiple processors can help in which of the following situations?

A. When the present processor is handling the load

B. When using a single-threaded application

C. When the present processor is overloaded

D. When using a multi-threaded application

---

6. Which of the following counters measure the number of threads waiting on the processor?

A. Server Work Queues: Queue Length

B. Server Work Queues: % Processor Time

C. System: Processor Queue Length

D. System: % Threads

7. You probably need to upgrade your processor if System Monitor indicates which of the following?

A. Average Pages/Sec 27.322

B. Avg. Disk sec/Transfer is 3.132

C. Average % Processor Time is 87%

D. Network Interface:Bytes Total/sec is 241.322

E. Avg. Mem sec/Transfer is 425.2

---

8. You probably need to upgrade your RAM if System Monitor indicates which of the following?

A. Average Pages/Sec 27.322

B. Avg. Disk sec/Transfer is 3.132

C. Average % Processor Time is 87%

D. Network Interface: Bytes Total/sec is 241.322

E. Avg. Mem sec/Transfer is 425.2

9. You probably need to upgrade your processor if System Monitor indicates which of the following?

A. Average % Processor Time is 87%

B. Avg. Disk sec/Transfer is 3.132

C. Average Pages/Sec 27.322

D. Network Interface: Bytes Total/sec is 241.322

E. Avg. Mem sec/Transfer is 425.2

---

10. You probably need to upgrade your RAM if System Monitor indicates which of the following?

A. Avg. Mem sec/Transfer is 425.2

B. Avg. Disk sec/Transfer is 3.132

C. Average % Processor Time is 87%

D. Network Interface: Bytes Total/sec is 241.322

E. Average Pages/Sec 27.322

11. Ideally, where should a paging file be placed in a Windows environment where the server operating system is located on the master hard drive (C:)?

A. On C:\Windows

B. On D: (a separate hard drive)

C. On E: (the CD-ROM drive)

D. Anywhere on C:

---

12. You are setting up a new server, you unsuccessfully attempt to use the PING utility to contact other servers in the domain. What should you check?

A. Check to see if BIND is being used.

B. Check to see if your default gateway is correct.

C. Check to see if your subnet mask matches theirs.

D. Check to see if WINS is being used.

13. How can you see resources used by a device in Windows 2003?

A. Go to the Start Menu button and choose the Run option. Type in WINMSD.EXE and click OK.

B. Go to the Start Menu button, then to All Programs, Accessories, System Tools, and System Information.

C. Right-click the My Computer option and select properties. Select the Hardware tab and choose Device Manager.

D. Right-click the My Network Places option and select properties. Select the Hardware tab and choose Device Manager.

---

14. If you don't have the money to add more RAM and you are using Windows 2003, what are some other options for addressing out of memory messages?

A. Decrease the temporary file size in your applications.

B. Increase the temporary file size in your applications.

C. Increase the paging file size.

D. Decrease the paging file size.

15. Which of the following methods of authentication are available in IIS 6.0 for 2003 Server?

A. Integrated Windows authentication

B. Digest authentication

C. Dual authentication

D. Microsoft .NET Passport authentication

---

16. How would you configure IIS to use Microsoft .NET Passport authentication?

A. In IIS Manager, expand Server_name, where Server_name is the name of the server, and then expand Web sites.

B. In the console tree, right-click the Web site, virtual directory, or file for which you want to configure authentication, and then click Properties. Click the Directory Security or File Security tab (as appropriate), and then under Anonymous and access control, click Edit.

C. Click to select the check box next to the Microsoft .NET Passport authentication method.

D. In the console tree, double-click the Web site, virtual directory, or file for which you want to configure authentication, and then click Properties. Click the Directory Security or File Security tab (as appropriate), and then under Anonymous and access control, click Open.

Chapter 4: Review Answers

1. What steps do you need to take after installing DHCP to ensure that it will provide users with IP addresses in your network?

***A. Configure a scope**

B. Slate a scope

***C. Start the DHCP service**

***D. Authorize the DHCP server**

E. Change the IP address of the DHCP server to a dynamic one

Explanation: After installing DHCP, the service must be configured and authorized. When you install and configure DHCP on a domain controller, the server is typically authorized when you add it to the DHCP console. When you install and configure the DHCP service on a member server or stand-alone server, it must be authorized.

---

2. You configure a scope for your newly installed DHCP service. Users are complaining that they aren't receiving IP addresses from the DHCP server. What should you do?

A. Reinstall the DHCP service

***B. Authorize the DHCP server**

C. Install WINS

D. Install RRAS

Explanation: To authorize a DHCP server, click Start, click Programs, click Administrative Tools and then click DHCP. Select the new DHCP server. If there is a red arrow in the lower-right corner of the server object, the server has not yet been authorized. Right-click the server, and then click Authorize. After a few moments, right-click the server again, and then click Refresh. There should be a green arrow in the lower-right corner to indicate that the server has been authorized.

3. You need to install the Windows Terminal Services, Remote Desktop Connection client from a Windows Server 2003. You have Terminal Services running on the 2003 Server. What steps do you need to take?

***A. Share the Client Setup Folder.**

B. Share the Server Setup Folder.

***C. Install the 32-Bit Terminal Services Client**

D. Install the 16-Bit Terminal Services Client

Explanation: First, you need to share the Client Setup Folder. On the Windows Server 2003 computer that is running Terminal Services, open Windows Explorer, and then locate the following folder: drive:\systemroot\System32\Clients\Tsclient\Win32 where drive is the drive that Windows is installed on and systemroot is the folder that contains the Windows installation files. Right-click the Win32 folder, and then click Sharing and Security. In the win32 Properties dialog box, click Share this folder, and then click OK. Next, you will need to install the 32-Bit Terminal Services Client. On the client computer, connect to the shared client installation folder on the server that is running Terminal Services. Click Start, and then click Run. In the Open, box type \\computername\Tsclient\Win32\Setup.exe, where computername is the computer name of the Windows Server 2003-based computer with the installation shared folder. Click OK. Install the client following the on-screen instructions.

---

4. You have a need to use Terminal Services and subsequently you need to reactivate a License Server. What steps should you take to do this?

A. In the console tree, double-click the license server that you want to reactivate, point to Advanced and then click Reissue Server.

***B. In the console tree, right-click the license server that you want to reactivate, point to Advanced and then click Reactivate Server.**

***C. After the Licensing Wizard starts, confirm that your name, your phone number (optional) and your e-mail address that are listed under Information Needed are correct, and then click Next.**

***D. Open the Licensing Terminal Services window.**

Explanation: To reactivate a License Server, open the Licensing Terminal Services window. In the console tree, right-click the license server that you want to reactivate, point to Advanced, and then click Reactivate Server. After the Licensing Wizard starts, confirm that your name, your phone number (optional) and your e-mail address that are listed under Information Needed are correct, and then click Next.

5. Multiple processors can help in which of the following situations?
   A. When the present processor is handling the load
   B. When using a single-threaded application

***C. When the present processor is overloaded**

***D. When using a multi-threaded application**

Explanation: Multiple processors can help when using a multi-threaded application or when the present processor is overloaded.

---

6. Which of the following counters measure the number of threads waiting on the processor?

***A. Server Work Queues: Queue Length**

   B. Server Work Queues: % Processor Time

***C. System: Processor Queue Length**

   D. System: % Threads

Explanation: The Server Work Queues: Queue Length and the counter measures the number of threads waiting on the processor.

7. You probably need to upgrade your processor if System Monitor indicates which of the following?

A. Average Pages/Sec 27.322

B. Avg. Disk sec/Transfer is 3.132

***C. Average % Processor Time is 87%**

D. Network Interface:Bytes Total/sec is 241.322

E. Avg. Mem sec/Transfer is 425.2

Explanation: An Avg. Disk sec/Transfer of 3.132 would indicate that the hard drive needs to be replaced, since it should be much lower, not even 1.0. An Average % Processor Time of 87% would indicate a need for a processor upgrade. If Average Pages/Sec is 27.322, then more RAM is needed, since the average should be more like 15 or less. Network Interface: Bytes Total/sec is 241.322 this is within the normal parameters for a NIC card.

---

8. You probably need to upgrade your RAM if System Monitor indicates which of the following?

***A. Average Pages/Sec 27.322**

B. Avg. Disk sec/Transfer is 3.132

C. Average % Processor Time is 87%

D. Network Interface: Bytes Total/sec is 241.322

E. Avg. Mem sec/Transfer is 425.2

Explanation: An Avg. Disk sec/Transfer of 3.132 would indicate that the hard drive needs to be replaced, since it should be much lower, not even 1.0. An Average % Processor Time of 87% would indicate a need for a processor upgrade. If Average Pages/Sec is 27.322, then more RAM is needed, since the average should be more like 15 or less. Network Interface: Bytes Total/sec is 241.322 this is within the normal parameters for a NIC card.

9. You probably need to upgrade your processor if System Monitor indicates which of the following?

***A. Average % Processor Time is 87%**

B. Avg. Disk sec/Transfer is 3.132

C. Average Pages/Sec 27.322

D. Network Interface:Bytes Total/sec is 241.322

E. Avg. Mem sec/Transfer is 425.2

Explanation: An Avg. Disk sec/Transfer of 3.132 would indicate that the hard drive needs to be replaced, since it should be much lower, not even 1.0. An Average % Processor Time of 87% would indicate a need for a processor upgrade. If Average Pages/Sec is 27.322, then more RAM is needed, since the average should be more like 15 or less. Network Interface: Bytes Total/sec is 241.322 this is within the normal parameters for a NIC card.

---

10. You probably need to upgrade your RAM if System Monitor indicates which of the following?

A. Avg. Mem sec/Transfer is 425.2

B. Avg. Disk sec/Transfer is 3.132

C. Average % Processor Time is 87%

D. Network Interface: Bytes Total/sec is 241.322

***E. Average Pages/Sec 27.322**

Explanation: An Avg. Disk sec/Transfer of 3.132 would indicate that the hard drive needs to be replaced, since it should be much lower, not even 1.0. An Average % Processor Time of 87% would indicate a need for a processor upgrade. If Average Pages/Sec is 27.322, then more RAM is needed, since the average should be more like 15 or less. Network Interface: Bytes Total/sec is 241.322 this is within the normal parameters for a NIC card.

11. Ideally, where should a paging file be placed in a Windows environment where the server operating system is located on the master hard drive (C:)?
    A. On C:\Windows
***B. On D: (a separate hard drive)**
    C. On E: (the CD-ROM drive)
    D. Anywhere on C:

Explanation: Ideally, a paging file should be placed on a separate hard drive from where the server operating system is located (in this example on D:).

---

12. You are setting up a new server, you unsuccessfully attempt to use the PING utility to contact other servers in the domain. What should you check?
    A. Check to see if BIND is being used.
***B. Check to see if your default gateway is correct.**
***C. Check to see if your subnet mask matches theirs.**
    D. Check to see if WINS is being used.

Explanation: You are setting up a new server, you unsuccessfully attempt to use the PING utility to contact other servers in the domain. Check to see if your subnet mask matches theirs and if your default gateway is correct. BIND (UNIX's answer to DNS) and WINS have nothing to do with pinging an IP address.

13. How can you see resources used by a device in Windows 2003?

***A. Go to the Start Menu button, and choose the Run option. Type in WINMSD.EXE and click OK.**

***B. Go to the Start Menu button, then to All Programs, Accessories, System Tools and System Information.**

***C. Right-click the My Computer option and select properties. Select the Hardware tab and choose Device Manager.**

D. Right-click the My Network Places option and select properties. Select the Hardware tab and choose Device Manager.

Explanation: If you want to view resources used by a device in Windows 2003, use System Information or Device Manager. To access System Information, use one of the following methods: go to the Start Menu button, and choose the Run option. Type in WINMSD.EXE and click OK. Or you can go to the Start Menu button, then to All Programs, Accessories, System Tools and System Information. To access Device Manager, right-click the My Computer option and select properties. Select the Hardware tab and choose Device Manager.

---

14. If you don't have the money to add more RAM and you are using Windows 2003, what are some other options for addressing out of memory messages?

A. Decrease the temporary file size in your applications.

***B. Increase the temporary file size in your applications.**

***C. Increase the paging file size.**

D. Decrease the paging file size.

Explanation: If you don't have the money to add more RAM and you are using Windows 2003, you can address out of memory messages by either increasing the paging file size (do this with the Advanced tab in the System applet in Control Panel) or increasing the temporary file size in your applications.

15. Which of the following methods of authentication are available in IIS 6.0 for 2003 Server?

***A. Integrated Windows authentication**

***B. Digest authentication**

***C. Dual authentication**

D. Microsoft .NET Passport authentication

Explanation: To configure authentication in IIS, start IIS Manager or open the IIS snap-in. Expand Server_name, where Server_name is the name of the server, and then expand Web sites. In the console tree, right-click the Web site, virtual directory, or file for which you want to configure authentication, and then click Properties. Click the Directory Security or File Security tab (as appropriate), and then under Anonymous and access control, click Edit. Click to select the check box next to the authentication method or methods that you want to use, and then click OK. The authentication methods that are set by default are Anonymous access and Integrated Windows authentication. When anonymous access is turned on, no authenticated user credentials are required to access the site. This option is best used when you want to grant public access to information that requires no security.

When a user tries to connect to your Web site, IIS assigns the connection to the IUSER_ComputerName account, where ComputerName is the name of the server on which IIS is running. By default, the IUSER_ComputerName account is a member of the Guests group. This group has security restrictions, imposed by NTFS file system permissions that designate the level of access and the type of content that is available to public users. To edit the Windows account used for anonymous access, click Browse in the Anonymous access box. Integrated Windows authentication (this used to be NTLM or Windows NT Challenge/Response authentication) sends user authentication information over the network as a Kerberos ticket, and provides a high level of security. Windows Integrated authentication uses Kerberos version 5 and NTLM authentication. To use this method, clients must use Microsoft Internet Explorer 2.0 or later.

Additionally, Windows Integrated authentication is not supported over HTTP proxy connections. This option is best used for an intranet, where both the user and Web server computers are in the same domain, and administrators can make sure that every user is using Internet Explorer 2.0 or later. Digest authentication requires a user ID and password, provides a medium level of security and may be used when you want to grant access to secure information from public networks. This method offers the same functionality as basic authentication. However, this method transmits user credentials across the network as an MD5 hash, or message digest, in which the original user name and password cannot be deciphered from the hash. To use this method, clients must use Microsoft Internet Explorer 5.0 or later, and the Web clients and Web servers must be members of, or be trusted by, the same domain. If you turn on digest authentication, type the realm name in the Realm box. Basic authentication requires a user ID and password, and provides a low level of security. User credentials are sent in clear text across the network. This format provides a low level of security because the password can be read by almost all protocol analyzers.

However, it is compatible with the widest number of Web clients. This option is best used when you want to grant access to information with little or no need for privacy. If you turn on basic authentication, type the domain name that you want to use in the Default domain box. You can also optionally enter a value in the Realm box. Microsoft .NET Passport authentication provides single sign-in security, which provides users with access to diverse services on the Internet. When you select this option, requests to IIS must contain valid .NET Passport credentials on either the query string or in the cookie.

If IIS does not detect .NET Passport credentials, requests are redirected to the .NET Passport logon page. You can also limit access based on source IP address, source network ID or source domain name.

---

16. How would you configure IIS to use Microsoft .NET Passport authentication?

***A. In IIS Manager, expand Server_name, where Server_name is the name of the server, and then expand Web sites.**

***B. In the console tree, right-click the Web site, virtual directory or file for which you want to configure authentication, and then click Properties. Click the Directory Security or File Security tab (as appropriate), and then under Anonymous and access control, click Edit.**

***C. Click to select the check box next to the Microsoft .NET Passport authentication method.**

D. In the console tree, double-click the Web site, virtual directory or file for which you want to configure authentication, and then click Properties. Click the Directory Security or File Security tab (as appropriate), and then under Anonymous and access control, click Open.

Explanation: To configure authentication in IIS, start IIS Manager or open the IIS snap-in. Expand Server_name, where Server_name is the name of the server, and then expand Web sites. In the console tree, right-click the Web site, virtual directory or file for which you want to configure authentication, and then click Properties. Click the Directory Security or File Security tab (as appropriate), and then under Anonymous and access control, click Edit. Click to select the check box next to the authentication method or methods that you want to use, and then click OK. The authentication methods that are set by default are Anonymous access and Integrated Windows authentication. When anonymous access is turned on, no authenticated user credentials are required to access the site. This option is best used when you want to grant public access to information that requires no security.

When a user tries to connect to your Web site, IIS assigns the connection to the IUSER_ComputerName account, where ComputerName is the name of the server on which IIS is running. By default, the IUSER_ComputerName account is a member of the Guests group. This group has security restrictions, imposed by NTFS file system permissions that designate the level of access and the type of content that is available to public users. To edit the Windows account used for anonymous access, click Browse in the Anonymous access box. Integrated Windows authentication (this used to be NTLM or Windows NT Challenge/Response authentication) sends user authentication information over the network as a Kerberos ticket, and provides a high level of security. Windows Integrated authentication uses Kerberos version 5 and NTLM authentication. To use this method, clients must use Microsoft Internet Explorer 2.0 or later.

Additionally, Windows Integrated authentication is not supported over HTTP proxy connections. This option is best used for an intranet, where both the user and Web server computers are in the same domain, and administrators can make sure that every user is using Internet Explorer 2.0 or later. Digest authentication requires a user ID and password, provides a medium level of security, and may be used when you want to grant access to secure information from public networks.

This method offers the same functionality as basic authentication. However, this method transmits user credentials across the network as an MD5 hash, or message digest, in which the original user name and password cannot be deciphered from the hash. To use this method, clients must use Microsoft Internet Explorer 5.0 or later, and the Web clients and Web servers must be members of, or be trusted by, the same domain. If you turn on digest authentication, type the realm name in the Realm box.

Basic authentication requires a user ID and password, and provides a low level of security. User credentials are sent in clear text across the network. This format provides a low level of security because almost all protocol analyzers can read the password. However, it is compatible with the widest number of Web clients. This option is best used when you want to grant access to information with little or no need for privacy. If you turn on basic authentication, type the domain name that you want to use in the Default domain box. You can also optionally enter a value in the Realm box. Microsoft .NET Passport authentication provides single sign-in security, which provides users with access to diverse services on the Internet. When you select this option, requests to IIS must contain valid .NET Passport credentials on either the query string or in the cookie. If IIS does not detect .NET Passport credentials, requests are redirected to the .NET Passport logon page. You can also limit access based on source IP address, source network ID or source domain name.

The objective of this chapter is to provide the reader with an understanding of the following:

5.1 Perform system recovery for a server

- **5.1.1 Implement Automated System Recovery (ASR)**
- **5.1.2 Restore data from shadow copy volumes**
- **5.1.3 Back up files and System State data to media**
- **5.1.4 Configure security for backup operations**

5.2 Manage backup procedures

- **5.2.1 Verify the successful completion of backup jobs**
- **5.2.2 Manage backup storage media**

5.3 Recover from server hardware failure

5.4 Restore backup data

5.5 Schedule backup jobs

Chapter 5: Disaster Recovery

Introduction:

It will happen to you. Sooner or later it ***will*** happen to you. Will you be ready? The main idea behind disaster recovery is in the name—to be able to recover from a disaster. Disaster recovery allows you to be able to return the effected system to a proper working state.

Some of the reasons you you may need to implement a part of your disaster recovery plans may include:

- A need (or desire) to revert to a previous version of a data file
- Missing or corrupt data files
- Missing or corrupt operating system files
- The system becomes unstable after you update a device driver or add a new hardware device or install a new application
- Hardware (hard drive) failure
- Total system failure.

Proper planning and a good set of tools will allow you to recover in as short a period of time as possible. You will have to provide the planning, but fortunately Windows Server 2003 provides a good set of basic tools to help you implement your plan. Careful use of these tools will allow you to recover from any of the failures mentioned above.

Getting Ready Questions

1. What is Automated System Recovery?
2. Define Shadow Copy.
3. What are the five different types of backup?
4. What is Safe Mode and when would you use it?
5. You have installed a new video driver and after logging on, you find that it is causing your system to freeze. Would the Last Known Good Configuration help you in this instance?

Getting Ready Answers

1. ASR is a tool that will help you collect information needed to repair and reconstruct your operating system and other system state files in case of a failure.
2. Shadow Copy is a feature of Windows Server 2003 that allows point-in-time, read-only copies of files that are currently stored on network shares.
3. The five different types of backup are Normal (Full), Copy, Differential, Incremental and Daily.
4. Safe Mode, entered by pressing F8, loads only the basic devices, drivers and services required to run and operate the system. You would use it when you suspect a recently installed application or driver is causing a problem.
5. No. The Last Known Good Configuration is updated each time Windows is started in normal mode and a user logs in and is authenticated. If you shut the system down without logging in, you do not overwrite the Last Known Good Configuration. However, in this instance, you have already logged on, so Last Known Good will not help you in this instance.

To make your system less prone to failures, investigate developing fault tolerant systems, especially for critical servers. A fault tolerant system is designed to continue operating even after a key component (hard drive, controller, power supply, etc.) fails. Several things you can do to make your system more fault tolerant (some of these will depend upon your hardware manufacturer and the model of systems you purchased) include:

- Adding an uninterruptible power supply (UPS) to protect the server due to a power failure. This will allow your server to shut down gracefully, better protecting key files and components. This is easy to add to any computer.
- Use multiple hard dive controllers to provide redundancy if one fails.
- Use one or more RAID arrays for your system and data file storage. This will help protect from data loss due to hard drive failure. *This will not take the place of a good back-up strategy!* RAID arrays can only help you recover if one physical disk is damaged. If more than one is damaged, you need to resort to plan B, your excellent set of backups!
- Consider multiples of everything, such as power supplies, etc. Your server hardware must be able to support these features. Investigate this with your hardware manufacturer.

Two other items that should be in your recovery toolbox are a good boot disk and the recovery console.

A boot disk (or Windows Startup Disk) is useful in helping you recover a critical file on your system hard disk. If your installation isn't corrupted in some other way, the boot disk can help you recover from:

- A damaged boot sector
- A damaged master boot record
- Virus infections of the master boot record
- Missing or damaged system startup files ntldr or ntdetect.com
- A damaged mirror set.

A boot disk is made by formatting a blank floppy, then copying the `boot.ini` file from your boot drive to the floppy. Then copy **ntldr** and **ntdetect.com** to the floppy. This disk is configuration specific, in that the boot.ini file will need to match the hard drive setup of your particular machine. The best way to do things is to have a seperate diskette for each machine. You can use a disk made on another machine if you have the same configuration on both machines, or if you modify the boot.ini to properly look for the boot and system partitions on the machine that needs repair.

The recover console is a utility you can add to your server installation that will provide several useful features and functions. What you are provided is a secure, NTFS-enabled, enhanced command prompt that you can use for operations in case you can't boot the system to safe mode. You can install it or run it from the operating system CD.

To install, follow these steps:

1. Insert your operating system CD while running Windows Server 2003.
2. Close **Autorun** if it is turned on.
3. At a command prompt, or in the run box, type in the following command, where d:\ is the drive letter of your CD drive: **d:\i386\winnt32 /cmdcons.** So, if your CD drive is drive h: the proper command would be **h:\i386\winnt32 /cmdcons**. You can also install it from a network share.
4. Click yes to install the recovery console.

You can access the recovery console from the extended startup options (pressing F8 at system boot).

5.1 Perform system recovery for a server

Performing a system recovery (either a partial or full recovery) for a server is a task with which any network administrator should be very familiar and comfortable. Different levels of failure call for different methods of recovery. Let's look at some of the tools provided in Windows Server 2003 and their function. In a later section, we'll investigate how to use the different tools to recover from a server failure.

5.1.1 Implement Automated System Recovery (ASR)

What is Automated System Recovery (ASR)? This is a tool that will help you collect information needed to repair and reconstruct your operating system and other system state files in case of a failure. The ASR is a set of a single floppy and a backup on removable media (or network file). ASR does not try to place all the necessary recovery information on a diskette, instead it makes a system backup and creates three information files on the floppy that describe the disk configurations, locations of various plug-and-play devices and system files on your server.

The ASR set is easy to make, and should be done BEFORE you implement a major change to your server as a fallback method, or final recovery. A major change may be defined as anything done in control panel, such as **Add/Remove Programs** or **Windows Components**, or any change to the hard disk configuration. Another possibility is to create a set after your install the basic operating system and before applications are installed. Saving this set would allow you to "start over" with a fresh server without the fun of completing reinstalling Windows.

The ASR diskette is not bootable, and it must be used with your original operating system CD or setup diskettes during the setup program.

To perform the following operation, you must be a member of the local Administrators group, the Backup Operators group or, if the computer is a member of the domain, the Domain Administrators group. You may also have the necessary permissions delegated to you. As a best practice, consider using the **Run As** feature so that you use these elevated permissions only when performing this operation.

To create an ASR set, perform the following steps:

1. Locate a blank floppy for the last step.
2. Start the Windows Server 2003 Backup program. Click on **Start | Programs | Accessories | System Tools**. Select **Backup**. (Could we hide that any deeper?) If the wizard wants to help you, just switch to advanced mode. Your screen should look like Figure 5.1.

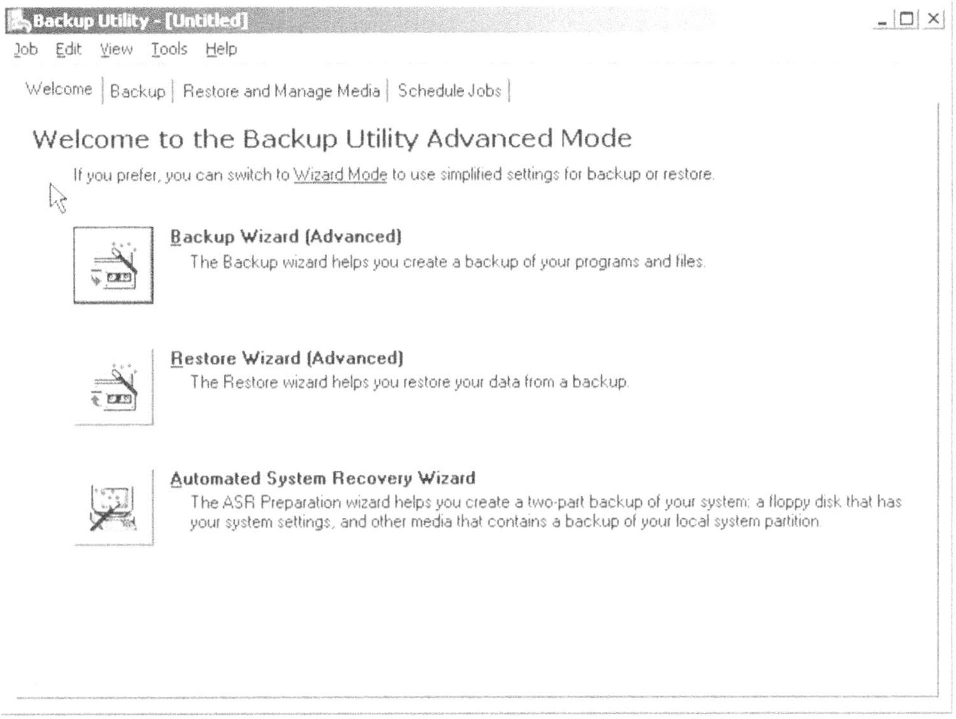

Figure 5-1: ASR Set.

3. Click on Automated System Recovery Wizard. The welcome screen is shown in Figure 5.2. Click **Next**.

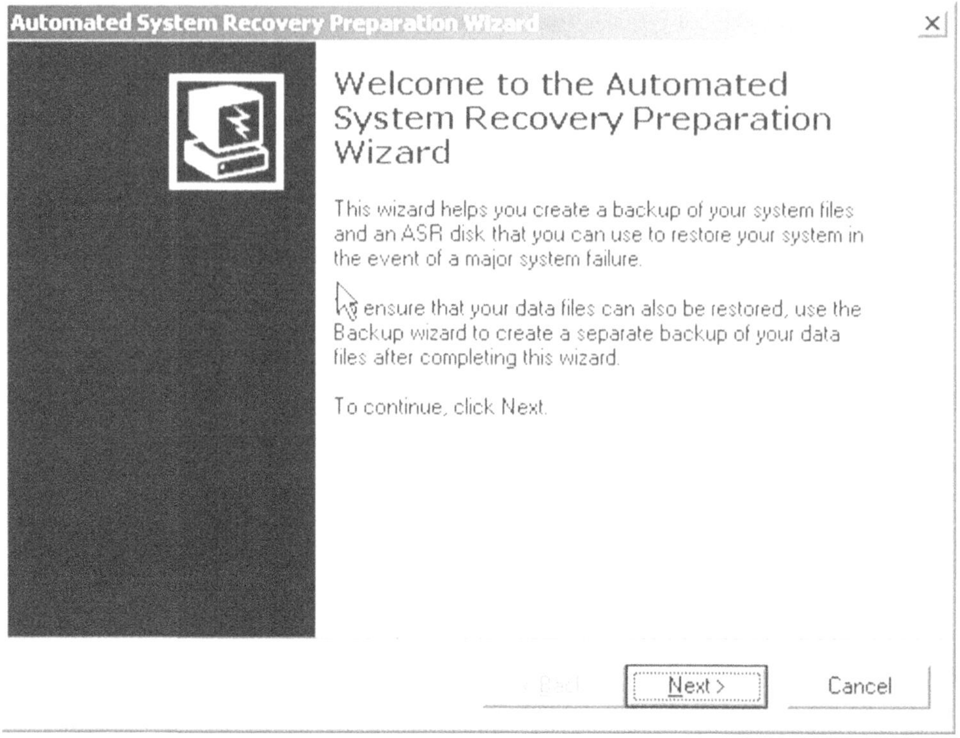

Figure 5-2: Automated System Recovery Wizard.

4. Welcome to the backup destination screen, as shown in Figure 5.3. Select the media type and the destination you desire. Click **Next** again.

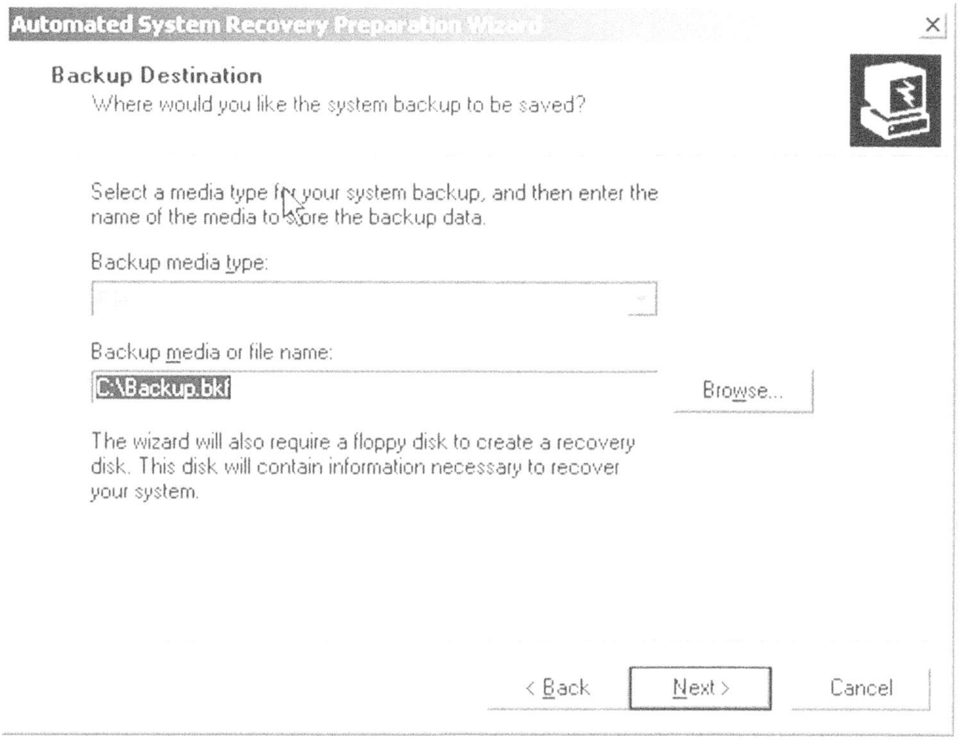

Figure 5-3: Backup Destination.

5. Verify your information and click **Finish** to exit the wizard and start the backup, as shown in Figure 5.4. The backup will begin, and you will see the backup progress box, as in Figure 5.5.

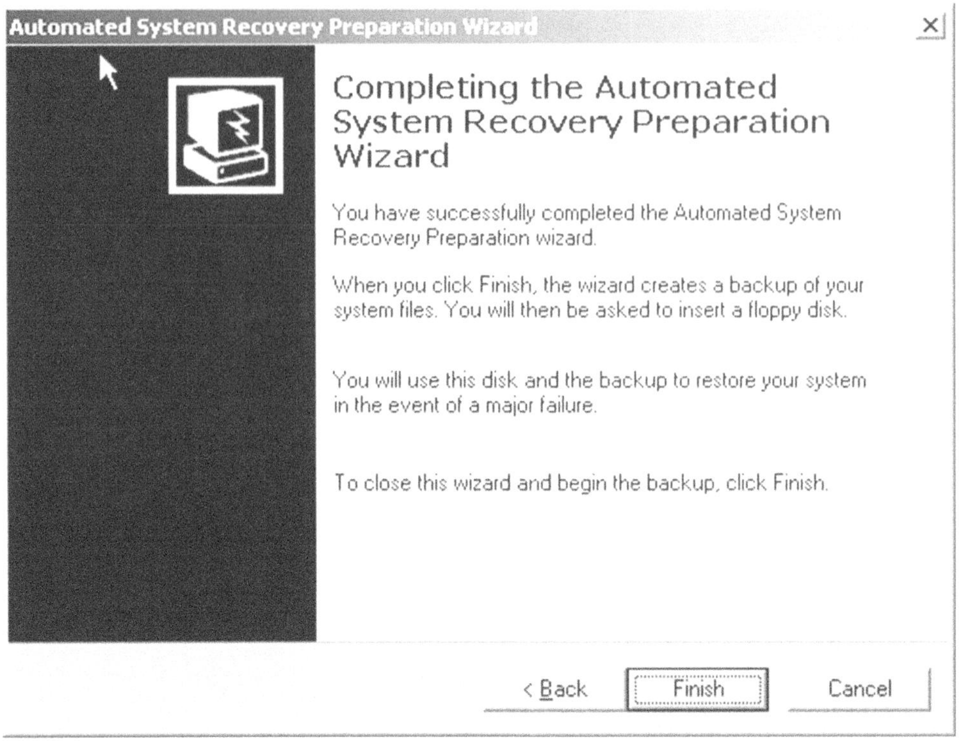

Figure 5-4: Backup Finish.

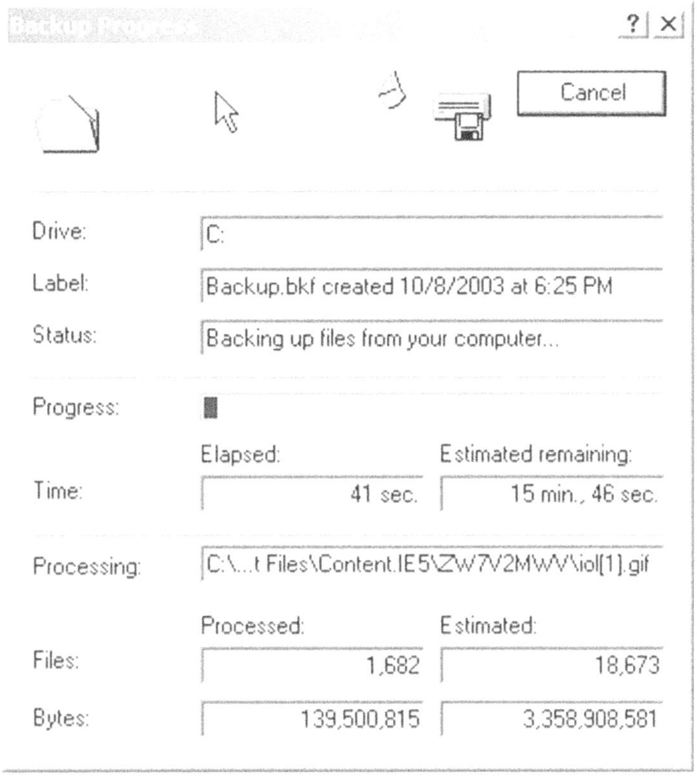

Figure 5-5: Backup Progress Display.

6. When the backup completes you will be queried for the blank floppy mentioned earlier. Insert it and click **OK** (Figure 5.6).

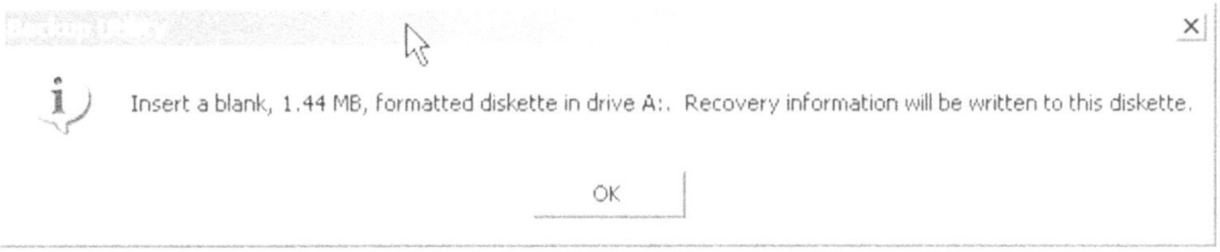

Figure 5-6: Backup Utility Insert.

7. Backup will write several configuration files to the floppy and confirms the process complete (Figure 5.7). Click **OK**, remove the floppy and store the floppy and the media in a safe place. Click **Close** to exit the backup program.

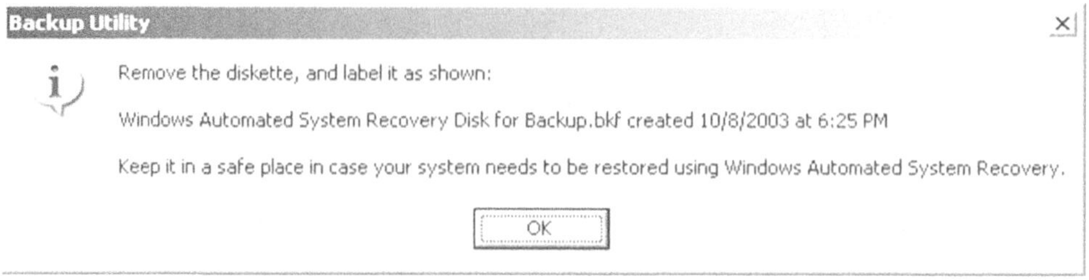

Figure 5-7: Backup Utility Remove.

To use the ASR set in a repair, insure that you have the correct ASR set and the Windows Server 2003 CD. Remember that the ASR set will only repair the operating system files. You must restore any applications or data separately.

To perform the following operation, you must be a member of the local Administrators group, the Backup Operators group or, if the computer is a member of the domain, the Domain Administrators group. You may also have the necessary permissions delegated to you. As a best practice, consider using the **Run As** feature so that you use these elevated permissions only when performing this operation.

Locate the following items:

- ASR floppy disk and backup media.
- Windows Server 2003 Operating System installation CD.
- Any separate driver diskettes you may have for a mass storage controller that does not appear on the operating system CD.

Follow these steps:

1. Place the installation CD in your CD drive and restart your computer. You may be prompted to press a key to start from CD.
2. If you have a separate driver file as mentioned above, press F6 when prompted in setup and insert the diskette as requested.
3. When the text-only portion of setup begins, press F2. You will then be prompted to insert the ASR floppy that matches the media you wish to restore.
4. At this point, follow the instructions on screen. The system will re-boot.
5. If you used a separate driver file as in step 2 above, press F6 again to use the diskette. Place the driver diskette in the floppy drive and follow the instructions on screen as you did in step 2.
6. Restore any necessary program or data backups.

The ASR gives you a very powerful tool to help protect your system data, and is much easier to use than utilities in previous versions of Windows.

5.1.2 Restore data from shadow copy volumes

Shadow Copy is a feature of Windows Server 2003 that allows point-in-time, read-only copies of files that are currently stored on network shares. With Shadow Copy enabled on a volume, you can examine the contents of a network share as it existed at a particular point in time. Client software must be installed, and the share must be accessed across the network. You must enable shadow copy on a volume by volume basis. All network shares on that volume are then "shadowed," not single shares. You can then schedule the frequency of the copy.

Shadow Copy will allow you to:

- Recover files that were deleted
- Recover files that were overwritten
- Allow "basic" version control while working on shared documents depending on the copy or archive schedule on the volume. You could possibly "see" what the document looked like this morning before you started working, if you may the copy at the appropriate time.

Shadow Copy is not enabled by default, due to the storage needed to support the feature. Shadow Copy should not be used as a replacement for regular system backups, as it only copies the network shares on the volumes for which it is enabled.

To configure Shadow Copy, open **Computer Management** in **Administrative Tools**. Then right-click on **Shared Folders**, select **All Tasks**, and click **Configure Shadow Copies** (Figure 5.8).

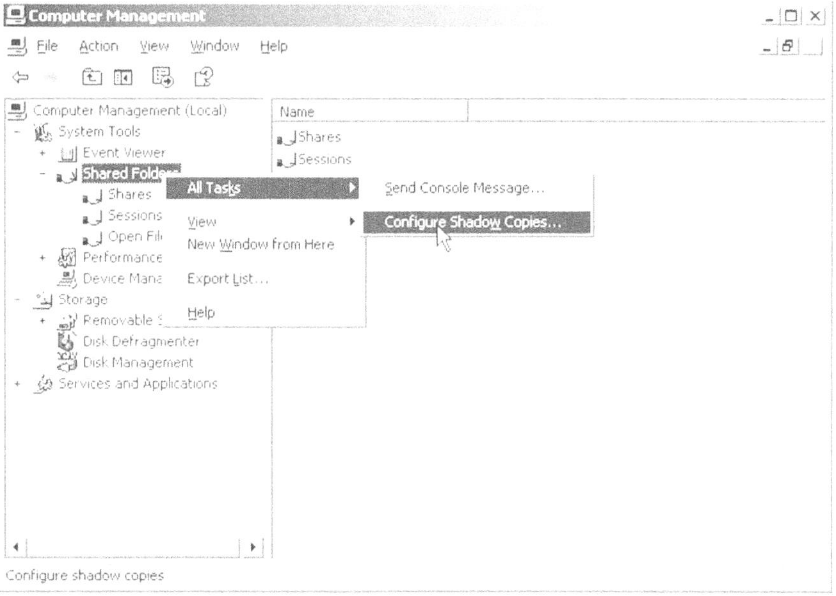

Figure 5-8: Start Shadow Copy.

You are then given the Shadow Copy dialog box, as shown in Figure 5.9. Here you can enable Shadow Copy and configure scheduling on the various volumes in the computer. Note the screen shot in Figure 5.9 shows drive C: enabled, and drives E: and F: disabled. Scheduling can be done by clicking on the settings button, and then selecting schedule. The default schedule is to make a copy at 7:00 a.m. and 12:00 noon, which may or may not be useful in your environment. You should not schedule a copy more than once an hour and you should avoid times of high usage on your server and network.

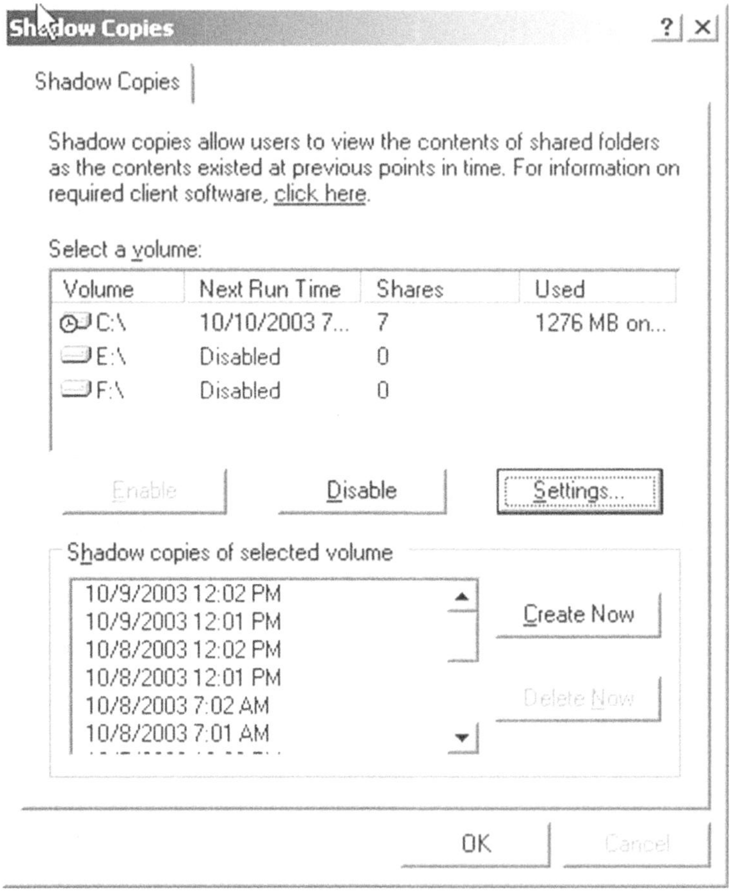

Figure 5-9: Configure Shadow Copy.

For the client to be able to use Shadow Copy, client software must be installed. Various methods can be used to distribute the software to the client desktop, including Group Policy, or accessing a shared folder across the network.

Okay, so you've gotten Shadow Copy configured on all your file servers on your network. You have the client software installed on all the workstations on your network. You want to use it to recover a file Kris just mistakenly deleted from the network share. She is saying something about a marketing project that's just slightly late and needs to be turned in today.

You make a copy every other hour, and Kris is quite happy to get the version that is 90 minutes old. How does the recovery all work? I'm glad you asked! It's pretty straight forward, but must be accomplished from the network client.

On the client machine, open Windows Explorer and move to the shared folder in question. Right-click on the share, and select properties. In the properties dialog box, select the pervious versions tab. You will now see the different versions of the share available to restore. Select a copy to work with (Figure 5.10).

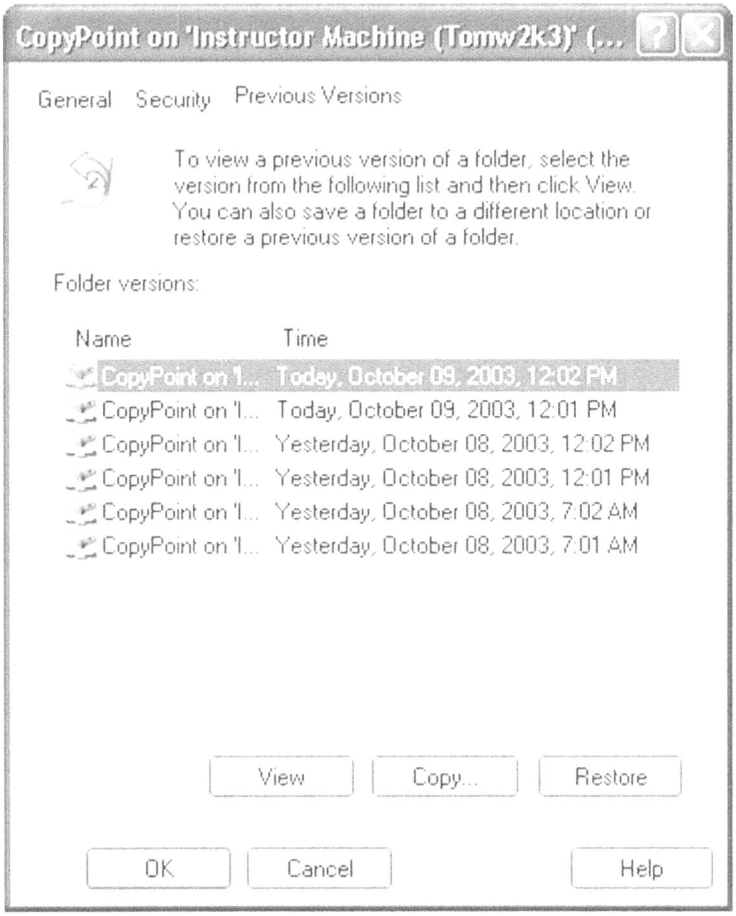

Figure 5-10: Previous Version of Backup.

If at this point you want to restore the entire folder, you can click on the restore button. BE CAREFUL, as this will restore the folder to its previous contents (overwriting the folder as it exists now). This may or may NOT be what you want. If a file exists now in the folder and did not exist in the version you wish to restore, the new file will be deleted. The safer route may be to copy the previous version to another location, and restore the deleted project file to the desired location.

A word about file permissions after these operations is called for. If you copy a file, it assumes the defaults of the target directory where you copy it. If you restore the file to the current location, the permissions are not changed. Restore or copy as necessary. In this case, copying the folder to another location, then moving the file in question back to the share where Kris can work with it would be the proper method of attack.

5.1.3 Back up files and System State data to media

What is backup? Backup is a process of copying files and folders from one location in a single operation. It is done to protect data from loss due to various reasons. If you are careful about performing backups on a regular basis, when a data loss occurs you will be able to recover from it. You should be able to recover from the loss of data amounting to anything from a single file to a complete hard drive or set of hard drives in a system.

Sounds great, doesn't it? I do all these things and magic will occur when I need it to. But now you may ask. "What should I backup? What is a regular basis? What is a regular backup? What is a good schedule?" Scheduling we'll talk about a bit later in this chapter. The others (and a few more) we'll answer here.

The frequency of your backups typically depends on two things:

- How critical is your data to your business?
- How frequently does it change?

The more critical the data, the more frequent your backup should be. The more frequently it changes, the more frequent your backup should be. A good rule of thumb to consider is "How much data loss can I afford to recover from without hurting my normal flow of business. Can I easily recreate the day's transactions and other changes?" Maybe a day is too long and you need to be thinking of a period of hours instead. You have to decide, depending upon the needs of your organization.

Let's discuss System State data for a minute. The System State data is what the computer uses to load, configure and run the operating system on your computer. Depending upon the type of Windows Server 2003 installation is on your server, this may include various things.

The following table outlines the type of data and on what type of server it would appear.

Component	When included in System State
Registry	Always
Boot files, Com+ Class registrations, including the system files	Always
Certificate Services	If server is a Certificate Server
Active Directory directory service	If it is a domain
SYSVOL Directory	If server is a domain controller
Cluster service information	If a member of a cluster
IIS metadirectory	If IIS is installed
System files that are under Windows File Protection	Always

Table 5-1: Backup: Type of Data.

The System State is backed up and restored as a unit. You cannot restore a portion of the System State due to the interdependence of the different sets of data. The data must be consistent across all parts of the System State backup, thus you are required to backup or restore as a unit.

The backup utility can be used to back up your entire server, selected portions of your server or the system state data. You can also use the backup utility to schedule a backup operation for you.

You can make several different types of data backups with the backup utility—five to be exact.

They are:

- Normal (or Full)
- Copy
- Differential
- Incremental
- Daily.

The different types allow you to make a complete backup of your selected data, or just changes in the data since the last time you made a backup. These different types target a specific category of data, such as all the files in a collection of folders, or all files on a selected volume that have changed since the last backup. This piece of magic involves the archive attribute. The archive attribute (or bit) is cleared or turned off every time a full backup or an incremental backup of a file is made. The archive bit is turned on (flipped on or switched on or flipped or toggled are also used to describe the action) every time a file or folder is changed after that backup. Other types of backups leave the archive bit alone. The reason why is described in the table below.

Backup Type	Description	Clears Archive Bit	Best Used For
Full or Normal	Backs up all selected files, regardless of the archive bit setting. Clears the archive bit for future operations. If the file is modified later, the archive bit is then set. This indicates the file has been changed and needs to be backed up again.	Yes	Baseline for future backup jobs. Always use the first time you create a backup set.
Copy	Backs up all selected files without changing the archive bit. This allows you to perform other types of backups on the files again later.	No	Making an additional tape or disk without disturbing the archive bit. Quite useful before a high risk operation (OS patch, driver upgrade, application upgrade, etc.) to allow you to recover the files to the exact state before said high risk operation.
Differential	Backs up all selected files and folders that were modified since the last full or incremental backup the files where the archive bit is turned on. The archive bit isn't modified, so you can perform other types of backups on these files again later. If you were to make another differential backup using the same selection set, you would backup the same file a second time.	No	Using a differential backup with the full backup set lets you restore to a point in time of your last differential set by just restoring two sets, the full backup set, and then the last differential set. While your backup time increases, the restore time is shorter than restoring several incremental backup sets.

Backup Type	Description	Clears Archive Bit	Best Used For
Incremental	This type of backup will back up all the selected files that have changed since the last incremental or full backup. It will the clear the archive bit on the files that were backed up. If you were to perform two incremental backups in a row, the files would not be backed up the second time, unless they were changed since the last incremental backup. This will take les media per backup set, as you are not copying all the files changed since the last full backup.	Yes	Networks that require a faster backup time due to a small maintenance window for the network. This method will take longer to restore that a full backup set and differentials, as to be sure you have the latest version of each file, you must restore all the incremental backup sets.
Daily	This type backs up only the files changed on that date, and ignores the setting of the archive bit. If a file was changed on the same day as the backup, it is backed up, even if it was just backed up by another type of backup. It ignores the archive bit setting.	No	If a copy of the files modified today are required for any reason in conjunction with another backup type.

Table 5-2: Backup Types.

You can select the type of media you desire to make your backup to. The various storage devices and media that are supported include tape drives, removable disks, recordable CD-ROM drives and logical drives on your local system.

You can combine different types of backups to allow for shorter backup times or shorter recovery times. The best scenario would be to make a complete backup of the system each day. Then to restore your system, you just need to restore that day's backup. You can also combine a normal or full backup with a differential or incremental backup. You should base your decision for a proper mix of types on the amount of time you can spend creating the backup, and the amount of time your can use to restore. Some sample scenarios follow.

Scenario One: Normal backup weekly combined with incremental backups every day.

On Sunday evening you perform a normal (full) backup. The archive bit on ALL files is reset. Each evening on Monday through Saturday you perform an incremental backup. Each backup saves the files changed that day, and also resets the archive bit on those files that were backed up. The evening backup on Monday through Saturday is done rather quickly (compared to the full backup on Sunday) as just the files changed that day are backed up.

If something were to happen to your server hardware on Saturday, to recover your files to the state of the last known good backup (made on Friday), you would have to first restore the full backup from the previous Sunday, and then each incremental backup made on Monday through Friday evening. This would insure your would get all the files that were changed during the week, as the files that were changed were only backed up on the day that they were changed.

Scenario Two: Normal backup weekly combined with differential backups every day

On Sunday evening you perform a normal (full) backup. The archive bit on ALL files is reset. Each evening on Monday through Saturday you perform a differential backup. Each backup saves the files changed since the full backup made on Sunday. The archive bit on these files is not changed. This way, on Monday you backup the files changed on Monday. On Tuesday, you backup the files changed on Monday and Tuesday, and so on through the week. The evening backup takes somewhat longer each evening, as you are backing up all files changed through the entire week.

Again, something happens to the server on Saturday, and you need to restore to the state the files were in on Friday evening when the backup was made. Here you need to restore the full backup made on Sunday, and the last differential backup made on Friday. Why just the two? Unlike the incremental backups made in scenario one, the last differential backup on Friday has all the files that were changed that week on one media set. Recovery time is reduced as compared to scenario one.

To backup using the Backup utility, follow these steps:

Start the Windows Server 2003 Backup program. Click on **Start | Programs | Accessories | System Tools**. Select **Backup**. If the wizard wants to help you, just switch to advanced mode. Your screen should look like Figure 5.11.

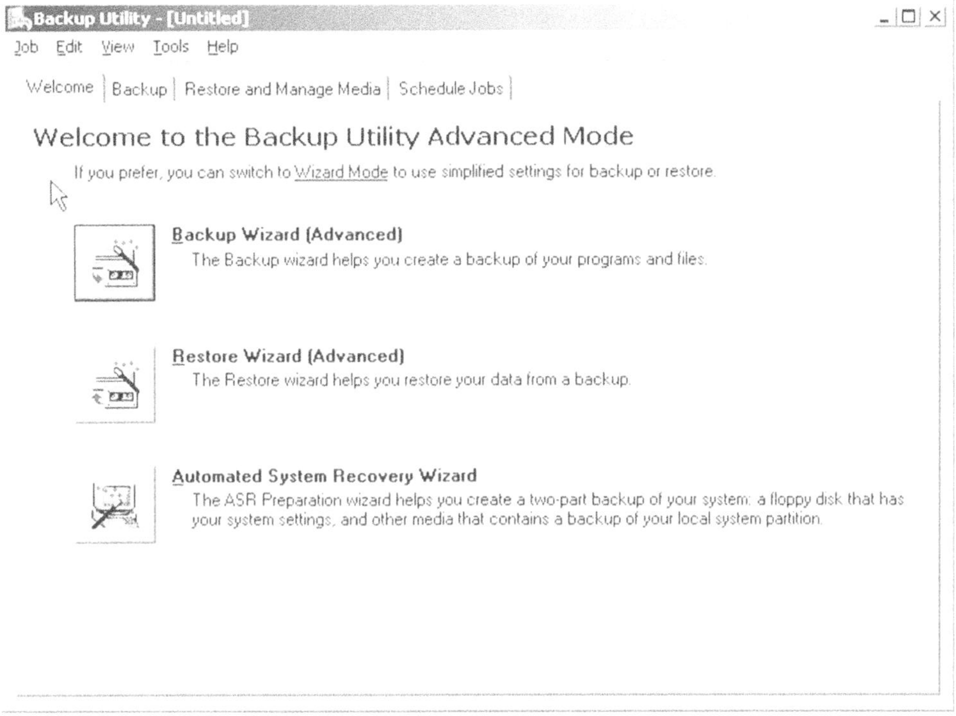

Figure 5-11: Backup Utility Advanced Mode.

Click on the **Backup Wizard** button. Again, if the wizard wants to help, click **Cancel**. You should get the selection box that appears in Figure 5.12.

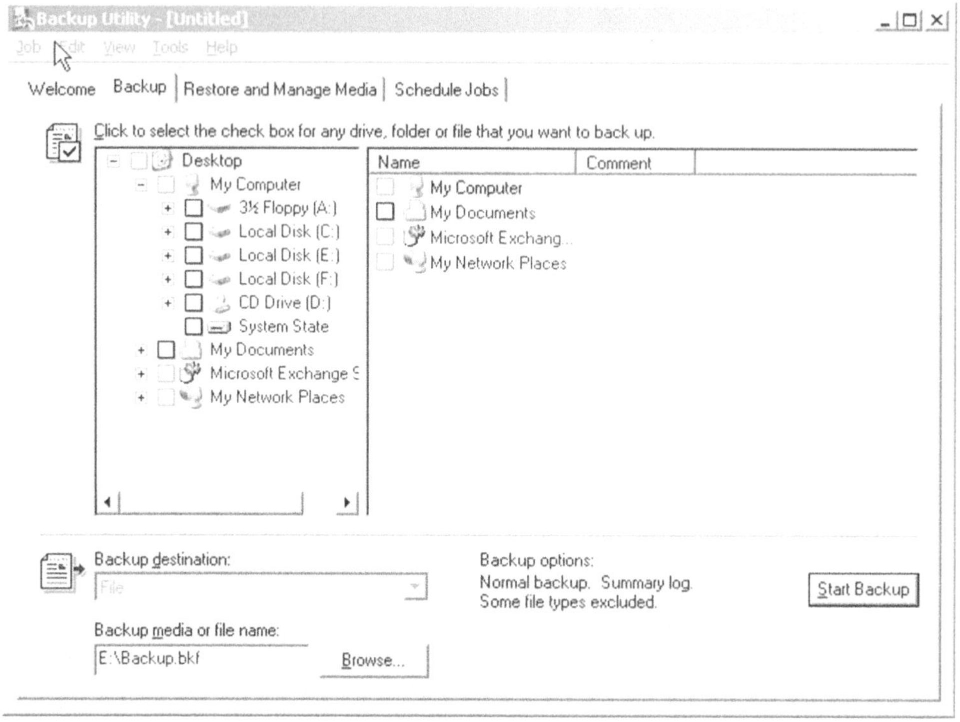

Figure 5-12: Configure Backup Utility Advance Mode.

At this point, I am going to backup the My Documents folder, so I'll select that. Your screen should appear something like the one in figure 5.13. Notice the blue check mark in the My Documents box. That means that particular folder and all of its contents will be backed up. Notice also that drive C: has a gray check mark by it. This means that some subfolder has been selected on that drive. You can click on the + boxes beside the drive to drill down to the selection. Notice also I have selected to backup this selection to a file (**`e:\backup.bkf`**) listed under the backup media or filename selection.

At this point, you can click the Start Backup button, and selections will be backed up.

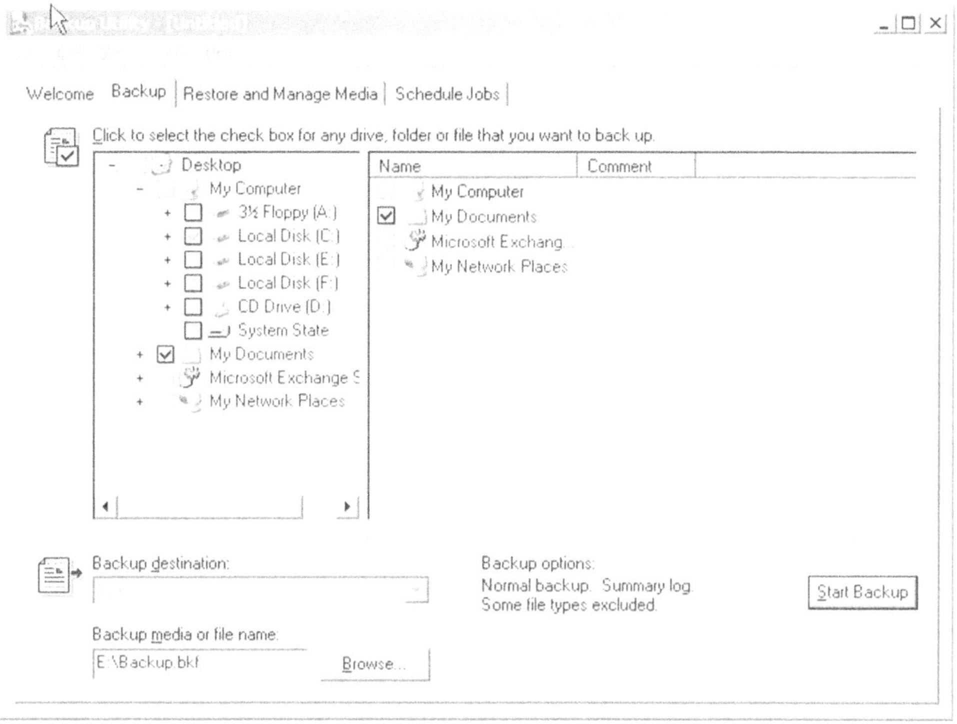

Figure 5-13: Backup Utility Media.

5.1.4 Configure security for backup operations

Who can backup data? You must have certain permissions or be granted certain user rights to be able to back up files and folders on a Windows Server 2003 machine. Typically you must be a member of the Administrators Group, the Backup Operators Group or the Server Operators Group to be able to back up and restore all files and folders on a particular machine. Any user can backup their own files and folders, and any files and folders that they have read permission for.

Administrators, Backup Operators and Server Operators can back up any file and folder because they have the **Backup Files and Directories** and **Restore Files and Directories** user rights granted to them by default. They also have **Modify** and **Full Control** permissions granted by default. Granting these rights and permissions to a regular user will allow them to backup and restore files and folders not belonging to them.

Some organizations create separate backup and restore groups to divide these tasks for security reasons. To do this, complete the following steps:

- Create a Backup Group in Active Directory Users and Computers.
- Create a Restore Group in Active Directory Users and Computers.
- Add the necessary members to each group.
- Add the Backup Group to the Backup files and directories Group Policy Object.
- Add the Restore Group to the Restore files and directories Group Policy Object.

The above Group Policy Objects can be found in the following group policy—**Computer Configuration | Windows Settings | Security Settings | Local Policies | User Rights Assignments**.

If you have a disk quota on your target drive, you may not be able to back up files and folders, if the quota keeps you from writing to the hard drive in question.

Pop Quiz 5.1

Pop Quiz 5.1 *Questions*

1. From what situations can the boot disk help you recover?
2. To create an ASR diskette and run ASR, of what group or groups should you be a member?
3. What is Shadow Copy?
4. What are the five different types of data backups that can be created with the backup utility?
5. Which form of backup will be faster during the backup (not restore) process, incremental or differential?

Pop Quiz 5.1 *Answers*

1. A boot disk can help you recover from a damaged boot sector, a damaged or infected master boot record, missing or damaged ntldr or ntdetect.com files or a damaged mirror set.
2. To create an ASR diskette and run ASR, you must be a member of the local Administrators group, the Backup Operators group or, if the computer is a member of the domain, the Domain Administrators group.
3. Shadow Copy is a feature of Windows Server 2003 that allows point-in-time, read-only copies of files that are currently stored on network shares.
4. The five different types of data backups are Normal (Full), Copy, Differential, Incremental and Daily.
5. Incremental will be the faster process during backup, as it clears the archive bit. Subsequently, only the files that have changed since the last full or incremental backup will be processed.

5.2 Manage backup procedures

Did it work? Did it really work?

5.2.1 Verify the successful completion of backup jobs

Aside from restoring your data to another server, or another location,—the best tests to see if you can really read the files you just backed up—one of the options you can select during the backup is **Verify Data After Backup Completes**. Options for backup are selected by selecting the **Tools** menu, then selecting **Options**, and then the **General Tab** from the main backup screen as shown in Figure 5.14. Note that the option is NOT selected by default, as it adds to the backup time. Select the desired checkbox, the click **Apply** and **OK** to exit the options dialog.

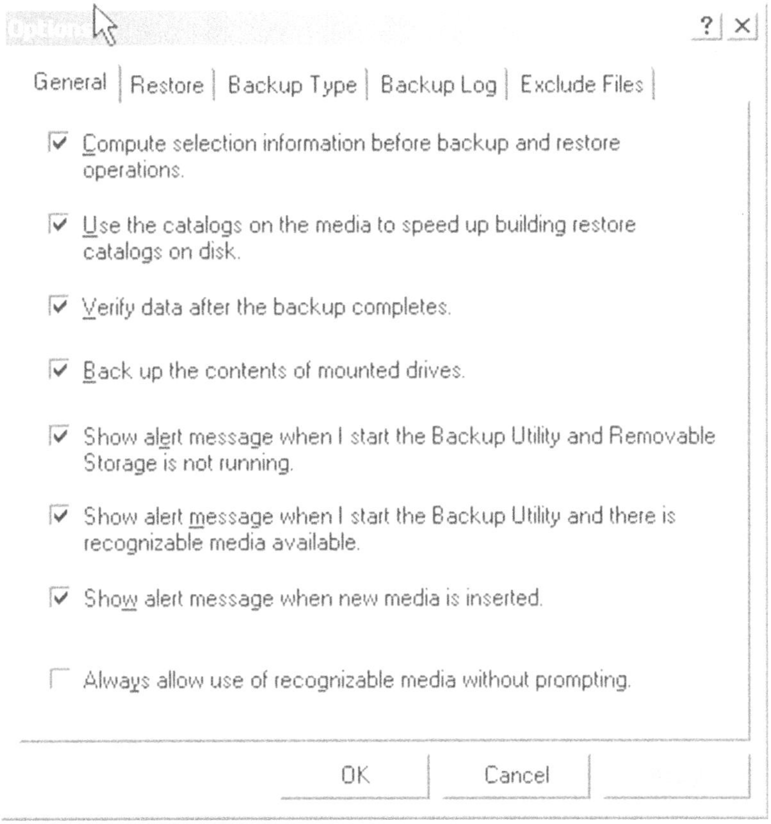

Figure 5-14: Backup Options Dialog.

What this option does is allows the Backup utility to compare the backed-up data and the original data on your hard disk to be sure that the two are the same. You should only verify backups of data files. Verifying system backups is a very difficult process because of the large number of changes that happen to system files on a continual basis. Be aware that some data files that were in use during your backup might also cause you to receive verification errors. You can usually disregard these errors. If you receive a large number of verification errors, there may be a problem with the media or the file you are using to back up data. If this happens, try using different media or designate another file and run your backup again.

Consulting log files created during backup is also an excellent way of checking the status of completion, and the success of your efforts. Also under **Tools**, **Options**, you then need to select the **Backup Log** tab, as shown in Figure 5.15. The default is summary, which will give you enough detail to see starts and stops, tape swaps and problem files. Detailed troubleshooting will require a detailed log. You can also keep a detailed log of each backup operation to exactly identify a particular file that you backed up and that you may wish to restore.

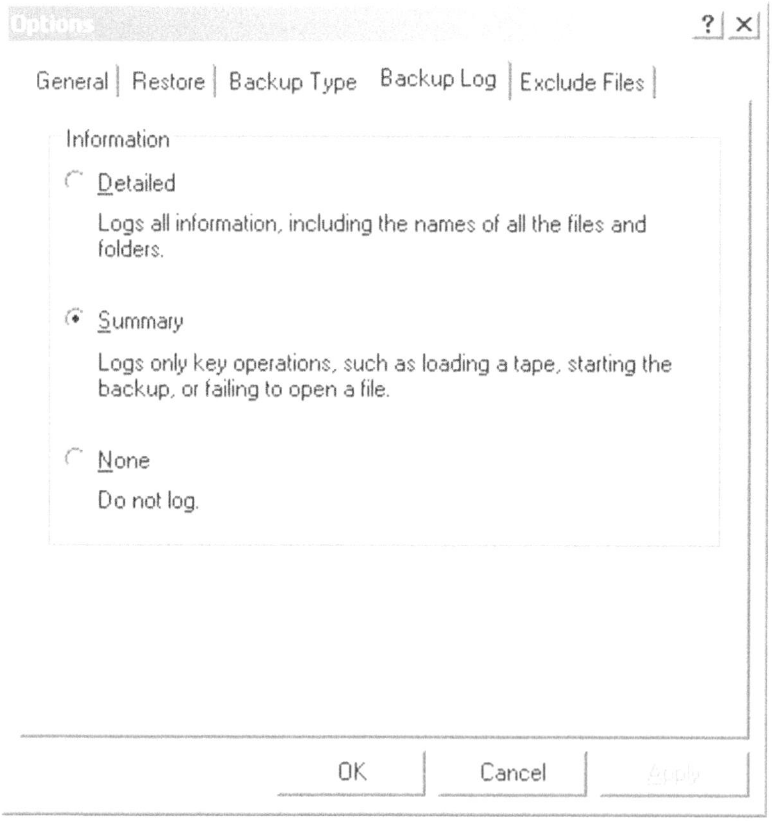

Figure 5-15: Backup Logs.

5.2.2 Manage backup storage media

Media catalogs allow you to easily manage the files and folders collected in your backups. If you are using removable media, the catalog can be created on-disk as well to speed the restore process. Samples of expanded on-disk catalogs are shown in Figure 5.16. Files can be selected to restore from these, and the proper media inserted into a tape drive. The catalog allows you to easily see the files and folders in a backup set. The catalog here shows the files and folders in a system state backup recently completely.

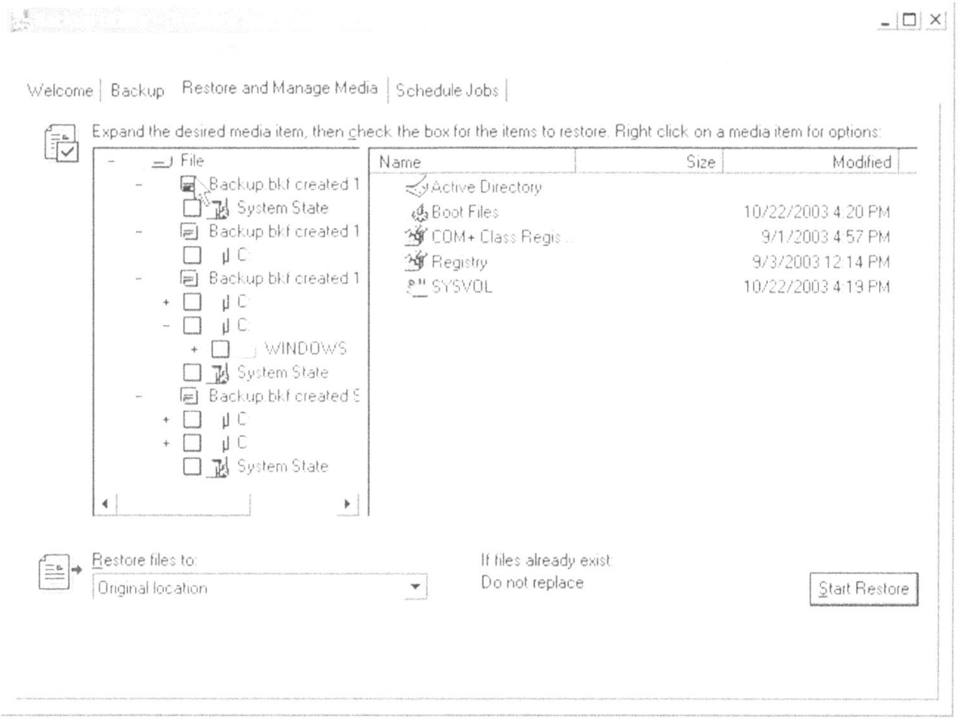

Figure 5-16: Backup Restore and Manage Mode.

The backup utility can also be used to perform some simple tape management. The options you will have available include format a tape, and pretension of a tape. These options appear if you have a tape drive installed in your computer.

5.3 Recover from server hardware failure

Lots and lots of red lights are blinking on the front of your server. Red lights on this server are never a "good thing." Careful examination reveals several lights you never even knew existed. Until now. Welcome to server hardware failure!

Fortunately, Windows Server 2003 provides some tools to help you recover from hardware failures. You need to be able to correctly identify the problem and choose the proper tool or tools to respond with. Two of those were mentioned at the beginning of this chapter, the **Windows Startup Disk** and the **Recovery Console**. Others include a good backup, a good System State Backup and a good ASR backup set. Still others are starting the system in **Safe Mode**, and using the **Last Known Good Configuration**.

If your system fails to start, you may be able to start it in safe mode. When starting in safe mode, Windows uses default settings and minimum device drivers, no network connection, the mouse driver and the video in video graphics adapter (VGA) mode. The idea is to remove all the "frills and extras" and let the system come up with very basic settings allowing you to troubleshoot. Some things you can do are change server settings, diagnose problems, remove newly installed software or hardware, install a service pack or other software patch or possibly reinstall the operating system. If the machine starts, you know the problem is something beyond the basic settings. If you have just added or changed something in the system, safe mode can be used to allow you to remove it or reverse the change you made.

Safe mode is entered by pressing F8 to display the advanced startup options during system boot. You have three options for safe mode. They are described in the following table. All three create a log file.

Option	Description	Example Use
Safe Mode	Loads only basic devices, drivers and services required to start and operate the system.	You suspect a recently installed application or driver is causing a problem.
Safe Mode with Networking	Same as Safe Mode, but also adds networking support	You need to verify networking is working properly, and/or you need access to the network to obtain files.
Safe Mode with Command Prompt	Same as safe mode, but with a command prompt instead of a graphical user interface.	You must use command-line troubleshooting tools. This mode will sometimes allow access when others fail.

Table 5-3: Backup Safe Mode Options.

The startup option **Last Known Good Configuration** allows you to use the registry and device configuration of the last successful system login which Windows saves at every successful login. This option gives you the ability to quickly recover from an incorrect driver or setting. The **Last Known Good Configuration** is updated each time Windows is started in normal mode and a user logs in and is authenticated. If you shut the system down without logging in, you do not overwrite the **Last Known Good Configuration**.

Last Known Good Configuration can be used to resolve startup problems. If you get a stop message or a message that one or more services failed to start immediately after a change, you can restart the computer without logging in, then select **Last Known Good Configuration**. You can then reverse the change just made, and try to correct it.

Note: It was mentioned earlier that **the Last Known Good Configuration** is only overwritten when starting in normal mode and logging in. If you were to start your system in **Safe Mode** and log in, but were unable to correct the problem, you could reboot and use the **Last Known Good Configuration**. **Safe Mode** does NOT overwrite the saved settings.

The Recovery Console is a tool that provides you with a command-line console on a system that is having a software problem that prevents the system from starting. It also allows you access the drives on your system. It loads a minimal version of Windows Server 2003. This allows you to possibly repair a system component that is keeping the system from starting without a complete reinstallation of the operating system.

When the system is started with the Recovery Console, you can enable or disable device drivers or services, read and write files to a local hard drive, format a hard drive, repair a boot sector or create a new boot sector or master boot record. The Recovery Console will allow you to work with a drive even if it is formatted with NTFS, and recognizes and enforces the NFTS file and folder permissions.

When using the Recovery Console, you must log in with the local administrator account and password. If it is installed, Recovery Console is one of the advanced startup options on a system. If it is not installed, or the system cannot access the partition the Recovery Console is installed on, you can run it from the operating system CD. Start the system from CD, then when prompted to repair or install, select repair.

Here are some general guidelines for using the various disaster recovery tools provided by Windows Server 2003.

Tool	Suggested Use
Safe Mode	Use when a problem causes your server not to start normally. Using the minimal services it operates with, you can determine if a recent change or other configuration issue has caused your problem, and correct it.
Last Know Good Configuration	Use for cases of incorrect configuration. You can reverse your most recent driver or other system changes since your last successful login, then boot normally and correct the issue.
Backup/Restore	Always have a good set of backups that protects your data and system settings. Restore (or restoring a shadow copy) will allow you to replace a missing or damaged file, or roll back to an earlier version of the file. Also, before some major system change or high risk operation, it is a good practice to make a system state backup (if the system files will be effected) or a copy backup (if data is effected) to allow you to recover (if necessary) to the point before the operation occurs. If the operation goes bad, you can use that backup to restore the state before you started. (Usually the time you really, really, really need such a backup is the time you didn't make one. Murphy's Law, and all that.)
Recovery Console	Use if you can't fix your problem with one of the startup options. You can replace files, etc. or attempt other manual recovery steps.
Automated System Recovery (ASR)	Use this tool instead of reinstalling Windows from scratch. It allows you to recover all the system settings, etc. that existed at the time the ASR set was made. Use this method as a last resort, as it does format disks. Keep in mind that you will also need a good data backup as the ASR only protects system files and settings.

Table 5-4: Backup Tools.

Pop Quiz 5.2

Pop Quiz 5.2 *Questions*

1. What does the option "Verify Data After Backup Completes" actually do?
2. Outside of Windows Startup Disk and Recovery Console, what are some of the other tools and recommendations provided by Windows 2003 to help you recover from hardware failures?
3. What is "Safe Mode"?
4. What is the Last Known Good Configuration?
5. If you start your system in Safe Mode and log in, which configuration will appear if you need to use "Last Known Good"?

Pop Quiz 5.2 *Answers*

1. What this option does is allows the Backup utility to compare the backed-up data and the original data on your hard disk to be sure that the two are the same.
2. Other tools and recommendations include a good backup, a good System State Backup and a good ASR backup set, as well as starting the system in Safe Mode, and using the Last Known Good Configuration.
3. When starting in Safe Mode, Windows uses default settings and minimum device drivers, no network connection, the mouse driver and the video in video graphics adapter (VGA) mode.
4. The Last Known Good Configuration is the registry settings and device configuration of the last successful system login.
5. The Last Known Good Configuration that exists, after you log in while in Safe Mode, remains the configuration that was created at your last successful login while in "Normal" mode.

5.4 Restore backup data

In Windows Server 2003, there are two major types of restores, using the Backup Utility and the ASR Restore. The ASR restore was covered in an earlier section.

Using the restore feature of the Backup Utility, you can restore files and folders to their original positions or to any disk you can access, restore files to FAT or NTFS formatted volumes or restore System State data.

Care must be taken to restore files and folders from NTFS volumes back to another NTFS volume. This will allow you to retain several file and folder features, like NTFS permissions, Encrypting File System (EFS) settings, disk quota information and other settings. You may also lose data. It has been the authors' experience that losing data is NOT usually the desired outcome when performing a restore operation.

To restore files and folders using the backup utility, start Backup and select the Restore and Manage Media tab. Your screen should look something like Figure 5.16 seen previously.

In the left pane, select the desired media item, and then select the files and folders you desire to restore.

You then need to designate the location for your restore. In the restore files to box, select one of the following:

- **Original location** – this replaces the files and folders back to their original locations.
- **Alternate location** – this allows you to type in or browse to a new location for the files. This option lets you relocate the files, but keeps the original folder structure. All the files and folders will appear in the new location.
- **Single folder** – this will place all the files into a single folder in the location you designate, but loses the original folder structure.

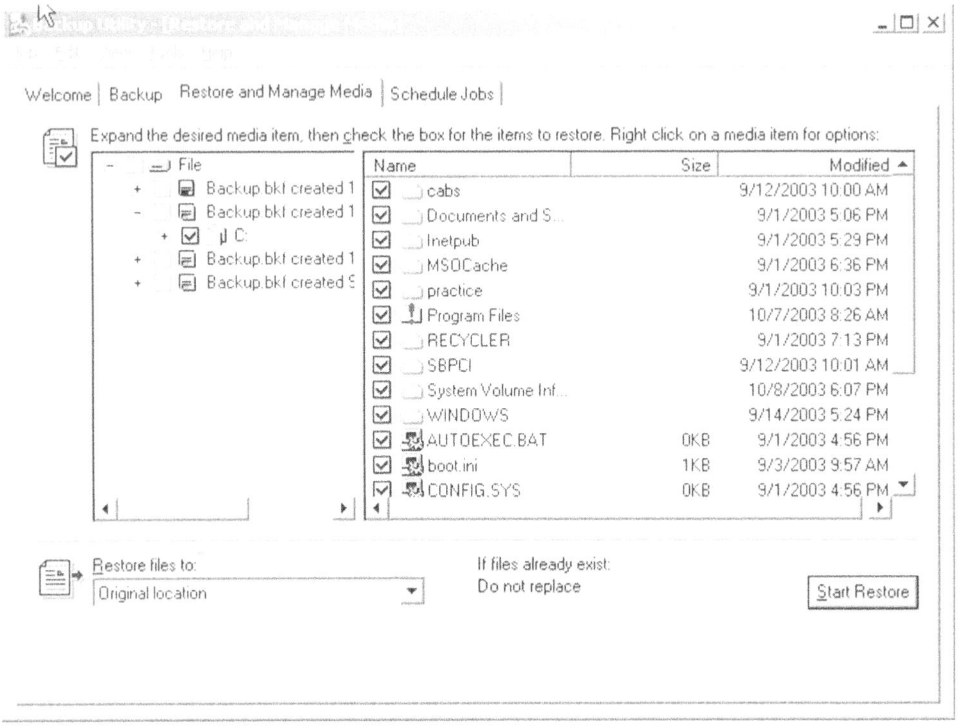

Figure 5-17: Backup Location Selection.

Figure 5.17 shows files from Drive C: being restored in their original location. Before you click on the **Start Restore** button, select the **Tools** menu, then click **Options**, and select the **Restore** tab. This will select the restore options for this operation. Select one of the following (Figure 5.18):

- Do not replace the file on my computer.
- Replace the file on disk only if the file on disk is older.
- Always replace the file on my computer.

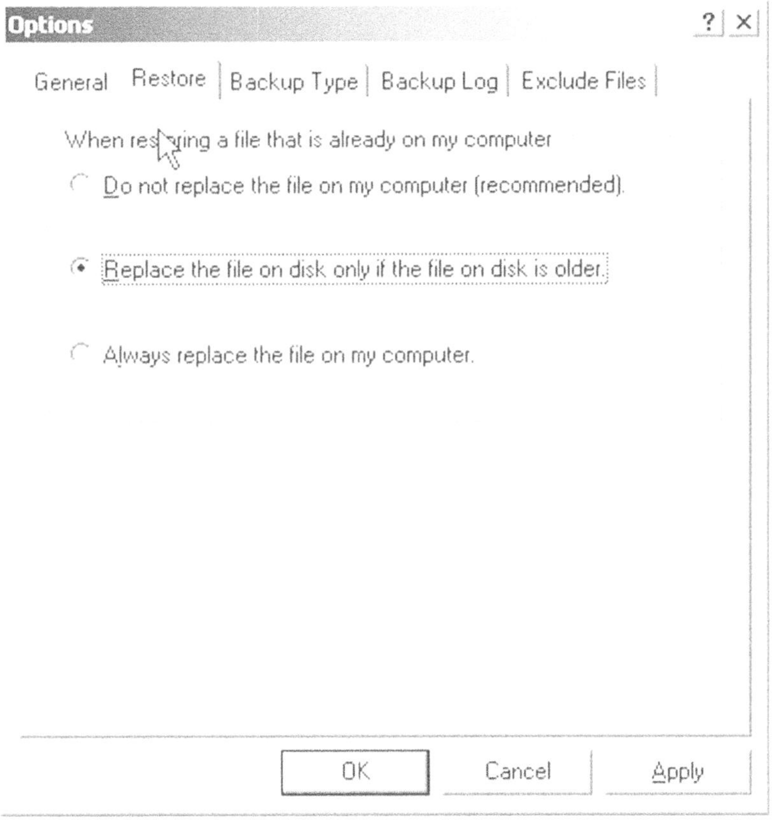

Figure 5-18: Backup Replace Files Option.

Click on **OK** to accept your restore options, then click on the **Start Restore** button to restore your files.

System State Data is restored the same way. Select a media set and expand it to reveal the System State Data selection. Select it, and click **Start Restore**. The restore will begin, replacing the System State files where they need to be placed.

Note: You MUST restore the complete System State, not just a part of it.

5.5 Schedule backup jobs

Why schedule backup jobs? Why not let the system worry about making the backup on the schedule you set up, instead of you trying to remember to backup the system as necessary. You can easily automate your backup plan to insure you have the backup sets you need to recover from various problems that may occur.

You can schedule a backup one of two ways:

- When creating a new backup job, or
- Selecting an existing job from the Scheduled Jobs tab in backup.

The Scheduled Backup options are the same as any other scheduled job in Windows Server 2003. They are shown in Table 5.5.

Schedule Option	Executes the operation
Once	Once at a specific time on a specific date
Daily	At the specified time each day
Weekly	At the specified time on each of the specified days of the week
Monthly	At the specified time once a month
At system startup	The next time the system is started
At logon	The next time the job owner logs on
When idle	When the system has been idle for a specified number of minutes

Table 5-5: Backup Schedule Options.

You will also be asked for user credentials to run the job. Be sure to provide a login and password of a user that has the necessary user rights and permissions, either directly assigned or through group membership.

Chapter 5: Summary

Congratulations! Even though you know that disaster will happen no matter how well you plan, you are now well prepared to recover from those disasters using tools such as a boot disk, a reliable backup, Safe Mode, ASR, Shadow Copy and Last Known Good.

While these skills won't elminate that horrible, sick feeling that comes over you when you discover a hard drive failure (or worse), having learned these tools will help you quickly get past the problem and get your network back onto prime performance with a minimum of time, trouble and data loss.

Chapter 5: Review Questions

1. What is true of using a backup method that uses a weekly normal and daily incrementals?

A. It requires less time for restoration

B. It requires more time for restoration

C. It increases the daily backup time

D. It minimizes the daily backup time

---

2. How can you install Recovery Console on a hard drive with Windows 2003?

A. Use the winnt32.exe command with the /cmdcons switch

B. Use the winnt32.exe command by itself

C. Use the winnt.exe command with the /cmdcons switch

D. Use the winnt32.exe command by itself

3. What is an incremental backup?

A. It is generally done just once a month.

B. It is a backup in which only files that have increased in size are backed up.

C. It is a normal backup.

D. It is not used as a daily backup method.

---

4. When using a normal and differential backup method, how many tapes will be required to restore the server?

A. 1 tapes

B. 2 tapes

C. 3 tapes

D. 4 tapes

E. 8 tapes

5. After noting the properties of the installed device driver, which of the following steps should you take when updating device drivers on a Windows Server 2003?

A. Note the properties of the updated driver, and install the new driver.

B. Test the new driver on a non-critical machine, note the properties of the updated driver, and install the new driver.

C. Simply install the new driver.

D. Install the new driver and rollback if necessary.

---

6. If a user tells you that they aren't able to log on their computer after installing a hardware device and it gave them the STOP message, what course of action would require the least effort?

A. Restarting by using safe mode

B. Performing a brand-new install of the operating system

C. Restarting with the last known good configuration

D. Restarting with the Windows 2003 CD-ROM and using Recovery Console

7. Which of the following scenarios is correct for using Last Known Good with System Restore if your 2003 server won't boot?

A. Just use Last Known Good; it won't work with System Restore.

B. Just use System Restore; it won't work with Last Known Good.

C. First, use the Last Known Good method to get the computer to boot and then use System Restore to get the previous state that you want.

D. Use System Restore and then use Last Known Good to get the state you want.

---

8. Which of the following statements are true regarding how System Restore works with drivers?

A. If unsigned drivers cause problems, you can revert to the restore point before the bad driver was installed.

B. If signed drivers cause problems, you can revert to the restore point before the bad driver was installed.

C. If signed drivers cause problems, there isn't a restore point created specifically before the bad signed driver was installed.

D. If unsigned drivers cause problems, there isn't a restore point created specifically before the bad signed driver was installed.

9. You attempt to restore a RAID 5 array on your 2003 Server box. However, when you attempt to run ASR, you get the following error message: Logical Disk Manager ASR Utility Error. The Logical Disk Manager encountered the following error while restoring the dynamic disk configuration on this system: Failed to commit the disk group creation transaction. Additional information: -25- . What is the cause of this error message?

A. ASR cannot be used with RAID arrays

B. One of the disks in the array is missing or corrupted

C. ASR cannot be used with RAID-5 arrays

D. The disk needs to be defragmented first before using ASR

---

10. What is the correct path to set up a restore point in Windows Server 2003?

A. Start | Programs | System Tools | Accessories | System Restore

B. Start | Programs | Accessories | Communication Tools | System Restore

C. Start | Programs | Accessories | System Tools | Disk Cleanup

D. Start | Programs | Accessories | Tools | System Restore

E. Start | Programs | Accessories | System Tools | System Restore

11. Which of the following executables starts the Volume Shadow Copy service?

A. Vscadmin.exe

B. Vssadmin.exe

C. Sssadmin.exe

D. Vsscopy.exe

---

12. How can you access shadow copies in 2003 Server?

A. In Device Manager, right-click Shares, point to All Tasks, and then click Configure Shadow Copies.

B. With the Copies tab of the Local Disk Properties dialog box.

C. In Computer Management, right-click Shares, point to All Tasks, and then click Configure Shadow Copies.

D. With the Shadow Copies tab of the Local Disk Properties dialog box.

13. When used with the NTBACKUP command, the /l switch can indicate what log file types?

A. e=edit

B. f=full

C. n=none

D. p=partial

E. s=summary

---

14. Which of the following NTBACKUP switches restricts access to a tape for the owner or members of the Administrators group?

A. The /I switch

B. The /v switch

C. The /r switch

D. The /m switch

E. The /e switch

15. Which of the following NTBACKUP switches verifies the data after the backup is complete?

A. The /a switch

B. The /r switch

C. The /v switch

D. The /m switch

E. The /t switch

---

16. When used with the NTBACKUP command, what does the /um switch do?

A. Locates the first available tape drive

B. Locates the first available hard drive

C. Formats the first available media

D. Uses the first available media for the current backup operation

E. Locates the first available media

Chapter 5: Review Answers

1. What is true of using a backup method that uses a weekly normal and daily incrementals?

A. It requires less time for restoration

***B. It requires more time for restoration**

C. It increases the daily backup time

***D. It minimizes the daily backup time**

Explanation: The backup method that uses a weekly normal and daily incrementals minimizes the daily backup time and it requires more time for restoration.

---

2. How can you install Recovery Console on a hard drive with Windows 2003?

***A. Use the winnt32.exe command with the /cmdcons switch**

B. Use the winnt32.exe command by itself

C. Use the winnt.exe command with the /cmdcons switch

D. Use the winnt32.exe command by itself

Explanation: Use the winnt32.exe command with the /cmdcons switch if you want to install Recovery Console on a hard drive with Windows 2003.

3. What is an incremental backup?
   A. It is generally done just once a month.
***B. It is a backup in which only files that have increased in size are backed up.**
   C. It is a normal backup.
   D. It is not used as a daily backup method.

Explanation: The incremental backup method is a backup where only files that have increased in size are backed up. It is generally done daily and to restore fully you would need all incremental since the last normal backup and the normal backup itself.

---

4. When using a normal and differential backup method, how many tapes will be required to restore the server?
***A. 1 tapes**
   B. 2 tapes
   C. 3 tapes
   D. 4 tapes
   E. 8 tapes

Explanation: When using a normal and differential backup method, two tapes will be required to restore the server. The normal backup tape catches everything, and the differential tape catches the difference since the last full backup tape.

5. After noting the properties of the installed device driver, which of the following steps should you take when updating device drivers on a Windows Server 2003?

A. Note the properties of the updated driver, and install the new driver.

***B. Test the new driver on a non-critical machine, note the properties of the updated driver, and install the new driver.**

C. Simply install the new driver.

D. Install the new driver and rollback if necessary.

Explanation: After noting the properties of the installed device driver, test the new driver on a non-critical machine, note the properties of the updated driver, and install the new driver.

---

6. If a user tells you that they aren't able to log on their computer after installing a hardware device and it gave them the STOP message, what course of action would require the least effort?

A. Restarting by using safe mode

B. Performing a brand-new install of the operating system

***C. Restarting with the last known good configuration**

D. Restarting with the Windows 2003 CD-ROM and using Recovery Console

Explanation: The option that requires the least effort in this scenario is the last known good configuration. Safe mode would be next in line as far as effort is concerned. Recovery Console and performing a brand-new install would require a great deal of effort.

7. Which of the following scenarios is correct for using Last Known Good with System Restore if your 2003 server won't boot?

A. Just use Last Known Good; it won't work with System Restore.

B. Just use System Restore; it won't work with Last Known Good.

***C. First, use the Last Known Good method to get the computer to boot and then use System Restore to get the previous state that you want.**

D. Use System Restore and then use Last Known Good to get the state you want.

Explanation: Last Known Good should be used when there is a non-bootable state. Once booted into either SafeMode or Normal Mode, System Restore can be used to capture optimal previous state. System Restore cannot be accessed unless the system is bootable into one of these modes.

---

8. Which of the following statements are true regarding how System Restore works with drivers?

***A. If unsigned drivers cause problems, you can revert to the restore point before the bad driver was installed.**

B. If signed drivers cause problems, you can revert to the restore point before the bad driver was installed.

***C. If signed drivers cause problems, there isn't a restore point created specifically before the bad signed driver was installed.**

D. If unsigned drivers cause problems, there isn't a restore point created specifically before the bad signed driver was installed.

Explanation: Using System Restore, if an unsigned driver installation appears to be the source of undesired system behavior, users can revert their systems to the restore point created automatically just before a driver was installed. In the event the device driver was signed, System Restore would not create a restore point. However, the effects of that device driver installation can still be reverted using System Restore, by restoring to the most recently created restore point before the driver was installed. This will revert changes made to the system by the driver, as well as any changes made after that restore point was created.

9. You attempt to restore a RAID 5 array on your 2003 Server box. However, when you attempt to run ASR, you get the following error message: Logical Disk Manager ASR Utility Error. The Logical Disk Manager encountered the following error while restoring the dynamic disk configuration on this system: Failed to commit the disk group creation transaction. Additional information: -25- . What is the cause of this error message?
A. ASR cannot be used with RAID arrays.
***B. One of the disks in the array is missing or corrupted.**
C. ASR cannot be used with RAID-5 arrays.
D. The disk needs to be defragmented first before using ASR.

Explanation: When you use Automated System Recovery (ASR) to restore disks that are in a redundant array of independent disks (RAID) set on a computer, you may receive the following error message: Logical Disk Manager ASR Utility Error. The Logical Disk Manager encountered the following error while restoring the dynamic disk configuration on this system: Failed to commit the disk group creation transaction. Additional information: -25- . This behavior may occur if there are corrupted or missing disks in the configuration.

---

10. What is the correct path to set up a restore point in Windows Server 2003?
A. Start | Programs | System Tools | Accessories | System Restore
B. Start | Programs | Accessories | Communication Tools | System Restore.
C. Start | Programs | Accessories | System Tools | Disk Cleanup.
D. Start | Programs | Accessories | Tools | System Restore.
***E. Start | Programs | Accessories | System Tools | System Restore**

Explanation: To set up a restore point in Windows Server 2003, go to Start | Programs | Accessories | System Tools | System Restore.

11. Which of the following executables starts the Volume Shadow Copy service?
    A. Vscadmin.exe

***B. Vssadmin.exe**

    C. Sssadmin.exe
    D. Vsscopy.exe

Explanation: You can access shadow copies of shared folders on the Shadow Copies tab of the Local Disk Properties dialog box. You can also view the same dialog box in the Computer Management snap-in. To do so, right-click Shares, point to All Tasks, and then click Configure Shadow Copies. The Vssadmin.exe tool is the command-line equivalent tool for the Volume Shadow Copy service.

---

12. How can you access shadow copies in 2003 Server?
    A. In Device Manager, right-click Shares, point to All Tasks, and then click Configure Shadow Copies.
    B. With the Copies tab of the Local Disk Properties dialog box.

***C. In Computer Management, right-click Shares, point to All Tasks, and then click Configure Shadow Copies.**

***D. With the Shadow Copies tab of the Local Disk Properties dialog box.**

Explanation: You can access shadow copies of shared folders on the Shadow Copies tab of the Local Disk Properties dialog box. You can also view the same dialog box in the Computer Management snap-in. To do so, right-click Shares, point to All Tasks, and then click Configure Shadow Copies. The Vssadmin.exe tool is the command-line equivalent tool of the Volume Shadow Copy service.

13. When used with the NTBACKUP command, the /l switch can indicate what log file types?

A. e=edit

***B. f=full**

***C. n=none**

D. p=partial

***E. s=summary**

Explanation: The systemstate parameter indicates that you want to back up the system state data. The bks file name parameter indicates the name of the backup selection file (.bks file) to be used for the backup operation. The /j switch indicates the job name to be used in the log file. The /p switch indicates the media pool from which you want to use media (you can't use the /a /g /f /t switches with this switch). The /g switch overwrites or appends to this tape. The /t switch overwrites or appends to this tape. The /n switch indicates the new tape name and can't be used with the /a switch. The /f switch indicates the logical disk path and file name and it cannot be used with the /p /g /t switches. The /d switch indicates a label for each backup set.

The /a switch performs an append operation and the /g or /t must be used with this switch, but not with the /p switch. The /v switch verifies the data after the backup is complete. The /r switch restricts access to this tape for the owner or members of the Administrators group. The /l:{f|s|n} switch indicates the type of log file: f=full, s=summary, n=none (with n, no log file is created). The /m switch indicates the backup type (normal, copy, differential, incremental, or daily). The /rs switch backs up the Removable Storage database. The /hc:{on|off} switch uses hardware compression on the tape drive. The /um switch locates the first available media, formats it, and uses it for the current backup operation.

14. Which of the following NTBACKUP switches restricts access to a tape for the owner or members of the Administrators group?
   A. The /I switch
   B. The /v switch
***C. The /r switch**
   D. The /m switch
   E. The /e switch

Explanation: The systemstate parameter indicates that you want to back up the system state data. The bks file name parameter indicates the name of the backup selection file (.bks file) to be used for the backup operation. The /j switch indicates the job name to be used in the log file. The /p switch indicates the media pool from which you want to use media (you can't use the /a /g /f /t switches with this switch). The /g switch overwrites or appends to this tape. The /t switch overwrites or appends to this tape. The /n switch indicates the new tape name and can't be used with the /a switch. The /f switch indicates the logical disk path and file name and it cannot be used with the /p /g /t switches. The /d switch indicates a label for each backup set.

The /a switch performs an append operation and the /g or /t must be used with this switch, but not with the /p switch. The /v switch verifies the data after the backup is complete. The /r switch restricts access to this tape for the owner or members of the Administrators group. The /l:{flsln} switch indicates the type of log file: f=full, s=summary, n=none (with n, no log file is created). The /m switch indicates the backup type (normal, copy, differential, incremental, or daily). The /rs switch backs up the Removable Storage database. The /hc:{onloff} switch uses hardware compression on the tape drive. The /um switch locates the first available media, formats it, and uses it for the current backup operation.

15. Which of the following NTBACKUP switches verifies the data after the backup is complete?
    A. The /a switch
    B. The /r switch
***C. The /v switch**
    D. The /m switch
    E. The /t switch

Explanation: The systemstate parameter indicates that you want to back up the system state data. The bks file name parameter indicates the name of the backup selection file (.bks file) to be used for the backup operation. The /j switch indicates the job name to be used in the log file. The /p switch indicates the media pool from which you want to use media (you can't use the /a /g /f /t switches with this switch). The /g switch overwrites or appends to this tape. The /t switch overwrites or appends to this tape. The /n switch indicates the new tape name and can't be used with the /a switch. The /f switch indicates the logical disk path and file name and it cannot be used with the /p /g /t switches. The /d switch indicates a label for each backup set.

The /a switch performs an append operation and the /g or /t must be used with this switch, but not with the /p switch. The /v switch verifies the data after the backup is complete. The /r switch restricts access to this tape for the owner or members of the Administrators group. The /l:{f|s|n} switch indicates the type of log file: f=full, s=summary, n=none (with n, no log file is created). The /m switch indicates the backup type (normal, copy, differential, incremental, or daily). The /rs switch backs up the Removable Storage database. The /hc:{on|off} switch uses hardware compression on the tape drive. The /um switch locates the first available media, formats it, and uses it for the current backup operation.

16. When used with the NTBACKUP command, what does the /um switch do?

A. Locates the first available tape drive

B. Locates the first available hard drive

***C. Formats the first available media**

***D. Uses the first available media for the current backup operation**

***E. Locates the first available media**

Explanation: The systemstate parameter indicates that you want to back up the system state data. The bks file name parameter indicates the name of the backup selection file (.bks file) to be used for the backup operation. The /j switch indicates the job name to be used in the log file. The /p switch indicates the media pool from which you want to use media (you can't use the /a /g /f /t switches with this switch). The /g switch overwrites or appends to this tape. The /t switch overwrites or appends to this tape. The /n switch indicates the new tape name and can't be used with the /a switch. The /f switch indicates the logical disk path and file name and it cannot be used with the /p /g /t switches. The /d switch indicates a label for each backup set.

The /a switch performs an append operation and the /g or /t must be used with this switch, but not with the /p switch. The /v switch verifies the data after the backup is complete. The /r switch restricts access to this tape for the owner or members of the Administrators group. The /l:{f|s|n} switch indicates the type of log file: f=full, s=summary, n=none (with n, no log file is created). The /m switch indicates the backup type (normal, copy, differential, incremental, or daily). The /rs switch backs up the Removable Storage database. The /hc:{on|off} switch uses hardware compression on the tape drive. The /um switch locates the first available media, formats it, and uses it for the current backup operation.

Total Recall

List of Tables and Figures

I Listing of all Tables

II Listing of all Figures

TotalRecall Gives You *Four* Levels of Computer Certification Practice Exams, Books, and eBooks

- Study formats and prices vary so you can choose one that best fits your level of knowledge and skills.
- Each format offers you either free or discounted access to our popular BeachFront Quizzer test engine. See description below.
- ALL come with our exclusive Money-Back Guarantee—pass the exam your first time or get money back!

1. InsideScoop Certification Success Series

Paperback books in the InsideScoop series offer a package of comprehensive study manual and CD-ROM of the BeachFront Quizzer test engine with answers/ explanations linked to relevant chapters in an integrated eBook. The study manual includes detailed information about each core exam topic with pre/post assessment quizzes; an abundance of figures, diagrams and photos; chapter summaries; helpful tips and time management techniques for test taking; lists of useful websites, articles and other learning resources; and an extensive glossary of 600 computer, IT, and telecommunications terms.

Books are $89.99

2. InsidersChoice Certification Success Series

Paperback books in the InsidersChoice series offer a package of comprehensive study manual and FREE download of the BeachFront Quizzer test engine with answers/ explanations linked to relevant chapters in an integrated eBook. The study manual includes detailed information about each core exam topic with pre/post assessment quizzes; an abundance of figures, diagrams and photos; chapter summaries; helpful tips and time management techniques for test taking; lists of useful websites, articles and other learning resources; and an extensive glossary of 600 computer, IT, and telecommunications terms.

Paperbacks are $59.99 and eBooks are $44.99

3. ExamInsight IT Certification System Series

Paperback books and eBooks in the ExamInsight series offer a package of compact study guide and 50% discount to purchase a download of the BeachFront Quizzer test engine with answers/ explanations linked to relevant chapters in an integrated eBook. The study guide includes compact information about each core exam topic with pre/post assessment quizzes; an abundance of figures, diagrams and photos; chapter summaries; helpful tips and time management techniques for test taking; and lists of useful websites, articles and other learning resources

Paperbacks are $39.99 and eBooks are $29.99

4. ExamWise IT Question Book Series

Paperback books and eBooks in the ExamWise series offer a package of Q&A workbook and 30-Day FREE access to a BeachFront Quizzer online practice exam. Each ExamWise Q&A workbook offers you approximately 300 practice questions organized by core exam topic. Questions are arranged in a unique format of two questions per right and page, with answers and brief explanations on the reverse page.

Paperbacks are $39.99 and eBooks are $29.99

The BeachFront Quizzer Test Engine Makes Passing Certification Exams as Easy as a Day at the Beach...

The BeachFront Quizzer test engine was pioneered in 1995 by Bruce Moran, an ex-NASA IT professional turned vocational computer instructor and certification trainer before launching his own book publishing operation in 2002. This popular test engine introduced interactive and adaptive features that other publishers have since tried to imitate, but never duplicate. It offers you four helpful study formats:

1) Adaptive technology generates 15-25 questions in 30-minute sessions to help you identify your strengths and weaknesses for each exam topic.

2) Study sessions help strengthen your weakest exam topics by generating up to 250 questions per topic until you can answer each correctly. Explanations for each question are linked to relevant chapters in an eBook study manual and often to web sites to help you develop a complete understanding of why an answer is correct. By focusing on your rough spots, we'll get you certified fast—guaranteed or get money back!

3) Simulated exams generate randomized questions about core exam topics in 60-90 minute sessions and then provide a score summary by topic. Taking multiple practice exams will build your confidence and ability to concentrate during the real deal!

4) Flash card drills present questions to answer mentally and then allow you to click F4 to display the correct answer.

Visit our web sites for more information:

www.TotalRecallPress.com / www.bfq.com

TotalRecall Certification Publications Microsoft

InsideScoop: TotalRecall's Complete Certification System Series:

InsideScoop to MCP / MCSE Certification: Exam 70-210
Managing Microsoft Windows 2000 Professional

InsideScoop to MCP / MCSE Certification: Exam 70-216
Implementing and Administering a Microsoft Windows 2000 Network Infrastructure

InsideScoop to MCP / MCSE Certification: Exam 70-217
Managing a Microsoft Directory Services Infrastructure

InsideScoop to MCP / MCSE Certification: Exam 70-219
Designing a Windows 2000 Directory Services Infrastructure

InsideScoop to MCP / MCSE Certification: Exam 70-220
Designing Security for a Microsoft Windows 2000 Network

InsideScoop to MCP / MCSE Certification: Exam 70-221
Designing a Microsoft Windows 2000 Network Infrastructure

InsideScoop to MCP / MCSE Certification: Exam 70-227
Installing, Configuring, and Administering Microsoft Internet Security and Acceleration (ISA) Server 2000, Enterprise Edition

InsideScoop to MCP / MCSE Certification: Exam 70-270
Installing, Configuring, and Administering Microsoft Windows XP Professional

InsideScoop to MCP / MCSE Certification: Exam 70-290
Managing and Maintaining a Microsoft Windows Server 2003 Environment

InsideScoop to MCP / MCSE Certification: Exam 70-291
Managing, and Maintaining a Microsoft Windows Server 2003 Network Infrastructure

InsideScoop to MCP / MCSE Certification: Exam 70-292
Managing and Maintaining a Microsoft Windows Server 2003 Environment for an MCSA Certified on Windows 2000

InsideScoop to MCP / MCSE Certification: Exam 70-293
Planning and Maintaining a Microsoft Windows Server 2003 Network Infrastructure

InsideScoop to MCP / MCSE Certification: Exam 70-294
Plan and Maintain a Microsoft Windows Server 2003 Active Directory Infrastructure

InsideScoop to MCP / MCSE Certification: Exam 70-296
Planning, Implementing, and Maintaining a Microsoft Windows Server 2003 Environment for an MCSE Certified on Windows

InsideScoop to MCP / MCSE Certification: Exam 70-297
Designing Microsoft Windows Server 2003 Active Directory and Network Infrastructure

InsideScoop to MCP / MCSE Certification: Exam 70-298
Designing Security for a Microsoft Server 2003 Network

InsideScoop to MCP / MCSE Certification: Exam 70-299
Implementing and Administering Security in a Microsoft Windows Server 2003 Network

ExamInsight: TotalRecall IT Insight Certification Book Series:

ExamInsight For MCP / MCSE Certification: **Exam 70-210**
Managing Microsoft Windows 2000 Professional

ExamInsight For MCP / MCSE Certification: **Exam 70-216**
Implementing and Administering a Microsoft Windows 2000 Network Infrastructure

ExamInsight For MCP / MCSE Certification: **Exam 70-217**
Managing a Microsoft Directory Services Infrastructure

ExamInsight For MCP / MCSE Certification: **Exam 70-219**
Designing a Windows 2000 Directory Services Infrastructure

ExamInsight For MCP / MCSE Certification: **Exam 70-220**
Designing Security for a Microsoft Windows 2000 Network

ExamInsight For MCP / MCSE Certification: **Exam 70-221**
Designing a Microsoft Windows 2000 Network Infrastructure

ExamInsight For MCP / MCSE Certification: **Exam 70-227**
Installing, Configuring, and Administering Microsoft Internet Security and Acceleration (ISA) Server 2000, Enterprise Edition

ExamInsight For MCP / MCSE Certification: **Exam 70-270**
Installing, Configuring, and Administering Microsoft Windows XP Professional

ExamInsight For MCP / MCSE Certification: **Exam 70-290**
Managing and Maintaining a Microsoft Windows Server 2003 Environment

ExamInsight For MCP / MCSE Certification: **Exam 70-291**
Managing, and Maintaining a Microsoft Windows Server 2003 Network Infrastructure

ExamInsight For MCP / MCSE Certification: **Exam 70-292**
Managing and Maintaining a Microsoft Windows Server 2003 Environment for an MCSA Certified on Windows 2000

ExamInsight For MCP / MCSE Certification: **Exam 70-293**
Planning and Maintaining a Microsoft Windows Server 2003 Network Infrastructure

ExamInsight For MCP / MCSE Certification: **Exam 70-294**
Plan and Maintain a Microsoft Windows Server 2003 Active Directory Infrastructure

InsidersChoice to MCP / MCSE Certification: **Exam 70-296**
Planning, Implementing, and Maintaining a Microsoft Windows Server 2003 Environment for an MCSE Certified on Windows

ExamInsight For MCP / MCSE Certification: **Exam 70-297**
Designing Microsoft Windows Server 2003 Active Directory and Network Infrastructure

ExamInsight For MCP / MCSE Certification: **Exam 70-298**
Designing Security for a Microsoft Server 2003 Network:

InsidersChoice to MCP / MCSE Certification: **Exam 70-299**
Implementing and Administering Security in a Microsoft Windows Server 2003 Network

InsidersChoice: TotalRecall's Insiders Certification System Series:

InsidersChoice to MCP / MCSE Certification: Exam 70-270
Installing, Configuring, and Administering Microsoft Windows XP Professional

InsidersChoice to MCP / MCSE Certification: Exam 70-290
Managing and Maintaining a Microsoft Windows Server 2003 Environment

InsidersChoice to MCP / MCSE Certification: Exam 70-291
Managing, and Maintaining a Microsoft Windows Server 2003 Network Infrastructure

InsidersChoice to MCP / MCSE Certification: Exam 70-292
Managing and Maintaining a Microsoft Windows Server 2003
Environment for an MCSA Certified on Windows 2000

InsidersChoice to MCP / MCSE Certification: Exam 70-293
Planning and Maintaining a Microsoft Windows Server 2003 Network Infrastructure

InsidersChoice to MCP / MCSE Certification: Exam 70-294
Plan and Maintain a Microsoft Windows Server 2003 Active Directory Infrastructure

InsidersChoice to MCP / MCSE Certification: Exam 70-296
Planning, Implementing, and Maintaining a Microsoft Windows Server 2003
Environment for an MCSE Certified on Windows

InsidersChoice to MCP / MCSE Certification: Exam 70-297
Designing Microsoft Windows Server 2003 Active Directory and Network Infrastructure

InsidersChoice to MCP / MCSE Certification: Exam 70-298
Designing Security for a Microsoft Server 2003 Network

InsidersChoice to MCP / MCSE Certification: Exam 70-299
Implementing and Administering Security in a Microsoft Windows Server 2003 Network

ExamWise: TotalRecall IT Insight Certification Book Series:

ExamWise For MCP / MCSE Certification: **Exam 70-210**
Managing Microsoft Windows 2000 Professional

ExamWise For MCP / MCSE Certification: **Exam 70-216**
Implementing and Administering a Microsoft Windows 2000 Network Infrastructure

ExamWise For MCP / MCSE Certification: **Exam 70-217**
Managing a Microsoft Directory Services Infrastructure

ExamWise For MCP / MCSE Certification: **Exam 70-219**
Designing a Windows 2000 Directory Services Infrastructure

ExamWise For MCP / MCSE Certification: **Exam 70-220**
Designing Security for a Microsoft Windows 2000 Network

ExamWise For MCP / MCSE Certification: **Exam 70-221**
Designing a Microsoft Windows 2000 Network Infrastructure

ExamWise For MCP / MCSE Certification: **Exam 70-227**
Installing, Configuring, and Administering Microsoft Internet Security and Acceleration (ISA) Server 2000, Enterprise Edition

ExamWise For MCP / MCSE Certification: **Exam 70-270**
Installing, Configuring, and Administering Microsoft Windows XP Professional

ExamWise For MCP / MCSE Certification: **Exam 70-290**
Managing and Maintaining a Microsoft Windows Server 2003 Environment

ExamWise For MCP / MCSE Certification: **Exam 70-291**
Managing, and Maintaining a Microsoft Windows Server 2003 Network Infrastructure

ExamWise For MCP / MCSE Certification: **Exam 70-292**
Managing and Maintaining a Microsoft Windows Server 2003 Environment for an MCSA Certified on Windows 2000

ExamWise For MCP / MCSE Certification: **Exam 70-293**
Planning and Maintaining a Microsoft Windows Server 2003 Network Infrastructure

ExamWise For MCP / MCSE Certification: **Exam 70-294**
Plan and Maintain a Microsoft Windows Server 2003 Active Directory Infrastructure

ExamWise For MCP / MCSE Certification: **Exam 70-296**
Planning, Implementing, and Maintaining a Microsoft Windows Server 2003 Environment for an MCSE Certified on Windows

ExamWise For MCP / MCSE Certification: **Exam 70-297**
Designing Microsoft Windows Server 2003 Active Directory and Network Infrastructure

ExamWise For MCP / MCSE Certification: **Exam 70-298**
Designing Security for a Microsoft Server 2003 Network

ExamWise For MCP / MCSE Certification: **Exam 70-299**
Implementing and Administering Security in a Microsoft Windows Server 2003 Network

TotalRecall Certification Publications
CompTIA Titles

InsideScoop: TotalRecall's Complete Certification System Series:

InsideScoop to CompTIA A+ Hardware:	Exam 220-301
InsideScoop to CompTIA A+ OS:	Exam 220-302
InsideScoop to CompTIA Network+:	Exam N10-001
InsideScoop to CompTIA Security+ (Second Edition):	Exam SY0-101

InsidersChoice: TotalRecall IT Insight Certification Book Series:

InsidersChoice to CompTIA A+ Hardware:	Exam 220-301
InsidersChoice to CompTIA A+ OS:	Exam 220-302
InsidersChoice to CompTIA Network+:	Exam N10-001
InsidersChoice to CompTIA Security+: (Second Edition):	Exam SY0-001

ExamInsight: TotalRecall IT Insight Certification Book Series:

ExamInsight For CompTIA A+ Hardware:	Exam 220-301
ExamInsight For CompTIA A+ OS:	Exam 220-302
ExamInsight For CompTIA Network+:	Exam N10-001
ExamInsight For CompTIA Security+: (Second Edition):	Exam SY0-001

ExamWise: The TotalRecall Question Book Series:

ExamWise For CompTIA A+ Hardware:	Exam 220-301
ExamWise For CompTIA A+ OS:	Exam 220-302
ExamWise For CompTIA Network+:	Exam N10-001
ExamWise For CompTIA Security+ (Second Edition):	Exam SY0-101
ExamWise For CompTIA I-Net+ Certification:	Exam IK0-002
ExamWise For CompTIA Server+ Certification:	Exam SK0-001

Money Back Book Guarantee

This guarantee applies only to books published by TotalRecall Publications, Inc.! We are so confident in our products that we are prepared to offer the following guarantee to YOU, our valued customer: If you do not pass your certification exam after two attempts, we will give money back!

Visit http://www.totalrecallpress.com/

Select "Money Back Book Guarantee" for details.

Registered book purchasers who qualify will receive:

1. 50% cash refund of purchase price
2. free TotalRecall book of equal value

NOTE: You must pay for shipping and handling.

To qualify for this TotalRecall Guarantee

you must meet these requirements and perform the following tasks:

1. Register your purchase at the TotalRecall web site
   http://www.totalrecallpress.com/
2. Fail the corresponding exam twice (No time Limit)
3. Contact TotalRecall for the RMA # and to claim this guarantee
   Send email to **mailto:Guarantee@totalrecallpress.com**
   Subject must contain your Membership # or Registration #

Ship the following to claim your refund:

1. RMA # from returned email
2. Documents of exam scores for both failed attempts
3. Return the Book to the following address:

TotalRecall Publications, Inc.
Attn: Corby Tate
1103 Middlecreek
Friendswood, TX 77546
888-992-3131 **bfquiz@swbell.net**
281-992-3131
281-482-5390 Fax http://www.bfq.com/ or http://www.bfqd.com

It's a Passing day here at the BeachFront.

Thank you for using the TotalRecall Certification Success Program.

Bruce Moran, President

70-290 Download Instructions

BeachFront Quizzer (BFQ) version 4.0 Special Edition

System Requirements: Windows 95 & 98, Windows NT, XP Windows 2000 and Server 2003 with a minimum of 6 MB hard disk space and 16 MB RAM

The Center For Technology Certification, Inc. will help you accomplish your Microsoft Certifications. This state of art software program is designed to cut your study time in half, and get you to a passing level in the easiest and shortest amount of time possible. The program will adapt to you personally, and then lay out a prioritized study plan that will visually show you your progress on a day to day basis. When the software has recognized that you are at a passing level in each objective category, you're ready to sit for the exam. It's really that easy!

Installation Instructions: 70-290 Special Edition Practice Exam with eBook
Visit http://www.technologyexams.com/download.php
Download and Install the latest version of the BFQ Engine: File Name Quiz32.exe

Visit http://snipurl.com/EI70290 and download the ExamInsight to 70-290 eBook ZIP file to a folder on your hard drive.

This will install all software files:
Open the WinZIP file and execute the 70-290SE.exe to install the questions.
Open the LicenseKey.txt file Copy and Insert the 12 digit number **License Key** when requested or type in the following License Key Numbers when requested.
TRP 70-290 SE Windows Server 2003 Environment Special Edition = 368671665867

The software is very user friendly.
After you get the program installed Open Click on the Help button menu Select contents for the on-screen manual. (You may want to print the Help File) You will follow a six step process that will lead you through the program efficiently. We are here to support you all the way. If you have any technical questions on the content, make sure you contact us. We are very proud of our pass rate, and we want you to contribute.

If you need additional assistance, visit our website http://www.totalrecallpress.com Please let me know that the download and installation worked properly.

Thank you for purchasing our product and Good Luck with your exam!

Sales: 877-654-2265, 727-450-0476
Technical Support: info@bfq.com 888-992-3131 or 281-992-3131 281-482-5390 Fax

Made in United States
Cleveland, OH
05 November 2026

47670550R00250